TEACHING AND LEARNING STRATEGIES FOR SUSTAINABLE DEVELOPMENT

INNOVATIONS IN HIGHER EDUCATION TEACHING AND LEARNING

Series Editor: Patrick Blessinger

Recent Volumes

Volume 1	Inquiry-based Learning for Faculty and Institutional Development: A Conceptual and Practical Resource for Educators – Edited by John M. Carfora and Patrick Blessinger
Volume 2	Inquiry-based Learning for the Arts, Humanities, and Social Sciences: A Conceptual and Practical Resource for Educators – Edited by Patrick Blessinger and John M. Carfora
Volume 3	Inquiry-based Learning for Multidisciplinary Programs: A Conceptual and Practical Resource for Educators – Edited by Patrick Blessinger and John M. Carfora
Volume 4	Inquiry-based Learning for Science, Technology, Engineering, and Math (STEM) Programs: A Conceptual and Practical Resource for Educators – Edited by Patrick Blessinger and John M. Carfora
Volume 5	University Partnerships for Community and School System Development – Edited by Barbara Cozza and Patrick Blessinger
Volume 6	Emerging Directions In Doctoral Education – Edited by Patrick Blessinger and Denise Stockley
Volume 7	University Partnerships for Academic Programs and Professional Development
Volume 8	University Partnerships for International Development
Volume 9	Engaging Dissonance
Volume 10	University Partnerships for Pre-service and Teacher Development
Volume 11	Refugee Education: Integration and Acceptance of Refugees in Mainstream Society
Volume 12	Contexts for Diversity and Gender Identities in Higher Education: International Perspectives on Equity and Inclusion – Edited by Jaimie Hoffman, Patrick Blessinger and Mandla Makhanya
Volume 13	Strategies, Policies, and Directions for Refugee Education – Edited by Enakshi Sengupta and Patrick Blessinger
Volume 14	Perspectives on Diverse Student Identities in Higher Education – Edited by Patrick Blessinger
Volume 15	Language, Teaching and Pedagogy for Refugee Education – Edited by Enakshi Sengupta and Patrick Blessinger
Volume 16	Strategies for Fostering Inclusive Classrooms in Higher Education – Edited by Jaimie Hoffman, Patrick Blessinger and Mandla Makhanya
Volume 17	Strategies for Facilitating Inclusive Campuses in Higher Education: International Perspectives on Equity and Inclusion – Edited by Jaimie Hoffman, Patrick Blessinger and Mandla Makhanya
Volume 18	Integrating Sustainable Development into the Curriculum – Edited by Enakshi Sengupta, Patrick Blessinger and Taisir Subhi Yamin

INNOVATIONS IN HIGHER EDUCATION TEACHING AND LEARNING VOLUME 19

TEACHING AND LEARNING STRATEGIES FOR SUSTAINABLE DEVELOPMENT

EDITED BY

ENAKSHI SENGUPTA
Centre for Advanced Research in Higher Education, New York, USA
International HETL Association, New York, USA

PATRICK BLESSINGER
St. John's University, New York, USA
International HETL Association, New York, USA

TAISIR SUBHI YAMIN
International Association of Educators for World Peace, Germany

Created in partnership with the International Higher Education Teaching and Learning Association

Higher Education Teaching & Learning

https://www.hetl.org/

emerald PUBLISHING

United Kingdom – North America – Japan
India – Malaysia – China

Emerald Publishing Limited
Howard House, Wagon Lane, Bingley BD16 1WA, UK

First edition 2020

British Library Cataloguing in Publication Data
A catalogue record for this book is available from the British Library

ISBN: 978-1-78973-640-3 (Print)
ISBN: 978-1-78973-639-7 (Online)
ISBN: 978-1-78973-641-0 (Epub)

ISSN: 2055-3641 (Series)

Printed and bound by CPI Group (UK) Ltd, Croydon, CR0 4YY

ISOQAR REGISTERED
Certificate Number 1985
ISO 14001

ISOQAR certified Management System, awarded to Emerald for adherence to Environmental standard ISO 14001:2004.

INVESTOR IN PEOPLE

CONTENTS

List of Contributors *vii*

Series Editors' Introduction *ix*

Foreword *xi*

PART I
PEDAGOGICAL APPROACHES

Chapter 1 Introduction to Teaching and Learning Strategies for Sustainable Development
Enakshi Sengupta, Patrick Blessinger and Tasir Subhi Yamin *3*

Chapter 2 Integrating Sustainability into the University: Academies for Learning
Audrey M. Dentith and Nancy V. Winfrey *15*

Chapter 3 An Interdisciplinary Problem-based Approach to Education for Sustainable Development
Bland Tomkinson and Rosemary Tomkinson *29*

Chapter 4 Using the SDGs to Promote Change and Nurture Connectivity in an Undergraduate Design Module
Jackie Malcolm and Keith R. Skene *41*

Chapter 5 Leading Assessment Practices to Foster Sustainability Learning in Engineering Classrooms
Margaret Jollands *57*

Chapter 6 Can the Anthropocene Provide a Tool for Meaningful Teaching of Sustainability in Higher Education?
Patrick Baughan *73*

Chapter 7 Deliberative Dialogue and Syllabus Deliberation as Innovative, Cross-disciplinary, and Sustainable Teaching Methods
Sharyn Lowenstein *83*

Chapter 8 Integrating Sustainable Development into the Whole Institution: Can the SDGs Bridge the Gap?
Stefanie Mallow and Hilligje van't Land 107

Chapter 9 Integrating Sustainable Development into the Postgraduate Curriculum in the UK: A Mixed Method Study
Gavin Melles 123

PART II
INNOVATIVE CASE STUDIES

Chapter 10 The Teaching Sustainability Mini-plot: A Faculty Learning Community Building Curriculum for Students' Sustainability Thinking
Jenny S. Wakefield and Christopher E. Grice 143

Chapter 11 Study Circle as an Innovative Tool for Promoting Lifelong Learning and Community Empowerment
Gwadabe Kurawa 159

Chapter 12 Student Perceptions of Engineers' Versus Teachers' Roles and Responsibilities in Contributing to Sustainable Development
Karin Edvardsson Björnberg, Inga-Britt Skogh and Lena Gumaelius 177

Chapter 13 Whakawhitinga Kōrero: Dialogues on Sustainability
Tonya Sweet, Andrea Milligan and Meegan Hall 197

Chapter 14 Campus as a Living Lab: Creating a Culture of Research and Learning in Sustainable Development
Angelique Pilon, John Madden, James Tansey and John Metras 213

About the Contributors 229

Name Index 241

Subject Index 249

LIST OF CONTRIBUTORS

Patrick Baughan	Advance HE, London, UK
Karin Edvardsson Björnberg	KTH Royal Institute of Technology, Stockholm, Sweden
Patrick Blessinger	International Higher Education Teaching and Learning, New York, USA
Audrey M. Dentith	North Carolina A&T State University in Greensboro
Christopher E. Grice	Brookhaven College, Texas, USA
Lena Gumaelius	KTH Royal Institute of Technology, Stockholm, Sweden
Meegan Hall	Victoria University of Wellington, Wellington, New Zealand
Margaret Jollands	RMIT University, Melbourne, Australia
Gwadabe Kurawa	Inter-agency Network for Education in Emergencies (INEE), Manchester, UK
Hilligje van't Land	International Association of Universities, Paris, France
Sharyn Lowenstein	Lasell College, MA, USA
John Madden	University of British Columbia, Vancouver, Canada
Jackie Malcolm	University of Dundee, Dundee, Scotland
Stefanie Mallow	International Association of Universities, Paris, France
Gavin Melles	Swinburne University, Melbourne, Australia
John Metras	University of British Columbia, Vancouver, Canada
Andrea Milligan	Victoria University of Wellington, Wellington, New Zealand

Angelique Pilon	University of British Columbia, Vancouver, Canada
Enakshi Sengupta	International Higher Education Teaching and Learning, New York, USA
Inga-Britt Skogh	KTH Royal Institute of Technology, Stockholm, Sweden
Keith R. Skene	Biosphere Research Institute, Angus, Scotland
Tonya Sweet	Victoria University of Wellington, Wellington, New Zealand
James Tansey	University of British Columbia, Vancouver, Canada
Bland Tomkinson	University of Manchester, UK
Rosemary Tomkinson	University of Manchester, UK
Jenny S. Wakefield	Dallas County Community College District, Texas, USA
Nancy V. Winfrey	Center for Creative Leadership, USA
Taisir Subhi Yamin	International Centre for Innovation in Education

SERIES EDITORS' INTRODUCTION

INNOVATIONS IN HIGHER EDUCATION TEACHING AND LEARNING

The purpose of this series is to publish current research and scholarship on innovative teaching and learning practices in higher education. The series is developed around the premise that teaching and learning is more effective when instructors and students are actively and meaningfully engaged in the teaching–learning process.

The main objectives of this series are to:

1. present how innovative teaching and learning practices are being used in higher education institutions around the world across a wide variety of disciplines and countries;
2. present the latest models, theories, concepts, paradigms, and frameworks that educators should consider when adopting, implementing, assessing, and evaluating innovative teaching and learning practices; and
3. consider the implications of theory and practice on policy, strategy, and leadership.

This series will appeal to anyone in higher education who is involved in the teaching and learning process from any discipline, institutional type, or nationality. The volumes in this series will focus on a variety of authentic case studies and other empirical research that illustrates how educators from around the world are using innovative approaches to create more effective and meaningful learning environments.

Innovation teaching and learning is any approach, strategy, method, practice, or means which has been shown to improve, enhance, or transform the teaching–learning environment. Innovation involves doing things differently or in a novel way to improve outcomes. In short, innovation is positive change. With respect to teaching and learning, innovation is the implementation of new or improved educational practices that result in improved educational and learning outcomes. This innovation can be any positive change related to teaching, curriculum, assessment, technology, or other tools, programs, policies, or processes that leads to improved educational and learning outcomes. Innovation can occur in institutional development, program development, professional development, or learning development.

The volumes in this series will not only highlight the benefits and theoretical frameworks of such innovations through authentic case studies and other empirical research but also look at the challenges and contexts associated with implementing and assessing innovative teaching and learning practices. The volumes represent all disciplines from a wide range of national, cultural, and organizational contexts. The volumes in this series will explore a wide variety of teaching and learning topics, such as active learning, integrative learning, transformative learning, inquiry-based learning, problem-based learning, meaningful learning, blended learning, creative learning, experiential learning, life-long and life-wide learning, global learning, learning assessment and analytics, student research, faculty and student learning communities, as well as other topics.

This series brings together distinguished scholars and educational practitioners from around the world to disseminate the latest knowledge on innovative teaching and learning scholarship and practices. The authors offer a range of disciplinary perspectives from different cultural contexts. This series provides a unique and valuable resource for instructors, administrators, and anyone interested in improving and transforming teaching and learning.

Patrick Blessinger
Founder, Executive Director, and Chief Research Scientist,
International HETL Association

Enakshi Sengupta
Associate Editor, International HETL Association

FOREWORD

Teaching is a practical approach to shape one's ideas through education. On the other hand, learning is the acquisition of knowledge or skills through study, experience, or being taught. It is the process of acquiring new or modifying existing knowledge, behaviour, skills, values, and preferences. Education is one of the most important factors for human development and society because it helps an individual to increase the mental and physical capacity as well as productivity. Teaching and learning strategies are a set of activities to accommodate different abilities, skills, and styles that allow every student/learner to participate and be able to achieve success.

Sustainability education is often referred to as Education for Sustainable Development (ESD), which has been defined as the type of education that allows every human being to acquire the knowledge, skills, attitudes, and values necessary to shape a sustainable future (UNESCO, 2014). ESD in Higher Institutions of Learning is based on student-centered approach with a focus on improving academic and higher-order thinking skills. It is also research based and aims at promoting environment for current and future generations. A well-structured curriculum should therefore include sustainable development issues, such as biodiversity, poverty reduction, climate change, sustainable consumption, etc. Council of the European Union (2010) states that ESD is essential for the achievement of a sustainable society and is therefore desirable at all levels of formal education and training as well as non-formal and informal learning. Institutions of Higher Learning all over the world are responding to political, economic, and social pressure to impart knowledge to students that will enable them to develop knowledge, values, and skills to improve the quality of life now and for the future.

In this book, authors provide practical examples and results from case studies in which teaching and learning strategies for sustainable development which enable students to use knowledge, skills, and values for sustainable development. The practical examples are from different countries, such as the United States of America, the UK, Sweden, New Zealand, Canada, Italy, Ghana, Zimbabwe, Nigeria, Australia, Costa Rica, Thailand, and others. There are numerous teaching and learning strategies, such as *Experiential Learning* in which students using prior experiences are engaged in critical thinking, problem-solving, decision-making, and applying ideas and skills to new situations; *Storytelling* in which students and faculty provide practical insight to environmental challenges that affect our planet; *Values Education* in which designed curricula contain attitudes and human values, such as social equity and peace, appropriate development, conservation, and democracy that are key in shaping a sustainable future; *Enquiry learning* in which students are given opportunity to think and develop problem-solving skills, discover, and create activities for sustainable development;

Appropriate assessment in which leading assessment practice is identified as fostering higher order thinking in solving complex multi-interdisciplinary problems; *Future problem-solving* in which curricula are designed to assist students to develop skills for analysing problems from a future perspective using research and group work; *Learning outside the classroom* in which students are provided with high quality learning activities by visiting local communities so that they appreciate first-hand experience and are able to practice skills of enquiry and value analysis and *Community problem-solving* in which students are given opportunity to develop practical skills that are needed in finding solutions to local challenges in the realm of sustainable future.

In a good number of cases, authors use multiple teaching and learning strategies which could be referred to as a hybrid approach for achieving sustainable development.

Apart from case studies, readers will also find the book useful to learn about a new program called ESD for 2030 which is intended to promote sustainable development for an entire institution which is referred to as "Whole Institution Approach for ESD." The book provides immense contribution to our genuine desire of incorporating strategies of teaching and learning for sustainable development in our respective curricula. However, it must be borne in mind that there is no case of "fit for all" in developing strategies of teaching and learning for sustainable development. Each Institution of Higher Learning should develop its own strategies by taking into account its own circumstances and respective regional perspective.

Andrew Ssemwanga (PhD)
Vice Chancellor
St Lawrence University – Uganda

PART I

PEDAGOGICAL APPROACHES

CHAPTER 1

INTRODUCTION TO TEACHING AND LEARNING STRATEGIES FOR SUSTAINABLE DEVELOPMENT

Enakshi Sengupta, Patrick Blessinger and Tasir Subhi Yamin

ABSTRACT

One of the most important issues plaguing our planet is the depletion of natural resources and climate change, creating new disasters, and global challenges. The international community has expressed its anguish and concern for these problems through several international forums and treaties. As a response, Education for Sustainable Development is a program that aims to educate students on these issues. Teaching sustainability to young graduates needs to be holistic and pluralistic in nature. Discourses and modules on sustainability help in making them sustainability conscious which will enhance the competencies of people and help them to live and act in a more sustainable way. This book has several chapters written by academics across the globe who have spoken about their experience of incorporating sustainability into their curriculum and adopting various pedagogical approach that has helped their students to learn and understand the subject. Sustainability has been part of the teaching and learning in general, and as part of management, engineering, medical, and design courses, for instance. This book helps us to understand how such teaching and learning strategies can be made more effective for students.

Keywords: Sustainability education; sustainable development; teaching strategies; curriculum strategies; citizenship education; pedagogical approach; stakeholders; social justice; awareness; sensitize; curriculum

Teaching and Learning Strategies for Sustainable Development:
Innovations in Higher Education Teaching and Learning, Volume 19, 3–14

ISSN: 2055-3641/doi:10.1108/S2055-364120200000019001

INTRODUCTION

> We hold the future in our hands. Together, we must ensure that our grandchildren will not have to ask why we failed to do the right thing and let them suffer the consequences. UN Secretary-General Ban Ki-moon (2007)

Sustainable development was defined in 1987 by Brundtland Commission Report as "development that meets the needs of the present without compromising the ability of future generations to meet their own needs." The concept advocates a future in which economic, social, and environmental factors are balanced toward an all-round development agenda with a view toward improved quality of life for all. The world is moving away from its shareholder's view of profit maximization and economic development toward one that is concerned about its stakeholders through social and environmental concerns. The major threats and damages caused to human through environmental concerns must be addressed through the sustainability paradigm. Sustainability is our focus toward future and is often considered as a long-term goal of our planet. Sustainable development is one of the various routes that one can adopt to achieve such a goal. Sustainable development affects all spheres of our lives, from our consumption pattern to good governance and includes technology transfer, teaching, training, and education in this field.

There are several underlying principles that encompass the sustainability concept in a holistic manner. These concepts range from poverty reduction, gender equality, environmental conservation, and preservation to social justice. The next generation needs to be trained and educated in sustainable development and that can only happen through a coordinated effort of both institutions of higher education and society. As Stern (2007, p. xxvi) noted,

> educating those currently at school about climate change will help shape and sustain future policy making, and a broad public and international debate will support today's policy-makers in taking strong action now.

Several studies have been conducted to measure the impact of sustainable education and the result has been very encouraging. Educating female students on sustainability has even resulted in larger impacts on carbon emissions abatement than direct low-carbon energy options (Wheeler & Hammer, 2010). Muttarak and Lutz (2014) explained that "public investment … through education can have a positive externality in reducing vulnerability and strengthening adaptive capacity amidst the challenges of a changing climate."

Academicians are constantly striving to formulate new educational approaches to motivate the learners on sustainability, create awareness, and help achieve necessary lifestyle issues. Government and other funding agencies are mobilizing support toward institutions of higher education to develop a new ecological vision and inculcate in young students a sense of global solidarity. There lies an urgent need to reorient the current teaching abilities to a curriculum that deals with sustainability and its goals. Students need to be sensitized about the natural resources that they have and how best that can be preserved. Policies, procedures, and governmental regulations go hand in hand with such teaching and learning strategies which work toward economic prosperity of the region without comprising the natural resources. An action plan needs to be prepared along with allocation of resources by every institute of higher education which can facilitate and implement a proper educational plan promoting sustainability.

Sustainability education is not only meant for students but also for the faculty. Capacity building programs should be in place so that the teachers are aware of the subject and have adequate knowledge to teach students. Teaching and learning strategies have undergone several changes in the past from nature and non-human environment to that of human welfare and health environment. The approach needs to be holistic in nature and not confined to undergraduate students but can even start from a basic education level. The strategy mainly focuses on: delivering basic education to students; re-orienting the existing education program with a focus toward sustainability; creating a general awareness among public and training in sustainability with a goal toward achieving lifestyle changes and consumption patterns; and improved public policies and decision-making to create a more sustainable society.

To attain a transition toward a sustainable society one needs a better understanding of the subject and a more positive attitude toward the concept. Yet the fundamental question remains as to how best this can be accomplished and what path one needs to charter in future? Academics delving into sustainability found that the only answer to their question is education. Education is the main solution that can empower individuals with the competence to deal with such critical ingredients for change.

Educating citizens starts with schools by training young generations which will help them learn as to how to address the issues in an effective manner. Education for Sustainable Development (ESD) was an effort that was overseen by UNESCO. In the last decade ESD was launched to help chalk out an approach to teaching and learning that promotes sustainable development in educational institutions. Since then it has become a global movement and the understanding of the concept of sustainability has evolved. UNESCO (2005) defined it as:

> Education for Sustainable Development means including key sustainable development issues into teaching and learning; for example, climate change, disaster risk reduction, biodiversity, poverty reduction, and sustainable consumption. It also requires participatory teaching and learning methods that motivate and empower learners to change their behavior and take action for sustainable development. Education for Sustainable Development consequently promotes competencies like critical thinking, imagining future scenarios and making decisions in a collaborative way.

LITERATURE REVIEW

ESD advocates a holistic perspective both toward content and the pedagogical approach. This holistic perspective recognizes that behind inculcating a sustainable viewpoint lies several socio-cultural factors and a conflict of interest between socioeconomic goals of society. These conflicts not only span over various disciplines but also tied to local and global perspectives with the present and future generations. Öhman (2008) identified three important aspects concerning holism: the first one being a connection between environmental, social, and economic dimensions leading to sustainable development issues; and the next being integration of the past, present, and future and a focus toward local, regional, and global issues.

While dealing with the issues of teaching and learning in ESD it focuses on developing skills and competence for sustainability. The approach is generally pluralistic in nature imbibing knowledge, views, and perspectives from different disciplines while dealing with sustainable issues. The thought behind incorporating various disciplines is that complexity of the issues and conflict of interest makes it impossible to teach a preconceived, pre-defined solution for every complex issue faced by the learners. This progressive and transformational approach develops the student's ability of critical thinking, enhancing their decision-making process through value-based and service learning. With the help of this approach students learn about the world based on their own understanding and develop competencies, which are needed to create a sustainable world. Holistic and pluralistic concept of sustainable education is intertwined and takes places through various interpretations of socio-economic and environmental perspectives.

According to Kopnina (2012) the concept of pluralism and holistic nature of teaching sustainability may be confusing as the subject has contradictions and paradoxes inherent in it. Kopnina (2012, p. 700) states that: "plural perspectives on ESD can lead practitioners into an essentially anthropocentric paradigm which can be counter-productive to the effort of fostering environmentally concerned citizenry." Wals (2010) also speaks about using deliberative method of holism and pluralism to solve the normative problems of teaching sustainability as no evidence has been gathered to reveal that simply teaching the concept of sustainability has resulted in changing human attitude and creating willingness among people to solve the sustainability issues plaguing our planet. Research on effects of teaching sustainability is rare and UNESCO (2014) in its recommendation has stated the need for more research, innovation, and monitoring needed to effectively develop the subject and the good practices of teaching sustainability.

A curriculum in sustainability requires faculty to identify issues, skills, and values essential to address the sustainability challenges and needs to integrate them in one unified course module as well as integrating it across courses and programs. Higher education institution (HEI) needs to identify which are the issues that need prioritization and reorient education toward achieving its sustainability goals. A reoriented curriculum helps to address the local issues and find a solution toward solving them. The curriculum is then culturally relevant and appropriate for the students. Certain faculty members have imported curriculum from other countries which may serve as a platform but needs customization to suit the local needs. A quality education in sustainability requires attention to individual learners need and a variety of techniques can be adopted by the teachers to attend to these needs. Traditional pedagogy of classroom teaching may not be enough in addressing the individual needs and experiential learning may be a better option for students to understand the basic concepts of sustainability.

CONCLUSION

Teaching sustainability remains a contested arena with challenges of developing a suitable curriculum that addresses the needs of the local community and equips students with problem-solving abilities in sustainability. The challenge remains that the concept may remain as lofty rhetoric or idealistic aims with little understanding of the subject and developing a creative and innovative approach toward the subject. The book has highlighted the best practices of teaching and learning sustainable development in various countries across several disciplines which can be adopted by other institutions of higher education.

CHAPTER OVERVIEWS

"Integrating Sustainability into the University: Academies for Learning," by Audrey M. Dentith and Nancy V. Winfrey, describes a curriculum and a pedagogical approach for universities that addresses the goals of sustainable education. It describes two educative initiatives that were hosted by universities that broaden the reach of faculty to include the local and regional communities. The Academy for the Critical inquiry of the Cultural Commons and the Ecojustice Leadership Academy were created and delivered in two separate sites in the United States. A discussion on the theoretical framework for the work as well as the learning theories that inform this curricular approach are integrated into the description of these university academies. Finally, a report on the learning of participants and a summary of the results of these efforts are included in the chapter.

"The Teaching Sustainability Mini-Pilot: A Faculty Learning Community Building Curriculum for Students' Sustainability Thinking," by Jenny S. Wakefield, Terry DiPaolo, and Christopher Grice, is about sustaining our planet for generations to come where one needs to recognize that humans have immense impact on the environment and an open and ongoing conversation is needed to generate informed actions toward sustainability. A sustainable future must grow from a change mindset, one of critical thinking, problem-solving, and continuous learning and active practice. In higher education, we are uniquely placed to share with students a sustainability-infused curriculum and other sustainability innovations toward such a change mindset. This research chapter focuses on how, in Texas, 10 Brookhaven college faculty self-selected to participate in a Teaching Sustainability Mini-Pilot during Fall semester 2018. The innovation was initiated to encourage students to become mindful of sustainability, inspired to get involved in sustainability efforts, and to become immersed in satisfactory real-world learning.

Participating faculty had agreed to include at least one assignment tied to sustainability in one of their courses. To capture the experiences of faculty in the mini-pilot, institutional review board approval was acquired, and faculty participated in focus group sessions or individual interviews. Data were analyzed using phenomenology. Analyzing the data three major themes emerged. These clustered around the idea of salient thinking and caring sharing awareness of sustainability with students for their own sake. The three themes were: (1) making sustainability learning visible through story and participatory action; (2) making sustainability learning visible through reflective discussions and paper submissions toward a changed mindset; and (3) making sustainability learning visible by starting with the text. The essence of the faculty experience was faculty concern for the future, a drive to share awareness with students of our fragile world, and a need to encourage students to take action for their own sake as well at their childrens' and grandchildren' sake.

"An Interdisciplinary Problem-based Approach to Education for Sustainable Development," by Bland Tomkinson and Rosemary Tomkinson, is based on the work of Charles Engel. Engel advocated that higher education should take a lead in remediating global challenges particularly those of sustainability. In this context, Engel took a broad view of the concept of sustainability, based largely on the Brundtland view of global challenges. Engel also proposed that successful approaches to facing the "wicked" problems of sustainability should be explored across disciplinary boundaries. To this end, the University of Manchester has been running a series of course modules focusing on these major challenges, largely run on interdisciplinary lines. Initially, the concept was explored across science and engineering schools, with the support of the Royal Academy of Engineering. As a leading authority on the use of problem-based learning, Engel had advised on the use of this approach as a means of addressing the wicked problems in interdisciplinary groups. The pilot modules were extensively evaluated and reported. Since that time the course units have developed and diversified, with extension to other schools, universities, and countries, and to postgraduate as well as undergraduate courses. The concept has also been explored in hybrid online format.

This chapter will re-introduce some of the original ideas and bring together the many threads that have emerged over the past 20 years. Governments, worldwide, try to restrain higher education to short-term outcomes – for example, student employability – is this the only path for higher education to be treading? That is an interesting challenge in itself. What can higher education do to help its graduates to become agents for change in the remediation of global wicked challenges? Does this impact on how institutions organize themselves and their curricula as well as the overall philosophy of higher education?

"Study circles as an innovative tool for promoting lifelong learning and community empowerment," by Gwadabe Kurawa, is based on The United Nations Sustainable Development Goal (SDG) 4 which aims at ensuring an inclusive, equitable quality education, and promoting lifelong learning opportunities for all. However, this may not be effectively realized, as this chapter demonstrates, through formal learning. Rather, an adoption of non-formal and informal learning along with formal learning is more likely to empower the general population to contribute toward development of a sustainable society. The chapter therefore critically examines the concepts of lifelong learning and the learning society and suggests that community learning can be a promising institutional medium for the promotion of adult and lifelong learning. The rationale for establishing community learning as a medium for lifelong learning is demonstrated through case studies from Zimbabwe and Sweden. This follows by comparing and contrasting the ways in which Sweden and Zimbabwe are promoting the lifelong learning for all.

"Using the SDGs to Promote Change and Nurture Connectivity in an Undergraduate Design Module," by Jackie Malcolm and Keith R. Skenea, is based on the SDGs introduced by the United Nations in 2016 to replace the millennium development goals. This chapter examines the impact of integrating these goals within a design challenge, as part of a level 3 undergraduate degree module. Design Values, Issues, and Ethics are an expansive module, aiming to broaden the students' discipline focus and allow them to expand their learning within a new landscape. This module promoted the utilization of nature-based intelligences to establish solutions to a community's basic need to survive and thrive. The SDGs were integrated through embedding them as part of a future-building scenario, supported by a series of exercises and seminars. Students were then asked to reflect on how the SDGs had impacted their design process, and to consider ethical and value dimensions.

"Student Perceptions of the Engineer's Versus Teacher's Roles and Responsibilities in Contributing to Sustainable Development," by Karin Edvardsson Björnberg, Inga-Britt Skogh, and Lena Gumaelius, highlights how students enrolled in a combined engineering and teacher education program given at the KTH Royal Institute of Technology understand the concept of sustainable development (SD) and the professional responsibilities of engineers versus teachers in contributing to this goal, focusing on four questions. A questionnaire was used to collect and analyze data focusing on five research questions: (1) How do the students conceptualize the notion of SD? (2) What sustainable development aspects are the students interested in? (3) Are there any gender differences in what aspects students are interested in? (4) How do the students perceive the roles and responsibilities of engineers versus teachers in contributing to SD? and (5) How confident are the students in their abilities to address sustainable development issues vocationally?

The data indicate a conventional view of sustainable development among the KTH students; a clear interest in sustainability issues; a tendency to ascribe significant but differentiated responsibilities to engineers/teachers; and a low degree of confidence in their own ability to adequately address sustainable development issues vocationally. The data indicate that there are differences between male and female students when looking at interest in different aspects. Female students are found to be slightly more interested than the male students. This gender difference is larger in relation to social aspects than ecological or economic aspects. It is suggested that future Sustainable Development Education (SDE) needs a shift of focus from what separates female and male students to what unites them. The observed "confidence gap" that exists between the stated degree of interest in and perceived importance of sustainability issues suggests the potential for significant improvement of the design of the CL program.

"Leading Assessment Practices to Foster Sustainability Learning in Engineering Classrooms," by Margaret Jollands, explains about a growing demand in industry for engineering graduates who can think sustainably. However, there are many barriers for academic staff to develop leading practice assessment to foster sustainability learning in engineering classrooms. There is no consensus on the definition of sustainability and its key competencies. Teaching resources are limited and staff capability in learner-oriented multidisciplinary systems engineering approaches are low hence staff are unclear what to teach and how to teach it. They rarely consider the best way to assess sustainability learning. Assessment is an integral part of teaching and learning and should be planned from the earliest stages. Current practice in assessment of student's understanding of sustainability includes case study, community projects, concept maps, and problem- or project-based learning.

However, only concept maps have been shown to significantly enhance student learning. There is a lack of rigorous evidence on best practice assessment. Staff may lack the capacity to use appropriate kinds of assessment, such as project-based learning. Traditional approaches to assessment such as tests and exams encourage surface learning, counter to the needs of sustainability for high-order thinking. Further work is needed to identify best practice for sustainability assessment. The definition of sustainable engineering practice should be updated with input from key stakeholders (industry and graduates). A hierarchical taxonomic framework should be developed to help staff select and align sustainability teaching approach, curriculum learning objectives, activities, and assessment. Current methods for assessing sustainability should be re-evaluated. Assessment methods using Bloom's or SOLO taxonomy should be investigated.

"Whakawhitinga Kōrero: Dialogues on Sustainability," by Tonya Sweet, Andrea Milligan, and Meegan Hall, is about Victoria University of Wellington in New Zealand (VUW) who is engaging with its responses and responsibilities to complex sustainability issues. However, the experience of academics championing sustainability indicates that interdisciplinary approaches to curriculum and pedagogy remain a particular challenge (Wood, Cornforth, Beals, Taylor, & Tallon, 2016). VUW is, of course, not alone in this. As Howlett, Ferreira, and Blomfield (2016) explain, "HEIs remain notoriously stubborn in changing their unidirectional, hierarchical and disciplinary approach to teaching" (p. 310). In many ways, affirming this challenge, this chapter shares insights from a 2016 attempt to establish a first-year course with a focus on sustainable development. Emerging from an impasse in the course development process, the course's eventual reincarnation in 2018 within the School of Design as Design Thinking for Sustainability (DSDN183) offered unexpected opportunities to engage in an interdisciplinary approach to sustainability education. This chapter considers how interdisciplinary approaches to sustainable development education could be enhanced through course design.

The chapter focuses particularly on a key pedagogical element developed for the course – a series of video dialogues between university and community-based sustainability experts, created to enable students to access understandings and research evidence about sustainability issues and each of the United Nations SDGs, through different disciplinary lenses. In contrast to strongly content-driven and normative approaches, the video dialogues are intended to provide students with opportunities to learn reflexively through exposure to differing visions for sustainable development, including indigenous perspectives. Used in this way, the video dialogues provide material for critical, creative, and iterative design thinking. The chapter concludes with thoughts and reflections on enhancing the transformative potential of sustainable development education through the use of pedagogical tools and approaches that support students' critical openness to addressing sustainability concerns.

"Can the Anthropocene Provide a Tool for Meaningful Teaching of Sustainability in Higher Education?" by Patrick Baughan, is on Anthropocene which is commonly explained as a current epoch that began when human activities started bearing a major impact on the natural world. As an area of study, it has a logical disciplinary home, addressed widely in geology (Gibbard & Walker, 2014). However, it is also gaining traction in other disciplines, especially the social sciences (Bonneuil & Fressoz, 2017). In most accounts, it involves examining how the relationship between humans and the planet has changed and what can be done to monitor the balance. Sustainability represents a more familiar challenge and discussion area in higher education. Nevertheless, two areas of questioning about it endure: what is sustainability and should students be taught about it? One established account is the "three-pillar model" which presents sustainability as an intersection of economic, social, and environmental issues (Brundtland Report, 1987).

There are, however, different views as to how sustainability curriculum change should be implemented (Hopkinson, Hughes, & Layer, 2008; Stubbs & Schapper, 2011) but students appear to want sustainability better represented in their institutions (Drayson, Bone, Agombar, & Kemp, 2013). This chapter considers whether the relatively recent focus on the Anthropocene can help us develop sustainability teaching in higher education. The project draws on desk-based research, comprising a review of academic sources on the Anthropocene and on sustainability, as well as teaching materials on these areas. I also draw on conversations with staff involved in teaching and researching the Anthropocene. The outcomes point to some support for further teaching about the Anthropocene and in a way which links to sustainability, and I argue that as a concept and proposition, the Anthropocene has potential for informing future sustainability teaching. However, the relationship between the Anthropocene and sustainability needs exploring further in follow-up research with both staff and learners.

"Campus as a Living Lab: Creating a Culture of Research and Learning in Sustainable Development," by Angelique Pilon, John Madden, James Tansey, and John Metras, describes that over the last 30 years, the University of British Columbia (UBC) in Vancouver, Canada has advanced sustainable development on campus through high- and mid-level policies and plans, initiatives driven from the academic faculty, and the operational staff at the university, dedicated department, and creative demonstration projects. These efforts have results in a culture of sustainability, ambitious goals, and strong collaborative relationships that combine to create an institutional environment that enables the Campus as a Living Lab (CLL) initiative. Launched in 2010, the CLL initiative utilizes the campus building and infrastructure as opportunities for research and learning.

Projects under the CLL bring together academic researchers, students, staff, and external partners in demonstrating and testing new ideas for sustainable development, and to share the lessons learned beyond the campus. These projects can range in scale from small and discrete educational or research projects, often led by students, to the design and construction of innovative buildings, with associated multiyear research programs. The results inform policies, plans, and projects on UBC campus, advance academic research, and support industry innovation.

CLL projects are opportunities for UBC students to participate in applied research and learning, that enhances their educational experience at the University. CLL provides a structured approach for UBC to develop research, innovation, and collaboration opportunities and explore integrated solutions that connect our campus operations with the well-being of our community, while providing unique learning opportunities for all our students.

"Deliberative Dialogue and Syllabus Deliberation As Innovative, Cross-Disciplinary, and Sustainable Teaching Methods," by Sharyn Lowenstein, argues that Deliberative Dialogues (DDs) are a form sustainable education, whose design, process focus, wide-tent approach, and interdisciplinary content align with best democratic practices in and out of the classroom. DDs are an effective method for bridging seemingly opposing forces in academia and the larger society: Narrow expertise versus interdisciplinarity, individual orientation versus collaboration, polarization, and prioritization of majority/privileged voice versus inclusivity and search for common ground. In this chapter, the author defines and describes deliberation and DDs, offer models, explores basic components, and analyzes her experiences in facilitating DDs in 35 classes across multiple disciplines in a small private university. She will look at the planning process, the logistics of running the DD, post-DD outcomes, and will make suggestions for future enhancements. Finally, she will explore a particular kind of DD, the Syllabus Deliberation method (also known as the negotiated or process syllabus).

"Integrating Sustainable Development into the Whole Institution: Can the SDGs Bridge the GAP?" by Stefanie Mallow and Hilligje van't Land, describes that in 2020, UNESCO will launch a new program called ESD for 2030. It is the follow-up program of the Global Action Programme (GAP) on ESD, which promotes the Whole Institution Approach (WIA) for ESD. This article will explore what the "WIA" means and how it translates in different contexts around the world. This part of the chapter will provide background information to understand the complexity of sustainable development in higher education and HEIs engage with Agenda 2030. The chapter will provide data and information based on an International Association of Universities (IAU) qualitative study conducted in fall 2018 and which looked at how the SDGs are changing the dynamics of HEIs and how they trigger new policy development and lead to innovation in teaching research and community engagement practice.

Based on the above, the chapter will present five case studies highlighting different approaches to integrating sustainable development into the whole institution. The universities analyzed are University of Bologna, University of Ghana, Siam University, University of Regina, and University of Costa Rica. The chapter will show that there is no one-size-fits-all approach and that each university has to engage with the SDGs on an individual level taking the regional needs into account. Yet, mutual learning is not only possible but also highly beneficial to all. Finally, this chapter will show that WIAs in combination with Agenda 2030 are great possibilities for universities around the world to not only engage with the Global Agenda, but also enhance their own possibilities.

"Integrating Sustainable Development into the Postgraduate Curriculum in the UK: A Mixed Method Study," by Gavin Melles, speaks about UK and a

Masters level discipline-specific courses in sustainability which integrates modules on the social, economic, and environmental issues of sustainable development. The postgraduate faculty teaching on these courses and the student cohorts enrolling in such courses bring varying attitudes, experiences, and beliefs to the ecological and anthropological discourses and practices about sustainable development. Existing studies of ESD have identified strengths and weaknesses in the knowledge and attitudes of students and faculty although few studies have focused on postgraduate cohorts and fewer still have attempted to compare and contrast students and lecturers. This mixed method case study analyses findings from data collected (2016–2017), student surveys ($n = 121$), and semi-structured interviews with faculty ($n = 21$) recruited from multiple university departments, centers, and programs ($n = 12$) to identify prevailing anthropocentric and ecocentric ideas and rationales about sustainable development and ESD. Findings suggest a strong orientation to mainstream sustainable development in both groups, but analysis identifies reasons for resisting a focus on extremes of "deep green" or "green wash" approaches. In addition, prevailing belief in academic neutrality, institutional and disciplinary factors, student pragmatism, and other drivers are highlighted. The study concludes by identifying potential paths from prevailing (experiential) education in sustainable development to more transformational approaches.

REFERENCES

Bonneuil, C., & Fressoz, J. (2017). *The shock of the Anthropocene: The earth, history and us*: London: Verso.

Brundtland Commission. (1987). *World Commission on Environment and Development (WCED)*. Our Common Future, New York, NY.

Drayson, R., Bone, E., Agombar, J., & Kemp, S. (2013). *Student attitudes towards and skills for sustainable development*. York: Higher Education Academy/National Union of Students.

Gibbard, P., & Walker, M. (2014). The term 'Anthropocene' in the context of formal geological classification. *Geological Society, London, Special Publications, 395*(1), 29–37.

Hopkinson, P., Hughes, P., & Layer, G. (2008). Sustainable graduates: Linking formal, informal and campus curricula to embed education for sustainable development in the student learning experience. *Environmental Education Research, 14*(4), 435–454.

Howlett, C., Ferreira, J.-A., & Blomfield, J. (2016). Teaching sustainable development in higher education: Building critical, reflective thinkers through an interdisciplinary approach. *International Journal of Sustainability in Higher Education, 17*(3), 305–321. https://doi.org/10.1108/IJSHE-07-2014-0102

Kopnina, H. (2012). Education for sustainable development (ESD): The turn away from 'environment' in environmental education? *Environmental Education Research, 2012*(18), 699–717.

Muttarak, R., & Lutz, W. (2014). Is education a key to reducing vulnerability to natural disasters and hence unavoidable climate change? *Ecology and Society, 19*(1), 42. http://dx.doi.org/10.5751/ES-06476190142

Öhman, J. (2008). *Values and democracy in education for sustainable development*. Malmö: Liber.

Stern, N. (2007). *The economics of climate change: The Stern review*. Cambridge: Cambridge University Press.

Stubbs, W., & Schapper, J. (2011). Two approaches to curriculum development for educating for sustainability and CSR. *International Journal of Sustainability in Higher Education, 12*(3), 259–268.

UNESCO. (2005). *United Nations Decade of Education for Sustainable Development (2005–2014): International Implementation Scheme*. Paris: UNESCO. Retrieved from http://unesdoc.unesco.org/images/0014/001486/148650E.pdf

UNESCO. (2014). Sustainable development begins with education: How education can contribute to the proposed post-2015 goals. Paris: UNESCO. Retrieved from http://unesdoc.unesco.org/images/0023/002305/230508e.pdf. Accessed on May 19, 2015.

Wheeler, D., & Hammer, D. (2010). *The economics of population policy for carbon emissions reduction in developing countries*. Washington, DC: Center for Global Development.

Wood, B. E., Cornforth, S., Beals, F., Taylor, M., & Tallon, R. (2016). Sustainability champions? Academic identities and sustainability curricula in higher education. *International Journal of Sustainability in Higher Education*, *17*(3), 342–360. https://doi.org/10.1108/IJSHE-12-2014-0171

CHAPTER 2

INTEGRATING SUSTAINABILITY INTO THE UNIVERSITY: ACADEMIES FOR LEARNING

Audrey M. Dentith and Nancy V. Winfrey

ABSTRACT

This chapter provides a theoretical framework that links ecojustice education to concepts of eco-intelligence and collective social intelligence. This theoretical framework informs the creation of innovative university academies that highlight sustainability and the revitalization of the cultural commons. The culture commons or those intergenerational face-to-face practices are evident in all communities worldwide. These practices include craft knowledge, the knowledge of growing, cultivating and preparing food, medicinal practices, and other forms of knowledge that are largely non-monetized and do not contribute to environmental degradation. Academies are sustained multiday events that incorporate the knowledge and work of activists, community members, faculty, and students who come together for the purpose of providing a platform for the discussion and resolution of critical environmental issues. Two examples are provided and details about the construction and execution of these events are provided.

Keywords: Ecojustice education; cultural commons; eco-intelligence; adult learning theories; enclosure; Vygotsky

Teaching and Learning Strategies for Sustainable Development:
Innovations in Higher Education Teaching and Learning, Volume 19, 15–28

ISSN: 2055-3641/doi:10.1108/S2055-364120200000019005

INTRODUCTION

In the past two generations, humans have degraded the Earth's ecosystems more rapidly than in any previous time in human history. The world's population doubled from 1960 to 2000 and the effects of the lifestyle enjoyed by millions of people over the past three generations have dramatically depleted natural resources and the viability of many species. Problems of pollution, carbon emissions, food insecurity, waste disposal, and water shortages now threaten people, animals, and ecological systems across the globe. This ravenous demand for natural resources and the rapid changes in social and economic life wrought on by corporate capitalism have dramatically altered the natural world. Certainly, we live in times of great ecological despair (Gore, 2006; Reid & the Millennium Ecosystem Assessment (Program), 2006).

In this time of great ecological despair, educators in universities committed to sustainable education believe that an increased focus on a sustainable curriculum and the education of adults in universities and the communities can influence everyone's need to live more ecologically balanced lives. Worldwide, there is a heightened interest and focus on education as the means of changing the mindsets and habits of people worldwide. Increasingly, education is also focused on policy issues including the ways that the actions of corporations and governments are working to thwart sustainability, indigenous cultural practices, and positive human/nature relations. Movements in education that seek to reduce or counter the forces that further degrade the environment and exacerbate poverty and alienation are more widely apparent than ever before (Albertini, 2002; Featherstone, 2000; Klein, 2001; Shiva, 2004, 2010). Education is now regarded as the central means to promote positive environmental change in the world. Thus, knowledge of engaged curriculum and adult learning theories are fundamental to this proposal.

In this chapter, we offer a curriculum and a pedagogical approach for universities that addresses the goals of sustainable education. We advocate for various educative initiatives including academies or extended symposiums hosted by universities that broaden the reach of faculty to include the local and regional communities. We include a discussion of the theoretical framework for our work as well as a discussion of the learning theories that inform this curricular approach. Finally, we report on the learning of participants and give a summary of the results of these efforts.

THE ACADEMIES

Our academies integrate the work of activists with the work of scholars to support sustainable goals not only in the university but also in the life of the community. We have organized several academies that feature activists, scholars, students, and other community members as presenters, authors, and students who come together to imagine a reworking of the university in which it becomes a true hub of engaged dialogue around the most pressing issues of our modern world – sustainability and ecological change.

One such example of our efforts was the *Academy for the Critical Inquiry of the Cultural Commons* that was held in the city of San Antonio, TX in the United States, at a large public university in the summer of 2012. In this five-day academy, activists, scholars, undergraduate and graduate students, faculty, and community members assembled to share their knowledge and experience of the cultural commons. The cultural commons, described in more detail below, are those largely non-monetized, intergenerational practices that are passed down from generation to generation in ways that do not contribute to the further degradation of the environment. These practices of mutually supported relationships, and local activities are always practiced in a face-to-face manner. They can inform the basis of the local economies and, as such, exist in direct contrast to the market economy. Highlighting, embracing, and extending the cultural commons was the organizing feature of this academy. The skills and knowledge of community members, the faculty, various activists, and students were highlighted in the events of this five-day format. Organic farmers, local-sourced restaurant chefs, faculty engaged in home gardening and canning, oral storytellers, water conservation activists, craftsmen, and Yogis, demonstrated their crafts while professors and graduate students presented papers and other artifacts related to living lives rich in the cultural commons and more ecologically sound lifestyles. Graduate students engaged in the scholarly pursuit of the cultural commons through sustained engagement within their communities alongside activists and scholars. Films were shown every evening including films on water shortages, indigenous populations, and waste disposal issues. A short film was produced on this academy. One additional way that other faculty in the College were encouraged to participate was through invited responses to the lectures. Various faculty were selected to offer opinions and insights from each of the scheduled speeches.

In 2016, an *Ecojustice Leadership Academy* was organized at a large public university in rural Appalachia in Boone, North Carolina in the United States. In this academy, professors committed to ecological living, gave lectures on international environmental programs, nature and beauty, the problems of digital knowledge, and the erosion of the cultural commons. Activists gave updates on their work with mountain top removal, coal ash disposal, and energy monopolies in the state of North Carolina. Poets recited their work and participants engaged in experiential activities that heightened their awareness of environmental issues and the need to be mindful and attentive to nature. Again, the focus on the cultural commons evident in this community was a central organizing focus. Warm up activities began each day and included experiential activities. For example, a simulation of the *Summit on Climate Change and Indigenous People*, a conference that took place in Alaska in 2009, was an example of one such activity. Films on the problems of coal ash disposal and overconsumption were featured. Importantly, students kept visual diaries of the week's activities, responding to their experiences in any form of expression (see Table 1 for a complete schedule of events).

Both of these academies were organized around a new or existing course. In the San Antonio academy, masters and doctoral students were enrolled in a class on curriculum theory in the Department of Education. Attendance was required although the format for this university class was unique. Students were immersed with the community participants and the scheduled speakers. They were given an assignment to complete as a measure of their learning, which included the development of an ethnographic experience researching the cultural commons in their communities. A full project that integrated theory into their research was required. Students were also invited to be interviewed for a film that was made on the project.

In the Boone academy, students were all doctoral students in educational leadership enrolled in a course created specifically for the general purposes of the academy called, *Ecojustice Leadership*. They were also immersed with the speakers and events for the week and were required to attend all events. As in the San Antonio program, community members were invited, as well as family, friends, other faculty,

Table 1. Ecojustice Leadership Academy @ Appalachian State University.

Day 1: Monday, May 16, 2016 Theme: *Revitalizing the Cultural Commons* Warm up: Experiential activity[a] Morning session (10–11.30 a.m.) Speaker: Dr Chet Bowers Title: *Characteristics of the Cultural Commons being undermined by the Digital Commons* Afternoon session (1–3 p.m.) Panel discussion Coral Coulter: Blue Ridge Women in Agriculture Emily Jackson: Appalachian Sustainability Agriculture Project Karen Sabo: Women's Fund of the Blue Ridge Break: 3–3.30 p.m. Film (4 p.m.): *Ancient Futures*	Day 3: Wednesday, May 18, 2016 Theme: *Sustainability and the Arts* Warm up: Experiential activity[a] Morning session (10–11.30 a.m.) Speaker: Dr Liz Rose Title: *Beauty and Productivity: Untethered Sisters* Afternoon session (1–3 p.m.) Panel discussion Mary Ray, Dept of Applied Design: On Sustainable Clothing Susan Musilli: Doctoral Program in Ed Leadership: Found Poetry Break: 3–3.30 p.m. Film: *The True Cost*
Day 2: Tuesday, May 17, 2016 Theme: *Leading Local Activism* Warm up: Experiential activity[a] Morning session (10–11.30 a.m.) Speaker: Dr Greg Reck Title: *Sustainability as a Radical Social Movement: A Personal Exploration* Break: 3–3.30 p.m. Afternoon session (1–3 p.m.) Panel discussion Amy Adams: Appalachian Voices Group Kim Porter: North Carolina Warn Tracy Edwards: Resident activist Film: *Sludge*	Day 4: Thursday, May 19, 2016 Theme: *Interdisciplinarity in Ecojustice Work* Warm up: Experiential activity[a] Morning session (10–11.30 a.m.) Speaker: Dr Jen Westerman Title: *Working on Earth: Class and Environmental Justice* Break: 3–3.30 p.m. Afternoon session (1–3 p.m.) Panel discussion Dr Lee Ball, Dept of University Sustainability: On Leading University Sustainability Efforts Tom Hansell: Center for Appalachian Studies: On Sustaining Local History and Culture Break: 3–3.30 p.m. Film: *After Coal*

Sponsored by the Reich College of Education.

and other students not enrolled in the class. To solidify their learning and meet the requirements for the program, enrolled students were required to complete a project that described a specific project of their design related to the course content.

Importantly several features of our work characterized these academies. First, attention to local knowledge and the particular issues that face people in these settings was central to the curriculum. In San Antonio, TX, water shortages, water deregulation, and the quality of food took center stage in this urban setting. In Appalachia, North Carolina, coal ash disposal, mountain-top coal removal, and energy monopolies were key areas of concern. Secondly, the curriculum was not only contextual, but purposely eclectic, organic, and integrated. Films, activist talks, demonstrations, academic lectures, and art characterized each of these endeavors and space was open for meaningful dialogue and exchange. Thirdly, an articulated ecojustice curriculum informed the content and activities. Fourth, attention was given to theories and methods of rethinking intelligence, fostering adult learning, and re-envisioning the role of the professor.

In the section that follows, we describe the curriculum framework for these academies.

THE ECOJUSTICE CURRICULUM FRAMEWORK

At the heart of this work are important curricular notions. An understanding of the tenets of ecojustice education is essential. Educational reforms in ecojustice education include the redressing of the following: the elimination of eco-racism, the colonization of other cultures; the need to revitalize the world's cultural commons; the need to pursue lifestyles that do not diminish the prospects for future generations; the need to respect the rights of nature; and, finally, an understanding of the environmental crisis as a cultural one. Specifically, ecojustice education regards the elimination of eco-racism or the practices that result in a disproportionate exposure among the poor and disenfranchised to the effects of pollution and overconsumption as paramount. The colonization of other cultures involves the continuing practice of appropriating resources to serve the wealthy and promoting Western values across the globe. Revitalizing the world's diversity of the cultural commons strengthens a community's self-reliance and promotes the discovery of human talent while not contributing to ecological destruction. Pursuing lifestyles that do not diminish the prospects for future generations requires us to shift our consciousness to one that recognizes the interconnectivity of all of the earth's systems including the acts of humans. Respecting the rights of nature and viewing all of nature not as a commodity but as viable, living organizations with the same rights as humans is essential. Finally, understanding the cultural roots of the problem we face to be at the heart of the ecological crisis. We are all socialized to think and act in specific ways. These practices are part of our cultural understanding which is at often odds with the needs of an eco-just world. Unfortunately, public schools and universities are driven by values that underlie the corporate world. However, there is hope that these mindsets can be changed. If we consider the changes that have already occurred in universities, particularly those shaped by activists, it is possible for us all to embrace these principles in our work (Bowers, 2011a; Martusewicz, Edmundson, & Lupinacci, 2011).

Here, we advocate for a curriculum that does three things: (1) embraces the cultural commons; (2) redresses our conceptions of intelligence; and (3) situates the professor as the mediator within the university community.

Embracing the Cultural Commons

There are two kinds of "commons": The *natural* and the *cultural commons*. The natural commons consists of those things that come directly from nature, that is, water, air, vegetation, and all aspects of our natural resources. Increasingly, these are being eroded by over-population, pollution, problems of waste disposal, climate change, ocean acidity, etc. The natural commons are also being constantly threatened by forces of industrialization and privatization (Bowers, 2006).

The cultural commons consist of the non-monetized knowledge that exists in every community. These include the craft knowledge, knowledge of gardening and food preparation, theater and most forms of art, ceremonies, medicinal practices, mentoring relations, knowledge of childbirth practices, rituals, yoga, games, meditation, and forms of intergenerational learning that take place face-to-face. These practices have endured for thousands of years, and are still evident in every community but often go unrecognized. These practices often do not contribute to ecological destruction and do not always involve the exchange of monies. These cultural commons are part of the intergenerational legacies that allow people to engage in practices and relationships that are largely outside of the mainstream consumer and monetized culture. These practices are typically intergenerational and have been passed on by face-to-face relationships. This inheritance might include all of the activities above, as well as mentoring and oral storytelling (Bowers, 2012).

These practices, habits, and customs vary from one culture to another. Ethnic groups often share some aspects of the cultural commons as part of their identity and heritage. In many cases, the cultural commons is, at times, the basis for the local economies as well as accompanying systems of mutual support that sustain their survival and means of intrinsic wealth and prosperity. This is in contrast to the liberal market economy which is most often driven by an incessant demand for a constant stream of new products (Bowers, 2006, 2012). Often times, the practices of the cultural commons are taken-for-granted by people. It is important to acknowledge that these practices are often not apparent to people because our culture over relies on individualism, change, and an adherence to a market liberal ideology (Bowers, 2011a).

Today, there is persistent erosion of many of our cultural commons. Bowers (2006) refers to this as *enclosure*. Today, many of the world's indigenous languages as well as erosion of processes of local democracy are widely apparent. The cultural commons are a means to counter the prevailing forces of such enclosure. The revitalization of the cultural commons, Bowers asserts, is of significant ecological importance. Their (re) emergence resists further degradation of the natural commons. Moreover, participation in the cultural commons enables people to discover personal interests, skills, and ways to engage with others in ways that strengthen the sense of community and mutual responsibility (Bowers, 2011a, 2012).

The cultural commons are foundational to the sustainability of local democracies. Local democracies can only exist in face-to-face relationships in which people understand the issues that will lead to the improvement of the way of life in a given community. There is a different kind of accountability in the face-to-face engagement. It is ground in moral values that are shaped by positive, engaged experiences (Bowers, 2016).

The revitalization of the cultural commons is a radical departure from consumer-laden and prevailing cultural practices. Efforts to revitalize the commons will ensure survival for billions of people in the years ahead as they struggle to survive in a world that is increasingly compromising its natural resources. Bowers (2016) thought that the revitalization of the cultural commons would reduce human impact on natural systems while offering opportunities for self-discovery and the cultivation of the talents of others. Bowers (2011a, 2011b) asserts that the revitalization of the cultural commons is a more radical proposal for social justice than the models thus far introduced in the West.

Bowers (2012) also asserted that not all of the cultural commons in a given community should be preserved. Some cultural commons include heinous customs such as those practiced by the Klu Klux Klan or violent street gangs. These should not be replicated, carried forward, or revitalized. Only those that support civil liberties and democratic practices should be sustained.

The activities of the academies described above center around the cultural commons. Bringing people together in interdependent relationships not only expands their awareness of the local cultural commons in their communities, but it also brings out their own personal talents and skills (Bowers, 2013).

Redressing Our Conceptions of Intelligence

Intelligence in the Western world has been largely characterized by an understanding of the autonomy of the individual. While the term ecology is widely used, it is little understood, particularly in terms of cultural and linguistic knowledge. Most understandings of ecology stem from an understanding of the cyclic and interdependent nature of the natural world. However, there exist *cultural ecologies*, such that an understanding of the ways that cultures are also nested within each other and totally dependent on the self-renewing capacity of the natural ecologies. Unfortunately, science has disregarded the nature of natural and cultural ecologies and has reduced all thinking to a reductionist approach. Certainly, the curriculum in most colleges and universities does not, in its current form, address intelligence as a relational concept. What is distinctive about eco-intelligence is that it involves noticing and responding to the information being communicated within and between the participants in the space of natural and cultural ecologies. It is about a conscious way of thinking and being that is systemic, evolutionary, and social (Bowers, 2017).

Eco-intelligence assumes that intelligence is part of a systemic, organic, and evolving community. Most professors have been educated to regard intelligence as a phenomenon evident in competitive, individualistic structures. Intelligence has largely been viewed as the manifestation of one's individual achievements, not as a phenomenon that is generated from the collective body of people and their ideas. We assert that intelligence is a relational phenomenon, one that relies on the interrelatedness of all human and non-human life. Such conceptions of intelligence can fundamentally alter the learning experiences of adults in the university and in the community. In our work in the academies, intelligence is conceived in a relational manner in that social relations do emanate from the exchanges of diverse people who hold different perspectives and values (Bowers, 2011a; Martusewicz et al., 2011).

This concept of ecological intelligence is very similar to notions of collective social intelligence. Such notions of intelligence are not only rooted in the history of the cultural commons, these have been supported by advances in neuroscience research over the last decade. Goleman (2006) introduced the term "social intelligence" based on exploration of brain functioning during interactions between people. Brain function is a complex and connected neurological process, and Goleman defines the "social brain" as a "set of distinct but fluid and wide-ranging neural networks that synchronize around relating to others" (p. 324). The process of relating to other people necessarily evolved over time to enable communities to navigate social currents, environmental events, and create processes for passing on intergenerational knowledge. Goleman explains that as people engage in complex social interactions and their collective neurons are activated, new circuitry in the brain develops to the degree that the interactions are valued by the community. These interactions, or connections between members of the community, are the essential fabric that sustains a relationship between the community and its natural systems. Any bioregion that includes a community of people has unique parameters that must be respected to maintain a sustainable relationship between the community and the natural resources upon which their lives depend: arable land, clean air, water, plants, and animals.

Social intelligence, according to Goleman (2006) can be organized into two broad categories: social awareness and social facility. Awareness refers to our attunement to another person, a quality of attention that goes beyond momentary connection to sustained presence and engagement. Social facility is the action taken as a result of that collective awareness. For example, neighbors might exchange greetings and lament the lack of community resources for recycling, but until they sustain a dialogue regarding their concern there is little social awareness in that neighborhood. Sustained engagement on the topic generates collective neural networks and energy toward action. In this case, a proposal to the city council from those neighbors who worked together to create solutions, demonstrates a new degree of social facility in that neighborhood.

Sherman (2016) builds on the same concept using the term "shared pool of attention" (p. 177). This "pool" is a collective resource, which unlike water or vegetation, is strengthened rather than depleted by use. In fact, Sherman argues that our collective life requires a sharing of attention to particular issues, and that meaning is created and deployed within the community in social interactions that sustain the framework of the community. A successful neighborhood recycling initiative could lead to increased collective awareness – a larger, more experienced "pool" – and new dialogue on other pressing community needs. Collective awareness and attention can be splintered, however, as contemporary capitalism weaves commodity forms into the community and meaningful components of the culture are profitably privatized. The subsequent social facility, or action, is therefore diluted or diminished.

Eco-intelligence as a relational phenomenon is a biological reality; neuroscience supports what we know about relationships, identifying and quantifying brain functionality during social interactions. Because the social brain's wiring is connecting individuals on a biological level, the parallel circuitry between them creates an instant shared sense of awareness, or attention, and is ultimately of importance. In that moment meaning is co-created. Over time this process supports a community as it collectively leverages diverse individual perspectives and local natural resources toward meaningful and sustainable action.

LEARNING IN THE ACADEMIES

Students reported high levels of learning in both of these academies. In the San Antonio academy, students reported that they were motivated to apply their new knowledge about ecology, and particularly knowledge of the cultural commons to their work in K-12 education. Several participants expressed interest in a variety of practices related to the evidence of the cultural commons in their communities.

In the Boone academy, students reported that they were surprised by how much they learned about environmental issues as a result of the class. They enjoyed the variety of learning experiences and the use of diverse learning modalities throughout the week. In addition, many commented on the spiritual experience of the week. Sharing poetry, watching films together, and discussing their responses to the activities, created a bonding experience among them, with some commenting that the information and discussion was so profound that the spiritual connectedness was "palpable." In their efforts to create action plans as a result of the academy, many reported on taking steps that were life-altering.

Lucio-Villegas (2015) conceives of adult education as basic skills associated with two different domains: employability and active citizenship. Employability is certainly an intended outcome of formal institutional programs, where diplomas, skills and competencies are developed for the labor market. Active citizenship is more concerned with equipping individuals to live a collective public life that is democratic and equitable, and often exists in the non-formal learning space of relevant, community engagement. Educating adults in this space, through an ecojustice lens, helps bring to the surface the deep cultural roots of social and ecological problems that are manifest in a particular community.

Toward active citizenship, Lucio-Villegas understands adult education as having six critical components: dialogue, participation, experience, diversity, a collective approach, and emancipative outcomes. Moving out of the classroom and into the community, via the two academies we outlined earlier, students and community members participated in a diverse, collective dialogue around specific community concerns that operationalized Lucio-Villegas' critical components. In reflective papers and post-academy focus groups, the student participants articulated their elevated learning, sense of community and responsibility, and inspiration to take emancipative action following the immersive experience. As Jared, one of the students shared,

> Over the course of the day, I think I moved from taking information in, hearing how it's applied, being outraged and then asking myself how am I going to do something about that?" (Dentith & Thompson, 2017, p. 72)

Here the work of Soviet psychologist Lev Vygotsky is relevant, and we provide his learning theory – within the broad concepts of adult education – as the pedagogical process within the scaffolding of this curriculum. Vygotsky was a social constructivist, building on the cognitive work of Piaget but situating individual learning within a social context. He argued that all cognitive functioning originates in social interaction and cannot be separated from the history and culture of the community. In other words, the sociocultural context shapes the way in which people construct meaning from their experience; the necessarily social process is mediated through a culture's symbols and language (Merriam & Bierema, 2014). All higher mental functions such as thinking, complex problem solving, and ethical decision making have their origins in human social life (Beliavsky, 2006). In fact, Vygotsky argued that this higher cognitive functionality is first manifest in collective behavior, as a form of cooperation with other people, and only afterwards becomes an internalized, individual developmental asset (Van der Veer & Valsiner, 1994).

Viewing sustainable education through this theoretical lens, the coalition of university faculty, students, community citizens, and local environmental activists, provides a base of diverse perspectives from individuals who, nonetheless share a common interest in sustainability and ecological change. Within this group, various dialogues are generated from people's experience, which, encourages them to create new experiences. In the process of creating and re-creating shared experiences new knowledge is co-created (Lucio-Villegas, 2015). Over time this new, collective behavior can become a positive, proactive social milieu where individual development is nurtured and sustained.

A second advantage of such a coalition is a balancing of power between university faculty and members of the local community. Rather than privatize education as a commodity that is limited to individuals of means, and perpetuate a hegemonic societal mindset valuing corporate capitalism at the expense of the natural world, universities can take the lead in convening dialogue with the communities whose footprint they share. The intersection of critical thinking skills and academic research of the university faculty, the logistical experience and passion of the activists, and the everyday epistemology of the community create a powerfully diverse and engaging dialogue. Again, we turn to Vygotsky for a theoretical frame for this phenomenon, his notion of the Zone of Proximal Development (Beliavsky, 2006).

Vygotsky's theory is that cognitive development exists along a continuum where individual learning is stable and consistent in terms of independent problem solving, on the one side, and where potential learning, which is dependent on guidance or collaboration, exists on the other end. The Zone of Proximal Development, the space between independent performance and aided performance (Beliavsky, 2006) is the place of rapid learning. In the case of our academy participants, the collective knowledge went *just beyond* that which is possible independently. In the case of our academy, each perspective lifts the collective knowledge *just beyond* that which is possible independently. In other words, the abstract theorizing of the university classroom gives students a basis for independent ecological decision-making, in collaboration with the wisdom of citizens who have attended to life in a particular place over many generations. When students develop these practices and the knowledge needed by those places, their learning is accelerated. The environment in which this learning takes place is not static, or peripheral in relation to social cognitive development, but constantly changeable and dynamic. As a result, the *zone* shifts in response to the changes in the individual and the relationship between the individual and the environment (Van der Veer & Valsiner, 1994). Taken as a collective phenomenon, as in the case of our academy, the potential for educational initiatives to shape the future of public awareness and action toward ecologically balanced lives is unlimited.

The unfortunate truth is that we live in an industrial culture that includes deeply ingrained social and ecological violence; beliefs that have infiltrated our behavior and shaped our modern culture (Martusewicz et al., 2011). Against this backdrop, the importance of collective dialogue cannot be overstated. The networks of support, trust, and reciprocity that have kept the traditional cultural commons alive can be re-generated and sustained through educational initiatives. The co-creation of language, meaning, and action-oriented partnerships around environmental issues is, in fact, a life changing experience. Sandy, a participant in the Ecojustice Leadership Academy explained, "I describe it as 'enlightenment' " (Dentith & Thompson, 2017, p. 71).

THE PROFESSOR AS MEDIATOR

In these academies, the role of the professor is distinct and differs from a traditional approach. According to Bowers (2013), the faculty or the teacher becomes a person who helps students to become aware of a community's traditions of self-sufficiency and mutual support. They illuminate the presence of the cultural commons in the local community through the work of the Academy. Highlighting the work of local activists is important, but contemplating the existence of the cultural commons brings out the abilities for all people to embrace the cultural commons and facilitate their proliferation. This pedagogical effort also helps students to recognize the ways that technologies and market forces threaten the cultural commons in contemporary life. This is not to say that some gains in scientific and industrial culture are not positive and have contributed to a better quality of life for many of the world's people. Certainly, the eradication of diseases has contributed to longevity and less suffering. Thus, the professor, as mediator, helps students to not only recognize the attributes of the cultural commons but also recognize the various ways that scientific and industrial cultures have made some positive contributions to human kind. It is the ability to discern the differences between those practices that erode the life-sustaining cultural commons with those activities that foster practices that embody sustainable practices and not contribute to the erosion of the environment (Bowers, 2013).

To operationalize the role of mediation requires faculty to reframe their voice as one of many equal voices in a generative dialogue, what Isaacs (1999) refers to as "the art of thinking together." As mentioned earlier, the success of the academy format depends on a balance of power between the university faculty, local activists, community members, and students. Academic culture celebrates critical thinking skills and, emboldened by the power of academic orthodoxy, can dominate the process of thinking together, overtly in comments and conclusions, or subtly, as in their tone of voice. A learning outcome for students is to experience the process of navigating the philosophical divide created by arrogant ideologies that compete for "market share," as it were, in terms of what students believe is best for the common good. They not only have the experience of thinking together in groups of people with differing agendas – as an equal voice – they also have the parallel experience of developing new knowledge *just beyond* that which would have been possible independently as students (Van der Veer & Valsiner, 1994). This is the Vygotsky's Zone of Proximal Development.

The challenge for university faculty in this non-traditional mediation role can be reduced by understanding the theoretical underpinnings of the curriculum and regarding the learning theories evident among adults, as described in this chapter. Social intelligence (Goleman, 2006) gives scientific credence to the process, and outcomes, of collaborative dialogue. The social brain, as Goleman uses the term, is a biological process supporting the network of relational intelligence that sustains the cultural commons. In this sense, the divide between progress and tradition is bridged by knowledge which is now available through advanced technologies. The role of the university faculty is critical, in this pedagogical approach, as the source of the mediation tools required to create and sustain a "living experience of inquiry *within* and *between* people" (Isaacs, 1999, p. 9, italics in the original) the result of which is a generative knowledge that only exists as a result of the different voices in the conversation.

CONCLUSIONS

We concur with environmental adult educator, Moema Veizzer, who suggested that in order to promote ecological perspectives and knowledge about ecological issues, we need to create learning opportunities that build stronger networks and partnerships with social movements (Viezzer, 1992 as cited in Clover, 2003). As curriculum scholars and adult educators, we are devoted to the pursuit of relevant knowledge in higher education. We are also committed to the goals of sustainability education as well as the need for universities to change the way they think about educating the public, namely that "life and education must never be separated. We must have more life in our universities and more universities in our lives" (Follett, 1918, p. 369).

We maintain that the university can play an important role in promoting ecological awareness, mindsets, and practices among young people that can lead to a new approach to sustainable life. Such consciousness and related practices, particularly those that can lead to the cultivation of the cultural commons and more self-sustaining lifestyles will be ever more important in the years to come.

REFERENCES

Albertini, C. (2002, September 17). Small is beautiful: Airports, Mcdonald's and hypermarkets in Mexico. *ZNet Commentary*. Reprinted in P. Rothenberg (Ed.), *Beyond borders: Thinking critically about global issues* (pp. 577–580). New York, NY: Worth Publishers.

Beliavsky, N. (2006). Revisiting Vygotsky and Gardner: Realizing human potential. *Journal of Esthetic Education, 40*(2), 1–11.

Bowers, C. A. (2006). *Revitalizing the cultural commons: Cultural and educational sites of resistance and affirmation*. New York, NY: Lexington Books.

Bowers, C. A. (2011a). *University reform in an era of global warming*. Eugene, OR: Ecojustice Press.

Bowers, C. A. (2011b). *Educational reforms for the 21st century*. Eugene, OR: Ecojustice Press.

Bowers, C. A. (2012). *The way forward: Educational reforms that focus on the cultural commons and the linguistic roots of the ecological/cultural crisis*. Eugene, OR: Ecojustice Press.

Bowers, C. A. (2013). *In the grip of the past*. Eugene, OR: Ecojustice Press.

Bowers, C. A. (2016). *Reforming higher education in an era of ecological crisis and growing digital insecurity*. Anoka, MN: Process Century Press.

Bowers, C. A. (2017). An ecojustice approach to educational reform in adult education. In A. M. Dentith & W. Griswold (Eds.), *Ecojustice adult education: Theory and practice in the cultivation of the cultural commons: New directions for adult and continuing education* (Vol. 153, pp. 53–64).

Clover, D. E. (2003). Environmental adult education: Critique and creativity in a globalizing world. In L. H. Hill & D. E. Clover (Eds.), *Environmental adult education: Ecological learning, theory, and practice for socioenvironmental change: New directions for adult and continuing education* (Vol. 99, pp. 5–15).

Dentith, A., & Thompson, O. (2017). Teaching adult ecojustice education. In A. Dentith & W. Griswold (Eds.), *Ecojustice adult education: Theory and practice in the cultivation of the cultural commons* (pp. 65–76). San Francisco, CA: Jossey-Bass Publishers.

Featherstone, L. (2000, May 15). The new student movement. In P. Rothenberg (Ed.), *Beyond borders: Thinking critically about global issues* (pp. 585–590). New York, NY: Worth Publishers.

Follett, M. P. (1918). *The new state: Group organization, the solution for popular government*. New York, NY: Longman Green.

Goleman, D. (2006). *Social intelligence: The new science of human relationships*. New York, NY: Bantam Books.

Gore, A. (2006). *An inconvenient truth: The planetary emergency of global warming and what we can do about it*. New York, NY: Rodale Press.

Isaacs, D. (1999). *Dialogue and the art of thinking together*. New York, NY: Doubleday.

Klein, N. (2001). Reclaiming the commons. *New Left Review, 9*, 81.

Lucio-Villegas, E. (2015). *Adult education in communities*. Rotterdam, The Netherlands: Sense Publishers.

Martusewicz, R. (2019). *A pedagogy of responsibility: Wendell Berry for ecojustice education*. New York, NY: Routledge Press.

Martusewicz, R. A., Edmundson, J., & Lupinacci, J. (2011). *Ecojustice education: Toward diverse, democratic, and sustainable communities*. New York, NY: Routledge.

Merriam, S., & Bierema, L. (2014). *Adult learning: Linking theory and practice*. San Francisco, CA: Jossey-Bass Publishers.

Reid, W. V., & Millennium Ecosystem Assessment (Program). (2006). *Bridging scales and knowledge systems: Concepts and applications in ecosystem assessment*. Washington, DC: Island Press.

Sherman, Z. (2016). Primitive accumulation in the cultural commons. *Review of Radical Political Economics, 48*(1), 176–188.

Shiva, V. (2004, May 13). Building water democracy: People's victory against coca-cola in Plachimada. *ZNet Commentary*. Reprinted on P. Rothenberg (Ed.), *Beyond borders: Thinking critically about global issues* (pp. 580–584). New York, NY: Worth Publishers.

Shiva, V. (2010). *Staying alive: Women, ecology and development*. Brooklyn, NY: South End Press.

Van der Veer, R., & Valsiner, J. (1994). *The Vygotsky reader*. Oxford: Blackwell Press.

Films

Beaver P. (Producer), & Hansell T. (Director). (2016). *After Coal* [Documentary]. United States: Center for Appalachian Studies at Appalachian State University.

Page J. (Producer), & Page J. & Walton E. (Director). (1993). *Ancient Futures* [Documentary]. United States: International Society for Ecology & Culture (ISEC).

Ross M. (Producer), & Morgan A. (Director). (2015). *The True Cost* [Documentary].

Salyer R. (Producer), & Salyer R. (Director). (2005). *Sludge* [Documentary]. United States: Appalshop.

United States: Life Is My Movie Entertainment Company (in association with) Untold Creative.

CHAPTER 3

AN INTERDISCIPLINARY PROBLEM-BASED APPROACH TO EDUCATION FOR SUSTAINABLE DEVELOPMENT

Bland Tomkinson and Rosemary Tomkinson

ABSTRACT

This chapter is based on the work of Professor Charles Engel who, sadly, passed away early in 2019. Some 20 years ago, Professor Engel was advocating that higher education should take a lead in remediating global challenges, particularly those of sustainability. He took a broad view of the concept of "sustainability," based largely on the Brundtland (1987) view of global challenges. Engel proposed that successful approaches to address the complex problems of sustainability should be explored across disciplinary boundaries. The University of Manchester developed a series of course modules focusing on these major challenges, largely run on interdisciplinary lines. Initially the concept was explored across science and engineering, with the support of the Royal Academy of Engineering. Charles Engel, a leading authority on its use, advised using Problem-Based Learning as a means of addressing the wicked problems in interdisciplinary groups. The pilot modules were extensively evaluated and reported. Since then the course units have developed and diversified, with extension to other schools, universities, countries, and to postgraduate courses. This transformative concept has also been explored in hybrid online format. The current chapter will re-introduce some of the original ideas and bring together the many threads that have emerged.

Teaching and Learning Strategies for Sustainable Development:
Innovations in Higher Education Teaching and Learning, Volume 19, 29–40

ISSN: 2055-3641/doi:10.1108/S2055-364120200000019006

Keywords: Sustainable development; problem-based learning; interdisciplinarity; wicked problems; transformative education; transferable skills

BEGINNINGS

The University of Manchester was formed in 2004 from a merger of the Victoria University of Manchester and the University of Manchester Institute of Science and Technology (UMIST). Prior to the merger, the two institutions collaborated in a number of areas, including a joint Teaching Research and Development Network (TRDN). In 2002 Charles Engel, at that time a Visiting Professor at the University of London's Institute of Education, posed a challenge to the audience at a TRDN Symposium, a challenge that he described as the "Ultimate Challenge" (see Engel, Tomkinson, & Warner, 2004). His postulation was that the major complex issues faced by the world would not be remedied by politicians, whose time horizon was the next election, nor by business leaders, whose time horizon was the next balance sheet. Instead, he suggested that such problems needed to be tackled by professionals with a longer time horizon, and in this they needed to be informed by higher education. Charles Engel's concept of sustainability was shaped by the Brundtland Report (1987) whose tenets can be summarized in a list of a number of significant challenges that face the future of the world:

- Economic burden of large national debts.
- Reduction of biodiversity.
- Pollution of air, soil, and water, with detrimental influences on the environment.
- Growth of world population, accompanied by increasing poverty in the developing world.
- Competition for limited water supplies, resulting in threats of armed conflict.
- The threats and consequences of climate change.

He postulated that these developments stimulate extremism, terrorism and migration that affect social stability.

Charles Engel went further and proposed that the remediation of world problems could best be achieved by interprofessional collaboration and also suggested that this then predicated interdisciplinary approaches in higher education. Moreover, he advocated that higher education needed to tackle the exploration of such issues using student-centered team-based approaches, such as problem-based learning.

According to Neufeld and Barrows (1974, p. 1042), in problem-based learning,

> the learner focuses on a problem ... which involves genuine intellectual effort. The learner brings to the problem all of his previous information and expertise as well as his ability to think rationally about it. As he begins to ask questions, certain issues become defined which will require further information search. After assembling appropriate information, he synthesizes a

> problem solution. The student learns to recognize that few problems ... are totally 'solved' and that wrestling with any one problem opens up many other questions...

Engel and Clarke (1979, p. 73) add that "Only the constant practice of formulating and answering searching questions is likely to create the habit of this form of continuing education."

PREPARING THE GROUND

Following the symposium the TRDN organized a number of meetings to consider global issues and related educational approaches. Typical of these was an evening meeting, attended by some students as well as faculty, at which a senior diplomat from New Zealand sketched out some of the problems facing small island communities, particularly in the light of climate change: an issue that has since gained greater international prominence. The participants then tried to tackle some of the issues in small interdisciplinary groups. Two of the key things to emerge from this exercise were: first, the need to spend time understanding the nature of the problem and; second, the need to understand that there may be no single "right" answer to the problem, the problem might be ameliorated but never "solved."

The approach took off in 2006 when the Teaching Support Unit in the Faculty of Engineering and Physical Sciences of the newly merged university managed to secure funding from the UK's Royal Academy of Engineering to appoint Charles Engel as a Visiting Professor in Engineering Design for Sustainable Development. He forewent part of his stipend for this position to appoint a Project Officer to work on the implementation of a pilot course unit in Education for Sustainable Development. From the beginning the course unit was envisaged to be delivered by a problem-based learning approach and to span a number of undergraduate programs. A number of advisory groups were set up, across the Faculty, to consider elements of the design and to help build support for the pilot (Tomkinson, 2008b, pp. 4–5).

THE PILOT

The pilot unit was made available to final year undergraduates on programs across the Faculty but not all programs were able to incorporate it: a number of the programs are entirely comprised of mandatory units in the final year, leaving no vacant space in the curriculum. The pilot unit was designed as entirely PBL, with academic researchers in a number of disciplines invited to submit scenarios for the five "problems" to be investigated during the semester. The submitted scenarios were sorted and modified to enable a progression and development of skills through the semester. The initial units were subject to a considerable amount of monitoring and evaluation, with some changes introduced following the mid-semester evaluation. The classes were supported by postdoctoral researchers, one to each group of about eight students. These facilitators were given initial training and took part in weekly monitoring meetings. Each weekly session was of two hours with an expectation that work would be undertaken on each project during the intervening week. Initially each group was allocated its own workspace for the sessions, but this later became two groups to a room. Individual students were allocated to groups to try to achieve a balance of subject disciplines, national origins, and gender within the groups.

The evaluation of the first implementation of the unit gave rise to some concerns that needed to be addressed, particularly concerning assessment. The model initially adopted was heavily influenced by the PBL approach to teaching medical students, but the nature of the problems faced, in looking at global issues of sustainability, was more complex than this. The principal change was to move from *modified essay questions* to an individual reflective report; changes were also made to the peer assessment of group reports.

The idea of sustainability issues being *wicked problems* (Rittel & Webber, 1974) was also introduced. Briefly, *wicked* problems have many of the following characteristics:

- No definitive formulation.
- No clear end, no "stopping rule."
- An answer that is "good or bad" rather than "right or wrong."
- No immediate or ultimate test of their resolution.
- Consequences to every solution, there is no possibility of learning by "trial and error."
- No well-described set of potential solutions.
- Essentially unique.
- Possibly symptomatic of another problem.
- Causes with no unique explanation.
- Expectations that their "owners" will find the "right" answer.

These characteristics are radically different to the *tame* problems with which students usually tend to be faced. Indeed, it has been suggested that universities tend to reduce the complexity of issues in order to make them simpler for students to tackle (van Dam-Mieras, 2006), particularly in science and engineering. In the field of global societal responsibility there is usually an additional complicating factor, in that different proposed solutions may appeal to different stakeholders and any such solution may disadvantage certain groups in society. Choosing a solution may then become a social and political issue rather than a technical one.

Jonassen (2000, p. 75) distinguishes a number of problem types and suggests that medical problems fall into the category of *Diagnosis-Solution* problems where the learning is to "...select and evaluate treatment options and monitor; apply problem schemas," whereas the more complex global issues would come under his category of *Dilemmas*, where the learning is of "reconciling complex, non-predictive, vexing decision with no solution...." Clearly, the approach to the design of problem scenarios and of assessment needs to reflect these differences. In the Manchester situation the need to structure the problem scenarios appropriately, as *Dilemmas* in Jonassen's schema, had been recognized but the assessment initially failed to follow suit, retaining a *Diagnosis-Solution* approach. Nonetheless, this soon became apparent and the assessment was realigned to the style of the problem scenarios.

The pilot course unit was evaluated against the criteria of acceptability, effectiveness, and sustainability. In terms of acceptability, the evaluation found high acceptance of the concepts both of PBL and interdisciplinarity (Tomkinson, 2008a, pp. 13–15) among both participating students and facilitators. In this case, it must be borne in mind that this was an optional unit that students chose to take. In terms of effectiveness, student results were good, with none failing the initial units, but there were also indications that students had developed their skills in a broader sense, with increases in deep learning and research skills. Sustainability – in the sense of maintaining the module – was trickier to evaluate. During the pilot phase additional resources were deployed than would normally be attributable to a single course unit. Some of these were, essentially, part of the monitoring and evaluation process, but the staff input was still higher than would normally be acceptable for a taught (as oppose to laboratory) module. Some authors of problem scenarios were paid, and this was an additional cost of this approach, whereas others treated the initial generation of the scenario as part of their research. Indeed, in some instances colleagues were able to use the ideas, generated by these student groups, in their own research. The question of resource utilization was to be addressed in later versions of the approach (see below). One serendipitous outcome was the amount of cross-cultural learning in the groups. An example of this was highlighted from the discussions on a scenario relating to post-earthquake building in Kashmir in a group that contained students from both India and Pakistan: students from China and South America suggested that they had learned much about the politics of the area from their fellow-students. On another occasion a Chinese student, who joined the course unit after it had started, was assigned to a mixed group where he was the only one from China. He protested at this and asked to be transferred to a group that had several Chinese students. This request was turned down. Interestingly, at the end of the semester that student sought out the lecturers and thanked them for insisting on his remaining in the allotted group; he felt that he had learned much more as a result.

DEVELOPMENT OF THE APPROACH

The intended next move was to extend the model outwards, upwards, and sideways. This step involved: first, extending the participation to a wider range of subject disciplines; second, trialing the unit at postgraduate level; and third, exporting the model to other universities. Initially, the last of these was pursued by extensive promulgation of the results of the pilot through conferences and journal papers. The extension to a wider range of subject disciplines gradually evolved but was not without its difficulties. At postgraduate level an optional unit was made available in a Masters program in Management of Projects but with an emphasis on the management of humanitarian aid projects. The undergraduate course unit had a value of 10 credits within a course total of 360 (or sometimes 480) credits, whereas a standard postgraduate course unit was valued at 15 credits (within a course total of 180 credits) and this meant extending the material and the assessment to fit with postgraduate criteria. Within the UK, the idea was also taken up by the University of Keele in a joint project with the Universities of Manchester and Staffordshire, with an emphasis on scaling up using digital technology. Outside the UK, a Masters Summer School was organized in Finland, by Kuovola and Mikkeli Universities, using the basic concepts but as an intensive short course and with a broader concept of subject matter.

The extension of the initial unit to a wider range of disciplines was accompanied by changes in responsibility for the unit, with its transference to the Business School within the university, so that no one engineering discipline was seen as having responsibility. The result of the widening of the range of participants had some unfortunate side-effects, with one school making the unit compulsory, thus swamping the interdisciplinary groups. The move from an optional unit to a compulsory one for these students also produced some difficulties: some students failed to see the significance of sustainability to their subject and some of their teachers had similar misgivings not only about the content but also about the teaching approach. In one case, this was tackled by running a unit for an individual school separate from the interdisciplinary unit. Unfortunately that did not entirely resolve matters with the teaching staff, who continued to criticize the approach and, in particular, the assessment method. That unit still exists but has a much more didactic structure. The main issues with the continuing interdisciplinary unit tend to be around: "transfer values": the students' home school has to make a financial transfer to the school operating the unit, and marking schemes that can differ between schools, making the integration of marks from the unit more difficult.

The development of a postgraduate unit was assisted, initially, by internal teaching development funds and then by a national teaching grant. These helped to pay for postdoctoral and postgraduate facilitators as well as for the evaluation of the unit (Bessant et al., 2013). After the external funding expired, the number of facilitators had to be reduced. The unit was lodged within a postgraduate Management of Projects course, whose students came from a range of disciplinary and cultural backgrounds. The students were largely divided between those with engineering degrees and those with business or management degrees, but there was also a smattering of other subjects. The unit was also offered to a small number of students taking a postgraduate degree in International Development Policy and Management and in this way some degree of interdisciplinarity was maintained. Many of the scenarios used had a sustainability focus, in its broadest sense (see above), and others had aspects of sustainability built in. This unit ran successfully for a number of years but had to change its title (and focus) because of pressure from others within the university who felt that they "owned" the subject. This unit is currently in abeyance, ostensibly because insufficient students take up the option, but more because of resistance from other teaching staff. Some of this resistance is philosophical (some of those holding key administrative positions prefer more didactic approaches) but more concern is expressed over the fact that students spend greater time on the unit than they do on others and assignment dates can conflict with the requirements of other units. There is also a view that the approach is less "efficient" because of its demands on staff and space resources, despite evidence that the approach is more effective in terms of learning. One of the consequences of pressures on staffing resource was a reduction in the number of postgraduate and postdoctoral facilitators. In terms of their input, this meant that less support was available to groups that were struggling with process but, more importantly, it also meant that facilitators were no longer available to take part in dialogue concerning the feedback, reducing this to a less effective paper exercise. Acting as a facilitator was also a development opportunity for the postdoctoral and postgraduate researchers who undertook the role, in many cases supporting their subsequent moves into academic posts, and the reduction in numbers meant that fewer individuals were able to take up this opportunity.

The national funding was granted for a proposal to examine the use of online working, in "blended" or "hybrid" approaches, as part of a mechanism to increase the number of students participating in the PBL approach while reducing the demands on space and facilitators. The funding also enabled the approach to be trialed in other UK universities. The use of some elements of online working was shown to be a feasible approach (Bessant et al., 2013; Tomkinson & Hutt, 2012) and some initial contacts were also made with a view to operating an online unit internationally (China, Finland, Malaysia, and USA). This last idea faced the problems of: incompatibility of university systems; time-zone differences, leading to communication having to be entirely asynchronous; and incompatibility of unit credit rating systems. The feedback from the trial suggested that use of online communication was viable but that students generally preferred face-to-face contact. Indeed, during the trial there were instances of students circumventing the use of online groups in favor of using the tools to set up face-to-face group meetings! This project also demonstrated the efficacy of the approach, not just in terms of the students' learning but also in their attitudes toward sustainability.

The "Summer School" approach adopted in Finland was an interesting, but challenging, one. Here Masters' students from a range of disciplines – many of them undertaking part-time degrees – were offered the opportunity to work together before starting on the dissertation element of their degrees. The format for this was an initial introduction to the approach followed by division into interdisciplinary groups with each group given a different "challenge," broadly relating to sustainable development. Topics included, for example, a question of building a tidal barrage across the Gulf of Bothnia or the Gulf of Finland or the Baltic Sea; siting and building an "Ecotown" in eastern Finland; the ecology of Finnish forests; maritime carbon emissions; and replacing school textbooks with "e-books." The groups were given one day in which to refine the problem into a more specific issue that needed to be tackled, to sketch out the information needs for tackling the challenge and to make a brief presentation. The groups were then given an afternoon in which to construct a relevant challenge to be tackled by another group – most of the rest of the week was then taken up with groups tackling the challenges set by their colleagues and presenting a report on progress. Within the timescale, the groups were not necessarily expected to come up with a viable solution. Online resources were available during this period. Apart from some interesting challenges and new ideas about sustainability, the students found that one of the chief benefits was in helping to develop the formulation and approach to their dissertation topics.

THE TRANSFORMATIVE NATURE OF EDUCATION FOR SUSTAINABLE DEVELOPMENT

Education for sustainable development needs to be transformative, rather than simply transmissive: that is, why some speak about Education for Sustainable Development, rather than Education about Sustainable Development. Mezirow (1997, 2003) describes transformative learning as transforming problematic frames of reference, which should make learners more inclusive, discriminating, open, reflective, and emotionally able to change. He suggests that current systems of education increasingly discourage this approach to learning rather than encouraging it.

Wals (2009, p. 11) argues that it

> calls for new kinds of learning that are not so much of a transmissive nature (i.e. learning as reproduction) but rather of a transformative nature (i.e. learning as change). The latter requires permeability between disciplines, schools and the wider community and between cultures, along with the capacity to integrate, connect, confront and reconcile multiple ways of looking at the world.

His report suggests 14 learning outcomes for education for sustainable development:

- Critical reflective thinking.
- Understanding complexity/systemic thinking.
- Futures thinking.
- Planning and managing change.
- Understanding interrelationships across disciplines.
- Applying learning in a variety of life-wide contexts.
- Decision-making, including in uncertain situations.
- Dealing with crises and risks.
- Acting with responsibility locally and globally.
- Ability to identify and clarify values.
- Acting with respect for others.
- Identifying stakeholders and their interests.
- Participating in democratic decision-making.
- Negotiating and consensus building.

Looking at Wals' list, it is apparent that many of the attributes sought are of skill rather than knowledge and this implies that professionals have to act as autonomous thinkers in a collaborative context rather than acting uncritically on received wisdom. These concepts are not easy to teach using conventional didactic approaches.

In a Delphi study, of best practice in embedding sustainable development in the education of engineers, Rosemary Tomkinson, Tomkinson, Engel, and Lawson (2008, p. 3) suggest

> Reflecting the weighting given to systems modelling, the dominant generic or transferable skill identified was that of dealing with complexity, but also being able to think "outside the box." Other skills felt to be important were those of communicating and networking – particularly across disciplines.

In terms of curriculum, the strength of feeling was that

> sustainable development should be embedded throughout and that student-centred learning methods, in particular role play and case studies, were most appropriate .... A significant number of respondents felt that sustainable development should form a compulsory element of the curriculum and others felt that making it compulsory was the only way to get students to take on board issues of sustainable development.

Blessinger (2018 *passim*) looks at paradigm shifts in higher education and suggests that

> [...] higher education should embrace a bold vision of higher education in the service of humanity and for the common good .... These paradigm shifts have caused educators to rethink higher education beyond the purely utilitarian perspective. In a world that is rapidly changing, higher education must engage in a continual renewal of itself at all levels and in all areas. Emerging trends in theory development tend to centre on a constructivist approach that contends that education is both individually and socially constructed. Within this approach, education is viewed as a social system where people attach values and meaning-making to their knowledge that, in turn, influences their understanding and interpretation of the world (that is, their worldview) and this worldview, in turn, helps shape their reality. In this paradigm, the intersubjective nature of society and education exemplifies the importance of how individual actions, values and ideas help shape their reality and perceptions.

The study of sustainable development needs to be set within political frameworks and national and local government administrations need to be seen as stakeholders in the process, not necessarily with the same view of desirable outcomes. Adopting cross-cultural groups as a basis for problem-based learning can help in this process. Interestingly, a small study (Hill, Tomkinson, Hiley, & Dobson, 2016), carried out within the sequence of course units elucidated above, found that differences in learning styles between students of different national origins were much less than the differences between students from different subject disciplines.

DISCUSSION

The original pilot study and some subsequent, related, studies have been subject to a considerable amount of evaluation, using questionnaires, nominal groups (see Delbecq, Van de Ven, & Gustafson, 1975), focus groups and more informal approaches. These studies found the interdisciplinary problem-based approach to be generally effective (see e.g., Bessant et al., 2013): but in the various developments of the basic approach some changes have been made to tailor the approach to different audiences.

Most notable in the changes wrought has been the approach to assessment. As has been noted above, many of the attributes sought are conative rather than cognitive and thus traditional approaches to student assessment are inappropriate. The pilot study started by borrowing the concept of *modified essay questions* (see e.g., Leeder, Feletti, & Engel, 1979) from medical PBL, but this was found to be difficult to structure in the new context and difficult for students to complete successfully. The change was made to use individual reflective reports to gauge the acquisition of skills: although this features some element of self-assessment, in that students are required to submit their own reflections on their own performance, the scripts are actually marked by the teaching staff. Subsequently it was found that some, less mature, groups of students struggled even with this approach and an element of *scaffolding* was incorporated into the reports. This required that students make interim *stage* reports, which could also be used for the process of giving feedback. Paradoxically, one of the criticisms of the approach, generally, has been the amount of assessment incorporated into the units. This is part of the paradox that students require greater feedback but this necessitates some form of assessment to generate the feedback. Moreover one of the sources of conflict with colleagues has been that students on problem-based modules are perceived to spend more time on their PBL assignments than they do on more conventional units.

Informal feedback from students suggests that the issue of spending more time on PBL assignments arises because they find the problems intrinsically more interesting and potentially more rewarding! One unsolicited statement from a student, fresh from a job interview stated

> I am more confident [than before taking the module] to work in a team, to co-operate, to try making compromises and negotiations in order to prevent conflicts. Overall, the scheme on working as a team in various projects is very helpful for my future career in the companies I pursue to work, so I am really happy and satisfied with this module which is totally different learning procedure than others.

Bessant et al. (2013) found that almost two-thirds of students undertaking a hybrid PBL course unit had changed their attitude toward sustainability or environmental issues: in this case the students were on programs suggest that they already had a high level of such awareness. The students also reported that they felt that their skills had been improved by the approach: 94% for teamwork; 75% for communication skills; and 78% for employability. The products of the approach clearly extend beyond the bounds of sustainability.

CONCLUSION

The concept of *wicked* problems provides a useful lens through which to examine the complex global problems of sustainability. As described in the earlier paragraphs, Education for Sustainable Development can be seen as a *wicked* problem in itself and one that would be worthy of tackling in small, interdisciplinary, problem-based groups. To some extent that is precisely the trajectory followed in the case described above, initially cross-disciplinary working groups were set up to inform the process and much of the initial grounding and trying to get colleagues on board was done both in an interdisciplinary way and by using appropriate scenarios. The development from the initial pilot study demonstrates that there is no single "right" answer to the problem: a feature of its *wickedness*! Nonetheless, the basic underlying ideas of problem-based learning have remained throughout.

A problem-based approach can be very effective in education for sustainable development, particularly if it can be delivered in interdisciplinary groups, but it needs to be carefully tailored to local circumstances and introduced with care, involving colleagues and senior administrators at the earliest stages. The evidence evinced above demonstrates that a PBL approach can deliver an education that is not only transformative, with regard to issues of sustainable development, but also one that develops generic skills that foster employability. Treating the teaching of sustainable development as comprising problems that have a straightforward answer does not do justice to the complexity of the issues involved and, in the minds of the authors, does not fulfill the characteristics of *higher* education.

ACKNOWLEDGMENTS

The original pilot study was supported by funds from the UK Royal Academy of Engineering; the study on using a hybrid approach was supported by the UK Higher Education Academy's National Teaching Fellows' scheme and the Finnish Summer School was supported by EU Erasmus funding. Initial funding toward the Managing Humanitarian Aid Projects unit came from the University of Manchester's Centre of Excellence in Enquiry-Based Learning.

REFERENCES

Bessant, S., Bailey, P., Robinson, Z., Tomkinson, C. B., Tomkinson, R., Ormerod, R. M., & Boast, R. (2013). Problem-based learning: A case study of sustainability education. Retrieved from http://www.keele.ac.uk/media/keeleuniversity/group/hybridpbl/PBL_ESD_Case Study_Bessant, et al.

Blessinger, P. (2018). Rethinking higher education in the service of humanity. *University World News*, July 13, p. 514.

Brundtland, G. H. (1987). *The Brundtland Report, World Commission on Environment and Development*. Oxford and New York: Oxford University Press.

van Dam-Mieras, R. (2006). Learning for sustainable development: Is it possible within the established higher education structures. In *Drivers and barriers for implementing sustainable development in higher education* (pp. 12–18).

Delbecq, A. L., Van de Ven, A. H., & Gustafson, D. H. (1975). *Group techniques for program planning: A guide to nominal group and Delphi processes*. Glenview, IL: Scott Foresman.

Engel, C., Tomkinson, B., & Warner, R. (2004). The ultimate challenge: Higher education, globalisation and change. *EDiNEB international conference*, Maastricht.

Engel, C. E., & Clarke, R. M. (1979). Medical education with a difference. Programmed Learning and Educational Technology, *16*(1), 70–87.

Hill, F., Tomkinson, B., Hiley, A., & Dobson, H. (2016). Learning style preferences: An examination of differences amongst students with different disciplinary backgrounds. *Innovations in Education and Teaching International*, *53*(2), 122–134.

Jonassen, D. H. (2000). Toward a design theory of problem solving. *Educational Technology Research and Development*, *48*(4), 63–85.

Leeder, S. R., Feletti, G. I., & Engel, C. E. (1979). Assessment: Help or hurdle? *Programmed Learning and Educational Technology*, *16*(4), 308–315.

Mezirow, J. (1997). Transformative learning: Theory to practice. *New Directions for Adult and Continuing Education*, *74*, 5–12.

Mezirow, J. (2003). Transformative learning as discourse. *Journal of Transformative Education*, *1*, 58–63.

Neufeld, V. R., & Barrows, H. S. (1974). The "McMaster Philosophy": An approach to medical education. *Academic Medicine*, *49*(11), 1040–1050.

Rittel, H. W., & Webber, M. M. (1974). Wicked problems. *Man-made Futures*, *26*(1), 272–280.

Tomkinson, B. (2008a). *Educating engineers for sustainable development: Report of a Royal Academy of Engineering sponsored pilot study*. Manchester: University of Manchester. Retrieved from http://www.osier.ac.uk/164. Accessed on November 29, 2018.

Tomkinson, B. (2008b). *Educating engineers for sustainable development: Appendices to a report of a Royal Academy of Engineering sponsored pilot study*. Manchester: University of Manchester. Retrieved from http://www.osier.ac.uk/165. Accessed on November 29, 2018.

Tomkinson, B., & Hutt, I. (2012). Online PBL: A route to sustainability education? Campus-Wide Information Systems, *29*(4), 291–303.

Tomkinson, R., Tomkinson, B., Engel, C., & Lawson, A. (2008). *Education for sustainable development in engineering: Report of a Delphi Consultation*. Loughborough: Engineering Subject Centre.

Wals, A. (Ed.). (2009). *Learning for a sustainable world: Review of contexts and structures for education for sustainable development*. Paris: UNESCO.

CHAPTER 4

USING THE SDGs TO PROMOTE CHANGE AND NURTURE CONNECTIVITY IN AN UNDERGRADUATE DESIGN MODULE

Jackie Malcolm and Keith R. Skene

ABSTRACT

The sustainable development goals (SDGs) were introduced by the United Nations in 2016 to replace the millennium development goals (MDGs). This chapter examines the impact of integrating these goals within a design challenge, as part of a level 3 undergraduate degree module. Design Values, Issues and Ethics is an expansive module, aiming to broaden the students' discipline focus and allow them to expand their learning within a new landscape. This module promotes the utilization of nature-based intelligences to establish solutions to a community's basic need to survive and thrive. The SDGs were integrated through embedding them as part of a future-building scenario, supported by a series of exercises and seminars. Students were then asked to reflect on how the SDGs had impacted their design process, and to consider ethical and value dimensions. These reflections were used to analyze the effectiveness of the SDGs as key principles for an ethical design intention. Integrating the SDGs within the design curriculum has served to promote a connectivity of systems that were largely separated prior to this pilot.

Teaching and Learning Strategies for Sustainable Development:
Innovations in Higher Education Teaching and Learning, Volume 19, 41–56

ISSN: 2055-3641/doi:10.1108/S2055-364120200000019007

Keywords: Future-building scenario; Indigenous knowledge; Reason Design Process; systems theory; value-based design; trade-offs

INTRODUCTION

Since its inception in 1948, the United Nations (UN) has played a key role in international development (Kumar, Kumar, & Vivekadhish, 2016). The United Nations Development Programme launched their seventeen sustainable development goals (SDGs), also known as the Global Goals, as part of Agenda 2030, in January 2016. This program was a "universal call to action to end poverty, protect the planet and ensure that all people enjoy peace and prosperity" (UNDP, 2018). The SDGs were a development of the earlier Millennium Development Goals (MDGs) launched in 2000, whose main focus was "to spare no effort to free our fellow men, women and children from the abject and dehumanizing conditions of extreme poverty" (UN, 2015, p. 3). These in turn stemmed from the OECD's International Development Goals of 1996.

Millennium Development Goals

In 2000, heads of state from 147 countries gathered in New York for the UN Millennium Summit, adopting the MDGs to target eight goals: the eradication of extreme hunger and poverty; universal primary education; promotion of gender equality and female empowerment; reduction in child mortality; improved maternal health; combatting HIV, malaria and other major diseases; and ensuring environmental stability and developing a partnership for global development. The program was set to run until 2015.

It is generally acknowledged that the MDGs had significant flaws. Some of these flaws were related to their design (Clemens, Kenny, & Moss, 2007). The MDGs also ignored the significant issues emerging within the developed world, such as excessive energy and resource use, obesity and increased political polarization, focusing only on issues in the developing world (Saith, 2007). Yet in considering issues for the developing world, they ignored important aspects such as urbanization, values and ethics, geo-political contexts, and indigenous thinking as valid knowledge (Breidlid, 2009). A significant gap in terms of environmental protection has also been recognized (McMichael & Butler, 2004). No roles were found for civil society organizations (Waage et al., 2010) with little emphasis on empowerment, human rights, social justice, nor equity (Fukuda-Parr, 2010; Langford, 2010). Security, disarmament, peace, and democracy were omitted, even though they underpin any true hope of sustainable development (Hill, Mansoor, & Claudio, 2010).

Furthermore, the MDGs were formulated by a non-representative group of experts with little input from grassroots movements nor post-development thinkers (Amin, 2006; Richard et al., 2011). This group was seen to represent a neoliberal agenda, based on private sector donor-centric solutions and globalization formulated around a Western agenda (Saith, 2007). Gender targets were restricted to parity in education (Abu-Ghaida & Klasen, 2004; Eyben, 2006; Hulme, 2010). Furthermore, significant errors in the data analysis used to report on progress have been identified (Attaran, 2005; Hickel, 2016) while goals were narrow and not interconnected (van Norren, 2012).

Sustainable Development Goals

The SDGs came to fruition from the vision of Paula Caballero, who, in 2010, was appointed as Director of Economic, Social and Environmental Affairs at the Ministry of Foreign Affairs within the Colombian government. Tasked with contributing to the Rio+20 Summit in 2012, she recognized that a replacement for the MDGs was necessary, given that the agreement governing the MDGs would terminate in 2015. Caballero also realized that there needed to be a greater emphasis on the three arenas: economics, society, and environment.

The outcomes, following years of discussion, were the 17 goals, 169 targets, and 304 indicators that comprise the SDGs. Also known as the Global Goals for Sustainable Development, the agreement was ratified in New York in September 2015, and will terminate in 2030. From their formulation onwards, weaknesses identified within the MDGs were noted and addressed (Fukuda-Parr, 2016; Maurice, 2015; Schmidt-Traub, Kroll, Teksoz, Durand-Delacre, & Sachs, 2017). There was a broad representation of all 193 member states as well as civil society groups. Developed countries now came under scrutiny, breaking the North–South aid agenda.

Processes now replaced targets, as evidenced by an entire goal (Goal 17) being dedicated to means of implementation. Flows replaced stocks. The basic principle of interconnectedness was prioritized, where no goal stands alone. This brought systems theory to the table, wherein trade-offs, feedback, and emergence are seen as essential elements (Skene, 2018). The planet and the human race are facing a period of social and environmental crisis like never before (Klein, 2014). We really are at a tipping point (Lenton et al., 2008). The SDGs, developed by the UN, are the fruits of the latest multinational effort to build toward a better future, recognizing that transformation is not an option, but a necessity. Stretching across economic, social, and environmental issues, the SDGs provide a context within which to generate a better world.

Sustainable Development Goals and Design

With the SDGs now taking the top chair at the global sustainability table, this chapter suggests that it is important that we examine two issues. Firstly, what is the relevance of the SDGs to design education, theory, and practice, and, conversely, what is the relevance of design to the SDGs?

Perhaps no area is more fundamental to a sustainable future than design. Design is the thought process comprising the creation of an entity (Miller, 2005). Skene and Murray (2015) observe that: "the story of design is the story of our relationship with the environment" (p. 280). Design is considered as the framework to challenge "wicked problems" which are difficult to solve due to complex interdependencies and inadequate information. Papanek (1984) suggests that "design is basic to all human activity" and that "it is the conscious and intuitive effort to impose meaningful order" (p. 4).

Yet design has the power both to sustain and to destroy. Schmidt and Donnert (as cited in Spangenberg, Faud-Luke, & Blincoe, 2010) warn that:

> Everything was fine in the ancient past. Nature produced no embarrassing shapes and colours, humans were busy struggling for survival and had no time to decorate their first wedges with scrolls. Everything was fine, because in the ancient past there were no designers. (p. 1485)

This warning reminds us that there can be good and bad design in terms of sustainability. Design in a vacuum is more likely to work against a sustainable planet. Setting design within an ecological context has the potential to provide transformative outcomes, for society and the environment (Spirn, 2014). A truly eco-centric design process will not only avoid the pitfalls of the MDGs, but also propel us toward a sustainable future, answering the "universal call to action to end poverty, protect the planet and ensure that all people enjoy peace and prosperity" (UNDP, 2018) that defines the SDGs. Design should not only be informed by the SDGs, but also, rather, the designer should take on a role of leadership in the process.

Therefore, we would suggest that there is no better arena within which to explore sustainable design than through the lens of the SDGs. At an even more fundamental level, both designers and sustainability practitioners face very similar challenges that are "complex, uncertain and contested by multiple stakeholders" (Maher, Maher, Mann, & McAlpine 2018, p. 1), where material supply chains and fluxes and flows are important. Thus, both fields have the potential to inform each other at a most basic level.

Papanek (1984) also promotes the idea that: "the solution to any design problem is to achieve the most with the least" and that by studying nature we can apply its "principles and processes to the needs of mankind" (p. 186). Ecology, on the other hand, seeks to "harmonize the human enterprise with how the world works as a physical system and how it ought to work as a moral system" (Orr, 2002, p. 3). While nature can inspire new design strategies to improve life on earth, there can often be a lack of connectivity, resulting in an ignorance of the impact such new intelligences might have beyond the immediate solution. Nurturing a systemic lens that is not simply human-centric, can influence the direction of a project, resulting in a solution based on mutualism.

The SDGs should matter to designers on many levels. In 2015, PricewaterhouseCoopers (PwC) found that 78% of individuals questioned stated that they were more likely to buy the goods and services of companies that sign up to the SDGs (PwC, 2015). Furthermore, 71% of businesses responded that they were planning how to engage with the SDGs. Thus, for the design student, it surely must be a priority to be familiar with the SDGs and be comfortable integrating them within the design process at both perceptual (Lakoff & Johnson, 1999) and conceptual (Bernstein et al., 2010) levels.

As early as November 2015, designers meeting at the Forward Thinking Conference in Oslo developed the Oslo Manifesto, which challenged the designer to ask how their work could contribute to the SDGs (DMI Review Staff, 2018). A more detailed manifesto, the Montréal Design Declaration, was launched in 2017, declaring that "All people deserve to live in a well-designed world" (MDD, 2017). Liedtke (2018) summarized the challenges of the SDG for designers as follows:

- "design for resource efficiency, creating more with fewer resources";
- "design for circularity, encouraging multiple uses of high-quality items"; and
- "design for social change and equality, encouraging consumption that is eco-intelligent, fair and moderate." (p. 87)

Looker (2017), having found that SDGs did not feature in any of the 58 design school program curricula examined in Canada, concluded that:

> By creating a stronger network between design associations, professional communities, and design schools, and by developing a toolkit for design educators, we can provide young designers with the skills to build a sustainable future. (p. 52)

Another important source of design wisdom for students comes from indigenous design, completely ignored by the MDGs, but often already meeting the SDGs, based on ancient practices. This is beautifully demonstrated in the work of the Mau Ogiek people, forest-dwelling hunter gatherers from Kenya, who embody sustainable practice in their culture and clothing design (Njeru, 2018). These people must work with extremely limited resources within closely knit social and environmental contexts, very much the vision of the SDGs.

FRAMING THE RESEARCH

To investigate the impact of the SDGs, when embedded within a design challenge, we worked with 28 undergraduate design students at level 3, who had chosen to undertake an expansive module, Design Values, Issues & Ethics, within the School of Art & Design at the University of Dundee. The intention of expansive modules is to broaden the student's discipline focus, while allowing them to expand their learning within a new landscape. This module promoted the utilization of nature-based intelligences, including biophilia, biomimicry, resilience, and symbiosis, to establish solutions to a community's basic need to survive and thrive. The students were drawn from a range of design disciplines: Product Design, Digital Interaction, Graphic Design, Textile Design, Interior and Environmental Design, and Jewellery & Silversmithing. The students worked in six multidisciplinary groups of four or five students on a design challenge that was systemic in nature: water, shelter, food, transport, clothing, and education. The module adopted a four-stage framework for participants to develop their concepts and acknowledge the complexity of designing with nature. Biophilia was used as the first step toward engaging students with nature, using their senses to stimulate their re-engagement within the natural environment. The course was taught in the University Botanic Garden, allowing access to a wealth of semi-natural habitats.

Secondly, biomimicry (literally mimicking nature) was introduced as a means of exploring how nature has overcome design challenges, and examining how these lessons could be adapted for the design challenge set for the students.

Thirdly, resilience was explored through a workshop where students worked in two teams to build an island, considering what humanity needs to survive and thrive within a particular environment, while questioning what is meant by our understanding of a "community."

Finally, symbiosis was investigated, where the interconnectivities of the design challenges were explored, using the SDGs as the drivers for understanding a systemic, value-based, design solution through their underpinning principles.

In order to explore these ideas and to examine the implications of implementing the SDGs into the design process, the students were asked to envisage a future where such concepts were central to the design process. To ensure this was robust, the Manoa scenario building method (Curry & Schultz, 2009) was used to stimulate conversations, facilitating a connectivity across water, housing, transport, food, governance, and education. The Manoa scenario building method is an eight-stage approach (see Schultz, 2015), used to exploring possible futures, based around lateral thinking and brain-storming. Future scenarios are envisaged and then interconnections are made, which in turn inform each scenario. Implication of such futures are explored and critiqued before finally developing a means of transition to the resultant best future. By situating this exploration within an ecological design module research project, students could test-drive the application of SDGs within the design process, both as practitioners and observers, allowing them to critically reflect on the utility of the SDGs in terms of ecological design. This chapter recounts these reflections and contextualizes the lessons learnt, both in terms of sustainability thinking and design.

FUTURE SCENARIO BUILDING

Future scenarios are now believed to be crucial in shaping the way in which people act and behave. Curry and Schultz (2009) critique future scenario building as shaping a human intention that can "create futures that are significant transformations of the present." Shaping future scenarios requires an acknowledgement that the present day scenario will change, needs to change, and that something better can be achieved. If we consider the SDGs within this context, we can examine the ways in which the SDGs can help to promote a new vision, through the design of scenarios, solutions, and strategies, for alternative futures that are environmentally and ethically just. List (2004) states that such scenarios require to be networked. This would suggest that using the SDGs to encourage future scenario building requires a level of connectivity that is holistic, allowing systems to flow in and out of each other.

Embedding the SDGs allowed the students to build an interconnected system, where each team could observe how one system might be reliant upon another system. Of course, what we must acknowledge is that by only analysing the six chosen systems, there were a number of missing systems from the whole, such as governance, economy, health and religion, or a belief system. The students were asked not to place their system within a present day context. They were asked to consider what a new community might look like, if our current society and available technology did not exist. This required imagination.

Making a decision about the location of their community became crucial in mapping resources, climate, and scenarios within a specific landscape. This then became the driver for the building of their community, giving consideration to the design challenge and how it might be shaped. Dei (2000) emphasizes that ethnic, indigenous knowledge, means knowledge consciousness arising locally emerging from long-term occupancy of a place. Indigenous wisdom became very important to the understanding of a community, where they are self-reliant and look to their immediate environment for resources to allow them to survive and thrive within that landscape. Njeru (2018), when discussing the sustainable practices of the Mau Ogiek people, living in Kenya, suggests that adopting indigenous wisdom plays a major role in the attainment of the SDGs. Indigenous practices are often forgotten when we are at the interface for design and community, and yet it has allowed ethnic groups to sustain their own cultures "leading to positive social, economic and environmental impacts" (Njeru, 2010, Introduction Section).

The Ethical Journey

We must acknowledge at this point that it appears to be very difficult to begin to erase all that the students know and understand about a society. To begin with, they constantly looked to include technology that is only available within our present day scenario. To encourage them to look beyond the constraints of existing institutional structures, we constantly took them beyond their expectations and asked them to consider a future scenario where they didn't have access to present day technology and current community structures. Presenting the students with various examples, such as the Kogi, descendants of the Tairona civilization (Ereira, 1992), encouraged discussion and debate around future scenarios and what a new community might begin to look like. It also encouraged the promotion of "Self-realisation" (Naess, 2008 p. 173), where the situated values of an individual required reflexivity.

Considering the ethical dimension, we must firstly understand where our own values are situated, bringing light to the cultures that have shaped the values we consider to be good and just. Establishing a value for the whole system requires us as a human species, to give value to all species. Justice must be applied to "animals, plants and landscapes" also (Naess, 2008, p. 173). Naess (2008) continues to discuss our "limited power and position within the whole" yet acknowledges the fact that there is still the "potential" for the individual to facilitate change (p. 174). He suggests that our "egos" are mere "fragments" and that we must look beyond our "self" to achieve a "self-realisation" that then allows us to design ethically, devoid of any cultural bias (p. 174). Naess (2008) suggests that this is born of "identification," where our values are constructed by our own identification, shaped by time as we grow and develop within this world. He suggests that where that "identity" has not been nurtured, then it "leads to indifference," where "distant objects or events which do not concern us are at best relegated to the indifferent background" (p. 174).

We would suggest that to promote an "identity" within us, that is, morally and ethically good and just, "self-realisation" is crucial to make the shift in behaviour needed for a more ethical future where care of all species is an aspect of our human nature and instinct. Edward Wilson (1978) examines this paradigm, considering the human instinct as a result of a set of triggers to the brain that enable us to act in a particular way. Shaped by science and culture, our instincts are also shaped by the constructs that define ourselves.

To facilitate such a shift in thinking about one's own values, we can reflect upon our own situated values to adopt a more ethical design intention and there is evidence as a result of this research to suggest that the SDGs can complement this journey, enabling the designer to work with the 17 goals to achieve a more sustainable and just future scenario. Once the students had critically reflected upon the institutional and cultural structures that had shaped their own values, and acknowledged they had been shaped from the moment they were born, they could then apply appropriate ethical considerations to their design challenge.

METHODS

To analyze the effectiveness of the SDGs as key principles for an ethical design intention, a survey was designed with 10 questions, ranging from simple requests for facts (e.g., What was your design challenge?) through to more complex, open-ended, opinion-seeking questions (e.g., Having explored the SDGs within the context of your project, would you change anything about the SDGs? If so, give an example.). The survey was made available to students via an online platform. A total of 21 of the 28 students participated, and all 21 students responded to all 10 questions. Results were analyzed and are summarized in the Results section.

RESULTS

What is your design challenge?

The students had been split into groups of four to five individuals and had drawn lots to choose one of six project themes. Of the 21 students who participated in the survey, one worked on a clothing challenge, three worked on an education challenge, four worked on a food challenge, four worked on a shelter challenge, five worked on a transport challenge, and four worked on a water challenge.

Were you aware of the SDGs before this module?

Thirty-three percent of students had encountered the SDGs before, while 67% had not encountered them at all.

If you were aware of the SDGs, where did you hear about them?

Of the seven students who had encountered the SDGs prior to this module, most had done so through school or university modules. Table 1 presents these findings.

Table 1. Basis of Knowledge of the SDGs, If Already Encountered.

Basis of Prior Knowledge of SDGs	Number of Students
High school conference	1
Previous module at Dundee University	2
High School courses	3
Media coverage	1

Which SDGs are related to your design challenge?

Fig. 1 summarizes the result for this question. Life on land, clean water and sanitation, good health and well-being, and sustainable cities and communities all scored highly, with over 70% of students including these, whereas less than 25% of students included quality education, decent work and economic growth, peace, justice and strong institutions and partnerships for goals as having any relationship with their projects.

What do you consider to be the values of the SDGs?

This open question provided a range of answers. Seven students identified equality as important, while living standards and planetary protection were identified by six students. Other values identified by a number of students included sustainability, helping

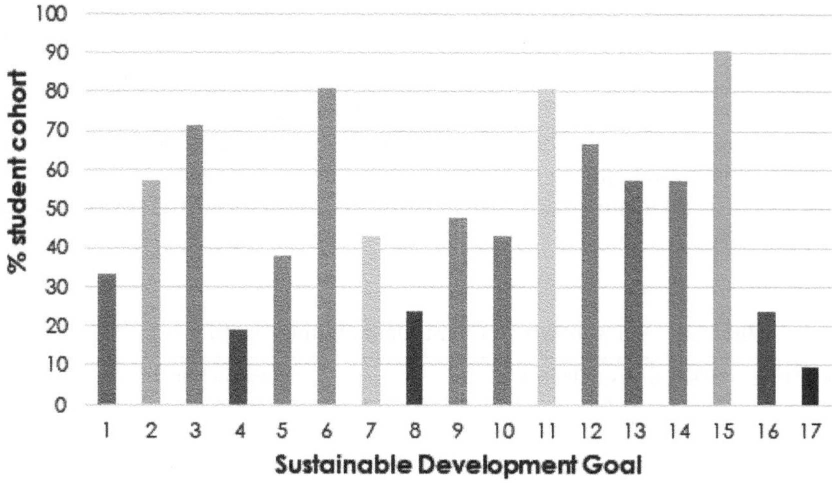

Fig. 1. Percentage of Students Recognizing the Relevance of Each of the SDGs to Their Projects.

Goals: 1. No poverty; 2. No hunger; 3. Good health and well-being; 4. Quality education; 5. Gender equality; 6. Clean water and sanitation; 7. Affordable and clean energy; 8. Decent work and economic growth; 9. Industry, innovation and infrastructure; 10. Reduced inequalities; 11. Sustainable cities and communities; 12. Responsible consumption and production; 13. Climate action; 14. Life below water; 15. Life on land; 16. Peace, justice and strong institutions; 17. Partnerships for the goals.

future generations, integration, community, and human health. Resilience, respect, unity, and empathy were among 13 values mentioned only by one student.

In what way do you find the SDGs helpful?

Results are summarized in Table 2. The most common use identified by students was help in improving design. Guidance, analysis, the bigger picture, and systems thinking also featured, while inspiration, raised awareness, and the promotion of both societal thinking and ethical design were identified by single students as important.

What aspects of your design have the SDGs made you think about?

Twenty-five different design aspects were identified as being highlighted by the SDGs. Most-cited aspects included materials (seven students), product life cycles (five students), and equal opportunities (four students). Three students identified clean water and sanitation, gender equality, and sustainability issues as important. Cultural issues, energy issues, food issues, life on land, life under the water, good health, recycling, renewable resources, and systems theory were each identified as significant by two students, while design trade-offs, education, geography, impact on society, sustainable communities, the human aspect, thought processes, well-being, and working with nature were each identified by one student.

Having explored the SDGs within your project, can you give an example of trade-offs, wherein it was impossible to maximize fulfillment of two or more SDGs because to maximize one would mean not being able to maximize another? How did you decide what trade-offs to make?

Table 3 presents the 10 trade-offs identified by the students. These mostly circle around issues relating to food production, human infrastructure, and life on land. One student identified a potential tension between social and environmental sustainability.

Table 2. Ways in Which the Students Found the SDGs Useful.

Useful Role of SDGs in Design Projects	Number of Students
Help improve design process	9
Act as a guide	5
Help analyze problems	5
Helped design toward a sustainable planet	3
Bigger picture	2
Help design toward human development	2
Promote systems thinking	2
Changed my outlook	1
Promote a thinking society	1
Promote ethical design	1
Raise awareness of other issues	1
They inspire action	1

Table 3. Examples of Trade-offs Identified by the Students.

Zero hunger – Life on land.
Zero hunger – Responsible production and consumption.
Decent work and economic growth – Reduced inequalities – Gender equality.
Decent work and economic growth – Climate action.
Sustainable cities and communities – Life on land.
Social SDGs – Sustainable SDGs.
Cost versus Sustainable design.
Life on land – Life under water.
Reduced inequalities – Sustainability.
Life under water – Aquatic transport.

Give an example of how two or more SDGs were connected within your project

Results are presented in Fig. 2. Students collectively identified many connections between the SDGs. Of interest is that three SDGs (Decent work and economic growth; Industry, innovation, and infrastructure; and Partnerships for the goals) were not seen as connecting with any other goals. In order to analyze

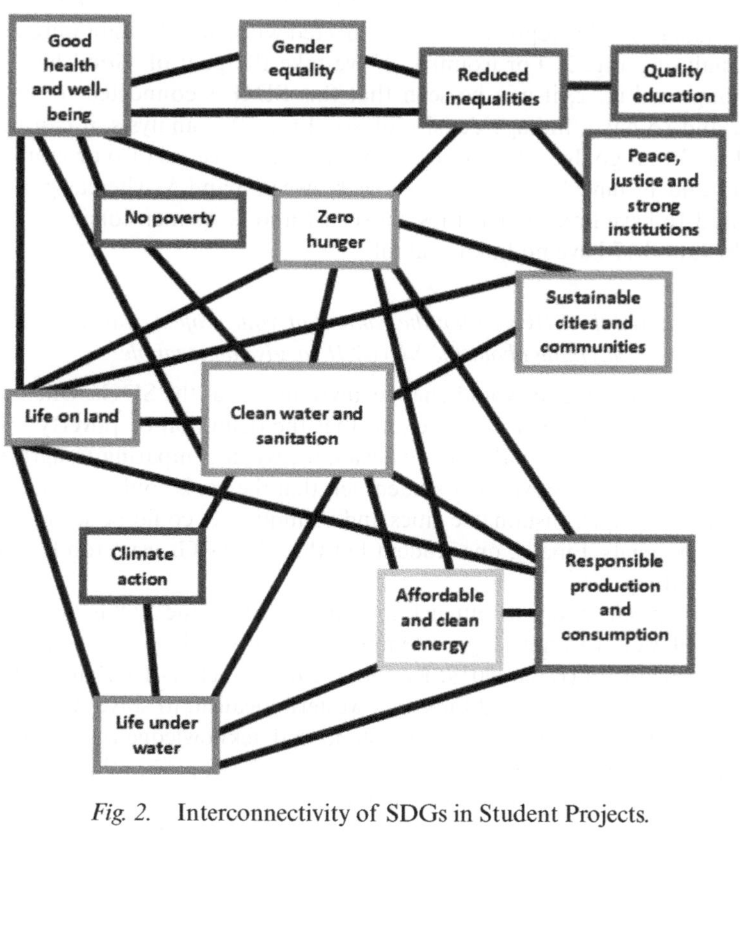

Fig. 2. Interconnectivity of SDGs in Student Projects.

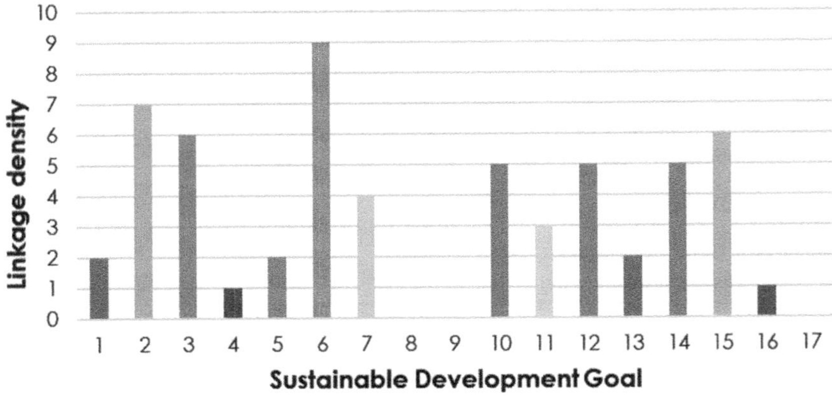

Fig. 3. Linkage Densities for SDGs Across All Projects (Goals Labeled as in Fig. 1).

connectivity further, a linkage density analysis was undertaken (Fig. 3). In this situation, linkage density simply refers to the number of other SDGs to which any particular SDG is reported to be connected with, and the data were derived from analysing Fig. 2. For example, if we take the goal of Good health and well-being, in Fig. 2, it can be seen that this SDG is connected to six other SDGs, and so has a linkage density of six. From this analysis, it can be seen from Fig. 3 that goals 2, 3, 6, and 15 have linkage densities of 6 or more, goals 7,10, 11 and 12 have linkage densities of between 3 and 5, whereas goals 1, 4, 5, 13, and 16 have linkage densities between 1 and 2. As mentioned previously, goals 8, 9, and 17 have no linkage at all.

Having explored the SDGs within the context of your project, would you change anything about the SDGs? If so, give an example

Only 15% of the students would change anything about the SDGs. One felt that the No poverty goal was too vague and that the definition of poverty was difficult to apply to hunter gatherers, for example, when comparing to agrarian or industrialized life styles. Another student felt that the goals could be teased apart further. For example, sustainable cities and communities could be separated into two separate goals. Finally, one student felt that the SDGs were too focused on western thinking.

This last point is key to our acknowledgment that the SDGs are largely a construct of western knowledge, attempting to address the global issues we are now concerned with (Buba, 2019; Kopnina, 2017; Salleh, 2016; Ziai, 2019). The question is whether we should look to a western idealism to solve such issues or whether we can use reflexivity to understand and acknowledge our situated values to achieve a level of "Self-realisation" (Naess, 2008, p. 173) that allows us to design systems that are conducive to all life.

INSIGHTS

Designing future scenarios can be challenged as being utopian, and the future will be shaped by the past and the present, driven by histories and cultures that have evolved within time and space. If the SDGs have been shaped by a western collection of values, it is important to acknowledge that time-tested indigenous methods can play a role in shaping a future that is socially, temporally, and spatially sustainable for all (Njeru, 2018). The SDGs can complement such wisdom, when used to connect and network the systems supporting life. At the outset, it was noted that only 33% of the student cohort had encountered the SDGs previously. This would indicate that all design programs should not expect prior knowledge of these important principles, and should seek to integrate them within their degree content.

This module, Design Values, Issues and Ethics, has previously run for seven years without the SDGs being discussed, or indeed the MDGs. A variety of alternative guiding design principles had been presented to the students: AIGA's Living Principles (AIGA, 2018), the Hannover Principles (McDonough, 1992), Life's Principles (Biomimicry 3.8, 2016), and the Reason Design Process (Malcolm, 2010) to encourage and promote an ethical design intention. Introducing the SDGs has provided us with the insights that they serve to promote a connectivity of systems that were largely separated prior to this pilot. The results of the survey presented us with rich data which suggested that the SDGs, when integrated into the undergraduate design curriculum, had potential to contribute to the transformation of the world and to securing a brighter future for the next generation.

When asked about the values of the SDGs one student stated that they could help achieve "complete equality and sustainability through all aspects of life, finding the perfect balance for each individual component." It was also recognized that they support and respect "different cultures," and were considered to be "all inclusive," rather than just focusing on "people who might be disadvantaged" and that they "affect everyone." What is most important was that the students saw the goals as "making sustainable systems more integrated and effective." This supports our notion that the goals did indeed promote connectivity, encouraging a design intention that went beyond the individual design challenge, and enhancing the learning experience by networking the six systems into one larger system.

The goals were considered to be "clear to understand" playing a "vital role in the development process" of their designs. It was suggested that the SDGs did in fact give clarity to the design challenges, and that they facilitated an understanding of the "bigger picture." Each design challenge therefore was not developed in isolation of the other systems, and while they "help[ed] to pinpoint the exact issue" they also "rais[ed] awareness of another one."

Reflecting on a shift in values, it was stated that the "SDGs had made [the student] think about how each element of a community not only impact[s] one another," but also the "foundations and values of a culture." David Orr (2004, p. xii) asks how we can be expected to "teach [young people] to love land and community when our society values such things far less than it does individualism or consumption"? The student's comment above suggests that by embedding the

SDGs within the design process, they have gone some way in helping to reinforce a value-based design intention that can envisage a new future scenario, built on a far more ethical vision. The student acknowledged that this was needed to "maintain a sustainable, equal and functioning system."

The methodology outlined above has provided us with insights into the ways in which the SDGs can underpin the principles of a design challenge, shaping a community to "survive and thrive," through an exploration of connectivity, cultural relevance, ethics and values, sovereignty, empowerment (both individual and ecological), actualization, sub-optimality, tribal issues, function/form issues, and ecological embeddedness.

Using student reflections, we have presented findings that critically observe the value of the SDGs within an educational landscape, where they have been used to promote the connectivity of fundamental human needs. Stafford-Smith et al. (2017, p. 911) highlighted the fact that targets set by the SDGs were "silent about inter-linkages and interdependencies among goals," suggesting that achieving the aims and objectives of the framework might not be realized. There has been evidence contained within the student responses to suggest that, if truly embedded within a design process, it is possible to use the SDGs to reinforce a systemic understanding of our place within the natural world and how we impact the environment.

This chapter has shown that by integrating the SDGs within the design process, the SDGs have gone some way in helping to reinforce a value-based design intention that can envisage a new future scenario. Furthermore, it is possible to use the SDGs to reinforce a systemic understanding of our place within the natural world and how we impact the environment. The SDGs can also underpin the principles of a design challenge, shaping a community to "survive and thrive," through an exploration of connectivity, cultural relevance, ethics and values, and ecological embeddedness.

There are clearly limitations to this study. The number of students was relatively small, anonymity prevented us from exploring other interesting aspects relating to geographic, cultural, and philosophical backgrounds. It was only the first year that this course had been run in this way. However, the findings are potentially useful, particularly in terms of them being the first study relating to this area, and it is intended to continue with the survey in future years, while using the findings to develop the module.

The challenges facing designers today cannot be solved merely by paying lip service to a set of guiding principles that are constructed by the very institutional constructions that are also the reason we are facing the destruction of the very life that sustains us. However, by using the SDGs, embedding them within a learning experience that uses reflexivity of the individual to encourage "Self-realisation," we can begin to make a shift toward a new landscape that nurtures, rather than destroys, all life.

REFERENCES

Abu-Ghaida, D., & Klasen, S. (2004). The costs of missing the millennium development goal on gender equity. *World Development*, *32*(7), 1075–1107.

AIGA. (2018). The living principles for design. Retrieved from https://www.aiga.org/the-living-principles-for-design. Accessed on November 16, 2018.

Amin, S. (2006). The millennium development goals: A critique from the South. *Monthly Review-an Independent Socialist Magazine, 57*(10). Retrieved from http://monthlyreview.org

Attaran, A. (2005). An immeasurable crisis? A criticism of the millennium development goals and why they cannot be measured. *PLoS Medicine, 2*(10), e318.

Bernstein, W., Ramanujan, D., Devanathan, S., Zhao, F., Ramani, K., & Sutherland, J. W. (2010). Development of a framework for sustainable conceptual design. In *17th CIRP international conference on life cycle engineering* (pp. 242–247).

Biomimicry 3.8. (2016). Life's principles. Retrieved from https://biomimicry.net/the-buzz/resources/designlens-lifes-principles/. Accessed on November 16, 2018.

Breidlid, A. (2009). Culture, indigenous knowledge systems and sustainable development: A critical view of education in an African context. *International Journal of Educational Development, 29*(2), 140–148.

Buba, I. A. (2019). Aid, intervention, and neocolonial 'Development'in Africa. *Journal of Intervention and Statebuilding, 13*(1), 131–138.

Clemens, M. A., Kenny, C. J., & Moss, T. J. (2007). The trouble with the MDGs: Confronting expectations of aid and development success. *World Development, 35*, 735–751.

Curry, A., & Schultz, W. (2009). Roads less travelled: Different methods, different futures. *Journal of Futures Studies, 13*(4), 35–60.

Dei, G. J. S. (2000). Rethinking the role of indigenous knowledges in the academy. *International Journal of Inclusive Education, 4*(2), 111–132.

DMI Review Staff. (2018). Design and the SDGs. *Design Management Review, 29*(1), 8–11.

Ereira, A. (1992). *The heart of the world.* London: Jonathan Cape.

Eyben, R. (2006). The road not taken: International aid's choice of Copenhagen over Beijing. *Third World Quarterly, 27*, 595–608.

Fukuda-Parr, S. (2010). Reducing inequality – The missing MDG: A content review of PRSPs and bilateral donor policy statements. *Ids Bulletin-Institute of Development Studies, 41*(1), 26–35.

Fukuda-Parr, S. (2016). From the millennium development goals to the sustainable development goals: Shifts in purpose, concept, and politics of global goal setting for development. *Gender & Development, 24*(1), 43–52.

Hickel, J. (2016). The true extent of global poverty and hunger: Questioning the good news narrative of the millennium development goals. *Third World Quarterly, 37*(5), 749–767.

Hill, P. S., Mansoor, G. F., & Claudio, F. (2010). Conflict in least-developed countries: Challenging the millennium development goals. *Bulletin of the World Health Organization, 88*, 562.

Hulme, D. (2010). Lessons from the making of the MDGs: Human development meets results-based management in an unfair world. *Ids Bulletin-Institute of Development Studies, 41*(1), 15–25.

Klein, N. (2014). *This changes everything: Capitalism v the climate.* London: Allen Lane.

Kopnina, H. (2017). Chapter 8. Future scenarios for sustainability education: The future we want? In P. B. Corcoran, J. P. Weakland & A. E. J. Wals (Eds.), *Envisioning futures for environmental and sustainability education* (pp. 44–60). Wageningen: Academic Publishers.

Kumar, S., Kumar, N., & Vivekadhish, S. (2016). Millennium development goals (MDGS) to sustainable development goals (SDGS): Addressing unfinished agenda and strengthening sustainable development and partnership. *Indian Journal of Community Medicine: Official Publication of Indian Association of Preventive & Social Medicine, 41*(1), 1.

Lakoff, G., & Johnson, M. (1999). *Philosophy in the Flesh.* New York, NY: Basic Books.

Langford, M. (2010). A poverty of rights: Six ways to fix the MDGs. *Ids Bulletin-Institute of Development Studies, 41*(1), 83–91.

Lenton, T. M., Held, H., Kriegler, E., Hall, J. W., Lucht, W., Rahmstorf, S., & Schellnhuber, H. J. (2008). Tipping elements in the earth's climate system. *Proceedings of the National Academy of Sciences, 105*(6), 1786–1793.

Liedtke, C. (2018). *Design for sustainability* (p. 85–88). Retrieved from https://www.sustainablegoals.org.uk/wp-content/uploads/2018/03/085-088-SDGs-LIEDTKE.pdf. Accessed on November 6, 2018.

List, D. (2004). Multiple pasts, converging presents, and alternative futures. *Futures, 36*, 23–43.

Looker, J. T. (2017). *A preliminary study of the United Nations sustainable development goals in Canadian industrial and graphic design school curricula.* Ph.D. thesis, Carleton University, Ottawa.

Maher, R., Maher, M., Mann, S., & McAlpine, C. A. (2018). Integrating design thinking with sustainability science: A research through design approach. *Sustainability Science*, *13*(6), 1565–1587.

Maurice, J. (2015). UN set to change the world with new development goals. *The Lancet*, *386*(9999), 1121–1124.

McDonough, W. (1992). *The Hannover principles*. Charlottesville, VA: University of Virginia.

Malcolm, J. (2010). Sustainability as an enhancement theme for the 21st Century design graduate: Should it become invisible? Higher Academy for Education: Art, Design Media Subject Centre.

McMichael, A. J., & Butler, C. D. (2004). Climate change, health, and development goals. *Lancet*, *364*, 2004–2006.

MDD. (2017). Retrieved from http://montrealdesigndeclaration.org/. Accessed on November 6, 2018.

Miller, W. R. (2005). *Definition of design*. Brooklyn, NY: Trimtab, Buckminster Fuller Institute.

Næss, A. (2008). *Ecology of Wisdom: Writings by Arne Næss*. Berkeley, CA: Counterpoint.

Njeru, S. N. (2018). Advancing Afrikan Indigenous sustainable practices for transformative development: The Mau Ogiek People, Kenya. *Proceeding of the 1st annual international conference*, 17–19 April, Machakos University, Kenya

Orr, D. (2002). *The nature of design: Ecology, culture, and human intention*. New York, NY: Oxford University Press.

Orr, D. (2004). *With earth in mind. On education, environment, and the human prospect*. Washington, DC: Island Press.

Papanek, V. (1984). *Design for the real world: Human ecology and social change*. London: Thames & Hudson.

PwC. (2015). *Make it your business: Engaging with the Sustainable Development Goals*. Retrieved from https://www.pwc.com/gx/en/sustainability/SDG/SDG%20Research_FINAL.pdf. Accessed on January 1, 2019.

Richard, F., Hercot, D., Ouedraogo, C., Delvaux, T., Samake, S., van Olmen, J., Conombo, G., ..., Vandemoortele, J. (2011). Sub-Saharan Africa and the health MDGs: The need to move beyond the 'quick impact' model. *Reproductive Health Matters*, *19*(38), 42–55.

Saith, A. (2007). Goals set for the poor, goalposts set by the rich. *International Institute of Asian Studies Newsletter*, *45*, 12–13.

Salleh, A. (2016). Climate, water, and livelihood skills: A post-development reading of the SDGs. *Globalizations*, *13*(6), 952–959.

Schmidt-Traub, G., Kroll, C., Teksoz, K., Durand-Delacre, D., & Sachs, J. D. (2017). National baselines for the sustainable development goals assessed in the SDG Index and Dashboards. *Nature Geoscience*, *10*(8), 547.

Schultz, W. (2015). Manoa: The future is not binary. *APF Compass*, April, 22–26.

Skene, K. R. (2018). Circles, spirals, pyramids and cubes: Why the circular economy cannot work. *Sustainability Science*, *13*, 479–492.

Skene, K. R., & Murray, A. (2015). *Sustainable economics: Context, challenges and opportunities for the 21st-century practitioner*. Sheffield: Greenleaf Publishing.

Spangenberg, J. H., Faud-Luke, A., & Blincoe, K. (2010). Design for sustainability (DfS): The interface of sustainable production and consumption. *Journal of Cleaner Production*, *18*(5), 1485–1493.

Spirn, A. W. (2014). Ecological urbanism: A framework for the design of resilient cities. In F. O. Ndubisi (Ed.), *The ecological design and planning reader* (pp. 557–571). Washington, DC: Island Press.

Stafford-Smith, M., Griggs, D., Gaffney, O., Ullah, F., Reyers, B., Kanie, N., Stigson, B., ..., O'Connell, D. (2017). Integration: The key to implementing the sustainable development goals. *Sustainability Science*, *12*(6), 911–919.

UN. (2015). *The millennium development goals report 2015*. New York, NY: United Nations.

UNDP. (2018). Retrieved from http://www.undp.org/content/undp/en/home/sustainable-development-goals.html. Accessed on November 5, 2018.

Van Norren, D. E. (2012). The wheel of development: The millennium development goals as a communication and development tool. *Third World Quarterly*, *33*, 825–836.

Waage, J., Banerji, R., Campbell, O., Chirwa, E., Collender, G., Dieltiens, V., & Unterhalter, E. (2010). The millennium development goals: A cross-sectoral analysis and principles for goal setting after 2015. *Lancet*, *376*, 991–1023.

Wilson, E. O. (1978). *On human nature*. Cambridge, MA: Harvard Press.

Ziai, A. (2019). Towards a more critical theory of 'development' in the 21st century. *Development and Change*, *50*(2), 458–467.

CHAPTER 5

LEADING ASSESSMENT PRACTICES TO FOSTER SUSTAINABILITY LEARNING IN ENGINEERING CLASSROOMS

Margaret Jollands

ABSTRACT

There is a growing demand in industry for engineering graduates who can think "sustainably." However, there are many barriers to developing assessment that fosters sustainability learning in engineering classrooms. There is no consensus on the definition of sustainability and its key competencies and teaching resources are limited.

Staff are unclear about what to teach, how to teach, and how to assess learning. Assessment is an integral part of teaching and learning and should be planned from the earliest stages, but this is rarely done. Engineering relies heavily on traditional assessments such as tests and examinations, but these are known to encourage surface learning. Sustainability is complex, multidisciplinary, and needs context, which requires higher-order thinking characteristic of deep learning.

Current assessment types for sustainability include examinations, case study, concept maps, and project-based learning. However, more research is needed to develop best practice assessments. Recommendations for teaching approach are to use a rigorous approach to instructional design, use a systems approach, and use a teaching model that promotes deep learning, incorporates context,

Teaching and Learning Strategies for Sustainable Development:
Innovations in Higher Education Teaching and Learning, Volume 19, 57–71

ISSN: 2055-3641/doi:10.1108/S2055-364120200000019008

and promotes alignment of learning objectives and assessment. Community-oriented assessments are recommended that feature the interdisciplinarity and complexity of sustainability and promote higher-order thinking.

Keywords: Bloom's taxonomy; sustainable engineering practice definition; "Closed-loop" project-based learning; contextualization for sustainability; Wicked problems; SOLO taxonomy

INTRODUCTION

This book offers both a welcome opportunity to address the issue of the lack of textbooks for engineering sustainability and contribute to the sustainability literature. This chapter addresses problems that arise when staff use traditional engineering assessment methods – the quiz, test, and exam – to test engineering students' understanding of sustainability. Our hypothesis is that measurement of students' understanding of sustainability needs specialist assessment.

There is a growing demand in industry for engineering graduates who can think "sustainably." This is now reflected internationally in professional body accreditation requirements for engineering graduates. The generic attributes in the Washington Accord (2014) include "Understand and evaluate the sustainability and impact of professional engineering work in the solution of complex engineering problems in societal and environmental contexts" (p. 15). Engineers Australia Stage 1 competencies for graduate engineers require "Understanding of the scope, principles, norms, accountabilities and bounds of sustainable engineering practice in a specific discipline" (Engineers Australia, 2017, p. 2).

However, there are several challenges for engineering academic staff to develop their students' *understanding of sustainable engineering practice*. Firstly, the definition of sustainability is contested. Some derive from the time-dependent and abstract sustainable development (SD) definition "Meets the needs of the present without compromising the ability of future generations to meet their own needs" (Brundtland, Khalid, & Agnelli, 1987, p. 41), while others follow the pragmatic "Appreciates the social, environmental and economic principles of sustainable engineering practice" (Engineers Australia, 2017, p. 3). A useful synthesis of definitions specifically for engineering by Carew and Mitchell (2002) identified nine principles and the processes to apply them, suggesting even the definition is complex. One consequence is that staff continue to teach curriculum that does not reflect a broad definition of sustainability. Many subjects have too narrow a focus on environmental aspects, neglecting integration of social and economic aspects (Holmberg & Samuelsson, 2006; Pappas, Pierrakos, & Nagel, 2013).

Secondly, faculty throughout higher education are being asked to change in too many ways in a short time. Leading authors on cultural change in education wrote that the most critical problem for educators is "not resistance to innovation, but the fragmentation, overload, and incoherence resulting from the uncritical and uncoordinated acceptance of too many different innovations"

(Fullan & Stiegelbauer, 1991, p. 197). There is a lack of consensus on what to teach: there is "a lack of empirical evidence, depth, and rigor in the discourse on key [sustainability] competencies" (Wiek, Withycombe, & Redman, 2011). There is a lack of resources with which to teach. Very few engineering disciplines have textbooks on sustainability. The few texts covering engineering may fail to represent the field in a broad sense, as they are written by experts from a particular discipline. Support for discipline-specific texts is provided by Holmberg and Samuelsson (2006), who describe sustainability as *inchoate*, that is, sustainability is without meaning if not given in context. There is a lack of consensus on best instructional design for sustainability: there is continuing debate about whether to add-on or integrate SD into the engineering curriculum (Mulder, Segalàs, & Cruz, 2005; Rydhagen & Dackman, 2011; Shing, 2015). Room must be made in the curriculum for new sustainability material: there may be resistance to displacing more traditional technical content to make room for the "new" sustainability curriculum, as this challenges academics' autonomy in relation to curriculum choice (Trowler & Cooper, 2002). And while it is reasonable to expect staff to be able to teach a wide range of discipline curriculum using contemporary approaches, staff capability to foster student understanding of sustainability is still developing. Sustainability requires a shift from teacher-oriented to learner-oriented approaches, as well as teaching skills in multi- and transdisciplinary contexts with societal complexity: "at the heart of this task is reorienting teacher education" (Holmberg & Samuelsson, 2006, p. 34).

Finally, a review of assessment practices is urgently needed. Assessment is an integral part of teaching and learning and should be planned from the earliest stages of development or change of curriculum (Boud & Associates, 2010). Assessment is critical, as without alignment among curriculum, approach, and assessment, students are likely to adopt a surface learning approach (Biggs, 1999). When curriculum and learning activities are reviewed, assessment must be reviewed as well, to ensure continued alignment. Alignment of curriculum, learning activities, and assessment are a critical element in many learning models, two of the most popular will be reviewed in the next section. The traditional methods of assessment in engineering (such as exercises, quizzes, tests, and examinations) tend to use a reductionist approach, which is counter to the need for students to adopt a systems learning approach to tackle sustainability problems (Byrne & Mullally, 2014; Holmberg & Samuelsson, 2006). The number of published studies is too small to identify the best approach to assessment for sustainability in engineering. Again, there is a lack of empirical evidence, depth, and rigor on the discourse of assessment for sustainability, at least in engineering. Further, staff may lack the capacity to use the kinds of assessment viewed as more suited to sustainability learning (Jollands, 2018; Segalàs, Ferrer-Balas, Svanström, Lundqvist, & Mulder, 2009).

It is not reasonable to expect all academic staff who teach sustainability to be experts in leading practice in teaching and learning. However, is it unreasonable to expect good sustainability teachers to be aware of the impact of their curriculum choices, teaching approach, and their assessment practices on student learning? This chapter briefly reviews these impacts.

This chapter first looks at the literature for instructional design and its importance in aligning models of learning with learning outcomes. Two widely used learning models and two useful taxonomic frameworks are also reviewed. These align curriculum and teacher approach with assessment, highlighting how the alignment impacts student learning. Then the types of approach commonly used in sustainability teaching are critiqued in terms the effect of the interdisciplinary nature and complexity of sustainability on student learning, highlighting why appropriate assessment methods are critical. The scant research on assessment is also reviewed. The Discussion section draws on themes from this literature to identify how sustainability teachers might enhance student learning. The assessment types commonly used in engineering are assessed against recommendations for assessment of sustainability learning. The chapter concludes that while more research is needed to identify best practice for sustainability assessment, recommendations can be made for the best teaching and assessment approaches.

The curriculum for sustainability learning is beyond the scope of this chapter. This is a relatively new field that is still evolving. Where relevant, in this chapter it is assumed that sustainability curriculum aims to develop systems thinking, interpersonal, anticipatory, normative, and sustainability transition competence (Wiek et al., 2011).

LITERATURE REVIEW

The Impact of Instructional Design on Student Achievement

Instructional design encompasses identification of a program's purpose, and crafting of its learning outcomes, curriculum and learning tasks, and delivery and evaluation. Instructional design describes the rigorous design processes used to develop relevant educational programs systematically, efficiently, and reliably. It ensures the resulting programs are effective, with congruence among their goals, teaching strategies, and program evaluation (Gustafson & Branch, 2002). Instructional design is increasingly identified as critical for successful learning in engineering (Felder, Brent, & Prince, 2011) but has rarely been undertaken across the whole curriculum in engineering (Litzinger, Lattuca, Hadgraft, & Newstetter, 2011).

Two Learning Models that Foreground Alignment

There are thousands of published studies that show the impact of instructional design on student learning and student achievement, based on a multitude of learning models. Two widely used models are those of Biggs and Bloom. These models foreground the importance of alignment between student learning and assessment. Biggs' 3P model (1999) posited that student learning outcomes depend on three factors: the student (prior knowledge, ability, and motivation); the teaching context (objectives, assessment, climate, and institutional procedures); and the learning activities (surface and deep). Bloom's revised taxonomy (Anderson et al., 2014) has two dimensions, cognitive process and knowledge.

It assists teachers in selecting learning objectives (each containing a cognitive process and knowledge domain). The learning objectives can then be used to develop curriculum, devise learning activities, and align assessment tasks.

Two Useful Frameworks for Sustainability Teaching

"A framework that is useful for teachers in renewing curriculum … must be coherent, systematic, detailed, comprehensive and specific" (Jollands, 2015, p. 9). A coherent framework is useful to teachers if it assists with organization of precise learning objectives and alignment with assessment (Anderson et al., 2014). It should also be adaptable to avoid obsolescence when the field evolves (Jollands, 2015). If it is hierarchical and taxonomic, learning tasks can be scaffolded for year level (Barrie, 2004, 2006). If it is detailed, comprehensive, and specific, it can assist with complexity (Biggs & Collis, 1982). All these features are needed in a framework for sustainability learning. Bloom's taxonomy was developed to assist teachers select and align learning objectives, curriculum, learning tasks, and assessments (Anderson et al., 2014). Its cognitive process has six dimensions: remember, understand, apply, analyze, evaluate, and create, and its knowledge scale has four dimensions: factual, conceptual, procedural, and meta-cognitive. The taxonomy has been used to develop scaffolded learning tasks in many courses (e.g., Banta, Griffin, Flateby, & Kahn, 2009; Pappas et al., 2013).

Bigg's SOLO taxonomy is another hierarchical tool that can be used to characterize the structural complexity of a learner's knowledge on their journey from novice to master. It notes two main changes in learning: increasing amount of detail in responses, as well as integration of the detail into a structural pattern (Biggs, 1999). It characterizes learners' development of understanding of a subject in multiple levels ranging from pre-structural (no understanding) through multi-structural (considers several aspects but fails to link them to a question) to extended abstract (relates given data to abstract principals) (Biggs & Collis, 1982). It facilitates teachers' development of highly specific tasks appropriate to each stage of learning (Biggs, 1999). The taxonomy has been used in a limited range of research and assessment of student work (Baillie & Toohey, 1997; Carew & Mitchell, 2002; Leung, 2000). The main disadvantage of the taxonomy is that markers must be well prepared and trained (Jollands, 2018; Leung, 2000).

These taxonomies may be used to develop a framework to select and align sustainability curriculum, learning objectives, activities, tasks, and assessment.

Teaching Approaches in Engineering Sustainability Classes

There are a wide variety of pedagogical approaches available for use in teachers' classrooms. In engineering sustainability classes, these range from traditional lectures to project-based learning (PjBL), and community-oriented approaches. The few studies that have reported on the quality of engineering students' learning outcomes in sustainability classes suggest sustainability learning should be approached differently from traditional engineering courses. One study found that students in traditional lecture-based sustainability classes had a *lower* understanding of sustainability at the end of the subject than the beginning.

In contrast, students in engineering classes characterized by a constructivist approach showed an enhanced understanding of sustainability (Segalàs, 2009; Segalàs, Ferrer-Balas, & Mulder, 2009, 2010). Unfortunately, the impact of assessment was not reported in these studies.

Other studies of engineering sustainability subjects reported on approaches to teaching, including PjBL (Byrne & Mullally, 2014), case study (Pappas et al., 2013; Segalàs & Tejedor, 2013), and a spine of PjBL design subjects (Jollands & Parthasarathy, 2013; Pappas et al., 2013).

PjBL is a common teaching approach in engineering programs. It was recommended in the seminal paper of Litzinger et al. (2011) as supporting the development of professional engineering practice. PjBL is learner-centered, active, and constructivist, where students solve authentic problems in groups inside and outside class. It involves finding solutions to large complex problems, usually conducted in groups. Groups are guided by a supervisor, but otherwise students learn independently. Assessment is generally a report and presentation (Prince & Felder, 2006).

However, evaluation of PjBL engineering programs shows mixed results. Some studies report that PjBL program graduates have capabilities superior to those from more traditional programs, in areas such as project management, and similar capability in technical areas (Jollands, Jolly, & Molyneaux, 2012; Kjærsdam, 2004). On the other hand, a meta-analysis of PjBL by Walker and Leary (2009) found no conclusive case for superiority of engineering graduates from PjBL than traditional programs. Recently PjBL approaches have been scaled back in several UK engineering departments (Graham, 2012). Only "closed-loop" PjBL appears to improve student learning significantly. In closed-loop PjBL, at the end of the project students must evaluate the quality of their sources, their own prior knowledge, and reflect on what improvements they could make in their reasoning (Walker & Leary, 2009). Litzinger et al. (2011) qualified their endorsement of PjBL with the proviso that developing skills

> to identify the nature and relevant context of the problem, what knowledge is needed to address it, and what methods are best suited to solve the problem *can only come with practice* in solving complex problems. (p. 134)

The meta-analyses indicate that PjBL programs must offer enough opportunities to practice, as well as reflection on learning, to be successful.

Community-oriented approaches "take into account the dynamic interaction and collaboration of multiple learners" in contrast to individual-oriented approaches where "students with different backgrounds and interests may follow different learning paths adapted to personal needs" (Segalàs, 2009, p. 77). The approach emphasizes that the learning that occurs with groups of peers can lead to deeper engagement and sense of agency when the group is co-ordinated well (Barron, 2000). This is distinct from community or service learning, which "combines academic study with community service" (Eyler, 2002, p. 517)

To summarize, the recommendations from the limited literature is that the best practice teaching approaches to develop sustainability thinking in engineering undergraduates include case studies, PjBL, and community-oriented learning.

Impact of assessment design on student approaches to learning

Do academic staff carefully consider a range of assessment choices, then select the most appropriate assessment practices, based on a consideration of the student cohort, level, and context? Or are staff selecting based on other criteria, such as the assessment most familiar or commonly used in their department? In the STEM higher education sector there is still an over-reliance on examinations, especially in engineering. This chapter posits that meta-cognitive awareness of assessment practices will lead to teachers making more effective assessment choices, depending on the demands of the task and the context. This idea is important for learners' development of their understanding of sustainability. Higher-order thinking is needed to understand sustainability as it is complex, and multi- and interdisciplinary (Carew & Mitchell, 2002; Holmberg & Samuelsson, 2006; Pappas et al., 2013). In addition, without context, sustainability is inchoate (Holmberg & Samuelsson, 2006). That is, sustainability is without meaning if not given in context.

Overview of Research in Assessment

There is a limited body of research work on assessment with few meta-analyses. Studies of student achievement have identified the significant impact of assessment (Biggs, 1999; Boud & Associates, 2010; Hattie, 2009). Further, in their seminal report Boud and Associates (2010) wrote "Assessment tasks, types, and means of deployment need to be fully aligned with all other aspects of the curriculum" (p. 3), but it was beyond the scope of their study to compare different kinds of assessment. In his analysis of meta-analyses of student achievement, Hattie (2009) wrote that assessment should:

- Encourage students to think through and solve problems by themselves or in a group.
- Set laboratories that aim to question, explain, and encourage higher-order thinking.
- Challenge and direct students' attention to important learning processes and outcomes.

There are no meta-analyses of assessment in the hundreds of meta-analyses of studies of student achievement included in the seminal work of Hattie (2009). This indicates that there is a lack of research on impact on student achievement of type of assessment.

The US National Institute for Learning Outcomes Assessment commissioned paper on innovations in assessment describes "three promising methods for providing authentic evidence of student learning" (Banta et al., 2009, p. 6) as it was suggested they offer a more complete picture of student achievement than other options. These are ePortfolios, CLAQWA rubrics, and online assessment communities.

There is a growing body of work on ePortfolios, but there is still insufficient research to determine their efficacy in engineering classes. CLAQWA rubrics are very detailed rubrics that facilitate higher interrater reliability, developed for identification of student writing deficiencies. While CLAQWA in combination with peer review has "demonstrated improvement" in one study (Flateby & Fehr, 2008, p. 904), use of CLAQWA alone is not an innovation that enhances student learning. Online assessment communities also enhance interrater reliability, by merging local with similar departments in other institutions, supporting faculty professional practice (Banta et al., 2009). However, they are also not an innovation that enhances student learning, and there is insufficient published evidence to gauge how effective they are.

Hence it is still too early to conclude that any of the three "promising" methods are effective.

In summary, there are no recent systematic rigorous studies of the effect of type of assessment on learning outcomes, depending on task, context, and discipline. The "promising" new assessment tools identified in the literature may have benefits, but the magnitude of the benefit, an indication of whether it is worthwhile to implement elsewhere, is, as yet, unknown.

Current Practice in Assessment for Sustainability in Engineering

The few text books available to teach sustainability in engineering classrooms provide little guidance on assessment. Mulder's *Sustainable Development for Engineers* (2006) provides student exercises, but these are too brief to provide any guidance on how to create high quality assessable tasks from the exercise ideas. Brennan's *Sustainable Process Engineering* (2013) provides no exercises or assessment tasks. Stasinoupolos, Smith, Hargroves, and Desha's *Whole System Design: An Integrated Approach to Sustainable Engineering* (2013) gives worked examples but no guidance on assessment per se.

In traditional engineering programs, examinations are a common form of assessment. One interesting study on "power" examinations looked at whether an examination could be set that would encourage deep learning about complex issues. Baillie and Toohey (1997) reported that an untimed open-book examination fostered a deeper approach to learning through setting of carefully chosen questions on challenging problems, evaluated using the SOLO taxonomy. A teaching approach was also adopted to help prepare the students for the different thinking required in such an examination. At the end of each class students discussed what kind of examination question might develop what they had just learnt, and students sat a mock exam. The combination of teaching and assessment approach resulted in a higher standard of answers in the examination. The study is frequently referenced in the literature on open-book examinations but there is no evidence that "power" exams have been widely adopted.

Reports and presentations are a common form of assessment in PjBL subjects (Prince & Felder, 2006). However, it is unclear whether these forms of assessment are better than examinations, as a meta-analysis of PjBL by Walker and Leary (2009) found no conclusive case for superiority of engineering graduates from PjBL than traditional programs.

The Concept map (Cmap) is another assessment tool that has been used to assess sustainability learning in some engineering departments. Cmaps are a graphical tool developed by Novak (1998) where students identify concepts and interlinks between concepts relevant to a specific question. Concept mapping emphasizes the main ideas, and helps students to synthesize the concepts, themes, and their main relationships in a visual display that helps recall. Cmaps are more detailed and nuanced than mind-maps, as Cmaps qualify the links between concepts with explanatory comments. Cmaps can be used pre- and post-test to evaluate learning (Segalàs, Ferrer-Balas, & Mulder, 2008). Students' Cmaps can be benchmarked against those drawn by sustainability experts (Segalàs, 2009). Cmaps are versatile and a useful complement to brainstorming, group work, reports, and presentations. Cmaps have been shown to enhance learning significantly, with effect sizes ranging from small (0.2) to large (0.8) (Hattie, 2009).

Research in Assessment for Sustainability in Engineering

There is a paucity of published research in assessment of student learning in engineering sustainability or sustainable practice development. There is insufficient research to draw firm conclusions on the most effective assessment type for student achievement in sustainability.

One report documented the views of sustainability experts, but rather surprisingly, only one offered views on assessment. The report – UNESCO Technical Paper No. 3 (Holmberg & Samuelsson, 2006) – captured the thoughts of 16 leading SD practitioners on the topic of embedding sustainability learning in the curriculum. One group described how they planned to embed SD into all programs through building capacity of SD staff "champions," and would evaluate success of the initiative on the basis of assessment types used for SD. They defined a basic level as "knowledge and basic concepts are evaluated through written exams" and an advanced level as "knowledge, skills, attitudes and values learning are evaluated in … Projects, field work and other final deliverables," applied to local issues (Lozano, Huisingh, & Delgado, 2006, p. 47). This clearly indicates the inferiority of examinations in assessing students' sustainability understanding. An evaluation of the impact of this approach on student learning has not yet been published.

Table 1 analyzes a selection of research papers describing instructional design and assessment with subject or program evaluation where available.

Each paper described in Table 1 focuses on one Engineering Department and one or a suite of subjects with embedded sustainability. The teaching approaches range from traditional lectures to PjBL or community-based learning. The assessments include an eclectic mix of reports and presentations, Cmaps, tests, case studies, essays, and posters. None included an exam. The disappointing research findings suggest none succeeded in transforming student learning and behavior: the results indicated students continued to approach sustainability in a traditional reductionist way, privileging technology over environment and social considerations.

In summary, there is a consensus that examinations are not a suitable assessment type for sustainability knowledge and understanding. Individual or group case studies, reports, and presentations are favored. However, the few research

Table 1. Publications on Sustainability Instructional Design, Assessment, and Research Outcomes.

Authors	Unit and Teaching Description	Assessment	Research Findings
Byrne and Mullaly (2014)	Problem-based learning in a first-year course	No exam; group assignment on a "wicked problem"; report and presentation	Students continued to take a reductionist approach, resisting indeterminacy, and complexity
Jollands and Parthasarathy (2013)	Project-based learning in a spine of design subjects from first to final year	No exams; tests on fundamentals; group assignment on a complex engineering project; design report and presentation; Cmaps	A comparison of students from second and fourth year showed increase in breadth and connectivity of ideas about sustainability, but the predominant focus on technology was unchanged
Pappas et al. (2013)	Systems approach; case study as encountered in engineering work; project-based learning in a spine of design courses; complexity increases over three years	No exam; individual case study analysis; group design project reports	Approach must be immersive to transform behaviour in students
Stanford et al. (2012)	Community-based final year capstone project based on real-world problem using jigsaw teams	Charrette document and presentation; final design documents and presentation	Sustainability was the focus of a minority of group members, so student learning varied from "minimal" to "significant."
Segalàs and Tejedor (2013)	Lectures. Case study analysis. Two week intensive at Masters level	No exam; individual poster and presentation; group case study report and presentation; Concept maps; individual essay	No research evaluation undertaken

results are not compelling. More work is needed to develop teaching approaches and assessments that transform sustainability learning in engineering.

DISCUSSION

In the absence of empirical evidence, depth, and rigor in the discourse on sustainability assessment, one hesitates to conclude what the best assessment methods might be. One can draw on research from other disciplinary practice to assess appropriateness for sustainability, but even here the literature lacks the depth and rigor to conclude with confidence what new assessment approaches could be introduced from the wider higher education community. While there are some "promising" ideas on assessment to consider, there is insufficient confidence to conclude those ideas will be a good fit to the sustainability task, the STEM discipline and the teaching context. This suggests it is beyond any current sustainability teacher to be aware of the impact of their curriculum choices, teaching approach, and their assessment practices on student learning.

Drawing on the broader literature on teaching and learning, one can identify directions for sustainability teachers to move that will enhance student learning, underpinned by credible research conclusions, and some new ideas to consider.

The recommendations for leading practice instructional design are to:

- Use a systematic, rigorous design approach to achieve efficient and reliable instructional design (Felder et al., 2011).
- Use a systems approach (Holmberg & Samuelsson, 2006).
- Use a teaching model that facilitates alignment between student learning and assessment, such as Biggs 3P model, to reduce the likelihood of students taking a surface approach to learning (Biggs, 1999).
- Develop a framework to facilitate selection and alignment of curriculum, learning objectives, activities, and assessment (Anderson et al., 2014; Biggs, 1999).
- Use "closed-loop" PjBL to improve student learning significantly (Walker & Leary, 2009) with multiple opportunities to practice complex problem-solving (Litzinger et al., 2011).

The recommendations for assessment are:

- Examinations should not be used, as the reductionist approach inherent in exams is counter to systems learning (Byrne & Mullally, 2014; Holmberg & Samuelsson, 2006) and promote surface learning (Hattie, 2009; Marzano, 1991), except if the examination is open-book essay based with questions that are challenging (Baillie & Toohey, 1997).
- Assessments should be community-oriented, that is, group based or peer based (Prince & Felder, 2006; Segalàs, 2009).
- Assessment methods must allow students to demonstrate the interdisciplinarity and complexity of sustainability (Carew & Mitchell, 2002; Holmberg & Samuelsson, 2006; Pappas et al., 2013).
- Assessment methods must encourage students to use higher-order thinking rather than knowledge retention (Hattie, 2009).

The common current practice examples of assessment described earlier are evaluated against this list of assessment recommendations in Table 2.

Table 2 shows that there is no straight-forward best assessment method for sustainability learning. Each assessment type has potential, but may not meet the recommendation unless designed or constrained in a particular way. The outcomes of each assessment type depends on explicit inclusion of community-orientation,

Table 2. Current Practice Assessments Compared to Recommendations for Assessment.

Assessment Type	Demonstrates Community-orientation, Interdisciplinarity, and Complexity	Encourages Higher-order Thinking Rather Than Knowledge Retention	Demonstrated Enhancement in Student Learning by Meta-analysis
Examination	No, except if open-book essay based	No, except if open-book essay based	Not demonstrated
Case study	For selected cases that are group based, interdisciplinary, and complex	Depends on assessment goals	Not demonstrated
Concept maps (Cmaps)	Meets, if undertaken in groups	Meets	Meets
Project-based learning in one course	For selected projects that are both interdisciplinary and complex	Depends on assessment goals	Does not meet
Project-based learning in a design spine	For selected projects that are both interdisciplinary and complex	Depends on assessment goals	Enhances breadth but may be too focused on technology

an interdisciplinary scope, a complex problem, activities, and goals that foster higher-order thinking. There are no rules of thumb: the impact of assessment choice on student learning depends on both task and context. The one area of consensus in assessment for sustainability – that examinations should not be used (Holmberg & Samuelsson, 2006) – is too limiting. Baillie and Toohey (1997) found that open-book "power" exams fostered a deeper approach to learning through setting of carefully chosen questions on challenging problems, evaluated using the SOLO taxonomy. Community-oriented learning has been shown to be transformative, for example, in humanitarian engineering (Brown, Price, Turner, & Colley, 2016). However, rigorous systematic research has not yet demonstrated this for sustainability. PjBL is widespread in engineering, but meta-analyses found no conclusive case for superiority of engineering graduates from PjBL than traditional programs, except for "closed-loop" PjBL. The only tool which meets all criteria is the Cmap. Cmaps are a versatile tool that may be used with other assessment approaches to significantly enhance understanding of sustainability.

CONCLUSIONS

Teaching in the evolving field of sustainability is fraught with difficulties for engineering academic staff. The definition of sustainability is not well understood by engineering academics, so there is no consensus on what to teach. There is a lack of teaching resources, as it is a new field. There is continuing debate about the best pedagogical approach, although community-oriented approaches such as PjBL show some benefits. There is no consensus on best assessment methods.

Many teachers lack the capability to use suitable assessment tools for sustainability, and some are so complex training is needed to mark reliably.

Instructional design is critical for successful learning in engineering but is rarely undertaken. Assessment should be planned along with curriculum and teaching approach. A hierarchical taxonomic framework is useful for teachers to select and align teaching approach, curriculum learning objectives, activities, and assessment, but none has been contextualized for sustainability learning. In the ideal situation, staff would be aware of the impact on student learning of their choices of assessment. However, there is a paucity of systematic rigorous research in effect of type of assessment on learning outcomes in any field, including sustainability. There is an over-reliance of examinations in engineering, which counters a systems approach, and fosters surface learning. Higher-order thinking is needed to understand the complex multi- and inter-disciplinary field of sustainability. Current practice in assessment of students' understanding of sustainability includes case study, community projects, Cmaps, and problem-based learning or PjBL. However, only Cmaps have been found to significantly enhance student achievement. Promising new ideas for assessment have been identified in other disciplines, but there is no evidence that these are suitable for sustainability.

In conclusion, future work should be undertaken to

- Revisit the definition of sustainable engineering practice, updated with input from industry and graduates.
- Develop a sustainable engineering practice framework that will help academic staff select and align best practice learning objectives, teaching approach, and assessment.
- Develop a consensus on what to teach and key sustainability competencies.
- Develop text books that are contextualized to discipline and provide detailed guidance on assessment.
- Re-evaluate the use of case study, PjBL, and community-oriented learning in assessing sustainability, as research to date has failed to find compelling evidence of their value.

REFERENCES

Anderson, L. W., Krathwohl, D. R., Airasian, P. W., Cruikshank, K. A., Mayer, R. E., & Pintrich, P. R. (2014). *A taxonomy for learning, teaching, and assessing: A revision of Bloom's taxonomy of educational objectives*. Harlow: Pearson New International.

Baillie, C., & Toohey, S. (1997). The 'power test': Its impact on student learning in a materials science course for engineering students. *Assessment & Evaluation in Higher Education, 22*(1), 33–48.

Banta, T. W., Griffin, M., Flateby, T. L., & Kahn, S. (2009). *Three promising alternatives for assessing college students' knowledge and skills.* NILOA Occasional Paper #2. Champaign, IL: NILOA

Barrie, S. C. (2004). A research-based approach to generic graduate attributes policy. *Higher Education Research and Development, 23*(3), 261–275.

Barrie, S. C. (2006). Understanding what we mean by the generic attributes of graduates. *Higher Education, 51*(2), 215–241.

Barron, B. (2000). Achieving coordination in collaborative problem-solving groups. *The Journal of the Learning Sciences, 9*(4), 403–436.

Biggs, J. (1999). *Teaching for quality learning at university.* Buckingham: SRHE & Open University Press.

Biggs, J. B., & Collis, K. F. (1982). *Evaluating the quality of learning: The SOLO taxonomy (structure of the observed learning outcome)*. New York, NY: Academic Press.

Boud, D., & Associates. (2010). *Assessment 2020. Seven propositions for assessment reform in higher education*. Sydney: Australian Learning and Teaching Council.

Brennan, D. (2013). *Sustainable process engineering: Concepts, strategies, evaluation and implementation*. Singapore: Pan Stanford Publishing.

Brown, N. J., Price, J., Turner, J. P., & Colley, A. (2016). Professional development within study abroad programs for engineering educators to gain confidence in preparing students to contribute to the sustainable development goals. In *27th annual conference of the Australasian association for engineering education*, Southern Cross University (pp. 96–105).

Brundtland, G. H., Khalid, M., & Agnelli, S. (1987). *Our common future*. New York, NY: UNESCO.

Byrne, E. P., & Mullally, G. (2014). Educating engineers to embrace complexity and context. *Engineering Sustainability*, *167*(ES6), 241–248.

Carew, A. L., & Mitchell, C. A. (2002). Characterizing undergraduate engineering students' understanding of sustainability. *European Journal of Engineering Education*, *27*(4), 349–361.

Engineers Australia. (2017). Stage 1 Competency Standard|Professional Engineer. Retrieved from https://www.engineersaustralia.org.au/resource-centre/resource/stage-1-competency-standard-professional-engineer

Eyler, J. (2002). Reflection: Linking service and learning – Linking students and communities. *Journal of Social Issues*, *58*(3), 517–534.

Felder, R. M., Brent, R., & Prince, M. J. (2011). Engineering instructional development: Programs, best practices, and recommendations. *Journal of Engineering Education*, *100*(1), 89–122.

Flateby, T. L., & Fehr, R. (2008). Assessing and improving writing in the engineering curriculum. *International Journal of Engineering Education*, *24*(5), 901–905.

Fullan, M., & Steigelbauer, S. (1991). *The new meaning of educational change* (2nd ed.). London: Cassel.

Graham, R. H. (2012). *Achieving excellence in engineering education: the ingredients of successful change*. London: Royal Academy of Engineering.

Gustafson, K. L., & Branch, R. M. (2002). Chapter 2. What is instructional design? In R. A. Resier & J. V. Dempsey (Eds.), *Trends and issues in instructional design and technology* (pp. 16–25). Boston, MA: Pearson.

Hattie, J. (2009). *Visible learning for teachers: a synthesis of over 800 meta-analyses relating to achievement*. London: Routledge.

Holmberg, J., & Samuelsson, B. E. (Eds.). (2006). *Drivers and barriers for implementing sustainable development in higher education: Education for Sustainable Development in Action Technical Paper No. 3.* Paris: UNESCO.

Jollands, M. (2015). A framework for graduate employability adapted for discipline differences. In *Proceedings of the higher education research and development society of Australia conference*, Melbourne (pp. 1–10).

Jollands, M. (2018). A comparison of assessment methods for engineering students' understanding of sustainability. In W. Leal Filho, J. Rogers, & U. Iyer-Raniga (Eds.), *Sustainable development research in the Asia-Pacific region*, Cham, DE, Springer (pp. 107–114)..

Jollands, M., Jolly, L, & Molyneaux, T. (2012). Project based learning as a contributing factor to graduates' work readiness. *European Journal of Engineering Education*, *37*(2), 143–154.

Jollands, M., & Parthasarathy, R. (2013). Developing engineering students' understanding of sustainability using project based learning. *Sustainability*, *5*(12), 5052–5066.

Kjærsdam, F. (2004). Technology transfer in a globalised world: Transferring between university and industry through cooperation and education. *World Transactions on Engineering and Technology Education*, *3*(1), 63–66.

Leung, C. F. (2000). Assessment for learning: Using SOLO taxonomy to measure design performance of design & technology students. *International Journal of Technology and Design Education*, *10*(2), 149–161.

Litzinger, T. A., Lattuca, L. R., Hadgraft, R. G., & Newstetter, W. C. (2011). Engineering education and the development of expertise. *Journal of Engineering Education*, *100*(1), 123–150.

Lozano, F. J., Huisingh, D., & Delgado, M. (2006). An integrated, interconnected, multi-disciplinary approach for fostering SD at the Monterrey Institute of Technology, Monterrey Campus. In J. Holmberg & B. E. Samuelsson (Eds.), *Drivers and barriers for implementing sustainable development in higher education: Education for sustainable development in Action Technical Paper No. 3* (pp. 37–47). Paris: UNESCO.

Marzano, R. J. (1991). Creating an educational paradigm centered on learning through teacher-directed, naturalistic enquiry. In L. Idol & B. Fly (Eds.), *Educational values and cognitive instruction: Implications for reform* (pp. 411–441). Hillsdate, NJ: L. Erlbaum Associates.

Mulder, K. (2006). *Sustainable development for engineers: A handbook and resource guide*. Sheffield: Greenleaf Publishing.

Mulder, K., Segalàs, J., & Cruz, Y. (2005). Training engineers for sustainable development, teaching experiences from three engineering institutions. In *Proceedings of European society for engineering education*, Ankara, Turkey (pp. 415–423).

Novak, J. D. (1998). *Learning, creating, and using knowledge: Concept maps as facilitative tools in schools and corporations*. Mahwah, NJ: L. Erlbaum & Assoc.

Pappas, E., Pierrakos, O., & Nagel, R. (2013). Using Bloom's taxonomy to teach sustainability in multiple contexts. *Journal of Cleaner Production, 48*, 54–64.

Prince, M. J., & Felder, R. M. (2006). Inductive teaching and learning methods: Definitions, comparisons, and research bases. *Journal of Engineering Education, 95*(2), 123–138.

Rydhagen, B., & Dackman, C. (2011). Integration of sustainable development in sanitary engineering education in Sweden. *European Journal of Engineering Education, 36*(1), 87–95.

Segalàs, J. (2009). *PhD dissertation engineering education for a sustainable future*. Barcelona: Universitat Politècnica de Catalunya.

Segalàs, J., Ferrer-Balas, D., & Mulder, K. F. (2008). Conceptual maps: Measuring learning processes of engineering students concerning sustainable development. *European Journal of Engineering Education, 33*, 297–306.

Segalàs, J., Ferrer-Balas, D., & Mulder, K. F. (2009). Introducing sustainable development in engineering education: Competences, pedagogy and curriculum. In *Proceedings of the European society for engineering education annual conference*, Rotterdam.

Segalàs J., Ferrer-Balas, D., & Mulder, K. F. (2010). What do engineering students learn in sustainability courses? The effect of the pedagogical approach. *Journal of Cleaner Production, 18*, 275–284.

Segalàs, J., Ferrer-Balas, D., Svanström, M., Lundqvist, U., & Mulder, K. F. (2009). What has to be learnt for sustainability? A comparison of bachelor engineering education competences at three European universities. *Sustainability Science, 4*, 17–27.

Segalàs, J., & Tejedor, G. (2013). ERASMUS Intensive Program in Sustainable Technology Development: Multicultural Constructive Community learning course for EESD applying Backcasting. In *Proceedings of the engineering education for sustainable development conference*, Cambridge (pp. 1–8).

Shing, C. K. (2015). *Sustainability integration into engineering curricula within five research universities in Malaysia.* Kuala Lumpur: University of Malaya.

Stansinoupolos, P., Smith, M. H., Hargroves, K., & Desha, C. (2013). *Whole system design: An integrated approach to sustainable engineering*. London: Earthscan.

Stanford, M. S., Benson, L. C., Alluri, P., Martin, W. D., Klotz, L. E., Ogle, J. H., ... & Schiff, S. (2012). Evaluating student and faculty outcomes for a real-world capstone project with sustainability considerations. *Journal of Professional Issues in Engineering Education and Practice, 139*(2), 123–133.

Trowler, P., & Cooper, A. (2002). Teaching and learning regimes: Implicit theories and recurrent practices in the enhancement of teaching and learning through educational development programmes. *Higher Education Research & Development, 21*(3), 221–240

Walker, A., & Leary, H. (2009). A problem based learning meta analysis: Differences cross problem types, implementation types, disciplines, and assessment levels. *Interdisciplinary Journal of Problem-based Learning, 3*(1), 6–28.

Washington Accord. (2014). *25 years Washington Accord 1989–2014*. International Engineering Alliance. Retrieved from http://www.ieagreements.org/assets/Uploads/Documents/History/25YearsWashingtonAccord-A5booklet-FINAL.pdf

Wiek, A., Withycombe, L., & Redman, C. L. (2011). Key competencies in sustainability: A reference framework for academic program development. *Sustainability Science, 6*(2), 203–218.

CHAPTER 6

CAN THE ANTHROPOCENE PROVIDE A TOOL FOR MEANINGFUL TEACHING OF SUSTAINABILITY IN HIGHER EDUCATION?

Patrick Baughan

ABSTRACT

The Anthropocene is commonly explained as a current epoch that began when human activities started bearing a major impact on the natural world. As an area of study, it has a logical disciplinary home, addressed widely in geology (Gibbard & Walker, 2014). However, it is also gaining traction in other disciplines, especially the social sciences (Bonneuil & Fressoz, 2017). In most accounts, it involves examining how the relationship between humans and the planet has changed and what can be done to monitor the balance.

Sustainability represents a more familiar challenge and discussion area in higher education. Nevertheless, two areas of questioning about it endure: what is sustainability and should students be taught about it? One established account is the "three-pillar model" which presents sustainability as an intersection of economic, social, and environmental issues (Brundtland Report, 1987). There are, however, different views as to how sustainability curriculum change should be implemented (Hopkinson, Hughes, & Layer, 2008; Stubbs & Schapper, 2011) but students appear to want sustainability better represented in their institutions (Drayson, Bone, Agombar, & Kemp, 2013).

Teaching and Learning Strategies for Sustainable Development:
Innovations in Higher Education Teaching and Learning, Volume 19, 73–82

ISSN: 2055-3641/doi:10.1108/S2055-364120200000019009

This chapter considers whether the relatively recent focus on the Anthropocene can help us develop sustainability teaching in higher education. My project draws on desk-based research, comprising a review of academic sources on the Anthropocene and on sustainability, as well as teaching materials on these areas. The author also draws on five conversations with staff involved in teaching and researching the Anthropocene.

The outcomes point to some support for further teaching about the Anthropocene and in a way which links to sustainability, and the author argues that as a concept and proposition, the Anthropocene has important potential for informing future sustainability teaching. However, the relationship between the Anthropocene and sustainability needs exploring further in follow-up research with both staff and learners.

Keywords: Anthropocene; sustainability; higher education; teaching; curriculum; geology; social science

BACKGROUND

The Anthropocene can be explained as

> [...] a proposed epoch that [began] when human activities started to have a significant global impact on Earth's geology and ecosystems .... It is the term approved by the *International Commission on Stratigraphy* to describe the geological age we are now living in, one in which human agency is affecting the planet more than any other force. (Watts, 2017, p. 54)

It has a logical disciplinary home, having been addressed widely in geology (Gibbard & Walker, 2014) but is gaining broader currency and has been the subject of discussion in other fields and disciplines, especially social science disciplines (Bonneuil & Fressoz, 2017; Steffen, Crutzen, & McNeill, 2007). In most accounts, study of the Anthropocene involves examining how the relationship between humans and the planet has changed geologically, and what can be done to monitor the balance.

Sustainability and the teaching of sustainability issues represent more familiar discussions in higher education policy and research. Nevertheless, at least two areas of doubt and debate regularly arise with respect to its development and implementation. First, how is sustainability best defined; and second, should students studying in higher education be taught it as part of their curricula – and if so how? Reid, Petocz, and Taylor (2009) are among the many authors who have discussed different interpretations of the term describing how sustainability represents a journey, an educational endeavor or is about types of work system. For others, such as Perrault and Clark (2017), sustainability is a list of behaviors that encompass what it means to "be sustainable." Wals and Jickling (2002) also consider the complications of understanding sustainability, suggesting

> Sustainability is as complex as life itself. The concept of sustainability is related to the social, economic, cultural, ethical and spiritual domain of our existence. It differs over time and space .... (p. 227)

One account that *is* established is the "three-pillar model" which presents sustainability as an intersection of economic, social, and environmental issues (Brundtland Report, 1987). Still, variation in understandings of sustainability do not provide the best starting point for considering its inclusion in teaching, though there have been many discipline-specific innovations addressing how sustainability has been blended and taught meaningfully in particular disciplinary contexts (Barlett & Chase, 2013; Johnston, 2013). But as I shall explore below, there remain different views as to *how* sustainability-based curriculum change should be implemented.

This chapter brings together the Anthropocene and sustainability, and looks at whether the former can provide a tool to address some of the ongoing curriculum-based concerns of the latter. It considers whether the Anthropocene can help us develop sustainability teaching in higher education and whether it can provide a more effective "way in" for teaching sustainability across the disciplines. The remainder of the chapter is organized as follows. In the next two sections, I further examine the Anthropocene and sustainability in higher education. Following this, the research approach I adopted for addressing the research questions is outlined, after which outcomes are presented. These sections are followed up with a discussion of the outcomes, some ideas for further research, and several recommendations.

At this stage, it should be pointed out that this chapter is based on an initial, small-scale study, drawing on literature reviews and informal conversations I have undertaken with staff teaching or writing about the Anthropocene. It is intended to offer a "thought-piece" and provoke further discussion and study. Thus, follow-on, larger scale investigations will be needed in the future. A summary of this project was previously presented at the European Conference of Educational Research (Baughan, 2018).

THE ANTHROPOCENE

In the previous section, I introduced the Anthropocene as an identified "epoch" to describe the current geological age, one characterized by the effects of human agency on the planet (Watts, 2017). To elaborate, Stephens, Hernandez, Roman, Graham, and Scholz (2008, p. 318) define the Anthropocene as an "…era of intense, irreversible human influence on the earth's systems." Arias-Maldonado (2016) argues that the Anthropocene, with its basis in geology and Earth system science "…plausibly suggests that human beings have colonized nature in a degree that has irreversibly altered the functioning of planetary systems" (p. 1), also providing an ongoing measure of the changing relationship between society and nature. To further our understanding of the term, it may help to unpack its origins in Ancient Greek language, "Anthrop" referring to "the age of humans" and "-cene" denouncing a particular geological time period. In fact, there are various theories concerning the Anthropocene (Crutzen, 2002; Lewis & Maslin, 2015), it being linked to several geological timescales. Other authors have questioned association of the term with a particular epoch or clear beginning

(Gibbard & Walker, 2014). Social scientists have been involved in discussing and critiquing aspects of the Anthropocene (Barnett & Campbell, 2010; Bonneuil & Fressoz, 2017).

Of note, researchers have reached different views about when the Anthropocene actually began, this being problematic to define as humans have been influencing their environments throughout their species' existence. Researchers have proposed five possible starting times, including the Industrial Revolution and Great Acceleration, the latter referring to major expansion in population, economic activity, urbanization, travel, technology, and consumption. Another reason why the notion is not straightforward lies in the fact that it is being investigated in different areas of science using different methods and criteria for examining the evidence (Castree, 2016). Lewis and Maslin (2015) argue that the importance of the Anthropocene – in terms of human beings bearing unprecedented consequences on planetary systems – means that we need to promote multiple understandings and definitions of the term, across the social sciences and humanities, as well as in geology.

Bringing the notion of the Anthropocene toward the focus of this project, a particular point of interest (and urgency) has been in its emphasis on human agency as the most environmentally problematic influence. This view provides, it is hypothesized here, a useful lever for informing the teaching and researching of sustainability, offering a visible example of its relevance to a wider audience. A further appeal for drawing on the Anthropocene in teaching sustainability lies in the argument that bearing in mind the number of debates and concerns surrounding the teaching of sustainability, which vary in different institutional settings and in different disciplines, new ideas about how we might approach sustainability teaching should be considered.

SUSTAINABILITY IN HIGHER EDUCATION

Caradonna (2016) opines that sustainability is "...a galvanizingly powerful term whose application subsumes a number of other movements, environmental perhaps most of all" (p. 3) later adding "Now almost anything can be viewed through the prism of sustainability ... sustainability has become an all-encompassing worldview ..." (pp. 177–178). Similarly, for Brew and Cahir (2013), a problem of definition is that sustainability is an overused term, adopted differentially by governments, institutions, and individuals. Indeed, these variations in understandings of sustainability may not always provide the best starting point for considering its inclusion in teaching, in spite of an impressive range of discipline-specific innovations, examples of which were cited above. In addition, there are different views as to *whether* and *how* sustainability-based curriculum change should be implemented. For example, several authors have discussed holistic integration (Hopkinson, Hughes, & Layer, 2008) while others offer more piecemeal approaches (Stubbs & Schapper, 2011). Nevertheless, student-based studies indicate that students want sustainability better represented in their institutions and curricula (Drayson, Bone, Agombar, & Kemp, 2013). These findings suggest that sustainability will remain on the international higher education agenda, and that, therefore, providers need to find effective ways of practising it and educating about it.

At this stage, it is useful to identify some of the accepted explanations of sustainability. Caradonna (2016) adds:

> The most common model of sustainability to emerge in recent years is the tripartite Venn diagram that illustrates the interconnectedness of the three "Es": environment, economy and social equality ... a fourth "E," education, is added to the diagram to reflect the importance of education in establishing a sustainable society. (p. 8)

In this approach, each of the "Es" may operate independently or in conjunction with one, two, or all three of the others. This broadly correlates with the "three-pillar model" which presents sustainability as an intersection of economic, social, and environmental issues (Brundtland Report, 1987). However, a criticism by Holden, Linnerud, and Banister (2017) should also be noted. These authors present an adjusted version of the model, additionally drawing on three "moral imperatives": satisfying human needs, ensuring social equity, and respecting environmental limits. Crucially, this adapted model views sustainable development as representing a set of *constraints* on human behavior, on the basis that human beings are exceeding limits of sustainability. Further, Perrault and Clark (2017) emphasize that sustainability is not just about the "here and now," but, when applied properly, must include a futures-based perspective because current consumption behavior should not prevent future generations from utilizing necessary resources for their own needs. Therefore, the view of sustainability I adopt (in this chapter and elsewhere) begins with the three-pillar model, but accepts the additional issues raised by Holden et al. (2017) and Perrault and Clark (2017). Further, I would, like others, opine that most sustainability issues can be contained within the environmental dimension; the social and economic issues encapsulated within accounts of sustainability are part of the environment that humans have created. In this sense, understanding sustainability through the study of the Anthropocene is also useful, as the latter acknowledges that the relationship between humans and the environment is central for study and is changing itself.

RESEARCH APPROACH

This chapter reports on a small-scale project which explored whether and how the concept or epoch of the Anthropocene might help inform sustainability teaching. In particular, it asks: what can the "lens" of the Anthropocene offer us for developing sustainability teaching in higher education? Does it provide a more suitable lens or "way in" for educating about sustainability? An important rationale for the study lies in well documented difficulties concerning the integration of sustainability in certain higher education curricula (see, for example, Vaughter, Wright, McKenzie, & Lidstone, 2013; Wood, Cornforth, Beals, Taylor, & Tallon, 2016).

The research approach taken for considering these questions involved two stages of inquiry. First, the larger part of the work was desk-based and explorative. This comprised a focused (and selective) review of literature on the Anthropocene and on sustainability in higher education, drawing on the fields of higher education research, geology, and social science. In addition, the review incorporated other sources including non-disciplinary-specific books (Bonneuil & Fressoz, 2017), media coverage (Watts, 2017), and teaching materials at higher education institutions at which I have worked. Example teaching materials about the Anthropocene can be found on various universities and other websites.[1] In addition for this first part of the project, I drew on previous literature reviews and empirical studies I have undertaken about sustainability in higher education and university curricula (Baughan, 2014, 2015). In these studies, I referred to the two underlying concerns in sustainability raised above: what it is and includes, and how, if at all, it should be included in the curriculum. The literature reviews and outcomes of these previous projects each offer perspectives about the problematized nature of sustainability, and the main challenges facing those trying to develop sustainability teaching and policy which informed the focus of this work. Finally, the process of undertaking this secondary work was informed by Foss and Waters (2007), who provide incremental steps for undertaking literature-based research. The literature obtained through this first tier of work is referred to throughout the chapter, but a number of additional points will be emphasized in the next (outcomes) section.

The second tier of research drew on five informal conversations that I undertook with teachers and researchers of the Anthropocene, all working at UK or other European-based universities. The colleagues involved were all actively teaching or researching about the Anthropocene, their disciplines including Geology, English Literature, and Education. These conversations were brief (10–15 minutes each) and relatively unstructured in their content. In each case, I explained my introduction to and interest in the Anthropocene, and asked the colleague concerned about their experiences of and perspectives on integrating the Anthropocene into sustainability teaching. In other words, my questions were very similar to the research questions raised above. For each conversation, I took brief notes during or after the event. All conversations are completely anonymized and I do not make claims of representivity in this work, it being based on a small convenience sample. Rather, the conversations are intended to provide a glimpse into ideas about the issues, with the intention that larger scale, more formal studies might now be undertaken.

OUTCOMES

This study was undertaken by way of a focused literature review and through conversations with higher education staff, with different disciplinary backgrounds, involved in Anthropocene teaching and research. The literature review supported the argument that there remain differences in interpretation about what sustainability encapsulates, whether it should be taught, and how it should be taught in different disciplines (see e.g., Witham, 2010, as well as the studies identified above). In turn, we may deduce from this that while sustainability in the curriculum represents an important area for learning, there are problems concerning its implementation. The Anthropocene may provide one mechanism by which to offer a less abstract and more "real-life" entry point into sustainability education. In this capacity, Arias-Maldonado (2016) who has previously considered sustainability and the Anthropocene in conjunction with one another (and in relation to environmental sociology), developed the idea of "The Anthropocenic Turn," a theory or "vantage point" through which to view sustainability. The author refers to the potential importance of developing an "Anthropocene-friendly" understanding of sustainability, his work elucidating the consequences that such an Anthropocenic Turn would have for sustainability studies.

The five informal conversations also point to tangible benefits which could be afforded by teaching about the Anthropocene. While the following quotations reflect brief conversations and the sentiments expressed need to be explored further, they clearly illustrate some advantages of foregrounding the Anthropocene in teaching:

> The Anthropocene as an area of study is … more specific. Not so blurred [as sustainability].
>
> It's [the Anthropocene] linked more obviously to our actions and our times.
>
> Better to teach about – more to show and look at. It lends itself to more teaching methods.
>
> More immediacy and less stale [than sustainability].
>
> Much better to teach about – more demonstrative … there is more to show and look at, and more easily.
>
> Sustainability is a very prevalent term and that can water it down. If it isn't applied to something it may not mean anything. Sustain what?
>
> Most definitions of sustainability emphasise sustaining the present, keeping going, and "business as usual." The Anthropocene tells us that this is not enough: that we need to do more than sustain, but actually make changes as well.
>
> The Anthropocene explodes the myth that things (the environment) will always be the same as they have been because that is not enough.

These quotations point to some enthusiasm for introducing the Anthropocene as a topic that could be included as a part of sustainability teaching. The comments indicate that it may have more resonance and immediacy with learners and, because of its specificity, would perhaps be simpler to understand (this is implied in the sixth quotation). However, respondents also indicated that it lends itself to a range of teaching methods – actual evidence and items could be used to illustrate or demonstrate the Anthropocene. Further, though not reflected in the quotations above, one respondent viewed the Anthropocene as a concept that could be used to theorize sustainability – a proposition that needs to be further considered. In the view of the author of this chapter, the final two quotations are particularly important: they raise questions about certain interpretations of sustainability and suggest that "maintenance" is not enough, that change is needed – recent activities and protests in areas such as climate change lend support this more urgent view. Consequently, in emphasizing the urgent, it may have more relevance and appeal in teaching. This participant added that the Anthropocene may also be a useful concept for making people reflect on what they value and what they may want to protect. However, most agreed that while attractive as a teaching idea, teaching the Anthropocene may raise its own disciplinary concerns and questions similar to the teaching of sustainability: for example, both lend themselves more to some disciplinary curricula than to others. In addition, the Anthropocene is different from sustainability and their relationship to one another may itself provide a discussion point in teaching and an area of further inquiry in relevant research. Not all accounts of sustainability necessarily link to the Anthropocene in the same way. Nevertheless, if the Anthropocene foregrounds urgent societal issues, it seems reasonable to argue that representatives of all disciplines have responsibility for considering the concept, its implications, and its link to their areas of focus.

Based on these findings, it is provisionally suggested that the Anthropocene has potential for informing future sustainability teaching. It provides one way to help reframe teaching from a more specific starting point, its focus on human agency the most visible example of this. In the final section, I elaborate on these findings and look ahead to further studies that might be undertaken.

DISCUSSION POINTS AND RECOMMENDATIONS

In light of the outcomes of this trial study, it is argued that the Anthropocene, while an important concept in its own right, also offers a valuable perspective and a lens through which to teach sustainability in higher education. It has potential benefit for informing and reframing the teaching of sustainability and is a concept worthy of further discussion in higher education itself. It is probably the case that in order to better understand the relationship between the Anthropocene and sustainability, further study is needed, but equally, previous literature and my own conversations indicate the Anthropocene should be considered and utilized when appropriate in sustainability teaching because it bestows several advantages – not least as it foregrounds current human impact on the natural environment which provides a clearer focus, and suggests, by its very nature, an urgency for human action. Indeed, it presents real, current, and urgent issues for attention.

There are limitations in this project which need to be acknowledged. First, the findings and conclusions offered are based on a small-scale study, which should be followed up using a larger sample base. In a future work, I would like to explore student views and ideas about teaching of the Anthropocene. Future research could draw on a more diverse sample base, featuring semi-structured interviews, focus groups, or an alternative methodology to capture the views and ideas of geologists, social scientists, and teachers of sustainability in other disciplines, at more institutions and organizations, and with varying levels of experience. Finally, while not a limitation of this study, it would be valuable to see related research undertaken in secondary and further education, and whether and how it is introduced in these earlier years of education.

The construct of the Anthropocene has its own limitations and critics. These include concerns that it might become viewed as another "buzzword" or subject to the same misuses as sustainability through "green-washing" ("...a way of exaggerating or fabricating the environmental benefits of a product, practice or service," Caradonna, 2016, p. 248). Nevertheless, although it is not being suggested here that the Anthropocene represents a replacement focus to sustainability, its more specific emphasis might enable existing sustainability and Education for Sustainable Development teaching to be better defined and understood by both educators and students.

To close this chapter, I would suggest a vital role for both the Anthropocene and sustainability in future sustainability teaching. On this, Castree (2016) makes a suitable point for us to take forward the ideas presented here:

> The Anthropocene deserves to become part of our lexicon – a way we understand who we are, what we're doing and what our responsibilities are as a species – as long as we remember that not all humans are equal contributors to our planetary maladies, with many being victims.

NOTE

1. One useful example of a teaching resource can be found at: https://medium.com/permaculture-3-0/teaching-the-anthropocene-b1b9339eb9e4.

REFERENCES

Arias-Maldonado, M. (2016). The Anthropocenic turn: Theorizing sustainability in a postnatural age. *Sustainability*, *8*, 10. doi:10.3390/su8010010

Barlett, P., & Chase, G. (2013). *Sustainability in higher education; stories and strategies for transformation (urban and industrial environments)*. Cambridge, MA: MIT Press.

Barnett, J., & Campbell, J. (2010). *Climate change and small island states: Power, knowledge and the South Pacific*. London: Earthscan.

Baughan, P. (2014). Conceptions of the sustainability–pedagogy relationship: Should sustainability issues be introduced in higher education curricula? *The International Journal of Pedagogy and Curriculum*, *20*(4), 53–63.

Baughan, P. (2015). Sustainability policy and sustainability in higher education curricula: The educational developer perspective. *International Journal for Academic Development*, *20*(4), 319–332.

Baughan, P. (2018). Beyond sustainability in higher education? Teaching, learning and the Anthropocene. Paper presented at the European conference of educational research, 4–7 September, Bolzano, Italy.

Bonneuil, C., & Fressoz, J. (2017). *The shock of the Anthropocene: The earth, history and us*. London: Verso.

Brew, A., & Cahir, J. (2013). Achieving sustainability in learning and teaching initiatives. *International Journal for Academic Development*. *19*(4), 341–352. doi:10.1080/1360144X.2013.848360

Brundtland Commission. (1987). *World Commission on Environment and Development (WCED)*. New York, NY: Our Common Future.

Caradonna, J. (2016). *Sustainability: A history*. Oxford: University of Oxford.

Castree, N. (2016, August 30). An official welcome to the Anthropocene epoch: But who gets to decide it's here? *The Conversation*. Retrieved from http://theconversation.com/an-official-welcome-to-the-anthropocene-epoch-but-who-gets-to-decide-its-here-57113. Accessed on April 14, 2019.

Crutzen, P. (2002). Geology of mankind. *Nature*, *415*(6867), 23.

Drayson, R., Bone, E., Agombar, J., & Kemp, S. (2013). *Student attitudes towards and skills for sustainable development*. York: Higher Education Academy/National Union of Students.

Foss, S., & Waters, W. (2007). *Destination dissertation: A traveler's guide to a Done dissertation.* Plymouth: Rowman and Littlefield.

Gibbard, P., & Walker, M. (2014). The term 'Anthropocene' in the context of formal geological classification. *Geological Society London Special Publications, 395*(1), 29–37.

Holden, E., Linnerud, K., & Banister, D. (2017). The imperatives of sustainable development. *Sustainable Development. 25*(3), 213–226. doi:10.1002/sd.1647.

Hopkinson, P., Hughes, P., & Layer, G. (2008). Sustainable graduates: Linking formal, informal and campus curricula to embed education for sustainable development in the student learning experience. *Environmental Education Research, 14*(4), 435–454.

Johnston, L. (Ed.). (2013). *Higher education for sustainability: Cases, challenges and opportunities from across the curriculum.* Oxon: Routledge.

Lewis, S., & Maslin, M. A. (2015). Defining the Anthropocene. *Nature, 519*(7542), 171–180.

Perrault, E., & Clark, S. (2017). Sustainability in the university student's mind: Are university endorsements, financial support, and programs making a difference? *Journal of Geoscience Education, 65*(2), 194–202.

Reid, A., Petocz, P., & Taylor, P. (2009). Business students' conceptions of sustainability. *Sustainability, 1*, 662–673. doi:10.3390/su1030662.

Steffen, W., Crutzen, P., & McNeill, J. (2007). The Anthropocene: Are humans now overwhelming the great forces of nature? *Ambio: A Journal of the Human Environment, 36*(8), 614–621.

Stephens, J., Hernandez, M., Roman, M., Graham, A., & Scholz, R. (2008). Higher education as a change agent for sustainability in different cultures and contexts. *International Journal of Sustainability in Higher Education, 9*(3), 317–338.

Stubbs, W., & Schapper, J. (2011). Two approaches to curriculum development for educating for sustainability and CSR. *International Journal of Sustainability in Higher Education, 12*(3), 259–268.

Vaughter, P., Wright, T., McKenzie, M., & Lidstone, L. (2013). Greening the Ivory Tower: A review of educational research on sustainability in post-secondary education. *Sustainability, 5*(5), 2252–2271.

Wals, A., & Jickling, B. (2002). Sustainability in higher education: From doublethink and news-peak to critical thinking and meaningful learning. *International Journal of Sustainability in Higher Education, 3*(3), 221–232.

Watts, J. (2017). Environment: Why everything else comes second. *The Guardian*, April 15, p. 54.

Witham, H. (2010). Embedding sustainable development in the higher education economics curriculum. *Higher Education Academy Economics Network.* Retrieved from http://www.economicsnetwork.ac.uk/projects/esd/ESDreport.pdf. Accessed on April 14, 2019.

Wood, B., Cornforth, S., Beals, F., Taylor, M., & Tallon, R. (2016). Sustainability champions? Academic identities and sustainability curricula in higher education. *International Journal of Sustainability in Higher Education, 17*(3), 342–360. doi:10.1108/IJSHE-12-2014-0171

CHAPTER 7

DELIBERATIVE DIALOGUE AND SYLLABUS DELIBERATION AS INNOVATIVE, CROSS-DISCIPLINARY, AND SUSTAINABLE TEACHING METHODS

Sharyn Lowenstein

ABSTRACT

This chapter argues that Deliberative Dialogues (DDs) are a form of Education for Sustainable Development, whose design, process focus, wide-tent approach, and interdisciplinarity align with best democratic practices. DDs are an effective method for bridging seemingly opposing forces in academia and the larger society: Narrow expertise versus interdisciplinarity, individual orientation versus collaboration, polarization and prioritization of majority/privileged voice versus inclusivity and search for common ground. This chapter will define and describe deliberation and DDs as useful for a wide range of disciplines, offer models, explore basic components, and analyze the author's participant researcher experience in crafting and facilitating DDs in 35 classes across multiple disciplines in a small private university. The chapter will look at the planning process, the logistics of running the DD, post-DD outcomes, and provide questions and suggestions for future enhancements. A particular kind of DD will be explored, the Syllabus Deliberation method (also known as the negotiated or process syllabus). Finally, the chapter will articulate findings related

Teaching and Learning Strategies for Sustainable Development:
Innovations in Higher Education Teaching and Learning, Volume 19, 83–105

ISSN: 2055-3641/doi:10.1108/S2055-364120200000019010

to the process of preparing for the deliberations, ways in which scaffolded activities improved, relationship between the dialogues and course curriculum, evolution of faculty and researcher-facilitator roles, challenges, and successes. Students' and faculty's perceptions of some outcomes are also included.

Keywords: Deliberative dialogue; deliberation; negotiated syllabus; process syllabus; democratic classroom practices; higher education; sustainable education

INTRODUCTION

Educating for Sustainable Development (ESD) and Sustainable Education are twin terms used to describe methodologies that push at the boundaries of educational culture: UNESCO (The United Nations Educational, Scientific, and Cultural Organization) notes that education for ESD is a holistic and transformative pedagogy that "empowers learners to take informed decisions and responsible actions for environmental integrity, economic viability and a just society, for present and future generations, while respecting cultural diversity" (UNESCO, n.d.). Rosalyn McKeown (2002) tells us that "ESD focuses largely on the major social, economic, and environmental issues that threaten the sustainability of the planet," including globalization, war, and human rights (p. 18). Stephen Sterling (2008), on the other hand, prefers the use of Sustainable Education, which he uses to highlight the learning outcome of critical awareness. According to Earl, Van Wynsberghe, Walter, and Straka (2018), the goal of Sustainable Education is behavior change, increased community/global agency, adaptability, cross-disciplinary thinking, and problem-solving. For the purposes of this chapter both terms are used.

To achieve the deep and broad goals identified above, however, a toolbox of strategic classroom activities is needed. Unfortunately, Earl et al. (2018) suggest that ESD lacks "innovative teaching methods" distinguishing it from other educational approaches. Warburton (2003) notes that we need to promote systems-level thinking by offering wide ranging content, illustrating interconnections, stressing dynamic processes over rigid structures, and helping students grapple with resource limits, environmental values, and equity. Warburton cites several deep learning principles for Sustainable Education including mastery combined with discovery learning, strategic use of personal experience, emphasis of principles over facts, and re-framing of learning as a process of asking more effective questions. The following section describes Deliberative Dialogue (DD) as a Sustainable Education best practice methodology promoting cross-disciplinary and out-of-the-box thinking, in which students are encouraged to explore the common good for future generations and grapple with the reality of limited resources.

What is Deliberation?

Deliberation is a collective thinking process that moves slowly and purposely, intended to include all the voices in the room and even, at times, a call for unexpressed opinions. Deliberation is "aimed at establishing a framework for mutual understanding and a common purpose that transcends mere ideas and opinion" (London, 2019, p. 1). Farland (2008) notes

> Deliberation is committed to exploring the range of positions taken in response to difficult social problems. Various positions are treated critically and fairly, and each approach, or "choice," is presented neutrally and without prejudice.

She goes on to say,

> Deliberative approaches stand in stark contrast to the culture of professional expertise in which the role of the academic professional is to employ specialized knowledge in order to endorse a particular pragmatic or conceptual solution. (p. 91)

Beyond juries, there are many forms of deliberation. *Involve*, a European-based organization and the "leading public participation charity on a mission to put people at the heart of decision-making," also identifies citizens' panels, citizen's juries, participatory budgeting practices, citizen report cards, and service co-design (Involve, 2019).

What is the Deliberative Dialogue?

The DD is a structured, engaging class discussion on a carefully framed and pressing social problem such as immigration, wealth distribution, food security, animal rights, or the opioid crisis. The intention of the DD is to gather as many diverse opinions as possible; therefore, it emphasizes student voice, group decision-making, and respectful disagreement. Distinguished by its more measured, methodical approach than is usually found in a conventional class discussion, it calls for testing of ideas, emphasizes thinking together over individual eloquence or persuasion, and shifting from one's personal perspective and individual agency to an analysis of the common good and collective action. Most especially, the DD also prompts deep listening, an increasingly rare occurrence in a polarized world.

Extensive research and practical applications of deliberative methods have been explored within disciplines, for example, within communication instruction (Abbott, McDorman, Timmerman, & Lamberton, 2016; Drury, 2015; Gastil, 2014; Ryfe, 2006) as well as in general education (Campus Compact, 2015); human service courses (Achankeng, 2018), and first year seminars (Harriger, McMillan, Buchanan, & Gustler, 2015). In addition, DD has been examined in terms of its outcomes (Drury, Derek, Goddard, & Wentzel, 2016; Gastil & Dillard, 1999; Knobloch & Gastil, 2015; Lawrence & Theis, 2014); facilitation styles (Dillard, 2013; Kaner, Lind, Toldi, Fisk, & Berger, 2014; National Issues Forum Handbook, 2006, 2016); and issue framing (Mathews, 2016).

The DD serves as a learning tool to promote democratic values such as empathy; inquiry; finding common ground; realizing and prioritizing one's values; understanding others' perspectives; analyzing the complexity and nuances of a social problem; figuring out the consequences of policies and regulations; and navigating the intersections of family, community, law enforcement, schools, racism, sexism, and many other isms. As Doherty (2008) notes, "Deliberative democracy principles and practices put [civic participants] at the center," as well as "collective learning, naming issues in terms of what people hold dear," and recognizing community strengths that can be tapped to enhance common challenges (p. 18).[1] London, a journalist observed,

> As I listened to people deliberating in the forums, I found that they were speaking in very different terms than I had anticipated. It seemed that while politicians and opinion leaders were telling one story, people in communities were telling another. Citizens were concerned about the deepening divide between the nation's rich and poor, not – as the press would have it – about obscure indicators on the state of the economy ... [Citizens] were neither as ideologically polarized nor as fixed in their political views as the news coverage and opinion polls had led me to expect. (p. 2)

There are many kinds of DDs; the DD model featured in this chapter draws from the US-based National Issues Forum/Kettering Institute (NIFI) foundation paradigm. NIFI is a non-partisan network of community groups, pre-school through higher education, and faith-based groups working on public issues (Grattan, Dedrick, & Dienstfrey, 2008). This model emphasizes the "ecology of democracy," that is to say,

> a metaphor describing the complex and interconnected parts of any community that must find ways to exist together in a place. The community is the place where people decide what their lives will be like within this ecology, and they can decide more or less deliberatively and democratically. Community-based decisions about how to educate and socialize the next generation, and how to maintain safety, prosperity, and health are the core of ecological work .... The ecology recognizes that individualism puts citizens in competition or at cross purposes, rather than in collaboration and coproduction of the common good. (Barker & Lovit, 2018, p. 19)

DDs take about 1.5 hours; they can be held in community settings such as town halls, veterans' centers, libraries, and churches, as well as in colleges and lower education. Some also happen online. In the community, DDs include one or more "moderators," one or more note-takers, and invited community members to serve as discussants.

Author's Context

During Spring 2017 the author was awarded a Sabbatical to study democracy in higher education and, in particular, democratic classroom practices; she gravitated toward DDs and a special variant, Syllabus Deliberations (SD) (see below), as particularly effective teaching tools. The author participated in two community DDs sponsored by the NIFI and became trained as a DD moderator.

Since Fall 2017 the author has been integrating SDs in her own classes and collaborating with faculty to integrate DDs other diverse classes, thus far facilitating a total of 35 DDs (with two faculty facilitating three different DDs on their own) in world history, interpersonal communication, public speaking, psychological testing, ethics, sociology, English, First Year Seminars, criminal justice, and social justice classes. When working outside of her own classes, the author and collaborating faculty have mutually decided on the topic, framing of the issue, purposes of the DD, and lead-up sessions.

The following section describes the DD process, followed by the author's findings based on her two-year journey of adaptive implementation. Findings are derived from collaborating faculty's written and oral feedback, student feedback through discussion and surveys, and the author's notes.

DELIBERATIVE DIALOGUE AT WORK

General Explanation

General Flow of Activity
Typically, an issue guide from NIFI has been used in its entirety or adapted; in some cases the author has written a new issue guide. The author visits the collaborating faculty's classroom prior to the DD and in the same or another session facilitates support (30 minute or longer scaffolded) activities that orient students to the DD session. During the DDs, the author has facilitated with faculty taking process notes. Post-DD, faculty, and author have discussed ways in which the DD might have impacted the course flow as well as the balance and relative importance of the idea exchange process versus the content of the DD (see Appendix 1). One faculty has later designed his own sessions.

Scaffolded (or Preparation) Activities
Scaffolded sessions are those that lead up to the DD day. These sessions can last from 30 minutes to over an hour, to align with course session format, content, and objectives. These activities can include an introduction to the rationale for doing a DD, other information on democratic practice and skill building components. During this session, the group investigates students' personal stakes in the upcoming issue, the ways in which they do (or don't) see their connection to the social problem, how it impacts their lives or the lives of others they care about, how it potentially links to other concerns they may have, and why this issue is important now and/or in the future.

Typically these sessions encourage discussion on the current polarization of US society and the erosion of democracy across the world. Sessions are designed to help students get out of their "comfort zones," develop various ways to disagree respectfully, and address questions about the issue, the issue guide, and the upcoming DD itself. Sessions prompt discussion regarding deliberating versus persuading or debating, and stress the importance of students contributing their opinions.

The preparation session includes the distribution of the issue guide, for which the faculty creates an assignment. Finally, the group discusses the guidelines of confidentiality, deep listening, disagreeing gracefully, respect, giving space to others to speak, and going out of our comfort zones. Ideally, guidelines are posted and visible on the DD day as well.

More on the Issue Guide

The NIFI has developed 11 issue guides on diverse topics (immigration, policing, climate, food security, wealth, and poverty) with guides generally ranging from 10 to 23 pages. (See Appendix 2 for example of an issue guide written by the author to supplement existing titles.) Effective issue guides for classroom use include the following four features: rationale, encouragement to participate, social issue definition, and treatment options and weighing of pros and cons:

Deliberative dialogue rationale. The rationale includes a call for more active civic engagement in a democratic society by "everyday people."

Encouragement to participate. The issue guide encourages maximum participation; prompts students to get out of their comfort zones; emphasizes deliberation and distinguishes it from voting, debate, or persuasion; suggests ways to disagree respectfully; and prompts those who more frequently talk to give space to the more reticent students.

Social issue definition. The purpose of this section is to explore the immediacy, urgency, and complexity of a problem. The social issue is typically framed by an open-ended question (such as "How can we enhance the civil rights of transgender individuals?"). In making the case for tackling the problem, the guide analyzes the components, prevalence, and impact of an issue. As well, the guide offers a range of local, community, and national approaches that either have been tried or might be considered. The goal is to present substantial – but not overwhelming – information.

Treatment options and weighing of pros and cons. The guide provides three or four options for taking action via individuals and local groups (families and consumers); schools and communities; police; legislation and regulation; media; businesses, and elected officials (see Appendix 2). Each of these options is presented with its possible tradeoffs including time, expense, possibility of overreach, conflict with other values or goals, impact on society or organizations, necessity for other pre-requisite or co-requisite action, need for more information, and the likelihood of unwanted outcomes such as increased community resistance.

Deliberative Dialogue Session Implementation

On DD day – ranging two days to two weeks from the scaffolded activity – the class reviews the order, general format, and guidelines of the dialogue discussion. Everyone is asked to take two or more pennies from a pile, and move one forward to mark each speaking turn, making verbal participation a very visual feature and emphasizing the importance of every voice. The group takes a few minutes to discuss criteria for a successful dialogue, elevating the principle of thinking together over achieving consensus. At the conclusion of the session a short verbal and written evaluation is implemented (see Appendix 3).

Reflections and Findings Related to Deliberative Dialogue in the Classroom

Below are findings related to preparation activities, personal stories, issue perception, opinion diversity, understanding and articulating tradeoffs among treatment options, group cohesion, (re)focusing, course linkage, as well as issue guide construction and use.

The author has found that enhanced preparation and assessment of students' readiness to participate increases DD student satisfaction, deepens learning and sharing, and develops the group. For example, the preparation/scaffolded session may indicate that the group members feel too personally affected by the issue to be able to discuss it, or they underestimate its impact. One of the best ways to help students uncover their personal stakes and develop self-empathy as well as empathy for others has been to encourage personal stories. According to Scott London, these stories "allow participants to identify with each other and recognize others' experiences as valid on their own terms – even when they may disagree about their 'positions' on an issue." One student's story elicits other students' stories: As these stories unfold and stack upon each other, they help build group confidence, increase trust, and promote lens shifting, that is, "seeing an issue through the eyes of another person, especially someone of a different culture or background" (London, 2019, p. 4).

Unlike the moderator out in the community, the facilitator in the classroom may need to push for everyone to speak through a variety of strategies: assuring that every opinion counts or asking students to imagine the issue from the point of view of another community stakeholders (e.g., a parent, a taxpayer, and a school principal). Most recently, the author has also left one empty chair, as a call to voice opinions that have not surfaced. The author has discovered that getting students to disagree (and do so respectfully), so critical to the entire DD process, is difficult for many. Publicly recognizing the first disagreement has been useful. The author has also found that some groups feel safer with more space between participants, and if the room has portable desks/tables, the group may use these to provide a protective "barrier."

Another finding is that the skills of weighing the tradeoffs do not seem to come naturally to students at any level (although students majoring in the social sciences have an easier time); therefore, the author has found the need to ask very pointed questions. ("Why is option x better in your opinion than option y?" "What advantages does one have over the other?" "For option z to work, what resources would need to be in place?" "How long might that take?" "How much would a cost versus b?") Teacher feedback (based on two sections of an advocacy writing course and two sections of a public speaking class) indicates that "The extent to which students considered tradeoffs among the various options" averaged 3 out of 4 (with 4 being highest).

One of the anticipated outcomes of the DD has been getting individuals to look at themselves as a part of the group and thinking of the group itself as an important entity. This idea also has not come naturally either, in the classroom or in the larger community. A facilitator, therefore, may wish to prompt the students to reflect on the group's formation and interaction. The author has developed an arsenal of such questions including the following: "How are we doing as a group?" "How much are we listening to each other?" "What else might we do to improve our group discussion?" "How satisfying is our discussion?" "What are we learning about each other?" "What seems to be our preferred option?" "What ways are people using to disagree?" "How can we increase our diversity of opinion?" "How brave are we as a group?" and "How can we give more equal 'air time'?".

Both teachers as well as students surveyed revealed that students felt heard and respected. For example, in a survey of 105 students across multiple sections of a World History course taught by the same professor,[2] on the question, "How much were you heard and respected?" students ranked themselves 9.25 out of 10, with 10 being highest. This sentiment was further echoed in students' definitions of the DD, including such representative descriptions as "a conversation free of hate, interruption and conflict" and "an open platform." This sentiment probably accounts for the finding that faculty saw one of the greatest benefits of the DD as helping the class build community. Indeed, one teacher commented:

> Despite the fact that the class already knew a lot about each other having delivered and listened to three individual speeches, the DD process seemed to increase solidarity, especially in the second group.

A second teacher wrote:

> I think this [community building] was one of the strengths of the Deliberative Dialogue particularly this semester. The dialogue helped students to develop practices and processes for creating and maintaining safe spaces for discussion of complex issues.

Within the DD session it has been easy to "get off-track" or at least leave the impression of getting off-track: One faculty wrote, "At times, the actual DD got a bit off-topic, leaving less time to discuss other aspects of the issue." As a response to this perception, the author has adapted two quick re-focusing techniques: the first is reminding students where they are in the issue guide: ("We have just finished up option #1" or "before we finish option #1 and move on to option #2, does anyone have anything else to add?") The second is marking time in a more clear-cut way: The facilitator (or, preferably, a designated time keeper) can signal the halfway point and about 15 minutes before the end of the discussion.

One of the interesting findings was the degree to which students' caring about the issue shifted in a positive direction: In the World History sections, on a 10-point scale, students' average self-reported ranking increased from 6.18 (pre-dialogue attitude) to 8.18 (post-dialogue). Considering these discussions lasted approximately one hour and the preparation sessions were under an hour, this movement is significant. For example, one student commented: "...agreements and disagreements matter in speaking with one another. This is a much bigger issue than anyone realizes." A second student noted, "...I care about this topic. I always felt like it wasn't important, but it is."

As far as the issue guides, the author has found it useful to refer students to class readings and discussions as they relate to the issue being discussed, rather than making assumptions that all students will automatically make these connections. Another important finding is that when faculty assign issue guide homework that goes beyond only reading it, for example, producing a summary, or answering questions, students come more prepared.

Writing an issue guide has involved an intense study period for the author: To prepare, the author has viewed select course readings, independently researched the social issue and the strategies that have been used or considered in addressing these issues, grappled with ways to frame the social issue as an open-ended question, and crafted the text. While it can be time consuming (10–20 hours or more), writing the issue guide can be a very rewarding experience, providing greater issue awareness for the author and informing the kinds of questions and prompting of students that moves the conversation forward. When the author has written the guides, collaborating faculty have usually appreciated the DD itself in a more nuanced way and seem to increase their personal stake, pointing out missing concepts, providing format support, and working on issue framing.

SYLLABUS DELIBERATION

A special form of DD, the SD, helps students better understand, develop personal stakes in, and collaborate on selected aspects of the syllabus. Also known as the negotiated or process syllabus, students may decide on percentage weights of course requirements, content, and/or evaluation procedures and values (Azarnoosh & Kargazari, 2017; Clarke, 1991; Harrell & Lam, 2019; Kaplan & Renard, 2015). The author's SDs within five of her own classes have focused solely on the weights of each of the major course requirements.[3]

Consistent with the goals of the DD, deliberating on the syllabus elicits student values, prompts consideration of tradeoffs, elevates the discussion of collective responsibility and accountability, and engages students in exploring their common ground and collective interests over individual needs and desires. The SD process places students at the center of their own learning. And, as with the DD, through the experience of the deliberation as well as its pre-deliberation scaffolded activities, students participate in a fundamental democratic practice of widening the tent for all voices.

Unlike the DD on a pressing social issue in which there may well be no clear consensus or decision, the goal of the SD is to finalize by consensus elements of the syllabus. Another difference between the SD and the DD on a pressing social issue is that with the latter there is clearly more emphasis on the interconnections among culture; power; local, regional, national, and even international factors; as well as the impact of racism, sexism, ageism, speciesism, depending on the issue being discussed. The SD, on the other hand, emphasizes power negotiation between the faculty member and the students as well as within the entire student group. A final difference is that while the DD provides three or four options (and various strategies within these options) for addressing pressing social issues, in the SD the students themselves are creating their own options and then deliberating upon them.

Reflections and Findings Related to Syllabus Deliberation

Below are findings related to SD scheduling, preparation activities, grade percentage significance, resisting the temptation to vote, group cohesion, personal stakes, opinion diversity, understanding, and articulating tradeoffs:

The SD should occur close to the beginning of the semester; the "sweet spot" seems to be session four (for twice-weekly classes) – allowing for enough time for students to get to know each other, ask course-related questions, and experience the professor's style. She has also found it important to call students' attention to the fact that the initial syllabus is but a draft, and that once the SD occurs, the syllabus will include the consensually agreed upon grading breakdown. (For emphasis, the initial syllabus can also embed a statement referring to the upcoming SD, which can also be identified in the course agenda page.)

When students and faculty come to the discussion with individual ideas on the weights/weight ranges and their rationales, the deliberation goes more smoothly. This weight analysis in advance of the SD places more responsibility on both the faculty to anticipate questions on the scope, purpose, parameters, length, depth, and format of papers and projects that constitute syllabus requirements, and on students, who now re-read and analyze the syllabus through a different lens. This cycle has led to more detailed syllabi, for example. In addition, after some trial and error, the author has shifted from leaving the initial weights completely open-ended to providing percentage ranges or upper or lower limits for some course requirements (as she has realized the point at which she is unwilling to compromise.)

When students do share their weights, they immediately realize they have different values and experiences insofar as individual learning preferences as well ability to demonstrate their knowledge. (Paraphrased examples of student comments include: "I don't do well on tests." "I am shy so attendance and participation should be lower." "I don't like to write about myself so I want a lower weight for the journals." "I am a visual learner." "I freeze when doing presentations.") Once students view the range of grading recommendations offered and listen to each other's reasoning, they begin to make additional proposals and counter-proposals, and these, the author found, should also be made immediately visible to keep track of these options. The facilitator must also help students understand their diverse rationales for assigning more or fewer percentage points: Some students want to award higher percentage points for those requirements they feel they can accomplish more easily, thus, improving their chances of a better grade. Others want higher points for those requirements they perceive as more difficult, thus giving themselves additional motivation. Eventually, with guidance, the class comes to realize that there are differences in student motivation, as well as the ways students think about their education and perceive their challenges and talents.

The author has found that the facilitator role dynamically fluctuates from traffic manager or moderator to coach, teacher, presenter, and task-master: At times it is important to remind students to consult the syllabus (again), directly teach such concepts as individual versus common interests, help students analyze their values/motivations for taking the class, and suggest ways to think about grading options. Inevitably, no matter how carefully built the syllabus, students' questions on requirements – including those specifically stated in the syllabus – interrupt the deliberation and at times threaten to derail the discussion altogether.

The SD – which after all calls for a group decision by the end of one class session or other limited time period – adds a certain amount of pressure and increases the intensity of the experience. It may be tempting to call a vote; indeed, the students sometimes press for it as a way to "settle" their differences and "compromise." However, a vote would most likely impact the quality of the deliberation, promote persuasion over deep listening, privilege the majority point of view, discourage outreach to those with minority opinion, and work against course investment. Instead, the author has utilized various polling techniques to see how close, or far, opinions range. (See Kaner et al., 2014 for more on polling techniques.) Following the polling, the author has asked each proposer to explain his/her position on the best choice grading option. It is at this point that the proposals (and counter-proposals) resemble the options so crucial in the DD on pressing social issues. And, in providing their rationales, students must discuss the merits of each grade scheme and tradeoff as it takes into account each of the other student-stakeholder preferences and needs.

While establishing personal stakes may be a challenge for the DD method, with the SD personal stakes are almost immediately palpable: Students' entire educational experience has trained them to value course grades. In addition, through the SD process, students multiply their personal stakes through their investment of more time to understand the course requirements and the ways in which they impact each of the class members. Collectively developing a scheme to set the weights of course requirements fair for all becomes a class problem whose solution is only reached with full input.

A SD survey of 15 students (with one student absent) in the author's Fall 18 First Year Seminar echoes many of the findings cited for the DD: In responding to the question "What was the best thing about our Syllabus Deliberation" students' representative comments included the following: "Everyone participated," "Coming up with reasonable weights," "That we had a choice." Asked to rank items on a five-point scale, the following statements produced the highest averages: "Everyone spoke" (4.0/5), "Everyone listened" (4.6/5), "I felt respected" (4.7/5), "I felt it was a free & open environment" (4.5/5), "I learned more about other members of the class" (4.3/5), and "I felt my voice mattered" (4.0/5).

Summing up salient points thus far, Table 1 compares the DD with the SD.

QUESTIONS AND PONDERINGS

The two related methodologies discussed in this chapter explore a very particular kind of student/teacher and student/student dialogue in which the faculty role becomes that of facilitator, and the goal changes from covering the curriculum and delivering content to nurturing deliberation on pressing topics, democratic practices, civic participation, navigation of diverse opinions, and collaborative decisions. One important takeaway for the author is the realization that although we tend to label most class exchanges as "discussions," as faculty we would greatly benefit from reflection on the discussion outcomes we want to achieve. For the author, the two-year trial and error process described in this chapter has raised many questions, some of which can be stated as: How do we signal expectations for our discussions? To what extent do our discussions help students tackle complex problems? To what extent do our discussions focus on disagreements and

Table 1. A Comparison between Deliberative Dialogue and Syllabus Deliberation.

Features	Deliberative Dialogue	Deliberative Syllabus
Discussion format	Deliberation	Deliberation
Scaffolded/ pre-dialogue activities	Yes	Yes
Civic thinking goals	Think together Understand personal stakes Listen deeply Build common ground Evaluate choices Distinguish between individual interests and group benefit Identify best option(s) Analyze trade-offs **Identify promising directions and themes** **Explore interconnections among issue and power dynamics within local, regional, national, and international factors**	Think together Understand personal stakes Listen deeply Build common ground Evaluate choices Distinguish between individual interests and group benefit Identify best option(s) Analyze trade-offs **Agree on specific document changes to be applied immediately** **Negotiate power between faculty and students**
Affective goals	Respect (give and receive) Develop the group Put student at the center Take risk to speak Take risk to disagree Navigate disagreement respectfully	Respect (give and receive) Develop the group Put student at the center Take risk to speak Take risk to disagree Navigate disagreement respectfully
Content focus	**Pressing social issue**	**Syllabus re-design**
Issue guide	**Yes, on pressing social issue**	**Syllabus and deliberation instructions substitute for guide**
Other materials	**Course readings**	**N/A**

Note: Text in bold indicates unique features.

what messages do we as faculty send about how to navigate these? Other than voting, what strategies do we utilize in helping classes make decisions and come to conclusions? To what extent do we value students finding their personal stake in issues?

The DD and SD can get nearly everyone within a class section – and sometimes all – to participate. The emphasis on the guidelines, the slow pace and the constant invitation to add to the discussion does eventually pay off in the dividend of respectful disagreement, community building, issue awareness, and enhanced caring. The DD can be a very promising tool for helping students reflect on their relationship with the wider society, for teasing out the many ways in which influence can be used and misused, for understanding how collective power can be harnessed to make impactful changes. Students begin to look a bit differently at the role of the media, schools, neighborhoods, laws, and law enforcement; the importance of voting; and ways of influencing local, state, and national government. When encouraged, they can see the impact of international trends on more local matters.

Crucial to the above, is the extent to which students learn deeply about the pressing issues. Faculty surveys from the advocacy writing and public speaking courses referenced above ranked 3 (out of a high of 4) on the question of the extent of student learning about the issues, defined as, "Awareness of nuances and interrelationships of the issues as well as awareness of additional strategies to address the problem; realization that the issues may be related to other classes they have taken and/or even larger social issues." Thus, between the promise of the methodology and the practical choices facilitators make in applying the methodology there is definitely room to increase students' understanding and analysis of social issues. Future DDs facilitated by the author will explore student participation in relationship to different kinds of issue guide assignments created by faculty as well as the clarity of faculty expectations for student preparation (including whether preparation grades are awarded).

If faculty are interested, the DD provides an opening for reflecting on social policy and advocacy. It can also be a launching pad for discussions on the kind of society in which students want to live, the legacy they wish to leave for their own children (and grandchildren), as well as issues of fairness and inclusiveness. The shift in the student–teacher roles can help anchor future discussions on the negotiation of power, learning and teaching values, student responsibility and accountability, and true exchange in the classroom and beyond.

There are three additional areas for improvement and continued exploration, issue investment, tradeoff assessment, and disagreeing: We must begin where the students are if we want them to be invested. Sometimes this means taking the discussion down a level or two so it becomes less abstract and more related to students' immediate lives. For example, in exploring the issue of animal rights, a class may discuss their relationships with pets or when they deliberate on the issue of "fast fashion," they might be prompted to venture into their closets, check clothing labels, and reflect on how their own clothing is produced. Sometimes helping students locate their personal stakes means allowing more time for personal stories and connections among group members. This can be seen as leading discussions off-track. It is a very delicate balance.

As Doherty (2008) notes, we have to keep in mind that deliberation involves two large set of skills: deliberation itself and learning how to work with potentially polarizing issues. It is easy to lose sight of these ambitious – but achievable – twin goals. Disagreeing and especially disagreeing gracefully for most is extremely difficult. Incorporating additional carefully sequenced exercises to help students feel more comfortable in expressing and accepting different viewpoints would certainly strengthen students' skills going into a deliberation either on a social issue or on the syllabus.

CONCLUSION

Both the DD on pressing social issues and the SD process are methods that support a holistic and transformative pedagogy, one that grows out of the Sustainable Education movement. The DD and DS methods emphasize collaboration, the common good, empathy, acceptance and negotiation of difference, deep listening, and community building. Through classroom use of these methods students and teacher take on new power-sharing roles, which require increased flexibility. As described in this chapter, the SD and the DD on pressing social issues can be incorporated into classes as individual methods or they can work in tandem, with the SD itself serving as a scaffolded activity for an eventual DD. Both can provide a platform to talk about democratic practices in and out of the classroom, and invite students to participate in a dynamic problem-solving process.

NOTES

1. Democratic practices have been described extensively throughout the literature. A select group of researchers includes the following: Boyte, 2015; Brower & Benenson, 2015; Johnson, 2015; Johnson et al, 2014; McDowell, 2015; Musil, 2009; National Task Force on Civic Learning and Democratic Engagement, 2012; Thomas, 2007; Westall, 2015. Full reference information cited in References.

2. The syllabus from my Restorative Justice Practices in Schools and Communities Spring 19 course contains the following paragraph: "During class four, January 30, we will be deliberating on the weights of each of the six course requirements. After this deliberation, the syllabus will be re-posted to Canvas with the weights you collaboratively decided. This deliberation allows the class to build its community and begin a process in which students and teacher navigate a more collaborative relationship. The syllabus deliberation, as with many restorative justice practices, allows the stakeholders more of a voice."

This particular deliberation actually lasted two classes, after which I re-posted the syllabus with the weights decided by the class. The revised syllabus contains the following paragraph: "During classes four and five, January 30 and February 4, we deliberated on the weights of each of the six course requirements. This re-posted syllabus reflects that deliberation. This deliberation allowed the class to build its community and begin a process in which students and teacher navigate a more collaborative relationship. The syllabus deliberation, as with many restorative justice practices, allows the stakeholders more of a voice, and explores questions of fairness and justice."

3. The author is indebted to Associate Professor, Denny Frey, who is also Dean of Curriculum Integration and Director of the RoseMary B. Fuss Teaching and Learning Center for providing this and the other calculations with respect to his World History sections.

REFERENCES

Abbott, J., McDorman, T. D., Timmerman, L., & Lamberton, J. (2016). *Public speaking & democratic participation: Speech, deliberation, and analysis in the civic realm*. New York, NY: Oxford University.

Achankeng, I, F. (2018). Deliberative dialogue as a teaching–learning experience in higher education. An application in some human services classroom practices. In E. Jean-François (Ed.), *Transactional perspectives on innovation in teaching and learning technologies*. Leiden: Brill/Sense.

Azarnoosh, M., & Kargazari, H. R. (2017). Negotiated syllabus. In A. Faravani, M. Zeraatphishe, M. Azamoosh, & H. R. Kargozari (Eds.), *Issues in syllabus design* (pp. 135–147). Rotterdam: SensePublishers.

Barker, D., & Lovitt, A. (Eds). (2018). *Higher Education Exchange*. Dayton, OH: Kettering Foundation.

Boyte, H. (Ed.). (2015). *Democracy's education: Public work, citizenship and the future of colleges and university*. Nashville, TN: Vanderbilt University Press.

Clarke, D. F. (1991, March). The negotiated syllabus: What is it and how is it likely to work? *Applied Linguistics*, *12*(1), 13–18. https://doi.org/10.1093/applin/12.1.13

Dedrick, J., Grattan, L., & Dienstfrey, H. (Eds.). (2008). *Deliberation and the work of higher education.* Dayton, OH: Kettering Foundation.

Dillard, K. (2013, August). Envisioning the role of facilitation in public deliberation. *Journal of Applied Communication Research, 41*(3), 217–235.

Doherty, J. (2008). Individual and community: Deliberative practices in a first-year seminar. In J. R. Dedrick, L. Grattan, & H. Diestfrey (Eds.), *Deliberation and the work of higher education* (pp. 59–87). Dayton, OH: Kettering Foundation.

Doherty, J., & A. Diebel with J. Hoereth, D. Hoffman, M. Kanengieter-Wildeson, W. Lawrence, D. E. Proctor, N. Ramos, & L. Strahley. (2018). Centers for public life: Learning a deliberative democratic practice. In D. Barker & A. Lovit (Eds.), *Higher Education Exchange.* Dayton, OH: Kettering Foundation.

Drury, S. (2015). Deliberation as communication instruction: A study of a climate change deliberation in an introductory biology course. *Journal on Excellence in College Teaching, 26*(4), 51–72.

Drury, S., Derek, A., Goddard, S., & Wentzel, J. (2016). Assessing deliberative pedagogy: Using a learning outcomes rubric to assess tradeoffs and tensions. *Journal of Public Deliberation, 12*(1).

Earl, A., VanWynsberghe, R., Walter, P., & Straka, T. (2018). Adaptive education applied to higher education for sustainability. International Journal of sustainability in Higher Education, 19(6), 1111–1120. https://doi.org/10.1108/IJSHE-08-2017-0131

Farland, M. (2008). The deliberative writing classroom: Public engagement and Aristotle in the core curriculum at Fordham University. In J. R. Dedrick, L. Grattan, & H. Diestfrey (Eds.), *Deliberation and the work of higher education* (pp. 89–112). Dayton, OH: Kettering Foundation.

Gastil, J. (2014). *Democracy in small groups: Participatory decision-making and communication* (2nd ed.). Scotts Valley, CA: CreateSpace Publishing.

Gastil, J., & Dillard, J. (1999, July). The aims, methods, and effects of deliberative civic education through the national issues forum. *Communication Education, 48*(3), 179–192.

Grattan, L., Dedrick, J., & Dienstfrey, H. (Eds.). (2008). *Deliberation & the work of higher education.* Dayton, OH: Kettering Foundation.

Harrell, K., & Lam, S. (2019). Empowering students through collective curriculum development in the college classroom. In S. Wurdinger, C. K. McDermott, K. Harell, & S. Hilton (Eds.), *Empowering our students for the future* (pp. 89–101). Lanham, MD: Rowman & Littlefield.

Harriger, K., McMillan, J., Buchanan, C., & Gustler, S. (2015). The long-term impact of learning to deliberate. *Diversity and Democracy – American Association of Colleges and Universities, 18*(4). Available at https://www.aacu.org/diversitydemocracy/2015/fall/harriger.

Involve. (2019). Retrieved from https://www.involve.org.uk

Kaner, S., Lind, J., Toldi, C., Fisk, S., & Berger, D. (2014). *Facilitators' guide to participatory decision-making.* San Francisco, CA: Jossey-Bass.

Kaplan, D. M., & Renard, M. K. (2015, January 9). Negotiating your syllabus: Building a collaborative contract. *Journal of Management Education. 39*(3). https://doi.org/10.177/1052562914564788

Knobloch, K., & Gastil, J. (2015). Civic (re)socialization: The educative effects of deliberative participation. Politics, 35(2), 183–200.

Lawrence, W., & Theis, J. (2014). Reimagining civic education in colleges and universities: The influence of deliberation on students' perceptions of political participation. *E-Journal of Public Affairs, 5*(2), 153–175.

London, S. (2019). Thinking together: The power of deliberative dialogue. Retrieved from http://scott.london/reports/dialogue.html. Accessed on March 19, 2019.

Mathews, D. (2016). *Naming and framing difficult issues to make sound decisions.* A Cousins Research Group Report on Democratic Practices. Dayton, OH: Kettering Foundation.

McKeown, R. (2002, July). Education for sustainable development toolkit. Retrieved from hppt://www.esdtoolkit.org

National Issues Forums. (2006). A handbook on how to convene and moderate deliberative public forums on divisive issues using the National Issues Forums Model. Retrieved from www.nifi.org/en/catalogue/product/handbook

National Issues Forums. (2016, June 30). Learning together: Moderating forums. Retrieved from https://www.org/en/catalogue/product/video-learning-together-moderating-deliberative-forums

National Task Force on Civic Learning and Democratic Engagement. (2012). A crucible moment: College learning and democracy's future. Washington, DC: AAC&U.

Ryfe, D. (2006). Narrative and deliberation in small group forums. Journal of Applied Communication Research, 34(1), 72–93.

Sterling, S. (2008). Sustainable education: Towards a deep learning response to unsustainability. *Policy & Practice: A Development Education Review, 6*, Spring, 63–68.

UNESCO. (n.d.). Retrieved from https://en.uesco.org/theses/education-sustainable-development/what-is-sed

Warburton, K. (2003). Deep learning and education for sustainability. *International Journal of Sustainability in Higher Education. 4*(1). https://doi.org/10.1108146763104555332

Westall, A. (2015). The relationship between democracy and sustainable development. Foundation for Democracy and Sustainable Development. Retrieved from https://www.fdsd.org/site/wp-content/uploads/2-15/06/the-relationship-between-democracy-and-sustainable-development.pdf

APPENDIX A

Deliberative Dialogue Description: FAQs
Sharyn Lowenstein, Ed.D.

What is a Deliberative Dialogue (DD)?

A DD is a structured discussion on a pressing social topic in which diverse opinions are sought and voiced. The goal is NOT to argue or debate per se, but, rather, through reasoning together, the group comes to an increased understanding about how to think about and act upon an issue.

What are some benefits?

- Civic skills: Facilitates civic engagement behaviors, including voicing one's opinion, listening carefully, disagreeing respectfully, perspective-taking, finding common ground and considering the common good. Reinforces the College's social responsibility mission.
- Connected learning: Can elevate a class discussion by asking students to consider the ramifications of a theory, practice, event. An effective DD encourages students to ask deeper questions about life purpose and the role of the civic participant in society.
- Public speaking: Promotes development of argument, evaluation and presentation of evidence, articulation of connections between one's own and another's point of view, question asking.
- Individual and Society KP: Emphasizes the relationship among individuals, families, communities, law enforcement, schools, government and policy.

How do classes prepare?

- An issue booklet is adapted or created based on the issue selected by the faculty member in coordination with the dialogue moderator (Sharyn Lowenstein).
- The issue booklet (averaging 6 – 10 pages) frames the issue, discusses its prevalence and impact, describes three or four options for addressing the problem, and identifies the pros and cons of each option.
- The faculty and moderator meet to develop (brief) pre-dialogue activities.

What happens during a DD?

While there are many variations, a 75-minute session can be sequenced as follows:

- First five minutes: re-introducing DD format and guidelines
- 10 minutes for expression of personal stakes
- 10 – 15 minutes discussion on each of the 3 or 4 options, taken sequentially
- Remainder for post-reflection discussion and individual surveys

What is the course faculty role?

- The course faculty meets with the moderator to select the issue, co-plan the sequence of activities leading up to the DD, and co-evaluate the entire process sometime after the DD.
- The faculty may simply observe the class, take notes, participate in the DD as one of the discussants, or co-moderate. Faculty may also help write the issue guide.

APPENDIX B

ISSUE GUIDE FOR PHIL 302

Framing question for Issue Guide: How should we best prepare our society to discuss the ethical issue of abortion with compassion and respect for all sides?

This issue guide grows out of our exploration of how to think ethically, and specifically how to think about the pressing issue of abortion. Authors we've read, such as Judith Jarvis Thomson (A Defense of Abortion), Mary Anne Warren (On the Moral and Legal Status of Abortion), Don Marquis (Why Abortion is Immoral) and Rosalind Hursthouse (Virtue Theory and Abortion) and many others raise important questions for us to think about. They also make the case that science alone cannot help us understand all the critical aspects of abortion, nor devise the best laws, regulations, policies, and institutions to protect whatever decisions our country makes surrounding abortion.

In untangling the abortion debates, the authors ask themselves (and, ultimately, the reader – us!) these kinds of questions:

- What is goodness?
- How do we make good decisions?
- What is justice?
- What does it mean to have rights? Are these rights contingent upon how easy or hard it is to grant them?
- Should we all strive to be the "good Samaritan?" The Minimally Decent Samaraitan? Something else?
- What does it mean to be 'human?' How do you determine the humanity of a being?'

These are not easy questions. They require immense soul searching, reading, deep thinking, and listening to each other. As society tries to answer these questions, we need well-honed communication skills, the ability and WILL to disagree respectfully without attacking each other. We need people to dare to move out of their comfort zones. We need a lifetime of practice in the art of real conversation and the flexibility to hold many even contradictory ideas in our heads at one time.

As we've all experienced, right now and during many times in the past, our country has been extremely divided. This has only worsened in the last several years. If we have discussions, these are often very superficial. In a democratic society we depend on open, frank discussions that allow us to hear each other and figure out how to address complex problems from which we cannot run away. Thus, our class, as part of our work as civic participants and members of US society will hold a respectful deliberative dialogue on March 4. This dialogue will allow us to practice, as the syllabus states, "how to think more clearly about important decisions and issues."

Society will hold a respectful deliberative dialogue on March 4. This dialogue will allow us to practice, as the syllabus states, "how to think more clearly about important decisions and issues."

The Deliberative Dialogue we will hold is a structured discussion in which all class members contribute ideas. The Deliberation is not about debate or persuasion; it's not about talking over each other. Rather, in this kind of discussion we will be thinking through the various, complicated aspects of making society more socially responsible. Sharyn Lowenstein will facilitate the discussion, taking us from one aspect to another, encouraging all to speak, encouraging differences of opinion. We ask that you join us in making the class open, safe, and welcoming.

The Deliberative Dialogue is a serious, adult discussion. These dialogues happen in many community settings, such as town hall meetings and juries. We invite you into this Dialogue not only as way to better understand what it means to be human but to become more practiced in the art of civic engagement. When you graduate Lasell, you will take with you many professional skills and much professional knowledge. You certainly will take with you the Core Intellectual Skills and Knowledge Perspectives and hopefully apply them to your work, your family life, and your community. It is our hope that you find the courage to talk about sensitive, complex topics as you take your part in society.

As you know, with abortion, there are many people on all sides of this complex problem. Even the 'experts' can't seem to agree on how best to deal with this complex problem. And that is exactly the reason that we are asking you to come prepared, to reflect on all your other class discussions and readings, to learn together, to search together, and to come to some conclusions. The idea of this dialogue is to entertain as many opinions as you can, to ask questions, and to listen with an open mind. At the end of the Dialogue we will try to come to some consensus. We are not asking you for your opinion on abortion specifically, but rather, to look at and 'weigh in' on the best options for helping our society prepare to discuss the ethical issue of abortion. This issue guide presents three areas that could make a difference, and in our Deliberative Dialogue we will look at which aspects as the most likely to contribute to helping people develop the skills, attitudes, and culture to hold discussion on how we decide about what is right regarding abortion.

Now some background:

It is important to know that different groups and organizations collect and report this data differently. According to "An Honest Analysis" (April 15, 2017) from the National Economics Editorial Us Abortion Statistics, which draws much of its data from the Centers for Disease Control, from 1973 to 2014 there have been approximately 44 million abortions in the US. Abort73.com (a much more conservative organization) reports that in 2014, 19% of all US pregnancies were terminated through abortions. Numbers appear to be dropping, according to National Economics Editorial. There have been several reasons proposed for this decline.

Including increased use of birth control for both men and women, anti-abortion laws, and changing culture. One factor that does NOT seem to be responsible for the decline is the frequency of sexual contact: National Economics Editorial comments that premarital sex rates have been "remarkably consistent" since the 1950's.

Options to Prepare Society to Discuss the Ethical Issue of Abortion

Option #1: What Schools Can Do

This option focuses on the kind of interventions that schools can undertake to promote critical thinking, listening, research, and ethical discussions.

Possible Actions	Tradeoffs
Develop/strengthen critical thinking and communication curriculum so that students have practical experience in reading, thinking, listening.	This is a long-term strategy and involves evaluating the current instruction we now have and develop ways to strengthen it.
Teach ethical ways of thinking beginning with elementary school and continuing through college.	Also a long-term strategy that may run into parental opposition, particularly in the lower levels.
Create a school culture in which students expect that all marginalized as well as majority opinions are heard.	Teachers need to be trained to participate fully, as would all other school personnel.
Create Ethics prizes, honor societies, clubs in college	

Option #2: Focus on Media

This option focuses on the ways that media (music, newspapers, websites, TV, movies, even art) promotes multiple points of view and discussion that is geared toward helping society resolve very deeply held and diverse ideas regarding how to handle abortion.

Possible Actions	Tradeoffs and Concerns
Find ways to increase newspaper funding so that stories are covered to promote conversation rather than disgust, fear, and knee jerk reactions.	Long-term strategies.
Develop watch dog organizations for all media that call out sensationalistic strategies.	We would need mechanism to grow these organizations for this purpose.

Option #3: Community and National Campaigns

This option focuses on tactics that include post-school ethics training

Possible Actions	Tradeoffs and Concerns
Create civic panels	Expense of facilitators, tracking of discussions, reporting back results
Require community service option after 18 years old in which young adults participate in training and ethnics discussions, including on issue of abortion. These young adults could then be placed in communities to work with elementary school –aged children in the schools and other youth organizations	Long-term strategy Expense

APPENDIX C

Post-Deliberative Dialogue Feedback Prompts for Written Response

1. As a group, what options do you favor?
2. Why do you favor these options?
3. What did you learn about yourself through the Deliberative Dialogue?
4. On a scale of 1 – 10, with 10 being 'fully heard and respected' how much do you think you were heard and respected during this Deliberative Dialogue? ________ Explain.
5. Before we started this Deliberative Dialogue, how much did you care about the issue of animal testing? (10 is the highest rating.) _______ Explain your rating.
6. How much do you now care about this issue? ________ Explain your rating.
7. How satisfying was this Deliberative Dialogue process? _________ Explain.
8. How would you describe Deliberative Dialogues to somebody else?
9. What questions/comments do you have about Deliberative Dialogues?

APPENDIX D

Post-syllabus Deliberation Prompts

On deliberative process:

- How satisfying was the process of the deliberation?
- How democratic was the deliberation?
- To what extent were minority opinions considered?
- To what extent did those with majority opinions try to reach out and understand/listen to those with minority opinions?
- Who had power in this deliberation? How did power flow during the activity?
- What did you learn about your own power and influence?

On preparation and learning:

- Looking back, how prepared were you for the syllabus deliberation?
- What did you learn about yourself? The other students?
- What did you learn about group decision-making?

On course investment and expectations:

- Before this deliberation, how invested were you regarding the percentage weights? (How much did you care about this class?)
- After this deliberation, how invested are you regarding the percentage weights? (How much do you care about this class?)
- To what extent has the syllabus deliberation changed your expectations for this course?
- To what extent has the deliberation changed the way you think about your role in this class? The role of the professor? The role of other students?

CHAPTER 8

INTEGRATING SUSTAINABLE DEVELOPMENT INTO THE WHOLE INSTITUTION: CAN THE SDGs[1] BRIDGE THE GAP[2]?

Stefanie Mallow and Hilligje van't Land

ABSTRACT

The Whole Institution Approach is part of UNESCO's Education for Sustainable Development program. This chapter explores what a "Whole Institution Approach" is and what it translates to in different higher education institutions around the world. This chapter provides background information to understand the complexity of sustainable development in higher education and how universities engage with the United Nations Agenda 2030. This chapter is based on an autumn 2018 International Association of Universities qualitative study, which looked at how the sustainable development goals (SDGs) are changing the dynamics of universities. To illustrate the findings, this chapter presents five case studies highlighting different approaches to integrating sustainable development into the whole institution. This chapter shows that there is no one-size-fits-all approach; each university engages with sustainable development and the SDGs in its own way. Finally, this chapter explains what the 2030 Agenda can mean for higher education institutions and more specifically Whole Institution Approaches.

Keywords: Sustainable development goals; higher education; Italy; Ghana; Canada; Costa Rica; Thailand; education for sustainable development; Agenda 2030

Teaching and Learning Strategies for Sustainable Development:
Innovations in Higher Education Teaching and Learning, Volume 19, 107–122

ISSN: 2055-3641/doi:10.1108/S2055-364120200000019011

INTRODUCTION

Sustainable development, commonly defined as "development that meets the needs of the present without compromising the ability of future generations to meet their own needs" (Brundtland Report, 1987), is growing in attention. Ever since in 2015 the United Nations General Assembly unanimously adopting *Transforming our world: Agenda 2030 for sustainable development*, commonly known as Agenda 2030, governments, civil society, higher education, and businesses are increasingly incorporating sustainable development into their strategic plans. This is visible in numerous statements and commitments that have been published since 2015 (e.g., higher education: Big Tent Consortium, 2018; businesses: UN Global Compact, 2016; governments: Ministry of Finance Ghana, 2018). The main part of Agenda 2030 are 17 Sustainable Development Goals (SDGs), divided into 169 targets and 244 indicators (United Nations, 2015).

Before the adoption of Agenda 2030, the higher education community continuously called for an inclusion of higher education in the post-2015 agenda as it was clear to many that without higher education and research, the 17 SDGs will never be reached (Hall, 2014). Higher education was eventually included in SDG 4.3, which calls to "ensure equal access for all women and men to affordable quality technical, vocational and tertiary education, including universities" (United Nations, 2015, p. 17). This bears a great potential for higher education institutions as well as for governments and civil societies working on the achievement of the SDGs.

The early 1990s saw heads of higher education institutions formally committing to sustainable development by signing joint statements and declarations (Lozano, Lukman, Lozano, Huisingh, & Lambrechts, 2013). However, a gap remained between this initial commitment and the actual actions of higher education institutions. Agenda 2030 could fill this gap. The Big Tent Consortium (2018), for example, called upon the higher education community to support the implementation of the SDGs that goes beyond the signing of statements.

Since the adoption of Agenda 2030 the International Association of Universities (IAU), witnessed a growing interest in sustainable development at higher education institutions globally. IAU is a global network of universities, founded in 1950 by UNESCO. Currently, IAU counts over 600 institutional members from more than 130 countries. Sustainable development has been part of the Association's strategic plan as early as 1993, and it is one of the pioneering organizations promoting sustainability at higher education institutions. Today, more and more universities around the world are approaching the Association with questions such as: what can we do with Agenda 2030? How can we address the SDGs? How can we make our university more sustainable? Given the broad scope of IAU Member Institutions, the answers to those questions vary. One suggestion for IAU's Members is to develop a so-called *Whole Institution Approach on Sustainable Development* as suggested by UNESCO.

Multiple UNESCO initiatives have advocated for Whole Institution Approaches in the past, the current name is *Global Action Programme on Education for Sustainable Development* (GAP ESD) (UNESCO, 2019b). At the end of 2019, a new program will be launched. As outlined in the draft framework of the 10-year plan entitled *Education for Sustainable Development: Towards achieving the SDGs (ESD for 2030)*, the new program will connect UNESCO's work on education for sustainable development (ESD) with Agenda 2030. As the authors of the draft framework put it: "The marriage of ESD and the SDGs is not only a necessity but a 'win–win' for both fields" (UNESCO, 2019a, p. 7).

In order to find out what Whole Institution Approaches at IAU Member universities look like and to inform the second iteration of the *IAU Global Survey on Higher Education and Research for Sustainable Development*, IAU conducted interviews with different actors at selected Member Institutions between September and October 2018. Five universities from different continents were selected, combined with additional research done on site and via desk research, to be presented in this chapter. This chapter will examine whether this "win–win" situation can also be applied to Whole Institution Approaches at universities around the world and fill the gaps of sustainability initiatives at many higher education institutions.

THE WHOLE INSTITUTION APPROACH FOR SUSTAINABLE DEVELOPMENT

The main difference between the SDGs and the previous development agenda is, that they are considered universal goals, aimed not only at developing countries but rather the whole world (Sachs, 2015). While the universal and broad nature of the SDGs has been criticized (The Economist, 2015), special advisor to the United Nations Jeffrey Sachs highlights that it might be exactly this what leads to the success of Agenda 2030: everyone can identify with the SDGs and interpret it differently (Sachs, 2015).

Different understandings about sustainable development are also observed among higher education institutions, which is important to understand Whole Institution Approaches. IAU conducted a second version of the Global Survey on Higher Education and Research for Sustainable Development (HESD) in June 2019. The survey received 536 responses, with universities from over 90 countries replying (Fig. 1).

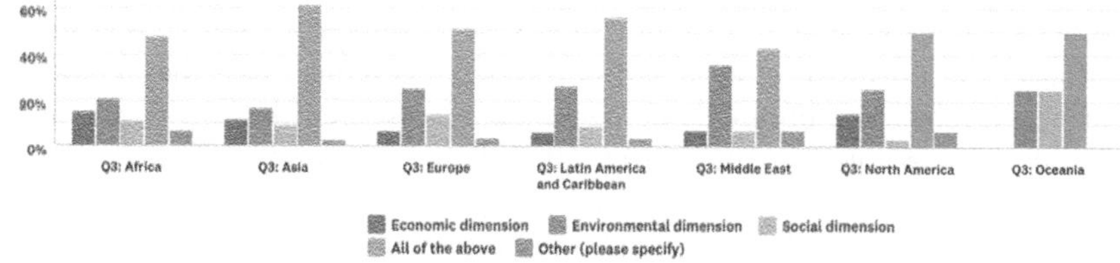

Fig. 1. Understandings of Sustainable Development at Higher Education Institutions (HEIs) (IAU 2nd Global Survey on HESD, Mallow & van't Land, 2020)

In many cases, sustainable development is still seen as the same as environmental protection. While this was the case at the beginning of the movement in the 1970s, sustainable development as defined in Agenda 2030 is a holistic concept, that requires systemic thinking and focuses on societal, economic, and cultural issues (United Nations, 2015). Although the environment is still predominating, 52% of the IAU Global Survey on HESD respondents indicated that sustainable development includes all dimensions. The case studies will show that developing a balanced Whole Institution Approach is nevertheless challenging.

It is also important to note that different cultural backgrounds and institutional settings require different strategies and for Whole Institution Approaches. Some universities are decentralized, with different faculties almost functioning as autonomous institutions. Others are very hierarchical, in which everything must be vetted through the head of the institution. Then there are public universities and private ones, big ones and small, old and young. Each university attracts its own students and brings in its own history and cultural values, and as different universities are, as different can be Whole Institution Approaches.

The understanding about Whole Institution Approaches for sustainable development advanced over the years along with the understanding of ESD and what sustainable development is (Wu & Shen, 2016). A rapid growth and fundamental shift happened when educating *about* sustainable development moved toward educating *for* sustainable development, which also required an increased focus on whole institutions (Hargreaves, 2008). Especially during the United Nations Decade on ESD (2005–2014), the Whole Institution Approach for sustainable development received a major push and began to spread throughout the world (Buckler & Creech, 2014).

Initially, it was mostly primary and secondary schools that started Whole School Approaches supported by UNESCO (Henderson & Tilbury, 2004). Higher education institutions soon followed, advocating for a name shift toward Whole Institution Approach, visible in a number of statements (e.g., HESI, 2012; IAU, 2014). However, it seems like the majority of work is still done in schools; a search of Google Scholar in March 2019 found 735 articles on Whole Institution Approach compared to 18,700 for Whole School Approach. This also explains why there is a large range of existing guidelines and standards for schools, including certifications like recognition as Eco-Schools (Foundation for Environmental Education, 2014) and a limited amount for universities (e.g., Sustainable Development Solutions Network (SDSN) Australia/Pacific, 2017).

Demand for guidelines is growing: the first *IAU Global Survey on HESD* conducted in 2016 confirmed that there is a rising interest in Whole Institution Approaches at universities: 69% of the respondents replied that they knew the concept. Nevertheless, only 45% of respondents answered that their institution had adopted a Whole Institution Approach. It can be assumed that the Whole Institution Approach was not a formal commitment at all institutions, since only 34% had a strategic plan for sustainable development, while 38% were developing a strategic plan for sustainable development (IAU, 2017).

Whole Institution Approaches for Sustainable Development have a great potential. In 2017, the SDSN Australia/Pacific published a guide called *Getting*

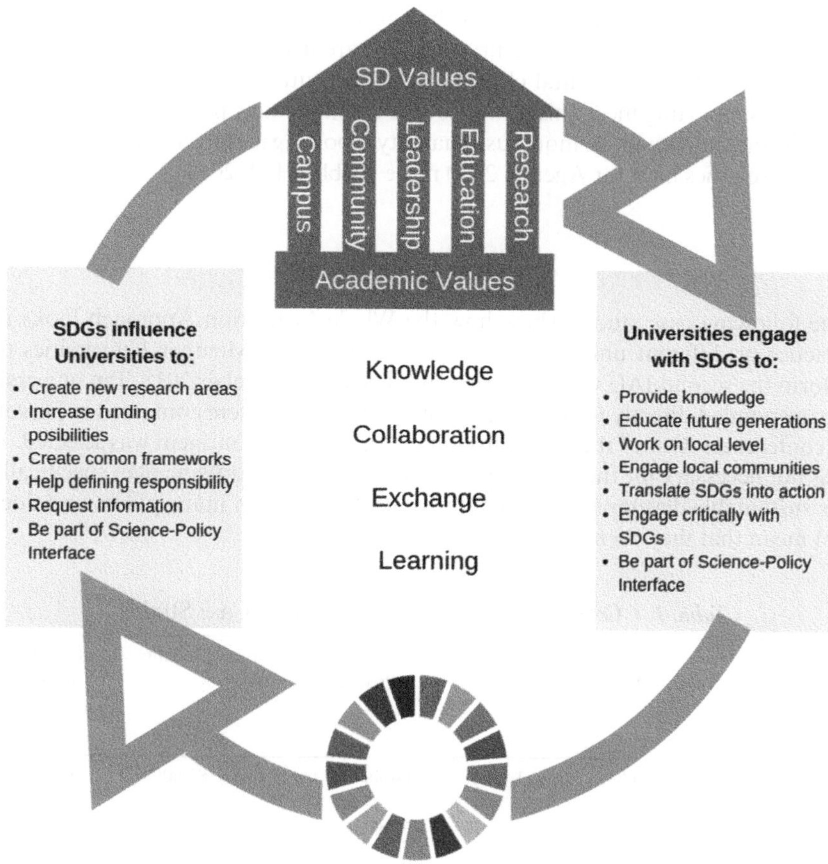

Fig. 2. Relationship of Universities and the SDGs. *Source*: Adapted from SDSN Australia/Pacific (2017).

Started with the SDGs in Universities. The authors speak about a "whole-of-university approach" toward the SDGs and provide the first guide to universities about how to integrate the SDGs (SDSN Australia/Pacific, 2017) (Fig. 2).

As shown in the graphic above, the relationship between higher education institutions and SDGs can be mutually beneficial. Thanks to Agenda 2030, there is an increased interest in sustainable development focused research, which has opened-up new funding streams such as the *SDG Fund.* The SDGs further provide universities worldwide with a new framework and help to define their social responsibilities, for example, in terms of offering values-based education and internationalization (Egron-Polak, 2018). In support to the SDGs, universities provide the necessary knowledge and research to inform policy-makers and they educate future generations and engage with local communities (SDSN Australia/Pacific, 2017). That way, they provide guidelines and support for the United Nations.

As the following case studies will show, using the 2030 Agenda as a baseline to map a university is one of the first steps toward a Whole Institution Approach that can lead to fundamental change of the institutions. Nevertheless, strategic plans and reporting mechanisms are not the norm in many parts of the world yet. Ideally, the future will see more sustainability reporting at universities to make the role universities have for Agenda 2030 more visible (Hall, 2014).

CASE STUDIES

The following case studies show how the Whole Institution Approach looks in practice at different universities. IAU issued a call for Member Universities to inform the second IAU Global Survey in HESD in September 2018. Ten universities responded directly to the call and an additional five were contacted in person at conferences. Out of those 15 universities, one for each continent was selected. It was not necessary for the included universities to have a strategic plan specifically for sustainable development, since this is not the norm in many places and does not mean that they do not have a de facto plan (Table 1).

Table 1. Overview Universities Selected for Case Studies.

Name	Founding Date	Location	Public/ Private	Campuses	Students	Strategic Plan for Sustainable Development (SD)
University of Bologna	1088	Italy, Europe	Public	5	85,000	Yes
University of Ghana	1948	Ghana, Africa	Public	3	38,000	No
University of Regina (UofR)	1974	Canada, North America	Public	2	15,568	Yes
Siam University	1965	Thailand, Asia	Private	1	15,000	No
University of Costa Rica (UCR)	1949	Costa Rica, Latin America	Public	7	45,000	No

Source: UofR (2015), University of Ghana (2014), UCR (2013), Siam University (n.d.), and University of Bologna (2016a).

The case studies are based on a mix of methods, with a special focus on the strategic plan of each university, where available. One semi-structured interview was conducted for each institution. In a few cases, questions were answered in writing, due to poor internet connection. Additionally, unstructured interviews during conferences and other meetings were conducted when we met representatives from the described universities. This was the case during the IAU International Conference 2018 in Kuala Lumpur, the IAU Workshop on HESD held in January 2019 at UNESCO in Paris, and the High Level Political Forum on Sustainable Development 2019 at the United Nations in New York.

Furthermore, four out of the five universities were visited in person between November 2017 and May 2019. During those site visits, additional documentation was acquired, and research conducted. Additional documentation was collected via desk research. Language was only an issue in the case of Siam University, because most official documents are in Thai. The other universities either produced reports in English or Spanish.

It would go beyond the scope of this chapter to explain all activities of the universities in detail. All of the five universities have initiatives that focus on including sustainable development in their teaching, conduct research related to sustainable development, aim to support the local community, and strive to make their campuses "greener." Therefore, the focus in this short analysis is the planning, conceptualization, and reasoning behind the Whole Institution Approaches, how the SDGs are involved and how this is related to the local (university) culture.

University of Bologna

The University of Bologna has already had a strong commitment to being a socially responsible and "green university" since 2009 (Paletta & Bonoli, 2019). Following the adoption of Agenda 2030, the University of Bologna founded AlmaGoals, a steering group within the University that focuses specifically on the SDGs. While the previous initiatives were beneficial to the development of the University, it was not until the integration of Agenda 2030 into the strategic plan by the leadership and the subsequent reporting on the SDGs that the University reinterpreted its teaching, research, community engagement, and campus operations (Paletta & Bonoli, 2019). The adoption of a strategic plan for the SDGs in 2016 makes the University of Bologna one of the first, if not the first, university to align with Agenda 2030, which it why it was chosen for this chapter.

The basis for AlmaGoals was an addition to the University's strategic plan 2016–2018. The university decided to focus on Agenda 2030 "[i]n order to implement a planning process for tackling the challenges posed by contemporary reality, particularly in relation to sustainable development," declaring sustainability as a development strategy (University of Bologna, 2016a, p. 11).

One of the first steps to put the idea of sustainability as a development strategy into action was designing a reporting tool and to map what the University of Bologna was already doing for the SDGs. Two comprehensive reports have been published since, highlighting how and where the University contributes to the SDGs (University of Bologna, 2016b, 2017) (Fig. 3).

The mapping allowed the University to see where its strengths are and monitor progress. In the 2017 report, 152 research projects were linked to the SDGs, 42 more than in 2016. Only two goals are not covered through research: SDG 1: No Poverty; and SDG 4: Quality Education. However, the University has 116 course units teaching about no poverty and a total 4,405 course units are addressing at least one of the goals (University of Bologna, 2017).

According to representatives from the University of Bologna who attended the IAU Workshop, the process of creating those reports was very beneficial for the whole university (personal communication, 2019, January 29). They highlighted, that it was sometimes a challenge to develop their own assessment methods, but it allowed to rethink activities and to promote Agenda 2030. It took the working group more than six months to determine benchmarks, collect the data and write the report (University of Bologna, 2016b).

Fig. 3. Research Projects Related to the SDGs at the University of Bologna (University of Bologna, 2017, p. 9).

Now it is important to translate knowledge to action and to create better ways for different actors in the University can engage with each other (personal communication, 2019, January 29). The University of Bologna has already taken action upon those challenges, by creating structures that aim for more engagement and essential change in the University (Paletta & Bonoli, 2019).

University of Ghana

Although the University of Ghana is not using "SDG-language" and is not using the SDGs' colorful marketing tools, it has adopted a de facto strategy that does directly contribute to the sustainable development of Ghana. The University was chosen as example for this chapter because of the way it engages with its country's commitment to Agenda 2030 and the way it is part of the policy-making processes of Ghana that involve the whole institution.

Ghana has a strong commitment to Agenda 2030, being one of the first countries to include the SDGs in its financial planning, contributing to the *Ghana Beyond Aid* vision of the current president Nana Akufo-Addo (Ministry of Finance Ghana, 2018). In Ghana, similar to other developing countries, the middle class is continuously growing, thus exacerbating issues with overcrowding, internet access, and maintaining an adequate qualified teacher-to-student ratio (University of Ghana, 2014). Therefore, the university is adapting to new situations accordingly and aims to be a "World Class research-intensive University" by 2024 while also giving back to the country (University of Ghana, 2014, p. 7).

Although the SDGs and Agenda 2030 are not particularly mentioned in the University's strategic plan, it has committed itself to actively supporting the government's plans for Agenda 2030 and the development of the country (P.E., personal communication, 2019, January 28). One example of this work is the work on the first SDG, poverty reduction. During an interview, a Member of the leadership team of the University of Ghana highlighted the University's commitment to reducing poverty in the country through the four main research areas that are a reoccurring theme at the University (G.N., personal communication, 2018, September 20):

- Malaria Research.
- Trans-disciplinary Research into Climate Change Adaptation.
- Enhancing Food Production and Processing.
- Development Policy and Poverty Monitoring and Evaluation.

The four examples show how poverty reduction is closely linked to health (SDG 3); climate change (SDG 13); ending hunger (SDG 2); peace, justice and strong institutions (SDG 16), and partnerships (SDG 17). According to the interviewee, the importance in addressing the SDGs as a whole institution is in focusing on areas of work most pressing to the country, hence translating the local issues to the global agenda and not vice versa. The University addresses those goals through interdisciplinary approaches, making them the core of its work (G.N., personal communication, 2018, September 20).

During the same interview, he also stressed the need to work further on gender equality (SDG 5), climate change adaption (SDG 13), and sanitation (SDG 6) in order to improve livelihoods in Ghana. Besides all the good work the University of Ghana is doing, he pointed out that there are major challenges on how to engage the University more effectively. The biggest challenge he named was inefficient or no communication about topics, especially about how to find funding. He also highlighted the need for national and global partnerships, because in his opinion it is impossible to reach the SDGs alone as one country or as one institution (G.N., personal communication, 2018, September 20). The development of the University is therefore also closely linked to the development of Ghana and what partnerships both can achieve.

University of Regina

The UofR in the Saskatchewan province in Canada had already publishes its strategic plan for sustainable development in 2015, the same year that Agenda 2030 was adopted. The UofR was included in this chapter, due to its unique engagement with the indigenous culture around it and how it encourages a change of mind-set. In the sustainable development plan the President and Vice-Chancellor writes:

> The University of Regina's Strategic Plan for Sustainability commits our campus community to playing a major role in "sustaining human wellbeing and the natural environment." This concept is beautifully articulated by a proverb attributed to First Peoples of centuries past: "We do not inherit the earth from our ancestors; we borrow it from our children" (UofR, 2015).

This concept is very similar to the understanding of sustainable development used in Agenda 2030. While the main point of the strategic plan of the UofR points toward environmental sustainability, the social, cultural, and economic parts are also connected. The plan of the University looks at five key concepts: leadership, waste, energy, transportation, and communication and engagement.

The sustainability commitment of the university is a good example of not only educating about sustainable development but rather for it. Unlike other plans, this one aims to change the mind-set of people and change the structure of how things are done at the university. One special part of the strategy is that it does not give specific tasks, but rather encourages everyone to do their best (University of Regina, 2015).

This is a new approach, which was developed through a sustainability tasks group that involved different stakeholders of the university and is also today constantly reviewing the process the University makes. One of the involved professors stated in an interview with IAU, that it was a change of mind-set that they wanted to encourage, and that other universities should also consider this, ideally through including the social sciences and humanities:

> You don't learn in most parts of the university how to change the human mindset; the humanities faculty is so central to all of this, it is the structure in the university that humanizes. However this faculty is often "forgotten" when it comes to [sustainable development]. Even though with [sustainable development] we're talking about the development of human capital. (Personal communication, 2019, September 18)

The way the University includes different stakeholders from diverse backgrounds is the strongest aspect of this Whole Institution Approach and unique from others. During a site-visit to the University in May 2019, it became apparent that unlike at the other institutions presented in this chapter, the main force behind sustainable development was not the leadership, but rather engaged students and professors. While this could be the reason for the different approach, it also includes more challenges according to the people met on-site, because it is more difficult to get funding and new ideas approved. However, some people hope that this will change for the next plan in 2020, because it should be easier to convince the leadership level thanks to Agenda 2030 (personal communication, 2019, May 6).

Siam University

In Thailand, the "Sufficiency Economy Philosophy," a lifestyle model introduced by the late King Bhumibol Adulyadej, shows a way of development that supports everybody. The philosophy has been compared to the SDGs in the recent publication *Sufficiency Economy Philosophy: Thailand's Path towards Sustainable Development Goals* (Ministry of Foreign Affairs of Thailand, 2017).

Siam University, a private university, situated in Thailand's capital Bangkok, combines the Sufficient Economy Philosophy with the SDGs in order for the university as a whole to embrace sustainability and through that develop the whole district into a sustainable one. This way of incorporating ideas into each other is the reason why Siam University was chosen for this chapter (Fig. 4).

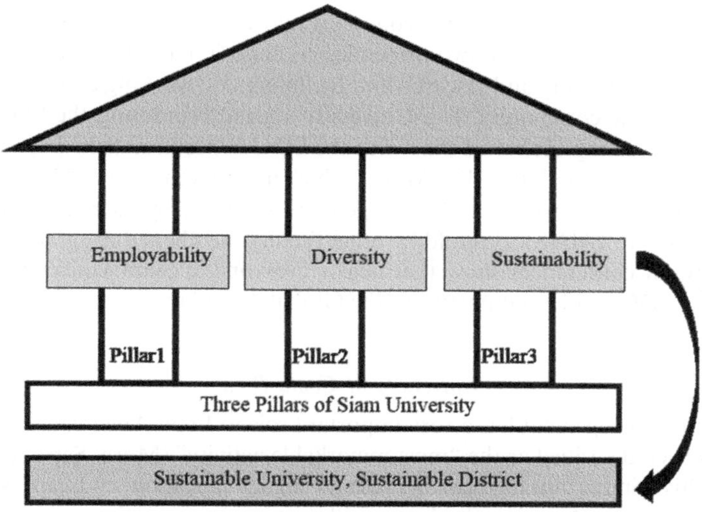

Fig. 4. The Three Pillars of Siam University.
Source: Adapted from Siam University (n.d.).

As can be seen in the above illustration, sustainability is one of the three pillars upon which the university rests and it is embedded in the mission and vision of the university. The university adopted a Whole Institution Approach, aiming to change the mind-set of the "3S" – Students, Staff, and Surrounding Communities. The university is used as living lab to teach all stakeholders in the university on how to live sustainable lifestyles (Siam University, n.d.).

During a 2018 interview the University President, Prof. Pornchai Mongkhonvanit, said that the university is continuously engaging with sustainable development. Initially, it was only one concept of many, until it became one of the core pillars of the university. In the future, the University wants to develop sustainable development further. This would mean that all stakeholders of the university know about sustainable development and know how to act on it. It will also be in the curriculum of all degrees (P.M., personal communication, 2018, October 8). The President further explained how the Whole Institution Approach is not only for students but also for everyone: the community around it can access the campus and use it as a "healthy space" and students are involved in community projects, such as cleaning the neighborhood and creating gardens. He also stressed, that the concept of sustainable development is flexible at the institution; lecturers and professors can choose how to approach it, which makes it easier for people to incorporate sustainability principles into the University (P.M., personal communication, 2018, October 8).

The President mentioned a project where Thai universities meet every two months to exchange on how they contribute to addressing the SDGs. Siam University is one of the leading universities in this project. The project is still rather new, and the process is not as fast as hoped. However, the President was able to engage other rectors in the quest to make universities more sustainable (P.M., personal communication, 2018, October 8).

To the President, Sufficiency Economy Philosophy and the SDGs are at the heart of his University. The two principles go hand in hand together, improving the quality of teaching and research and the living and working conditions of all members of the community. The University started promoting the SDGs on a large scale, creating their own pins with the SDG Wheel and their logo and distributing tote bags with the SDG Wheel, which includes the words "Think Freely, Work Wisely." The two materials were generously shared by the President during various visits to IAU. Stories told by other faculty members during unstructured interviews at conferences show that nearly everyone at Siam University knows about the SDGs and is supportive to the Global Agenda.

University of Costa Rica

Community engagement has a very important role in Latin American universities and has been described as the "most remarkable activity" (Mora, Serra, & Vieira, 2018). This is important to know, because the higher education landscape is rapidly changing in Latin America. Student enrollment rates are continuously increasing on the continent and equity increased over the last few years (Ferreyra, Avitabile, Álvarez, Paz, & Urzúa, 2017). At the same time, trust in higher education is declining and university autonomy is under threat, making it more important than ever to have a solid foundation in academic values in the region (Ferreyra et al., 2017). The UCR has been chosen as a representative of the region for this chapter, due to the way that it addresses those challenges through the SDGs.

The UCR is the oldest, biggest, and most prestigious public university in the small Central American state, making it a role model to other universities in Costa Rica. The Rectorate of the University published a book about its commitment to the 2030 Agenda in 2019, highlighting the need for all sectors to work together to achieve the SDGs (Jensen & Angulo, 2019). In the prologue, the rector Prof. Henning Jensen confirms the important role the UCR has within society and that the University is committed to contribute to transformational social change in the country. The University will continue to harmonize its work with the SDGs, finding solutions to global challenges with other actors (Jensen & Angulo, 2019).

To make the link to Agenda 2030 more visible, a working group mapped the UCRs activities along the lines of all 17 SDGs, sorting them according to the University's strategies, further highlighting the areas were work still remains to be done. The rectorate further identified five main roles through which the University wants to contribute to Agenda 2030 (Jensen & Angulo, 2019, p. 15):

1. Accessible education, inclusive of equity, quality, and promoting opportunities.
2. Contribution to the social, economic, and environmental development of the Costa Rican territory.

3. Leading role in the fields of science, technology, and innovation.
4. Support to the central and local governments for the implementation of mechanisms for action and follow-up of the SDGs.
5. Dissemination of the teamwork of different entities of the institution, for the development of the SDGs.

The five points are essentially outlining a Whole Institution Approach for the SDGs, always in connection with the needs of Costa Rica. This translates, for example, to all undergraduate students doing 300 hours of community work in order to be able to graduate that way the University gives back to the community and educates students (H.J., personal communication, 2019, July 10).

Although academic freedom and trust in Costa Rican higher education is better off than other Latin American countries, such as Mexico and Venezuela, and the academic landscape is changing at a smaller rate, challenges remain (Ferreyra et al., 2017). In Costa Rica, it is the current fiscal reform that threatens to reduce funding for education, in particular higher education that challenges the UCR (H.J., personal communication, 2018, November 14). Agenda 2030 might be a way to reconnect the University with the government and to show the value it has through globally agreed challenges (Jensen & Angulo, 2019, p. 10).

DISCUSSION

Can the SDGs bridge the gap? This is the question asked in the title of this chapter. Is Agenda 2030 really the answer to the structural issues that the current ESD program of UNESCO has, as suggested in the new plan (UNESCO, 2019a)? All of the people interviewed for this chapter, and most of the people asked informally during related conferences recognized that the SDGs are not perfect, but a good tool to "get work done" (M.A., personal communication, 2019, October 10). They agreed that through the backing of the United Nations, it has become easier to convince people of the need of sustainability initiatives at their universities.

The University of Bologna, the Siam University, and the UCR all started to use the language, the images, and the topics of the 2030 Agenda in their Whole Institution Approaches. The University of Bologna took the SDGs as a chance to start changing the structure of its university, while Siam University incorporated them into the institutions philosophy. The UCR used them to highlight its importance to the government. While all of those concepts are different, they have one thing in common: connecting the Global Agenda to the local university and changing through that both.

On the other hand, neither the University of Ghana nor the UofR use the SDGs in a broad scale, at least not to this date, mostly because the strategic plans were developed before 2015. However, they promote Agenda 2030 through events, workshops, and conferences and engage with the basic ideas and concepts of it. The advantage of this is that the Whole Institution Approach is developed alongside local needs, leaving space to include the Global Agenda at a later stage.

Knowledge and understanding about the issues addressed in Agenda 2030 is constantly under review and is developing at universities around the world. This is also the case for initiatives for sustainable development at universities. The SDGs provide for many a bridge to be able to communicate better and to benchmark initiatives.

CONCLUSION

As the five examples show, sustainable development, and increasingly Agenda 2030, is part of many universities. Whole institution approaches to sustainable development that are benchmarked against the SDGs are on the rise. This development is important, since it provides higher education institutions with a joint idea to take on responsibility. While individual projects and courses about sustainable development have existed for a long time at higher education institutions, the Whole Institution Approach takes their commitment to a new level. Furthermore, having a common framework for action will make it easier to report and measure what higher education institutions are doing in support of Agenda 2030. This is needed, to ensure that higher education can further strengthen its involvement in development agendas.

Of course, there are also limitations and risks toward a Whole Institution Approach for sustainable development that includes the SDGs. One is the limited knowledge about sustainable development. Another one is that sustainable development is still too often associated with the natural sciences, which excludes the humanities and social sciences departments. Additionally, it is at first costly to start the processes, because the institution needs to be mapped and afterwards changes implemented. As well, it would take some time to convince all stakeholders within the institution that sustainability is important for all, especially at those already facing financial and other structural issues. Those are just some of the obstacles that one can find on the road to a Whole Institution Approach. Yet, all interviewed people confirmed that it is worth the effort.

It is too early to assess the impact Agenda 2030 has in terms of mobilizing initiatives at higher education institutions and to see to what extend they will be fruitful. Yet, it is safe to say that the SDGs are mobilizing people across all backgrounds, including university professors, vice-chancellors, international office staff, and, in particular, students. Briefly put, Agenda 2030 is a new chance for higher education institutions to not only influence global agendas, but also to rethink and reorganize their own work and commitment. It proves hopeful to see that much is happening; if the transformation that has been initiated is pursued properly into the future we can be even more hopeful that universities will lead the way and will help orchestrate the mind-set change required to address the Global Goals in the best possible way.

NOTES

1. United Nations Sustainable Development Goals.
2. UNESCO Global Action Programme on Education for Sustainable Development.

REFERENCES

Big Tent Consortium. (2018). *International Higher Education Declaration to support the implementation of the United Nations sustainable development goals*. Big Tent Consortium. Retrieved from http://www.guninetwork.org/files/international_higher_education_declaration_to_support_the_implementation_of_the_united_nations_sustainable_development_goals_eng.pdf. Accessed on March 25, 2019.

Brundtland Report. (1987). Report of the World Commission on Environment and Development: Our Common Future. United Nations General Assembly document A/42/427., New York.

Buckler, C., & Creech, H. (2014). *Shaping the future we want: UN Decade of Education for Sustainable Development* (2005–2014). Paris: UNESCO.

Egron-Polak, E. (2018, February 6). *Sustainable development goals: A new framework for the future of international higher education?* World Education Views and Reviews. Retrieved from https://wenr.wes.org/2018/02/sustainable-development-goals-a-new-framework-for-the-future-of-international-higher-education. Accessed on July 10, 2018.

Ferreyra, M. M., Avitabile, C., Álvarez, J. B., Paz, F. H., & Urzúa, A. S. (2017). *At a crossroads: Higher education in Latin America and the Caribbean*. Washington, DC: The World Bank.

Foundation for Environmental Education. (2014). Retrieved from https://www.ecoschools.global/. Accessed on July 31, 2019.

Hall, B. L. (2014). Let's make some noise! Higher Education and the Post-2015 Development Agenda. *IAU Horizons*, *20*(3), 23–24.

Hargreaves, L. G. (2008). The whole-school approach to education for sustainable development: From pilot projects to systemic change. *Education for Sustainable Development*, *6*, 69–74.

Henderson, K., & Tilbury, D. (2004). Whole-school approaches to sustainability: An international review of whole school sustainability programs. Report prepared by the Australian Research Institute in Education for Sustainability (ARIES) for The Department of the Environment and Heritage, Australian Government.

HESI. (2012, July 20–22). Commitment to sustainable practices of Rio de Janeiro. Retrieved from https://sustainabledevelopment.un.org/content/documents/1889HEI%20Declaration%20English%20new%20version.pdf. Accessed on March 4, 2019.

International Association of University (IAU). (2014). *IAU Iquitos statement on higher education for sustainable development*. Iquitos: IAU.

International Association of Universities (IAU). (2017). Higher *education paving the way to sustainable development: A global perspective*. Paris: IAU. Retrieved from http://iau-hesd.net/sites/default/files/documents/higher-education-paving-the-way-to-sd-iau-2017.pdf. Accessed on July 10, 2018.

Jensen, H., & Angulo, Y. (2019). *Desarollo Sostenible: Aportes de la Universidad de Costa Rica para el alcance de los objetivos de Desarrollo Sostenible de la Agenda* 2030. San Jose, CA: UCR.

Lozano, R., Lukman, R., Lozano, F. J., Huisingh, D., & Lambrechts, W. (2013). Declarations for sustainability in higher education: Becoming better leaders, through addressing the university system. *Journal of Cleaner Production*, *48*, 10–19.

Mallow, S., & van't Land, H. (2020). *Higher education for the sustainable development goals: 2nd IAU Global Survey on HESD*. Paris: IAU.

Ministry of Finance Ghana. (2018). Ghana's SDG Budget Baseline report. *Retrieved from* https://www.mofep.gov.gh/sites/default/files/news/Ghana's-SDG-Budget-Baseline-Report-Aug-09-18.pdf. Accessed on July 31, 2019.

Ministry of Foreign Affairs of Thailand. (2017). Sufficiency *economy philosophy*: Thailand's *path towards sustainable development goals*. Bangkok: A special publication of the Bangkok Post for the Ministry of Foreign Affairs of Thailand. Retrieved from http://www.mfa.go.th/dvifa/contents/files/articles-20170626-142701-203959.pdf. Accessed on March 8, 2019.

Mora, O.-G., Serra, M. A., & Vieira, M.-J. (2018). Social engagement in Latin American Universities. *Higher Education Policy*, *31*(4), 513–534.

Paletta, A., & Bonoli, A. (2019). Governing the university in the perspective of the United Nations 2030 Agenda: The case of the University of Bologna. *International Journal of Sustainability in Higher Education*, *20*(3), 500–514.

Sachs, J. (2015). Achieving the sustainable development goals. *Journal of International Business Ethics*, *8*(2), 53–62.

Siam University. (n.d.). *IAU global cluster*. IAU HESD Portal. Retrieved from http://iau-hesd.net/sites/default/files/siam_university_cluster_profile.pdf. Accessed on August 6, 2019.

Sustainable Development Solutions Network (SDSN) Australia/Pacific. (2017). Getting started with the SDGs in universities: A guide for universities, higher education institutions, and the academic sector. Melbourne: Australia, New Zealand and Pacific Edition.

The Economist. (2015, March 26). The 169 commandments. Retrieved from https://www.economist.com/leaders/2015/03/26/the-169-commandments. Accessed on July 9, 2018.

UN Global Compact. (2016). *CEO statement of support for the sustainable development goals*. UNGC. Retrieved from http://www.unglobalcompact.org.au/2016/09/07/gcna-launches-ceo-statement-of-support-for-the-sdgs. Accessed on July 31, 2019.

University of Costa Rica (UCR). (2013). *Plan Estratético Institutional* 2013-2017. San José, CA: Universidad de Costa Rica.

UNESCO. (2019a). *SDG 4: Education 2030: Part II, Education for sustainable development beyond 2019*. Paris: UNESCO. Retrieved from https://unesdoc.unesco.org/ark:/48223/pf0000366797.locale=en. Accessed on April 15, 2019.

UNESCO. (2019b, July 31). *Transforming learning and training environments*. Priority Action Area 2. Retrieved from https://en.unesco.org/gap/priority-action-areas/transforming-learning

United Nations. (2015). *A/RES/70/1 transforming our world: The 2030 agenda for sustainable development*. New York, NY: Author.

University of Bologna. (2016a). *Strategic Plan* 2016–2018. Bologna: Author.

University of Bologna. (2016b). Reporting on U.N. *sustainable development goals*. Bologna: Alma Mater Studiorum – Università di Bologna.

University of Bologna. (2017). Reporting on U.N. *sustainable development goals*. Bologna: Alma Mater Studiorum – Università di Bologna.

University of Ghana. (2014). Strategic *plan* 2014–2024. Accra: Public Affairs Directorate.

University of Regina (UofR). (2015). *Strategic plan for sustainability* 2015 – 2020. Regina: UofR.

Wu, Y.-C. J., & Shen, J.-P. (2016). Higher education for sustainable development: A systematic review. *International Journal of Sustainability in Higher Education, 17*(5), 633–651.

CHAPTER 9

INTEGRATING SUSTAINABLE DEVELOPMENT INTO THE POSTGRADUATE CURRICULUM IN THE UK: A MIXED METHOD STUDY

Gavin Melles

ABSTRACT

*In the UK, Masters level discipline-specific courses in sustainability integrate modules on the social, economic, and environmental issues of sustainable development. The postgraduate faculty teaching on these courses and the student cohorts enrolling in such courses bring varying attitudes, experiences, and beliefs to the ecological and anthropological discourses and practices about sustainable development. Existing studies of education for sustainable development (ESD) have identified strengths and weaknesses in the knowledge and attitudes of students and faculty although few studies have focused on postgraduate cohorts and fewer still have attempted to compare and contrast students and lecturers. This mixed method case study analyses findings from data collected (2016–2017) from student surveys (*n = *121) and semi-structured interviews with faculty (*n = *21) recruited from multiple university departments, centers, and programs (*n = *12) to identify prevailing anthropocentric and eco-centric ideas and rationales about sustainable development and ESD. Findings suggest a strong orientation to mainstream sustainable development in both groups but analysis identifies reasons for resisting a focus on extremes*

Teaching and Learning Strategies for Sustainable Development:
Innovations in Higher Education Teaching and Learning, Volume 19, 123–140

ISSN: 2055-3641/doi:10.1108/S2055-364120200000019012

of "deep green" or "green wash" approaches. In addition, prevailing belief in academic neutrality, institutional and disciplinary factors, student pragmatism, and other drivers are highlighted. The study concludes by identifying potential paths from prevailing (experiential) education in sustainable development to more transformational approaches.

Keywords: Education for sustainable development; United Kingdom; postgraduate; faculty; students; strong and weak sustainability; interview; survey

INTRODUCTION

Analysis of the UN decade of Education for Sustainable Development (ESD) (2004–2015) indicate mixed outcomes in terms of the depth of engagement of universities, students, and faculty. Ashford (2004) has suggested that important concepts and values of ESD can be swallowed up by the restrictions of higher education politics and curriculum. Thus, Wals (2012) concluded that ESD faces efficiency and management reforms in universities, which are "arguably undergoing a process of neo-liberalisation" (Sylvestre, Wright, & Sherren, 2013, p. 1358). Other pressures such as academic neutrality and increasing industry relationships (Mulder, 2010) reinforce the resistance of universities to addressing the ideological and political challenges strong sustainable development commitments suggest, for example, alternative economics (Amador, Martinho, Bacelar-Nicolau, Caeiro, & Oliveira, 2015). These and other obstacles suggest that we are still some distance from developing transformative ESD courses that challenge the mainstream (see e.g., Sipos, Battisti, & Grimm, 2008).

These pressures have led to the mainstreaming of conventional ecological modernization arguments in ESD, which places emphasis on policy, legislation, and other measures to control pollution and emissions while allowing for continued economic growth (e.g., Coffey & Marston, 2013). Following prior work focused on a continuum of very weak to very strong positions on sustainable development (e.g., Gibbs, Longhurst, & Braithwaite, 1998, p. 1353), Baker (2013) maps the different eco-centric and anthropocentric discourses available to ESD in her ladder of sustainable development (see Table 1). This locates conventional ecological modernization as a hybrid appeal to weak, populist, and strong positions (Adams, 2009). This study asks to what extent students and faculty in postgraduate sustainability oriented courses, and particularly at the postgraduate level, adopt conventional approaches and why.

Postgraduate Taught Courses: Faculty and Student Perspectives

Postgraduate taught courses integrating sustainability concepts and practices offer an intense environment to enroll committed and engaged student cohorts, and explore a broad range of principles and approaches (Fenner, Ainger, Cruickshank, & Guthrie, 2005; Grierson & Hyland, 2011; Naeem & Peach, 2011; Stubbs & Cocklin, 2008). Faculty teaching on these courses also bring different attitudes, experience, and knowledge to teaching and learning (Christie, Miller,

Table 1. The Ladder of Sustainable Development: The Global Focus (Baker, 2013).

Model of Sustainable Development	Normative Principles	Type of Development	Nature	Spatial Focus	Governance	Technology	Policy Integration	Policy Tools	Civil Society: State Relationship	Philosophy
Ideal Model	Principles take precedent over pragmatic considerations (participation; equity, gender equality, justice; common but differentiated responsibilities)	Right livelihood; meeting needs not wants; biophysical limits guide development	Nature has intrinsic value; no substitution allowed; strict limits on resource use, aided by population reductions	Bioregionalism; extensive local self-sufficiency	Decentralization of political, legal, social, and economic institutions	Labor-intensive appropriate, green technology; new approach to valuing work	Environmental policy integration; principled priority to environment	Internalisation of sustainable development norms through ongoing socialization, reducing need for tools	Bottom-up community structures and control; equitable participation	**Ecocentric**
Strong Sustainable Development	Principles enter into international law and into governance arrangements	Changes in patterns and levels of consumption; shift from growth to non-material aspects of development; necessary development in Third World	Maintenance of critical natural capital and biodiversity	Heightened local economic self-sufficiency, promoted in the context of global markets; green and fair trade	Partnership and shared responsibility across multilevels of governance (international, national, regional, & local); use of good governance principles	Ecological modernization of production; mixed labor- and capital-intensive technology	Integration of environmental considerations at sector level; green planning and design	Sustainable development indicators; wide range of policy tools; green accounting	Democratic participation; open dialogue to envisage alternative futures	↑
Weak Sustainable Development	Declaratory commitment to principles stronger than practice	Decoupling; reuse, recycling, and repair of consumer goods; product life-cycle management	Substitution of natural capital with human capital; harvesting of biodiversity resources	Initial moves to local economic self-sufficiency; minor initiatives to alleviate the power of global markets	Some institutional reform and innovation; move to global regulation	End-of-pipe technical solutions; mixed labor- and capital-intensive technology	Addressing pollution at source; some policy co-ordination across sectors	Environmental indicators; market-led policy tools and voluntary agreements	Top-down initiatives; limited state-civil society dialogue; elite participation	
Pollution Control	Pragmatic not principled approach	Exponential, market-led growth	Resource exploitation; marketization and further closure of the commons; nature has use-value	Globalization; shift of production to less regulated locations	"Command and control" state-led regulation of pollution	Capital-intensive technology; progressive automation	"End-of-pipe" approach to pollution management	Conventional accounting	Dialogue between the state and economic interests	**Anthropocentric**

Cooke, & White, 2015; Cotton, Warren, Maiboroda, & Bailey, 2007; Reid & Petocz, 2006). Attitudes and experiences of both students and faculty are influenced by and also adapt to the organizational environment of ESD, which according to current studies is more or less conducive to promoting critical reflection on sustainability issues (Higgins & Thomas, 2016; Leal Filho, 2015; Lovren, 2017).

Previous studies of undergraduates have identified significant knowledge gaps and modest ability of students to put principles into practice (e.g., Azapagic, Perdan, & Shallcross, 2005; Barth & Timm, 2011; Kagawa, 2007; Nejati & Nejati, 2013; Tuncer, 2008). Studies of postgraduate students have found similar mixed knowledge and experience, and some resistance to strong ideological ESD positions (Brody & Ryu, 2006; Corney, 2006; Zeegers & Clark, 2014). Knowledge and attitudes of faculty have also suggested mixed acceptance of the relevance of ESD to universities as a whole (Leal Filho & Pace, 2016; Lozano et al., 2015; O'Byrne, Dripps, & Nicholas, 2015; Ryan & Tilbury, 2013; Sylvestre et al., 2013). In sum, these studies altogether suggest a general "dissonance" in student and faculty attitudes to sustainable development in general.

Theory: Ladder Framework Underlying this Study

A number of methods and instruments have been used to examine attitudes of students to sustainability and sustainable development, including reflective journals (Zeegers & Clark, 2014) and survey instruments (e.g., Kagawa, 2007; Tuncer, 2008). Few studies explicitly focus on the dichotomy between anthropocentric and eco-centric attitudes or the multidimensional nature of the concept (e.g., Connelly, 2007) as described above (see table 1). Kopnina (2013) describes the development and testing of the Eco-centric and Anthropocentric Attitudes toward the Environment scale (EAATSD), which dichotomizes attitudes between these two extremes. In a recent study (Kopnina & Cocis, 2017) employing the scale, it is shown that enrolment in a sustainability course at undergraduate has no effect on developing more ecocentric attitudes.

More complex models of the multiple dimensions of anthropocentric and eco-centric approaches, such as that of Baker (2013), include a range of other factors (see Table 1). This fact and given the range of caveats about the value and interpretation of surveys as defining fixed attitudes (Mendes, Thomas, & Cleaver, 2011), this study employed and analyzed the survey as a form of open discussion with this cohort rather than as a test. This study employed Baker's (2013) ladder to examine student (survey) and faculty (interview) attitudes to eco-centric and anthropocentric arguments. The ladder of sustainable development was used to develop a draft set of questions (content validity) and appeared to have face validity. The questions were modified following feedback from two anonymous reviewers and the survey then submitted in pilot form to students at Swinburne University for further evaluation and comment. This feedback provided further inputs, which were incorporated into the final version of the survey.

Simultaneously, a semi-structured interview with faculty ($n = 21$) conducted in late 2016 face to face and via phone addressed four broad topics of the meanings of sustainable development, the translation of principles into ESD curriculum, the meaning of strong and weak positions, and lecturer personal experiences and assessment of their student cohorts. Student survey and faculty interview overlapped in content regarding attitudes to sustainable development. For analysis, NVivo Plus 12 was used to develop thematic insights from initial substantive coding of interviews. As a result, this study allows for a comparison of student cohort positions on conventional and alternative issues identified in faculty interviews to see the degree of consensus and dissensus.

MATERIAL AND METHODS

This study focused specifically on postgraduate (MSc/MPhil) students and faculty in Environment & Sustainability taught programs. Studies comparing university student and teacher perceptions to examine similarities and differences have employed similar tools, for example, surveys (e.g., Brinkworth, McCann, Matthews, & Nordström, 2009). Since this study used two different quantitative (survey) and qualitative (interview) methods it represents a mixed method approach (Brannen, 2005). Currently, there is a strong trend in certain fields including education and health research to such approaches (Small, 2011), which eschew dichotomizing qualitative and quantitative "paradigms" as fundamentally incompatible, preferring a pragmatic logic encouraging use of method mixes (Feilzer, 2010).

Through recruitment at 10 UK institutions (Table 2) the study obtained a student sample ($n = 121$) and faculty sample ($n = 21$). The survey recruitment returned a varied response rate to the question list, with a 6.6–9.9% loss in sections of the survey. The study used Expected Maximization to replace these. Cronbach Alpha for $n = 39$ without reversing questions was 0.745 (0.802 based on standardized items); removal of Q10 on market-led growth would have increased Alpha to 0.783. Judging by the variable means and range obtained, the most divisive questions proved to be those promoting conventional market-led growth. The interview study meanwhile invited approximately 30 UK academics at relevant institutions to take part in the interview. A final sample of 21 was recruited following this.

This interview study was cross-institutional, focused on an academic cohort working in MSc (or similar) programs. The study employed active interviewing principles to contextualize responses and distinguish views on sustainable development from practices of ESD (as in Wright & Horst, 2013). Active interviewing focuses on the active co-construction of responses to interview questions often with respect to broader discourses (Holstein & Gubrium, 1995). As Alvesson and Karreman (2000) note the problem in qualitative organizational studies such as this study is how to move from interview interaction to the broader discourses of society (Alvesson & Karreman, 2000, p. 1132). Baker's ladder of sustainable development was used as a proxy for four possible sustainable development discourses: deep green, strong eco-centric, weak (mainstream) ecological modernization, and weak market environmentalism, as described in Table 1.

Institutions and Programs

Twelve institutions responded to the invitation to participate. Students recruited to the survey were undertaking a unit (either compulsory or elective) addressing the human and material aspects of sustainable development.

Table 2. Study Recruited Institutions and Programs.

Institution	Key Program(s)	Survey	Interviews
Bath University School of Management	MSc in Sustainability and Management	01	1
Brunel University	Sustainability, Entrepreneurship & Design MSc	06	2
Cambridge University School of Engineering	MPhil Engineering and Sustainable Development	14	2
Edinburgh University Edinburgh College of the Art	Advanced Sustainable Design (MSc)	03	2
Cardiff University School of Architecture	Theory and Practice of Sustainable Design (MSc); Sustainable Mega Buildings (MSc)	05	2
Glasgow University Adam Smith Business School	Environment & Sustainable Development MSc; Sustainable Energy MSc	01	2
Lancaster University Environment Centre	MSc Energy and the Environment; MSc Vulcanology	11	2
Manchester Metropolitan University	MSc Environmental Management & Sustainability	0	1
Strathclyde University School of Civil Engineering	Environmental and Sustainability Studies MSc; Global Sustainable Cities MSc	20	2
UCL Faculty of the Built Environment (Bartlett)	MSc Environment and Sustainable Development	03	1
University of Edinburgh School of Geosciences	MSc in Environmental Sustainability MSc Sustainable Resource Management	15	2
University of London SOAS	MSc Sustainable Development MSc Poverty Reduction	15	2
Unstated		27	0
Total		121	21

Survey Results and Analysis

The survey explicitly examined a set of underlying concepts for which sub-scales were tested. This produced nine factors explaining 65% of variance, with the first two factors dividing between strong and weak positions, and collecting questions oriented to these two positions. Reliability tests (and Cronbach's alpha) on several sub-scales proved meaningful, for example, Nature matters (alpha 0.705; Q6, 11, 12, and 13); need for pervasive Government Policy and Legislation (alpha 0.816; Q21, 22, 30, 31, 32, and 9); reactions to mainstream growth, voluntary commitments and technology (alpha 0.786; Q10, 18, 26, 27, and 35). Thus, the factor analysis supported the claim that sustainable development was multidimensional. As noted below, future refinement of the questionnaire to reduce questions and overlapping content might produce even clearer factor loadings and improved reliability.

Consensus and Disagreement

Survey questions, which are listed in number order (Q1–39), aimed to provoke agreement and disagreement with eco-centric and anthropocentric positions as measured by range, mean, and standard deviation (see Table 3). Although reliability and other measures were applied (as described above) unlike Kopnina (2013) and the EEATSD scale (Kopnina & Cocis, 2017) the survey did not dichotomize into two but rather four positions (as described above), including questions about political representation, alternative economics, rights, and equity (see below). This study did not aim to develop a universally reliable test of attitudes but rather explore the potential of developing a broad survey based on the

Table 3. Student Survey Statistics.

Questions	Min.	Max.	Mean	SD
Equity, justice, and other key principles should be observed and legally reinforced	3	7	6.34	0.832
Developed and developing nations have equal responsibility for solutions	1	7	6.21	1.064
Developed countries have greater historical responsibility	1	7	5.99	1.275
Practical issues such as job creation are more important than principles, for example, equity	1	7	3.83	1.759
Human needs not wants should be a development and growth priority	3	7	6.00	0.962
Biophysical limits should determine sustainable development practice	2	7	6.03	0.982
Excessive consumption gaps between rich and poor should be controlled	2	7	5.42	1.433
Well-being is more important than income	3	7	5.98	1.017
Recycling in industry should be mandated and strictly controlled	4	7	6.49	0.686
Market-led growth is the key to sustainable development	1	7	3.41	1.758
Nature has intrinsic value which cannot be substituted	2	7	6.20	1.007
Biodiversity must not be sacrificed for growth and development	4	7	6.21	0.798
Critical natural capital needs protecting from development demands	2	7	6.39	0.841
Nature can be seen as ecosystem services for development	1	7	4.85	1.742
Converting the environment for development purposes is acceptable	1	7	3.54	1.482
Development should focus on the local rather than the global economy	2	7	5.44	1.004
Green and fair trade practices should be universal	2	7	5.85	1.196
Sustainable development needs globally competitive local firms	1	7	3.90	1.469
Offshoring jobs for development ends is acceptable	1	7	4.12	1.518
Decentralized institutional authority	1	7	5.02	1.221
Local, state, and national government levels need to coordinate better	4	7	6.37	0.594
National regulation of pollution is essential	4	7	6.27	0.657
Global agreements, for example, Kyoto, have been effective	1	7	4.12	1.421
Locally appropriate farming is the key to successful development	1	7	3.55	1.598
Agriculture should aim to balance technology and labor	2	7	5.03	1.242
A growing world population needs another green revolution	1	7	4.45	1.643
GM farming should be encouraged	1	7	4.00	1.713

Table 3. (*Continued*)

Questions	Min.	Max.	Mean	SD
Voluntary control of emissions and pollution in industry works	1	7	3.30	1.939
Environmental management systems should address Co2e sources	1	7	6.06	1.103
Ecologically sensitive planning should be universal	1	7	6.26	0.893
Government sectors need to be better coordinated for decision-making	4	7	6.32	0.710
There should be a range of sustainability policy tools	3	7	6.36	0.678
Impact assessment should be employed for planning and development decisions	3	7	6.28	0.751
Mainstream sustainable development understanding will replace laws	1	7	3.72	1.576
Voluntary tools and commitments are enough for sustainable development	1	7	5.01	1.486
Bottom-up community governance leads to sustainable solutions	2	7	4.89	1.147
There should be equitable participation, for example, gender, for development decisions	2	7	5.73	1.188
Open dialogue between citizens and government matters	3	7	6.20	0.708
Elected representatives alone can make key development decisions	1	7	3.54	1.626

"ladder" to see the cohort's position on strong and weak paradigms or discourses as described above and compare results to faculty views.

The general conclusion from the survey was that extreme positions regarding economic models, politics, governance, and policy met with resistance. Justification for rejecting such positions was made clearer in the open-ended comments (see below) available. Broadly speaking, however, there is scepticism about voluntary controls and processes, for example, human capacity to "see the point," global agreements, etc., while also scepticism about local versus global dichotomies.

Qualitative Comments on "Radical" Positions

Although only one quarter of respondents added caveats and elaborations, contentious issues pitting different strong and weak concepts, for example, market-led growth, practice versus principle, citizens and representation, global competitiveness, and convert environment for development provoked disagreement. There was skepticism about voluntary commitments in general, including global agreements (non-enforceable).

Thus, question (Q4) on the choice between practice or principle was divisive (3.83, SD 1.759). Some measure of the different opinions can be seen in the following qualitative caveats:

> Where job creation is important, it is often used as a justification for continuing known activities that are bad for the environment, for example, the Heathrow runway will "create new jobs."

> Gender equality and other social equalities should be seen as primarily important to form the foundation principles and practices if not dealt with at the forefront could be exacerbated by development.
>
> I don't agree with statements which suggest we can only do one thing or the other. That is not really development. Jobs can be created in ways, which promote principles and practice – we really need those jobs more anyway.
>
> Depends on where in the world you are. Building the right kind of infrastructure and creating jobs in developed countries is important to keep them going, it is also very important in developing countries but there they might be facing bigger issues when it comes to gender equality.

Likewise question (Q10) on the importance of market-led growth (3.41, SD 1.758)

> Market-led gives rise to too many negative externalities and fails to address inequalities. It needs to be restrained by redistributive policies. Pure market forces neglect social and environmental aspects, and winners will always protect own interests.
>
> The key to sustainable development is to reach social agreements made on the basis of rationality (science-based evidence), but been aware that our decisions are taken only on the base of what we know, and there are many uncertainties. Therefore flexibility to changing policy and management paths is essential.

Converting environment for development (Q15, 3.54, SD 1.482)

> One to one trades should not be encouraged, however innovations in agro-forestry housing, etc., have shown that it is possible to co-manage to maintain bio-diversity and the environmental services land or forests provide with human productive activities.
>
> Partly disagree, the local landscape is important and shouldn't be sacrificed for developments, but if absolutely necessary for development compromise must be made, that is, increase building capacity or locate in the least sensitive area.
>
> This needs to be regulated and strictly controlled. The recent government's decision to relax planning laws is uniformed and a fundamental mistake. Brownfield development needs to be moved up the agenda government's agenda (again).

Success of global agreements (4.12, SD 1.421)

> Have been successful in raising awareness and creating global movements for change, have been less unsuccessful in achieving enforcement of standards and agreements leading to change.
>
> It depends what they have been effective in doing really. In terms of halting climate change and moving us toward sustainability, they made a small start (though many would say this was not good enough – it has obviously not been but international agreements are hard and maybe it was good.
>
> So far they have been more symbolic than effective. I hope that Paris Agreement will be a shift towards more effective climate change agreement, however it is not ambitious enough.

Overall, faculty and students reject deep green "ideological" commitments and statements, preferring compromise positions. Dichotomies such as local versus global, labor versus technology, and forms of strong state control and intervention, for example, to control consumption, met with resistance. There was high level of agreement about certain mainstream principles, for example, the value of nature, equality, need for policy tools, and the need for control of industry excesses, since voluntary measures and approaches did not work.

Scepticism about the capacity of society to take sustainability on board could be linked to this. Most discussion was around trade-offs between nature and development or growth needs, for example, off-shoring, global competitivity. As exemplified, qualitative comments provided additional insight on the capacity of this cohort to nuance and rationalize their (quantitative) responses. Suggestions about radical political, for example, bottom-up governance, economic, for example, privileging local farming and economies, or environmental change interventions in the survey provoked disagreement. Positions that were morally sound but had limited direct implications for individuals, for example, support needs not wants, wide range of policy tools, open dialogue matters, were uncontentious and agreed to. Additional comments (not quoted above) also showed students citing specific examples from their own countries.

Faculty Interviews

As noted above faculty interviews were categorized under broad category headings as defined by the interview prompts and the content of interview as "directly expressed in the interview" (Vaismoradi, Jones, Turunen, & Snelgrove, 2016, p. 102). The analysis process produced seven such interdependent descriptive category headings: curriculum structure, focus, and history; discipline considerations and views; interpreting strong and weak views; lecturer experiences and transformation; organizational contrasts and tensions; sustainability principles and practices; and student characteristics and consequences. It is out of these category and sub-category headings that thematic insights were identified.

Curriculum Structure, Focus, and History

Under this category were gathered quotes, ideas, and comments on the core, electives, and program structure of specific courses, course development and history comments, dissertation characteristics for each program, experiential opportunities for students, and focus areas and themes of programs. The program structures for each degree (see Table 1) allow for a degree of flexibility in subject choice and the program development and history in each location was often linked to particular charismatic individuals, emergence of (sustainability) research centers, and other factors.

> I think the sustainable development program within the CeDeP programs uh actually it has its roots going back well before we were in SOAS – I think it probably started in the late nineties and it was inspired by the Rio agenda from 1992 – trying to get the a bit of a balance between those three dimensions. [SOAS]

> So in the early years we used a lot of input from MIT in various ways and there faculty would come over here and deliver modules. We did a bit by video link which in those days was scary. It's much better now of course. [CAM]

> And then when he retired uh I and we had a separate class on strategic environmental assessment that I taught. And I couldn't possibly teach uh a whole class on uh sustainability just because of my ridiculously already very high teaching load. [STRATH]

Given that each program also had a specific disciplinary home, multiple course foci, for example, sustainable consumption, industrial ecology, were possible within broad sustainability influenced areas. There was no stipulation that dissertations had to necessarily address a key sustainable development issue or principles. The key insight from this topic area was that strong, neutral, and weak positions treatment was variously treated curriculum structures, and that a range of strategic and historical issues gave rise to the courses. Experiential activities, for example, field visits, footprint measuring activities, etc., were an important component of courses albeit not all, for example, those with an economic focus.

Discipline Considerations and Views

As intimated above in the brief program descriptions, sustainable development is taught from a specific disciplinary home or perspective, and any core unit about general principles is integrated into a specific degree, for example, vulcanology, architecture, biodiversity and conservation, business and Corporate Social Responsibility (CSR), etc., with (potentially) limited direct association with conventional sustainability questions. Thus, faculty views are ultimately colored or modified by the discipline focus in business, management, architecture, engineering, etc., where the programs had their bases as others have noted (e.g., Cebrián, Grace, & Humphris, 2015; Cotton et al., 2007; Green, 2013). This was an area with strong tie-ups with faculty views and experiences. The insight from this dimension of the interview was a reminder that all positions on sustainable development are colored by disciplinary affiliations, and there is no abstract position outside of these disciplinary configurations. This suggests that attempts to find such abstract principles are flawed although whether discipline is significant influence on views is not yet clear.

Interpreting Strong and Weak Views: Natural Versus Human Capital Focus

Notwithstanding the above comments and limitations, interview responses to questions about strong and weak views as reflected in Baker's framework revealed a continuum of responses and positions. One conceptual difficulty was that the majority had an understanding of weak (human capital can substitute for natural capital) and strong sustainability (substitutability is not encouraged), as widely understood in ecological economics but were not familiar with strong and weak sustainable development as a broader political, social, and moral issue; (only) two respondents referred specifically to the ladder framework, for example,

> Well yes for the program in fact we have a unit in the program called policy for sustainable development. And the basic premise of this unit – we're using the ladder of sustainable development for international and national policy as well as legislation. [MMU]

On this basis, across the interview set a continuum of positions emerged relative to strong and weak sustainable development: (1) little or no awareness of the contrast; (2) awareness of (the related) strong and weak sustainability but not the "expanded" concept, for example,

> [Sure] and I'm not aware of there being a weak or strong sustainable development. If somebody has made that distinction and they've explained it that's something that's passed me by. And I'd be quite interested if you have a source that I could read about that. (ED)

(3) personal interpretation of strong and weak sustainable development; (4) clear understanding of the broader concept; and (5) rejection of the relevance of the (standard) distinction, for example,

> The strong and weak sustainability means to me – a debate mostly it took place in the nineties – and between two random and absurd perspectives in my opinion because one was very technological optimistic, no? [UCL]

In general, there was an explicit and implicit recognition of the question of nature and economic trade-offs whether labeled strong and weak or not, while questions of more "radical" socio-political or economic change, for example, degrowth theses, while occasionally acknowledged were not central concepts. Some of this "ignorance" of the broader issues probably arose from conventional disciplinary focus on natural science or economic issues. Some interviewees simply rejected the dichotomy and debate as outdated or irrelevant to the specific sustainability decisions in a specific context.

> For me there are – there are always an end in mind. So, as long as you know what is sustainable and what isn't. It shouldn't be strong or weak. It should just be sustainable or not. [BRUN]

When I explained the broader concept, several interviewees acknowledged that the issues were addressed either implicitly or by a different lecturer or course, for example,

> Ok I think that theme and those topics do some up [yeah] not in a not it's just that I'm not familiar with the technical phrases but those exact themes do come up in several of our programs. [LANC]

Much like definitions of the terms sustainability and sustainable development themselves there is generally scepticism across the cohort toward a focus on specific terms and a preference for (at this level) emphasis on the underlying debates and principles.

Lecturer Experiences and Transformation

It is possible to forget that views and attitudes on these issues are not only articulated in the context of the interview as isolated conceptual issues but also as related to personal biographies and influential experiences:

> I was also involved in fisheries work i did a big report for … FAO in the OPEC era because they wanted to explore higher oil prices um fisheries and uh you know all these sort of things. [GLAS]

> And before I joined this lecture position at, I worked with the United Nations in Southeast Asian countries. And I looked at the damage different industries and different products were doing to the environment. [BRUN]

> I worked for a practice in the late eighties early nineties, which was one of the first actually to say sustainability in a more holistic way. So I was looking at – um the impact of sustainability on human health, local economies, and all this kind of thing. So – as a designer an in practice I was interested in in doing that. [ECA]

Such experiences are related (albeit not by all) as decisive in the academic career trajectory and eventual focus and attitudes. In terms of insight, two concepts stood out: not all lecturers associate their interest or involvement in teaching with personal biographies and events; and for those who do their current position on the issues, for example, nature, economics, and growth, they link to such histories.

Organizational Contrasts and Tensions

This particular theme identified comments about interinstitutional tensions, developments, and differences of opinion about the meaning and practice of sustainable development, stretching from "neutral" recognition of different views to comments on almost incompatible views and barriers. Under this general heading, respondents referred to: general limitations across the university relative to ESD; specific disciplinary differences with other areas about meanings; certain individuals within departments who created potential obstacles; and structural and related issues, for example, courses closing or numbers increasing due to certain agendas.

> Because we're not here to change attitudes and behaviours – universities are not an advocacy body who should promote a particular viewpoint with a particular set of values. [MMU]

> And there's been a lot of movement within our university in the past couple of years. Due to some personal changes, which have meant that people who have been scared – been sustainability interested but scared have been enabled to come forward. And so that's now – so now we have I think strong sustainability. [Bath]

> Talk to some of my other colleagues in this department and that aspect of sustainability wouldn't be present – for them it's about ecological sustainability in terms of how do you sustain a [don't take more wood out of the forest than you put in] yeah as opposed to say what about the social benefits and costs. I mean it's just completely off topic as far as they're concerned. [LAN]

The insights from this topic have been mentioned above. Again to reiterate teaching sustainability and sustainable development takes place in an environment where a plurality of views is normal and some of those views are potential barriers to progress in ESD.

Sustainability Principles, Definitions, and Practices

Sustainable development, and even more so sustainability, was described as anything from a meaningless term to a critical driver of future life on earth. Environmental thresholds and triple bottom line trade-offs at a range of scales also featured as inevitable and even sometimes as a defunct perspective.

> Because again that interpretation of the trade-off is a bit of a nineteen nineties or eighties perspective where it assumes that there will be winners and losers and yes in the mainstream that's what happens. But perhaps this is one of the reasons why sustainable development isn't progressing fast. [MMU]

> And similarly with this idea of trade-offs. I actually find that a really self-defeating way of talking about sustainability. Because of course trade-offs are something that we see everywhere. Again a trade-off is normal. [Bath]

Under the thematic banner of social, ethics and equity issues, meanwhile, participants talked about personal and broader moral justice, societal challenges, and principles. These included the importance of collective approaches to behavior change and education, for example, citizen science, civil society organizations, and eco-villages. These observations overlapped with the universally accepted complex and "wicked" nature of the issues, which ESD should integrate as a learning goal – and the need to promote participatory decision-making. Around the theme of the relationship between economics, growth and nature, comments, and observations clustered around interpretations of where to draw the line between development and economic growth within an environmentally compromised setting.

> And I find it very interesting uh to contrast um . in now relatively gung ho kind of economicy sort of growth scenarios on the one hand with sort of WWF state of the world – state of the planet reports, which is arguing that we're already in serious overshoot. uh and even though you question the methodology and all the rest of it ... if it applied consistently the message is that things ... do seem to be getting worse rather than better [even on a precautionary sort of principle] indeed. [GLASG]

Students Characteristics and Consequences

The overwhelming conclusion from comments about students was that lecturers saw this cohort as a committed if occasionally naïve group, whose own practices, including after graduation and during, showed contradiction with sustainability principles.

> But that involves um for example one person within a year had a consultancy job and was proud that she had her first company car [right] ah [ok] yeah I mean well I mean she does wind-farm development and has to speak to people and all the rest. So she has to get out there and um. So [mm] and and others as well it. [EDIN]

On an individual organization basis, the typically mixed discipline classes brought advantages and challenges of knowledge gaps and disciplinary difference to the ESD enterprise. The majority of lecturers also described the overall aim as the education of change-makers for industry and society, who would play a key role in business, policy, design, and other areas.

> They're sort of rebuilding their – what they [world view] world view yeah. So there are moments when that happens in the program which is good. I think that's part of what we're trying to do. [Brunel]

Graduate outcomes did not always lead to such personal change (as noted above).

DISCUSSION & CONCLUSION

Sustainable development is a multidimensional concept with broad ideological, ethical, political, and economic consequences. The ladder of sustainable development integrates these factors into a framework that extends across eco-centric and anthropometric positions. Explicitly addressing this complexity should form part of HESD pedagogy, and there are some indications this is happening. Evaluating student knowledge before, during, and after education should also address this complexity, especially at the postgraduate level.

This study trialed a survey with a cohort of UK postgraduate taught students (n = 121), and interviews with faculty (n = 21) with a view to examining their relative positions with respect to strong and weak sustainable development. This study addressing a postgraduate cohort found students willing and able to take a position on a wider range of dimensions. Student respondents from a wide range of countries and backgrounds took an overall pragmatic attitude to moral versus practical issues, and showed a general resistance to strong interventions. Faculty interviews also showed a cohort with mixed backgrounds and disciplinary focus, who also in general took a pragmatic view of sustainability principles and practices. There was broad consensus on the importance of principles, while anthropocentric development demands could win out over the environment. In sum there seemed to be limited support for strong positions on sustainable development. These data and analysis may suggest it is important (and realistic) to encourage pluralistic views of sustainable development and where possible to expose students to all the different strands.

ACKNOWLEDGMENTS

The study was conducted in the UK during a nominated fellowship at the Institute for Advanced Studies in Humanities, Edinburgh University, in late 2016. Author gratefully acknowledges the IASH support.

REFERENCES

Adams, W. M. (2009). *Green development: Environment and sustainability in a developing world* (3rd ed.). Abingdon: Routledge Taylor & Francis Group.

Alvesson, M., & Karreman, D. (2000). Varieties of discourse: On the study of organizations through discourse analysis. *Human Relations*, *53*(9), 1125–1149. https://doi.org/10.1177/0018726700539002

Amador, F., Martinho, A. P., Bacelar-Nicolau, P., Caeiro, S., & Oliveira, C. P. (2015). Education for sustainable development in higher education: Evaluating coherence between theory and praxis. *Assessment and Evaluation in Higher Education*, *40*(6), 867–882. https://doi.org/10.1080/02602938.2015.1054783

Azapagic, A., Perdan, S., & Shallcross, D. (2005). How much do engineering students know about sustainable development? The findings of an international survey and possible implications for the engineering curriculum. *European Journal of Engineering Education*, *30*(1), 1–19. https://doi.org/10.1080/03043790512331313804

Baker, S. (2013). *Sustainable development*. London: Routledge Taylor & Francis Group.

Barth, M., & Timm, J. (2011). Higher education for sustainable development: Students' perspectives on an innovative approach to educational change. *Journal of Social Sciences*, *7*(1), 13–23. https://doi.org/10.3844/jssp.2011.13.23

Brannen, J. (2005). Mixing methods: The entry of qualitative and quantitative approaches into the research process. *International Journal of Social Research Methodology: Theory and Practice*, *8*(3), 173–184. https://doi.org/10.1080/13645570500154642

Brinkworth, R., McCann, B., Matthews, C., & Nordström, K. (2009). First year expectations and experiences: Student and teacher perspectives. *Higher Education*, *58*(2), 157–173. https://doi.org/10.1007/s10734-008-9188-3

Brody, S. D., & Ryu, H. (2006). Measuring the educational impacts of a graduate course on sustainable development. *Environmental Education Research*, *12*(2), 179–199. https://doi.org/10.1080/13504620600688955

Cebrián, G., Grace, M., & Humphris, D. (2015). Academic staff engagement in education for sustainable development. *Journal of Cleaner Production*, *106*, 79–86. https://doi.org/10.1016/j.jclepro.2014.12.010

Christie, B. A., Miller, K. K., Cooke, R., & White, J. G. (2015). Environmental sustainability in higher education: What do academics think? *Environmental Education Research*, *21*(5), 655–686. https://doi.org/10.1080/13504622.2013.879697

Connelly, S. (2007). Mapping sustainable development as a contested concept. *Local Environment*, *12*(3), 259–278. https://doi.org/10.1080/13549830601183289

Corney, G. (2006). Education for sustainable development: An empirical study of the tensions and challenges faced by geography student teachers. *International Research in Geographical and Environmental Education*, *15*(3), 224–240. https://doi.org/10.2167/irgee194.0

Cotton, D., Warren, M. F., Maiboroda, O., & Bailey, I. (2007). Sustainable development, higher education and pedagogy: A study of lecturers' beliefs and attitudes. *Environmental Education Research*, *13*(5), 579–597. https://doi.org/10.1080/13504620701659061

Feilzer, M. Y. (2010). Doing mixed methods research pragmatically: Implications for the rediscovery of pragmatism as a research paradigm. *Journal of Mixed Methods Research*, *4*(1), 6–16. https://doi.org/10.1177/1558689809349691

Fenner, R. A., Ainger, C. M., Cruickshank, H. J., & Guthrie, P. M. (2005). Embedding sustainable development at Cambridge University Engineering Department. *International Journal of Sustainability in Higher Education*, *6*(3), 229–241. https://doi.org/10.1108/14676370510607205

Gibbs, D. C., Longhurst, J., & Braithwaite, C. (1998). "Struggling with sustainability": Weak and strong interpretations of sustainable development within local authority policy. *Environment and Planning A*, *30*(8), 1351–1365. https://doi.org/10.1068/a301351

Green, T. L. (2013). Teaching (un)sustainability? University sustainability commitments and student experiences of introductory economics. *Ecological Economics*, *94*(2013), 135–142. https://doi.org/10.1016/j.ecolecon.2013.08.003

Grierson, D., & Hyland, C. (2011). Learning for change: Cross-disciplinary postgraduate programmes in sustainability. *The International Journal of Environmental, Cultural, Economic and Social Sustainability*, *7*(3), 37–50. Retrieved from http://strathprints.strath.ac.uk/31813/

Higgins, B., & Thomas, I. (2016). Education for sustainability in universities: Challenges and opportunities for change. *Australian Journal of Environmental Education*, *32*(1), 91–108. https://doi.org/10.1017/aee.2015.56

Holstein, J., & Gubrium, J. (1995). *The Active Interview*. Thousand Oaks, CA: SAGE Publications, Inc. https://doi.org/10.4135/9781412986120

Kagawa, F. (2007). Dissonance in students' perceptions of sustainable development and sustainability: Implications for curriculum change. *International Journal of Sustainability in Higher Education*, *8*(3), 317–338. https://doi.org/10.1108/14676370710817174

Kopnina, H. (2013). Evaluating education for sustainable development (ESD): Using ecocentric and anthropocentric attitudes toward the sustainable development (EAATSD) scale. *Environment, Development and Sustainability*, *15*(3), 607–623. https://doi.org/10.1007/s10668-012-9395-z

Kopnina, H., & Cocis, A. (2017). Testing ecocentric and anthropocentric attitudes toward the sustainable development (EAATSD) scale with Bachelor students. *European Journal of Sociology and Anthropology*, *2*(1), 1–16. https://doi.org/10.20897/ejsa.201702

Leal Filho, W. (2015). Education for sustainable development in higher education: Reviewing needs. In W. Leal Filho & P. Pace (Eds.), *Transformative approaches to sustainable development at universities* (pp. 3–12). Cham: Springer. https://doi.org/10.1007/978-3-319-08837-2_1

Leal Filho, W., & Pace, P. (2016). Teaching education for sustainable development at university level: Implications on learning programmes at higher education. In W. Leal Filho & P. Pace (Eds.), *Teaching education for sustainable development at university level* (pp. 1–6). Geneva: Springer International Publishing. https://doi.org/10.1007/978-3-319-32928-4_1

Lovren, V. O. (2017). Promoting sustainability in institutions of higher education: The perspective of university teachers. In W. Leal Filho, U. M. Azeiteiro, F. Alves, & P. Molthan-Hill (Eds.), *Handbook of theory and practice of sustainabiity development in higher education Volume 4 World Sustainability Series* (pp. 475–490). Cham: Springer International Publishing AG. https://doi.org/10.1007/978-3-319-47877-7_32

Lozano, R., Ceulemans, K., Alonso-Almeida, M., Huisingh, D., Lozano, F. J., Waas, T., …, Hugé, J. (2015). A review of commitment and implementation of sustainable development in higher education: Results from a worldwide survey. *Journal of Cleaner Production*, *108*(June), 1–18. https://doi.org/10.1016/j.jclepro.2014.09.048

Mendes, P., Thomas, C., & Cleaver, E. (2011). The meaning of prompt feedback and other student perceptions of feedback: Should National Student Survey scores be taken at face value? *Engineering Education*, *6*(1), 31–39. https://doi.org/10.11120/ened.2011.06010031

Mulder, K. F. (2010). Don't preach. Practice! Value laden statements in academic sustainability education. *International Journal of Sustainability in Higher Education*, *11*(1), 74–85. https://doi.org/10.1108/14676371011010066

Naeem, M. A., & Peach, N. W. (2011). Promotion of sustainability in postgraduate education in the Asia Pacific region. *International Journal of Sustainability in Higher Education*, *12*(3), 280–290. https://doi.org/10.1108/14676371111148063

Nejati, M., & Nejati, M. (2013). Assessment of sustainable university factors from the perspective of university students. *Journal of Cleaner Production*, *48*, 101–107. https://doi.org/10.1016/j.jclepro.2012.09.006

O'Byrne, D., Dripps, W., & Nicholas, K. A. (2015). Teaching and learning sustainability: An assessment of the curriculum content and structure of sustainability degree programs in higher education. *Sustainability Science*, *10*(1), 43–59. https://doi.org/10.1007/s11625-014-0251-y

Reid, A., & Petocz, P. (2006). University lecturers' understanding of sustainability. *Higher Education*, *51*(1), 105–123. https://doi.org/10.1007/s10734-004-6379-4

Ryan, A., & Tilbury, D. (2013). Uncharted waters: Voyages for education for sustainable development in the higher education curriculum. *Curriculum Journal*, *24*(2), 272–294 https://doi.org/10.1080/09585176.2013.779287

Schwarz, N. U. (1999). Self-reports: How the questions shape the answers. *American Psychologist*, *54*(2), 93–105. https://doi.org/10.1037/0003-066X.54.2.93

Sipos, Y., Battisti, B., & Grimm, K. (2008). Achieving transformative sustainability learning: Engaging head, hands and heart. *International Journal of Sustainability in Higher Education*, *9*(1), 68–86. https://doi.org/10.1108/14676370810842193

Small, M. L. (2011). How to conduct a mixed methods study: Recent trends in a rapidly growing literature. *Annual Review of Sociology*, *37*(1), 57–86. https://doi.org/10.1146/annurev.soc.012809.102657

Stubbs, W., & Cocklin, C. (2008). Teaching sustainability to business students: Shifting mindsets. *International Journal of Sustainability in Higher Education*, *9*(3), 206–221. https://doi.org/10.1108/14676370810885844

Sylvestre, P., Wright, T., & Sherren, K. (2013). Exploring faculty conceptualizations of sustainability in higher education: Cultural barriers to organizational change and potential resolutions. *Journal of Education for Sustainable Development*, *7*(2), 223–244. https://doi.org/10.1177/0973408214526491

Tuncer, G. (2008). University students' perception on sustainable development: A case study from Turkey. *International Research in Geographical and Environmental Education*, *17*(3), 212–226. https://doi.org/10.1080/10382040802168297

Vaismoradi, M., Jones, J., Turunen, H., & Snelgrove, S. (2016). Theme development in qualitative content analysis and thematic analysis. *Journal of Nursing Education and Practice*, *6*(5), 100–110. https://doi.org/10.5430/jnep.v6n5p100

Wals, A. E. J. (2012). *Shaping the education of tomorrow: 2012 Full-length Report on the UN Decade of Education for Sustainable Development*. Paris: United Nations Educational, Scientific and Cultural Organization. Retrieved from http://unesdoc.unesco.org/images/0021/002166/216606e.pdf 102

Wright, T., & Horst, N. (2013). Exploring the ambiguity: What faculty leaders really think of sustainability in higher education. *International Journal of Sustainability in Higher Education, 14*(2), 209–227. https://doi.org/10.1108/14676371311312905

Zeegers, Y., & Clark, I. F. (2014). Students' perceptions of education for sustainable development. *International Journal of Sustainability in Higher Education*, *15*(2), 242–253. https://doi.org/10.1108/IJSHE-09-2012-0079

PART II

INNOVATIVE CASE STUDIES

CHAPTER 10

THE TEACHING SUSTAINABILITY MINI-PILOT: A FACULTY LEARNING COMMUNITY BUILDING CURRICULUM FOR STUDENTS' SUSTAINABILITY THINKING

Jenny S. Wakefield and Christopher E. Grice

ABSTRACT

Humans have immense impact on our environment and open and ongoing conversations are needed to generate informed actions toward sustainability. A sustainable future must grow from a changed mindset, one of critical thinking, problem-solving, and continuous learning and active practice. In higher education we are uniquely placed to share with students a sustainability-infused curriculum toward such a changed mindset. At Brookhaven College faculty self-selected to participate in a Teaching Sustainability Mini-Pilot during Fall semester 2018. The innovation was initiated to encourage students to become mindful of sustainability, inspired to get involved in sustainability efforts, and to become immersed in satisfactory real-world learning.

Keywords: Sustainability; community college; faculty learning community; focus group; interdisciplinary; sustainability-across-the-curriculum; sustainability curriculum; phenomenology; teaching sustainability mini-pilot; real-world learning

Teaching and Learning Strategies for Sustainable Development: Innovations in Higher Education Teaching and Learning, Volume 19, 143–158

ISSN: 2055-3641/doi:10.1108/S2055-364120200000019013

In *Plato's Republic*, published in 380 BC, Glaucon and Socrates discussed the unsustainable lifestyle in which humans lived in the feverish city with all of its temptations, desires, perceived needs, and the never-ending consumption (Bloom, 1991). Philosophy professor Joseph DesJardins (2007) paralleled this notion by suggesting that in the current paradigm – more than 2,400 years after Socrates – the trend is still for businesses to produce and cater to consumers' requests and perceived needs. Consumption has stimulated us to adopt a "buy and throw" mentality where perceptually necessary items are often considered earned rewards for hard work or replacements for happiness, or limited free time (DesJardins, 2007).

The economic market system depends on consumption. But as environmental resources are rapidly depleted, overconsumption has become an unsustainable way of living. However, overconsumption does not cover the full picture of what is meant by unsustainable living. Many definitions for sustainability exist and these definitions often stem from individual learning or training, observed efforts, or trends. Fisher and McAdams (2015) conducted survey research at a medium-size university in the United States and explored 552 student responses on how they conceptualize sustainability. The researchers found that students' understanding of the definition of sustainability was influenced by the kind of course they were taking as well as "the factors that they perceived as important to the definition of the term" (p. 417). The authors noted that students did not have one single idea of what sustainability is.

Not fully understanding the definition of sustainability impacts communication (Djordjevic & Cotton, 2011; Reid & Petocz, 2006) and possible actions toward sustaining our world for future generations. Our chapter informs on the teaching sustainability mini-pilot (TSMP) that took place at Brookhaven College (BHC) in Fall 2018. Through this curricular innovation, faculty aspired to enhance student awareness and understanding of sustainability. Both our definition and the participating faculty definition of sustainability development (SD), aligns with the *United Nations Commission on Environment and Development 1987 Brundtland Report*: "Sustainability development is development that meets the needs of the present without compromising the ability of future generations to meet their own needs" (ch. 2, 54).

If we are to sustain our planet for generations to come, we need to recognize that humans have immense impact on our environment and that an open and ongoing conversation is needed to generate informed actions toward sustainability. We need to include our college students in these conversations. As Adams (2013) noted, higher education (HE) institutions, faculty, and scholarly communities hold a privileged position at the forefront of knowledge about the trends that impact people on our planet. Adams (2018) also conjectured that universities exert "significant influence over a large proportion of the world's future leaders" (p. 332), further stressing the need for educational institutions and teachers to take actions to teach about sustainability. In recent years, the influencing power of HE institutions has informed a range of initiatives by the American Associations of Universities and Colleges focused on personal, civic, and social responsibility. For example, the Core Commitments initiative aims "to reclaim and revitalize the academy's role in fostering students' development of personal and social responsibility."[1]

In the authors' home state of Texas, the Texas Education Code prescribes that institutions offering undergraduate academic degree programs develop and implement the Texas Core Curriculum (19 Tex. Admin. Code § 4.28 2019). The purpose is to prepare college students to face the challenges they will encounter as they enter the world of work to earn a living and for them to be exposed to and able to live in social harmony with a variety of people from different cultures in a physical and economically sustainable natural world.

By adopting the core curriculum, faculty from Texas HE institutions facilitate students' development toward the core objectives. Through assessment methods and observing students actively engage in sustainability volunteer work, it can be determined whether students are indeed demonstrating the necessary skills to live in a diverse, intellectual, and changing world. The six Texas core objectives are critical thinking, communication, empirical and quantitative skills, teamwork, personal responsibility, and social responsibility (LEAP Texas, 2019a). All these core objectives align well with teaching SD topics.

In this chapter, we share findings from the implementation of the TSMP project of the President's Sustainability Committee, developed by faculty at BHC. Ten faculty members at this community college participated in a learning community to encourage each other to incorporate sustainability curriculum, assessments, and volunteer work in their courses to make students aware of and inspire them to critically think about and discuss the social, economic, and environmental implications of sustainability.

REVIEW OF LITERATURE

Faculty Learning Communities

Instructors often join Faculty Learning Communities (FLC) not only to learn specifics on topics they're interested in but also because these groups can unravel additional objectives and opportunities together that can be accomplished (Cox, 1999). Natkin and Kolbe (2015), for example, noted how interaction among fellow faculty on a topic may help to increase faculty interest and generate an understanding of sustainability. As part of the college sustainability initiative at BHC, faculty self-selected to participate in a FLC on how to incorporate sustainability topics into the curriculum.

The FLC discussed what an initial TSMP would look like – one where each participating faculty member would include at least one SD assignment in one of their courses. In tandem with the formation of the FLC, rich debate and discussion with faculty, advocates, and allies coupled with two years of research (Brookhaven's annual Sustainability Survey) identified three core challenges to achieve the goal of enhancing student awareness of sustainability through curriculum implementation. The President's Sustainability Committee and the FLC participants recognized: (1) the faculty's professional and personal development in teaching sustainability varies greatly; (2) disciplines across the college use different curricula models (e.g., prescriptive vs. descriptive); and (3) part-time faculty constitutes a large segment of instructional employees. To address challenges, and since the participating faculty-both full-time and adjuncts-taught courses in various areas, it was determined that an interdisciplinary approach would be best.

The TSMP project was initiated during the Fall 2018 semester to encourage college students to become mindful of sustainability, and to inspire them to become involved in sustainability efforts and immersed in satisfactory, real-world learning through discussions, assignments, volunteer opportunities, and textbook reading. Ten faculty members participated in the TSMP.

Although several studies from Four-year universities exist that explain how faculty teach sustainability to their students, and some studies exist that reflect data evaluating these initiatives, few studies were found that shared findings from a faculty-driven experience at a community college. Brookhaven faculty designed a model, implemented the model throughout several disciplines, and data were gathered from the faculty's shared experiences. By sharing this model, conversations may be furthered on how to improve the TSMP model for future iterations. Offering the model for more educators to replicate should help them take similar curricular steps toward education on sustainability. Additionally, it is important to note that community colleges are eager participants in the conversations about teaching with SD goals in mind.

We will begin by briefly discussing some existing literature about incorporating SD in a HE curriculum, further describe the Brookhaven FLC and the TSMP project, introduce the data collection method used, and discuss the findings from the research. We conclude by sharing faculty-lived experiences of curricular sustainability implementations in the TSMP.

Educating Sustainability

Although the opportunity to educate with a sustainability mindset has existed for many years, sustainability education has been part of the educational landscape for only a few decades. Incorporating "environment" into HE "can be traced to the 1970s and 1980s when pressing environmental issues led to such fields as environmental engineering and environmental studies" (Wals & Blewitt, 2010, p. 56). However, it was not until the 1990s that HE educators truly began to understand the impacts humans have on both the ecosystem and human life, and the important role HE has in encouraging society to learn about and take action on these issues (University Leaders for a Sustainable Future (ULSF), 2015). The *Talloires Declaration*, composed in 1990, is a 10-point document of the "first official statement made by university administrators of a commitment to sustainability in higher education" (ULSF, 2015, para 5). The document, now signed by more than 500 universities, draws up an "action plan for incorporating environmental literacy and sustainability into university teaching and practice" (ULSF, 2015, para 5).

Faculty awareness of the need to educate the student population on sustainability through a sustainability curriculum has grown, as has initiatives for faculty to work on course designs or course edits that include sustainability curriculum. Research reporting is an important function of four-year institutions as it benefits faculty and instructional designers who review innovations that worked in practice and allow research to be replicated. Two example implementations from our current decade follow:

Dmochowski, Garofalo, Fisher, Greene, and Gambogi (2016) shared an interdisciplinary case study from Penn State University where faculty worked without incentives other than being able to conduct research and be assisted by paid undergraduate student research assistants during the summer months. Faculty first attended a workshop to learn about sustainability curriculum and then worked with their student assistants who aided with research, finding sustainability materials, and creating assignments and assessments for the faculty. The research study did not go into specifics about what type of courses were designed or what assignments and assessments were created by student assistants.

Stubbs and Schapper's (2011) Australian study described two teaching approaches: They suggested that incorporating corporate sustainability (CS), and corporate social responsibility (CSR) into the curriculum can effectively prepare students to respond to challenges related to education for sustainability. CS believed to be a more pedagogical frame, develops students to become change agents, trains them to question their world view, and includes "development of communication, negotiation, critical analysis, and chance management skills" (p. 262) as part of the curriculum. CSR requires research and "appropriate learning processes that contribute to the critical analysis and evaluation of business and its relation to society" (p. 263). Both approaches "equip students to respond effectively to the challenges of CSR and CS" (p. 265).

CONCEPTUAL FRAMEWORK

Although several four-year university research studies exist showing faculty teaching sustainability to their students, few studies show research that shares the experience from these initiatives, for example, how the curriculum was implemented. Even fewer studies cover research from faculty-driven experiences at community colleges. We know, however, that initiatives at community colleges are increasing sustainability awareness among students, as evidenced by community college webpages. In Pennsylvania, for example, Dickinson Community College offers more than 100 courses each year for students to learn about sustainability within the three main sustainability areas: social, economic, and environmental (Dickinson, 2019). Estrella Mountain Community College in Arizona offers sustainability-infused courses, and a sustainability and ecological literacy academic certificate (Estrella Mountain, 2019) and Onondaga Community College in New York provides an array of courses in various disciplines that are sustainability-infused (Onondaga, 2019). At DCCCD a 3-tier Sustainability Scholar program is underway that reward students with a recognition at graduation if they take at least three "sustainability-marked courses."

The Association for the Advancement of Sustainability in Higher Education (AASHE) noted in their 2010 publication *A Call to Action* that colleges and universities are appropriate test sites for trying out models and practices; however, they also emphasized that the important task for these colleges and universities is grounded in how well we will be able to educate students about sustainability.

Our research reflects one attempt by faculty at a community college to share their work on educating their students on sustainability and how they chose to include assignments and volunteer work in their curriculum.

Study Aim and Research Question

The guiding research questions in our study were "How did TSMP faculty incorporate sustainability curriculum in their courses? And, what drives faculty to include sustainability teaching into the curriculum?"

METHODOLOGY

Purpose and Setting

The purpose of this study was to collect lived experience data from faculty who have instructed students about sustainability in their BHC courses during the Fall 2018 semester. BHC is part of Dallas County Community College District (DCCCD) and is located in central Texas. The DCCCD sustainability goals are those to conserve energy and resources, minimize waste, provide education on sustainability and an understanding of our world while also building a healthy and sustainable future for Dallas County, and to engage the local, regional, and national community on sustainability efforts.

During the last 10 years, the district has worked to lead efforts and share ideas toward building a sustainable future though means of action, interaction, and education. Among several coordinated initiatives are the DCCCD Sustainability Team, student and faculty-run clubs and projects, events such as Recycle Mania and the Sustainability Summit Conference, academic offerings, and service-learning opportunities. The DCCCD Board of Directors and the chancellor support not only sustainability district-wide but also community sustainability efforts, and have aligned with the UN SD goals with the overarching district goals to provide support and encouragement for each college, and its faculty, to teach about sustainability.

In the fall of 2016, Dr Thom Chesney, president at Brookhaven, initiated a committee with the purpose to develop, assess, and continually improve college efforts for sustainability initiatives with the commitment to

- institutionalize sustainability practices in alignment with board and college strategic priorities;
- achieve carbon neutrality, zero waste, and positive water balance;
- collaborate with the community to raise awareness of sustainability and support planning to achieve a desirable future for all; and
- teach sustainability (President's Sustainability Committee, 2019).

During the years following, several initiatives were started leading up to the fall semester of 2018, when 10 Brookhaven faculty members self-selected to participate in a faculty-initiated FLC: the TSMP. These educators agreed to include at least one assignment in one of their courses in an effort to more broadly introduce

SD through course curriculum, or volunteer service for extra credit. The TSMP was created for college students to become engaged in SD through the curriculum and to involve students in satisfying, real-world learning related to sustainability efforts.

Objective

Results from the 2017 BHC Sustainability Survey of employees suggested that: (1) sustainability is important for the holistic vitality of the campus and local community; (2) it aligns to the college's mission; and (3) it was seen that it provides students with a competitive edge economically and academically. These survey results, from a cross-section of 169 Brookhaven employees, served as the guiding principles behind the mini-pilot. The goal was to experientially try out a model that aligned to the college's mission of equipping students with the skills and relationships necessary for twenty-first century leadership. The model was specifically designed for Brookhaven faculty by Brookhaven faculty. It is important to share with others how such a model was designed and implemented so that conversations may be furthered on how to improve the model for future iterations and allow for model replication at other institutions.

Participants, Recruitment, and Subjects Taught

The 10 faculty members were made up of three females and seven males. Invitations to faculty went out before the winter break including a link to a Doodle for scheduling focus groups at a convenient time. A follow-up email went out after the break, and one reminder email went out the day before the focus group session. Participants unable to attend the focus group sessions were invited individually via email. Two TSMP faculty members who were unable to attend were interviewed individually.

Classes that the participants taught included the following topical courses: Biology; Geology: Environmental Science and Earth Science for Non-Science Majors; English for speakers of other languages (ESOL); Introduction to Physical Fitness/Wellness for Early College High School (ECHS) Students; Introduction to Philosophy; Introduction to Ethics; Introduction to Sociology; Texas Government; Visual Communications; and Yoga.

The type of assignments and assessments included were:

- Textbook chapters – discussions in class or online in forums.
- Selection of outside articles (news and research) forums.
- Research observations, blogging.
- Research literature review or formal paper.
- Extra credit: Windmill Garden attendance/support, community project, paper submission.

Data Collection

Data were collected in two 50-minute focus group sessions and individual interviews. Faculty signed an Institutional Review Board-approved consent form for their anonymous participation. The facilitator took notes and kept track of time;

eight minutes per question were allocated. Participants were encouraged to record their answers on a large post-it sheet on the table in front of them while another group member spoke so to capture as many thoughts and comments as possible. Participants took turns pulling 10 questions from a box, reading them aloud in the order, and answering. When the reader had answered the question, other faculty around the table took turns answering. Interviewee participants answered all questions in order written on the question sheet.

Method

A descriptive research design was used. Phenomenology is a research method that allows the researcher to study a lived experience with, or a perception toward, a phenomenon. This qualitative research method looks at the phenomenon of interest. The phenomenon in this study – the object – was to learn from faculty at BHC how sustainability topics were incorporated into the faculty's curriculum and to identify the essence of the faculty experience as they incorporated sustainability curriculum into coursework. Using phenomenology, the main researcher looked at the commonality of the shared experience that the faculty participants had as they incorporated sustainability assignments into their courses in this initial TSMP.

In qualitative research, validity is a snapshot of "what is" before us – in this case, data gathered in the focus group discussions and the interviews. Reliability for this research was established by aligning with phenomenologist Edmund Husserl's (1962) suggestion of performing an epoché – to "bracket out" the personal "own" experience and, additionally, by aligning with Colaizzi's (1978) suggestion of returning to the subjects for confirmation purposes.

The main researcher performed the epoché by writing a subjectivity statement. The anonymous data gathered included notes taken during the focus group sessions, notes written by participants during the sessions, and individual interview data. All data were transcribed and sent back to the subjects. This process, known as "returning to the subjects" is often utilized to ensure that participants can add to the transcript what they feel was missed and correct any statements they feel are incorrect or incomplete. None of the participants chose to correct or add to the data.

Following Creswell's recommendation when taking a phenomenological approach, the data were then analyzed by searching for "significant statements, sentences, and quotes" (Creswell, 2013, p. 82) that enlighten the participants' reasoning and experience with incorporating curricular sustainability assignments in their courses. This step is followed by clustering and organizing clusters into themes toward finding the *essence* (the gist) of the experience. Three main themes emerged from the data.

PRESENTATION OF DATA

The first and largest theme *Making Sustainability Learning Visible through Story and Participatory Action* emerged from faculty implementations of storytelling discussions, reflective, and participatory activities. Several of these were embedded in the fabric of the community college community: the community colleges are known to have lower tuition costs than four-year institutions and for having a diverse population, as they serve people from all walks of life including ECHS students, typical students, adult learners, workforce training, and general education readiness learners. Three of the faculty specifically noted during the focus group conversations that Brookhaven has a large diversity in its student population. Students come to the community college from all over the United States and from different countries to study.

A professor mentioned that his students of diverse backgrounds "trust each other" and he saw this trust emerge in the classroom conversations as they learned from each other's real-world stories. He said, "My students learn best through story … we are all content experts." He emphasized that "Coming together from diverse backgrounds, we have a lot to learn from each other" and he included his students in each classroom discussion not lecturing but listening and learning from his students. His students earned extra credit for working on the Brookhaven Windmill garden project – a 4,600 square foot garden built by employees, students, and community members to recognize "nature's critical role in our world."[2] This assignment worked well in his biology curriculum as students were able to listen and learn hands-on as they helped with the flora and fauna of the garden.

Faculty used both overt and covert methods to include sustainability into the curriculum. In this study, only one faculty member used the covert approach: "My approach was not to mention the topic at all" noted a geology faculty member. Given the diversity of students in his classes, he took a storytelling approach but also asked students questions through his "survival of the fittest" method. He asked questions such as "What is the environment? How do we maintain it? What is the environment if you are a barren wood, a deer, or a human being?" His reasoning for not using the word *sustainability*, per se, was that he wanted students to "think" and share from their perspective (e.g., country of origin and experiences), without tying the questions and class discussions to any definition or word that may not be clear to the students. He also told students stories about what happens when humans interfere with nature. One of his stories was about the lionfish who started life in home aquariums but was let out into the ocean; it adapted so well that the lionfish became an invasive predator who now threatens to overtake native fish species who have to seek deeper waters to survive. Stories like this allow students to think critically and to consider their lifeworld in a natural way. As a response to this covert approach of teaching sustainability topics through storytelling, another focus group member noted that "This way of using storytelling may be a natural way of introducing the [sustainability] principles to students."

The Learning and Teaching as a Communicative Action (LTCA) theory provides support for interaction with content and idea sharing but also allows for critical reflection and creative self-expressions, leading to building personal agency (Wakefield, Warren, & Alsobrook, 2011, p. 581). A professor teaching three sections of *Introduction to Sociology* focused on social equity and encouraged his students to consider social reflections. He mentioned that the subject was already part of what he would normally teach in his course; however, he additionally incorporated outside readings on food consumption which was new for his teaching. He allowed his students three different choices of assignments where two included having students reflect by telling personal stories through blogging about their growing understanding of, and their lived experiences with, sustainability. One of the two assignments was "Living a Month of Meatless Mondays." He explained:

> Students would opt to have no meat on Monday. They conducted mini-ethnographies where they answered questions such as: "How did people respond to their meatless Mondays?" "What is good affordable food?" "How do people respond when they learn they no longer eat meat?" Someone did a video of cooking with family, a vegetarian paella. Most students did a blog. Students enjoyed the meatless Mondays, but also found it was a challenge.

Another option included a narrative assignment provided by this faculty member. Students chose a local farmer's market and made participant observations. This student-centered assignment was a combination of authentic learning and knowledge-construction. Students answered questions such as "How was the process?" and "What was it like?" Different farmer's markets were different, he acknowledged. Students were in charge and would reflect on their observations at the markets based on their experiences. He reported that, in some instances, the visit to the farmer's markets became family outings. He had one mixed class of traditional college students and ECHS students. He observed that the ECHS students took their parents to the markets. "It was actually a family event and they discussed that."

Critical thinking is a part of problem-based learning, a strategy to help learners "develop flexible knowledge that they can apply to problems" (Hmelo-Silver, 2013, p. 25). The problem-based learning strategy requires learners to learn while solving problems. A professor teaching Environmental Science had been encouraging her students to volunteer for the college recycling program for quite some time. Students pick up trash bins across the college campus and separate out the trash from the recyclables. She said, "They figure out how much is recycling and how much is garbage. They bag it, weigh it, and take it to the bins where it is supposed to go. They don't realize how little recycling actually goes on" until they participate in this activity.

This theme was the largest and in summary captured the sense of story, reflection, and active learning (Fig. 1).

The second theme, *Making Sustainability Learning Visible by Starting with the Text*, emerged from how faculty incorporated sustainability curriculum into their courses. Several of the professors noted that they felt more comfortable including SD in their courses when starting with a textbook that already included a chapter or two on the topic. Subjects taught were in many ways interdisciplinary: Philosophy, Ethics, Health/PE, Geology, ESOL, and Visual Communications. Students read from the text and then discussed the topics, either in the classroom or on online discussion boards. Some faculty would also supplement the reading by adding news articles or research papers to share real-world scenarios and implications from sustainability.

An English as Second Language and Yoga faculty member who interviewed individually, identified herself as a sustainability veteran who began incorporating

Fig. 1. Volunteer students gathered recycle bins from around campus. The contents were separated, weighed, and students determined actual recycles, compared to the trash placed in these bins..

Left: Bags of trash and recyclable after students separated out trash. *Right:* Students using a scale to weigh trash. Photos by Carrie Schweitzer.

sustainability in her courses about 30 years ago when she was working at University of Oregon on an environmental team. In her teaching, she noted,

> I purposefully choose textbooks that have chapters that lend themselves to sustainability. I also bring in materials from the outside research. For example, in my Yoga class, I try to stop them from drinking brown soda. I bring articles about the dangers of the ingredients that are in brown soda. I talk about the dangers of harmful chemicals in cleaners, hand sanitizers, pollution, and about the water quality, wherever you are, and they get shocked by that.

A professor teaching ECHS students about health and nutrition shared that she had "one whole chapter on pollutions" and that she spent a lot of time discussing environmental health with her students. She noted that talking about "nutrition easily ties to meat production" which sparked questions about whether it is realistic to stop eating meat.

Teaching both Philosophy and Ethics, a professor noted that he included three weeks of sustainability in his Introduction to Ethics course and two weeks in his Introduction to Philosophy course toward the end of the semester. His were selected readings and discussion forums for the students on environmental philosophy, a topic that bridged both subjects. He noted, "The gist of students appeared to be *more* interested." He added that for his next iteration he would try not to have the sustainability assignments so late in the course to avoid student energy loss, as tends to happen when finals are moving closer.

In summary, this theme captured students' reflective thinking after reading a text or assigned articles, thereafter, discussing these either in the classroom or on forums providing their insight.

The third theme *Making Sustainability Learning Visible through Reflective Papers* was closely related to the first theme in that it had students reveal their thinking. Two of the faculty had their students reflect through paper submissions and on blogs. The sociology faculty mentioned earlier provided his students the option to conduct a thematic review of literature. His students were asked to find research on food consumption and to do a mini-literature review. A faculty member included the 17 UN goals in his Texas Government course as a course banner to raise students' curiosity and spark questions. As a signature assignment, students were to write a policy paper about health, voter protection, or similar; however, because of the emphasis on sustainability at BHC, the social science department also included a choice for an environmental topic. He reported that "40% of students chose the environmental topic. They wrote about things like fracking, in part because we created an environment conducive to them doing it." This faculty member also offered students an extra credit opportunity to author a paper on any two of the UN SD goals.

In summary, this theme captured thinking about and responding to literature and real-world events related to sustainability and responding through reflective and scholarly writing.

The Essence of the TSMP Experience

At the center of the faculty sustainability teaching experience were concerns for the future, a drive to share awareness with learners of our fragile world, and a need to encourage students to take action for their own sake as well their children and grandchildren. The essence of the experience emerged through comments such as the following:

> Our mother Earth is in danger of extinction through our actions. If they want life as they know it: being able to breathe, having plenty of water to drink, to continue then, it is important that they get involved. They themselves and their children and children's children will inhabit what we leave behind.

Another eloquently put comment was: "It's important [that we incorporate sustainability in the curriculum] because we have a problem that we cannot fix before we educate everyone. Education is the perfect place to start." Another faculty added "We are preparing them for more than our discipline. Any time we can do something in our classroom that helps them be better citizens for our planet ... that is important." Yet another professor noted that "[it is important to] tailor course to student's background, based on needs, interests, and cultural understanding – culturally relative [as it will be meaningful and memorable to the students]." Another noted about incorporating sustainability in the curriculum that

> I think it has raised the level of social responsibility. Students' awareness of their responsibility socially, sustaining our resources, things that they can do on a daily basis such as not using plastic straws, or not using disposable water bottles, but get one that they can re-fill....

SUMMARY OF THEMES

A sustainable future must grow from a changed mindset to one of critical thinking, problem-solving, and continuous learning and practice. Ritchhart and Perkins (2008) provided six main anchors for what they called "salient thinking," that is, bringing thinking out into the open for others to critique, discuss, and learn from. The authors argued that (p. 58):

- Learning is a consequence of thinking.
- Good thinking is not only a matter of skills, but also a matter of dispositions.
- The development of thinking is a social endeavor.
- Fostering thinking requires making thinking visible.
- Classroom culture sets the tone for learning and shapes what is learned.
- Schools must be cultures of thinking for teachers.

Additionally, Ritchhart, Church, and Morrison (2011) noted that "for thinking to occur students must first have something to think about and be asked to think" (p. 30). Providing students with a starting point to think about SD through a curricular innovation was also the method chosen by TSMP faculty. And, at the essence of the instructors' experience was the concern about the future and their fundamental need to encourage students to take action for their own sake as well as future generations.

The three themes emerged from the data illuminate how TSMP faculty incorporated sustainability curriculum in their courses:

Theme 1: Making Sustainability Learning Visible Through Story and Participatory Action

This theme emerged from faculty sharing stories with their students related to sustainability but also from students sharing their own stories and thoughts. Here we also found students engaging in participatory events such as volunteering for opportunities where they were directly exposed to sustainability initiatives.

Theme 2: Making Sustainability Learning Visible by Starting with the Text

This theme emerged from how faculty incorporated sustainability curriculum in their courses. This was most often done by starting with the textbook and then adding additional, current, and significant readings for students to ponder. This allowed students to go beyond the textbook and learn from more recent research and events to give them a better idea of current reality. One of the professors mentioned students would become "astonished" by this reality.

Theme 3: Making Sustainability Learning Visible through Reflective Paper Submissions Toward a Changed Mindset

This theme included students' considerations and thinking around sustainability. Students reflected on blogs and authored papers and literature reviews to dive deeper into learning about sustainability topics they had often not considered before.

LIMITATIONS, IMPLICATIONS, AND OUTCOMES

This research study provides a snapshot from Brookhaven Community College, where faculty were actively engaged in sustainability teaching. The snapshot was taken after 10 faculty members incorporated a semester of sustainability curriculum in the FLC TSMP pilot project. The TSMP model was designed by self-selected faculty who agreed to incorporate sustainability assignments into their course curriculum. These faculty members wanted to open dialogues about SD and have their students contemplate and discuss relevant, real-world issues toward a changed mindset – a new view toward a sustainable world. This project included student engagement in authentic learning to provide a crossroad between textbook learning and addressing hands-on issues in the near environment. In several instances, thinking and authentic learning became truly visible as students not only discussed issues in the classroom but also volunteered to engage in authentic learning through volunteering and service-learning.

The TSMP at BHC and its sustainability FLC represent one model to introduce real-world sustainability learning to students at different levels taking classes in a variety of topics. At BHC, faculty approached the incorporation of sustainability curriculum either overtly or covertly in an effort to engage and change students' mindset – the attitudes and awareness of students – about our changing world while also encouraging sustainability efforts. This was accomplished by promoting sustainability using knowledge co-creation, inquiry-based learning, student-centered learning, participatory, and authentic learning strategies. These types of strategies reside in the constructivist paradigm, where instructor–teaching methods facilitates active knowledge-construction toward a personal change of mindset in the learner toward personal understanding and comprehension of sustainability.

The findings show how a sustainability FLC may emerge when interested, engaged, and determined faculty volunteer to try meet the goal of serving students with a sustainability-infused curriculum. More research studies that share the design, work, and outcome of voluntary faculty curricular innovations toward sustainability are needed. Specifically, studies that describe the process, method, and outcomes would be valuable so that others may replicate initiatives.

At BHC faculty continue to work on teaching sustainability, and a new district-wide initiative is underway: "Reframing the Curriculum." Campus facilitators train their own faculty on how to integrate SD topics and assessments in a diverse spectrum of courses. As time progresses, BHC educators strive to have more faculty participate in the FLC intertwining sustainability themes into curriculum for the benefit of informed and inspired learners who think critically and act on the social, economic, and environmental implications of sustainability.

ACKNOWLEDGMENTS

The authors wish to recognize Terry DiPaolo for encouraging the research, Carrie Schweitzer and the "Brookhaven College Teaching and Sustainability Mini Pilot faculty" collectively, and this book's chapter peer reviewers, as well as Linda McSwain, and Anna H. Wakefield for assisting with proofreading and suggestions for improvements.

NOTES

1. See https://www.aacu.org/core_commitments
2. Windmill garden: https://www.brookhavencollege.edu/aboutbhc/sustainability/pages/the-windmill-garden.aspx

REFERENCES

AASHE. (2010). Sustainability curriculum in higher education: A call to action. Retrieved from https://eric.ed.gov/?id=ED537521. Accessed on March 23, 2019.

Adams, C. A. (2013). Sustainability reporting and performance management in universities. *Sustainability Accounting, Management and Policy Journal*, *4*(3), 384–392.

Adams, C. A. (2018). Debate: Integrating reporting and accounting for sustainable development across generations by universities. *Public Money & Management*, *38*(5), 332–334. doi:10.1080/09540962.2018.1477580

Bloom, A. (1991). *The republic of Plato. Translated, with notes, an interpretive essay, and a new introduction*. New York, NY: The Perseus Books Group.

Colaizzi, P. (1978). Psychological research as the phenomenologist views it. In R. Valle & M. Kings (Eds.), *Existential phenomenological alternative for psychology* (pp. 48–71). New York, NY: Oxford University Press.

Cox, M. D. (1999). Peer consultation and faculty learning communities. *New Directions for Teaching and Learning*, *1999*(79), 39–49.

Creswell, J. W. (2013). *Qualitative inquiry & research design: Choosing among five approaches* (3rd ed.). Thousand Oaks, CA: Sage Publications, Inc.

DesJardins, J. R. (2007). *Business, ethics, and the environment: Imagining a sustainable future*. Upper Saddle River, NJ: Pearson Prentice Hall.

Dickinson Community College. (2019, March 23). Sustainability curriculum. Retrieved from https://www.dickinson.edu/info/20052/sustainability/2219/sustainability_courses

Djordjevic, A., & Cotton, D. R. E. (2011). Communicating the sustainability message in higher education institutions. *International Journal of Sustainability in Higher Education*, *12*(4), 381–394. doi:10.1108/14676371111168296

Dmochowski, J. E., Garofalo, D., Fisher, S., Greene, A., & Gambogi, D. (2016). Integrating sustainability across the university curriculum. *International Journal of Sustainability in Higher Education*, *17*(5), 652–670. doi:10.1108/IJSHE-10-2014-0154

Estrella Mountain Community College. (2019, March 23). Sustainability in the curriculum. Retrieved from https://www.estrellamountain.edu/sustainability/curriculum

Fisher, P. B., & McAdams, E. (2015). Gaps in sustainability education: The impact of higher education coursework on perceptions of sustainability. *International Journal of Sustainability in Higher Education*, *16*(4), 407–720. doi:10.1108/IJSHE-08-2013-0106

Hmelo-Silver, C. (2013). Creating a learning space in problem-based learning. *Interdisciplinary Journal of Problem-based Learning*, *7*(1), 24–39.

Husserl, E. (1962). Ideas: General introduction to pure phenomenology. New York, NY: Collier Books.

LEAP Texas. (2019a). Core objectives. Retrieved from http://leaptx.org/coreobjectives/social-responsibility/

Natkin, L. W., & Kolbe, T. (2015). Enhancing sustainability curricula through faculty learning communities. *International Journal of Sustainability in Higher Education*, *17*(4), 540–558.

Onondaga Community College. (2019, March 23). Sustainability in the curriculum. Retrieved from http://www.sunyocc.edu/index.aspx?menu=91&collside=489&id=28275

President's Sustainability Committee. (2019, March 23). Retrieved from https://bit.ly/2Z4JxRA

Reid, A., & Petocz, P. (2006). University lecturers' understanding of sustainability. *Higher Education*, *51*(1), 105–123. doi:10.1007/s10734-004-6379-4

Ritchhart, R., Church, M., & Morrison, K. (2011). *Making thinking visible: How to promote engagement, understanding, and independence for all learners*. San Francisco, CA: Jossey-Bass.

Ritchhart, R., & Perkins, D. (2008). Making thinking visible. *Educational Leadership*, *65*(5), 57–61.

Stubbs, W., & Schapper, J. (2011). Two approaches to curriculum development for educating for sustainability and CSR. *International Journal of Sustainability in Higher Education*, *12*(3), 259–268. doi:10.1108/14676371111148045

United Nations Commission on Environment and Development. (1987). The Brundtland Report (Report Chapter 2). Retrieved from https://en.wikisource.org/wiki/Brundtland_Report/Chapter_2._Towards_Sustainable_Development

University Leaders for a Sustainable Future (ULSF). (2015). About. Retrieved from http://ulsf.org/about/#history. Accessed on March 17, 2019.

Wals, A. E. J., & Blewitt, J. (2010). Third-wave sustainability in higher education: Some (Inter)national trends and developments. In P Jones, D. Selbye, & S. Sterling (Eds.). *Sustainability education perspectives and practice across higher education* (pp. 55–72). New York, NY: Earthscan, Taylor and Francis.

Wakefield, J. S., Warren, S. J., & Alsobrook, M. (2011). Learning and teaching as communicative actions: A mixed-methods Twitter study. *Knowledge Management & E-Learning: An International Journal*, *3*(4), 563–584.

CHAPTER 11

STUDY CIRCLE AS AN INNOVATIVE TOOL FOR PROMOTING LIFELONG LEARNING AND COMMUNITY EMPOWERMENT

Gwadabe Kurawa

ABSTRACT

The United Nations Sustainable Development Goal 4 aimed at ensuring an inclusive, equitable, quality education, and promoting lifelong learning opportunities for all. However, this may not be effectively realized, as this chapter demonstrates, through formal learning or education alone. Rather, an adoption of non-formal and informal learning alongside formal learning is more likely to empower the general population to contribute toward the development of a sustainable society. This chapter therefore critically examines the concepts of lifelong learning and the learning society and suggests that community learning, or study circles, can be a promising institutional medium for the promotion of adult and lifelong learning. The rationale for establishing a study circle as a medium for lifelong learning is demonstrated through case studies from Zimbabwe and Sweden. This follows by comparing and contrasting the ways in which Sweden and Zimbabwe promote lifelong learning for all.

Keywords: Sustainable Development Goals; Millennium Development Goals; lifelong learning; learning society; study circles; sustainable society; education; community learning

Teaching and Learning Strategies for Sustainable Development:
Innovations in Higher Education Teaching and Learning, Volume 19, 159–175

ISSN: 2055-3641/doi:10.1108/S2055-364120200000019014

INTRODUCTION

The United Nations (UN) Sustainable Development Goals (SDGs) respond to the topics on economic growth, social development, and environmental sustainability (UN, 2015a). The 17 SDGs are further broken down into 169 targets. United Nations Educational, Scientific and Cultural Organization (UNESCO, 2017) has articulated learning objectives for the 17 SDGs and the activities needed to realize them. This chapter focuses only on SDG 4 – meeting the needs of children, young persons, and adults. The argument in this chapter is that lifelong learning for all is a basic feature of SDG 4 and study circles are an important vehicle for promoting lifelong learning to empower those at the margins of the society in both developed and developing countries.

The chapter is organized as follows: It begins with an overview of SDGs and lifelong learning. The concept of "learning society" is then discussed under a separate section, and focused on three different perspectives identified in the literature. This is followed by a description of study circle as an innovative approach for promoting lifelong learning and empowering those living at the margins of the society. The discussion on study circles continues with two case studies from Zimbabwe and Sweden and provides concluding thoughts after analyzing the link between Adult Learning and Education (ALE) and SDG 4 targets.

SUSTAINABLE DEVELOPMENT GOALS

In September 2016, the UNESCO Institute for Lifelong Learning (UIL) brought together international professionals to analyze the value of SDGs for lifelong learning, and to explore the possibilities and limitations of education as a facilitator of sustainability and development. This commences with the UN 2030 Agenda for Sustainable Development, referred to as "Transforming our World," which acknowledges the important role of lifelong learning in achieving sustainable development (UN, 2015a). Among the 17 SDGs specified in the Agenda SDG 4, with its associated 10 targets, urges Member States to "ensure inclusive and equitable quality education and promote lifelong learning opportunities for all" (UN, 2016).

It is important to note that prior to the 17 SDGs, there have long been global activities and support for lifelong learning as essential to development. For example, Education for All (World Education Forum (WEF), 2000) and the Millennium Development Goals (MDGs) (UN, 2015b) already foregrounded the existing agenda of the SDGs and argued for the centrality of a lifelong learning approach in attending to environmental and social problems. In addition to this, and in the same year 2015, UNESCO identified not only lifelong learning as one of the bedrocks of its own new agenda – the Education 2030 Framework for Action – but has also made efforts to promote lifelong learning as an essential component of the SDGs (UNESCO, 2017).

This ambitious UN 2030 plan, "Transforming our World," increased the number of goals, from the initial eight in the MDGs, formulated in 2000 to be achieved by 2015, to 17 SDGs to be realized by 2030. Education, under this

UN 2030 agenda, was also elected as a specific development goal (UN, 2015a). Thus, the focus of education was expanded from schooling to lifelong learning, where adult education, higher education, and technical education become part of the continuum supported by the global education community in the realization of sustainability. It is interesting to note that although the MDGs generally focused on Global South, the SDGs target all nations across the world.

In particular, the formulation of SDG 4 resulted from a two-year consultation process involving international experts in the field of education and Member States in transforming the future education plan. These discussions lead to the WEF, which met in Incheon, Republic of Korea, in May 2015. The meeting resulted in a document entitled Education 2030 (UNESCO, 2016a), which comprises both the Incheon Declaration and the Education 2030 Framework for Action.

The aim of these statements is to aid the implementation of SDG 4. SDG 4 also specified some learning objectives for all SDGs to be achieved by 2030 (see Education for Sustainable Development Goals: Learning Objectives, UNESCO, 2017) This chapter focuses on SDG 4, but will not discuss the interplay between SDG 4 and other 16 SDGs, in addressing the needs of those at the margins of the society. The notion of lifelong learning for all is a core feature of SDG 4.

LIFELONG LEARNING

The UIL, in an effort to provide leadership, has worked across and with many countries to provide guidance and encourage nations to commit to SDG 4 (UNESCO, 2016a). UIL has long been engaged with the plan of lifelong learning through a number of its programs supporting literacy, policy development, adult learning, and education. This concern with lifelong learning is explained in two seminal reports: Learning to be: The World of Education Today and Tomorrow (Faure et al., 1972) and Learning: The Treasure Within (Delors et al., 1996), UIL, which is the only UN agency assigned with the responsibility for lifelong learning, collates and categorizes data on national lifelong learning policies and strategies, researches lifelong learning across the globe, and collaborates with countries in their attempts to promote learning. UIL has an online Collection of Lifelong Learning Policies and Strategies, which are accessible online, and these collections are worthy of commendation in terms leadership on promoting this global agenda (see e.g., Daniele & Raul, 2018; Yang & Yorozu, 2015; Yorozu, 2017, which are the latest books in the series). This chapter draws on the conceptualization of lifelong learning in these publications UIL describes lifelong learning as:

> rooted in the integration of learning and living, covering learning activities for people of all ages (children, young people, adults and the elderly, girls and boys, women and men) in all life-wide contexts (homes, schools, workplace and community among others) and through a variety of modalities (formal, non-formal and informal) which together meet a wide range of learning needs and demands…. (UIL, 2015, p. 2)

This definition of lifelong learning, which reflects emancipatory, humanistic, and democratic values, is now viewed as “a philosophy, a conceptual framework and an organising principle of all forms of education" (UIL, 2010, p. 5) which is "intended to improve people's quality of life" (UNESCO, 2016b, p. 9). Meanwhile, WEF suggests that:

> to complement and supplement formal schooling, broad and flexible lifelong learning opportunities should be provided through non-formal pathways with adequate resources and mechanisms and through stimulating informal learning, including through use of ICT. (WEF, 2016, p. 30)

It follows from the above that SDG 4 generally is intended to ensure the provision of equitable educational opportunities from a holistic and lifelong learning point of view. It aims at helping children, youth, and adults to successfully complete compulsory basic education resulting in good and pertinent learning outcomes which may serve as a foundation of lifelong learning. This broader scope of SDG 4 also seeks to provide equal opportunities in terms of access to non-formal, and informal education and training opportunities for individuals for the span of their life.

This form of learning throughout life or lifelong learning opportunities should, the SDG 4 further advised, be provided to all age groups, including adults, beginning at early childhood "in all settings and at all levels of education" (WEF, 2016, p. 33). Conversely, such forms of learning "should be embedded in education systems" through

> [...] the provision of multiple and flexible learning pathways and entry points and re-entry points at all ages and all educational levels, strengthened links between formal and non-formal structures, and recognition, validation and accreditation of the knowledge, skills and competencies acquired through non-formal and informal education. (WEF, 2016, p. 33)

This holistic method points to the economic, cultural and other resources required to make learning happen both inside and outside formal learning settings (like e.g., schools and community centers). This chapter is guided by this definition of lifelong learning in a learning society that enhances learning for all.

LEARNING SOCIETY

The concept of the learning society is elusive and contested, as there are many definitions and perspectives attributed to it. As such, this chapter focuses on three perspectives of the learning society identified by Ranson, Rikowski, Nixon, Mckeown, and Butterfield (1995). The first perspective sees the learning society largely focusing on skills development for the labor market (Rikowski, Ainley, & Ranson, 1996). The authors on argue that this is a limited economic perspective that enjoyed considerable support from national and international businesses and governments with their "skills revolution" and by commentators who conceive the learning society mainly as a means to achieve economic growth and employability. The "society" component in this view is, they conclude, substituted for by "economy." This view reflects Human Capital theory which is focused on people's competences and qualities acquired through education and learning which promote productivity.

The second interpretation of learning society paid more attention to effective knowledge for work (Cooley, 1993). The emphasis here is on the potential role of modern information technologies in producing satisfying work and for companies to be infused with democratic processes (Rikowski et al., 1996). This assumption is somewhat similar to the first one. They both suggested that the possibility of succeeding to function in the society by individuals is by getting paid employment. This implied that economic inclusion addresses social exclusion and education plays a major role in shaping how individuals lead their adult life. This is a fixed and accepted notion of normal life, which overlooks how, often, inclusion is problematic.

Of course, people are also interested in non-economic returns on learning with regard to health, life satisfaction, and civic participation. The latter is one prerequisite to social cohesion and functioning citizenship at a societal level and therefore a factor of high political and societal relevance (Ruber, Rees, & Schmidt-Hertha, 2018). This resonates with the third definition considers the learning society as a society which integrates learning for citizenship (Ranson, 1994). This form of learning encourages, Ranson (1994) argues, active involvement in the community and accumulation of human capital. It is learning for life through active participation in social life itself throughout the lifetime of the learner (Ranson, 1994). This is the view of learning society adopted in this chapter. Put simply, the question of how we can build a learning society is asked. WEF (2016), UIL (2015), and Ranson et al. (1995) acknowledge several aspects requiring development. One such aspect – the development of community learning (one of the lifelong learning systems) – is examined below.

STUDY CIRCLE

The study circle is an innovative approach aimed at addressing adult learning and the problems and issues those adults face daily, and empowering those who are perceived as disadvantaged in a society (Oliver, 1987). However, before presenting the features of a study circle and the manner of its operation, this chapter briefly analyses the notion of empowerment. Empowerment is, Wallerstein and Bernstein (1988) contend, a process of social action that promotes participation by individuals and groups with the aim of improving their lives and solving problems that are important in their communities.

However, this interpretation differs from that adopted in the discourse of the new capitalism. For example, a chief executive officer (CEO) of a company may be sanctioned by the board directors of the company to make cuts, leading to the redundancy of certain members of staff. The CEO, and perhaps other corporate employees, may be seduced into performing better by bonus payments tied to their performance results. In this sense, empowerment can also be interpreted as exploitation. This chapter "opposes the reduction of the term (empowerment) as it is used in the current fashion of individual self-assertion, upward mobility and the psychological experience of feeling privileged" (Lather, 1991, p. 3). Empowerment is therefore conceived in this chapter "to mean analysing ideas about the causes of powerlessness, recognising systematic oppressive forces, and acting both individually and collectively to change the conditions of our lives" (Lather, 1991, p. 4). It is important to note here that this interpretation of empowerment closely correlates with the study circle characteristics described below.

As initially stated, study circles are a simple, effective, and manageable method for promoting lifelong community learning (Oliver, 1987) in both developed and developing countries, as will be shown in this chapter. Study circles comprise an informal group of five to 10 members interacting in a democratic and participatory manner (Leighninger, 1996). Members voluntarily and collectively meet frequently in order to study and learn about specific social or political issues affecting their lives (Brevskolan, 1980). The three aspects of shared learning, respect for individual views, and equal membership of the group act not only to promote dialogue, bring new insights, and create new knowledge but can also increase the confidence of individuals and communities who have long been oppressed and marginalized. In addition, members study at their own pace and utilize their individual experiences and knowledge (Christie, 1998). Group members organize the study circle meetings and take responsibility for facilitating them (Oliver, 1987). The participants also select and process the reading material according to their individual and group needs and simultaneously learn how to utilize the shared knowledge and seek more information (Brevskolan, 1980). The materials used during the meetings must be directly relevant to the communities and reflect local content as much as possible, with the ultimate aim of contributing toward improving and enriching their lives and social conditions.

Another important point to note here is that study circles differ from conventional forms of schooling (Brevskolan, 1980). Competition between students, demands for academic achievement and teacher-centered pedagogy are not followed. Although some study circle institutions, such as Folk High Schools (FHS) in Sweden, receive financial support from government, courses offered by FHS rarely lead to qualifications (Christie, 1998). Studies undertaken through study circles in FHS are based on the presumption that the circle members have an inherent desire to learn (Brevskolan, 1980). The increase in knowledge and improved ability of the members to understand relevant social problems and interact with their surrounding world are perceived to be sufficient benefits (Brevskolan, 1980). As such, the circles do not require a formal setting, such as a classroom, as members can meet wherever they deem appropriate: members' homes, a rural library, under a tree, or at a community center (Oliver, 1987). They are also flexible in relation to timing and can be organized around the schedules of the group members. The resources required to set up a study circle are not extensive.

In summary, study circles can be described as a process through which participants gain an enhanced understanding or insight into the issues under consideration. Through their studies, participants acquire the skills to put their lives into perspective and examine issues within a wider social context (Brevskolan, 1980). The origin of the study circle concept is discussed in case study 2, which considers study circles in Sweden, but the chapter turns firstly to case study 1 below which examines the manner in which a study circle was established in Zimbabwe.

CASE STUDY 1: ZIMBABWE

Study Circles in Zimbabwe

The population of Zimbabwe exceeds 14 million (UN World Population Prospects, 2019b). Recent estimates suggest that during the years 2011–2017 extreme poverty may have risen by one half, from 22.5 percent to 33 percent. This figure will be far greater in rural areas. Welfare inequality also rose from 43 percent in 2011 to 45 percent in 2017, with low social service delivery outcomes in rural areas resulting in severe spatial poverty traps. Moreover, various economic and political events in late 2018 and early 2019 may have led to the further impoverishment of the population, with rapid food price inflation potentially increasing the proportion of food insecure people to 51 percent (ZIMVAC, 2019). Growing difficulties for rural residents in accessing formal learning and education, driven by high transport costs and a severe contraction in the real wages of public servants, are excluding a growing proportion of the population from essential services.

It is reported that significant international aid has been received by Zimbabwe for many years since its independence in 1980 (Naido, 2001). Nevertheless, the poor and marginalized people in the country have benefitted minimally from such donor assistance as a result of increasing corruption and gross mismanagement. This is responsible, Naido (2001) claims, for the existence of widening inequality between socioeconomic groups and a significant rise in the proportion of families at risk of poverty or social exclusion. As a result, a loss of enthusiasm has been seen among many Zimbabweans toward participating in discussions surrounding socioeconomic, political, and environmental issues, as well as diminished confidence in addressing such social problems either as individuals or communities. Consequently, some community initiatives have been developed to increase the participation of marginalized individuals and rural communities in discussions concerning their social problems and to promote sustainable and democratic development in the country (Naido, 2001). The study circle is one such initiative.

Naido (2001) analyzed the study circle set up by the Africa Book Development Trust (ABDT) in 1997. The program, which was initially introduced to marginalized rural communities in the Matabeleland South and Midlands Provinces, is based on the philosophy that communities should be trained to develop such skills and knowledge as would allow them to discuss and understand their own social problems. The training, in the form of a study circle, commences by involving communities in village- and ward-level workshops. These workshops are organized by the ABDT and utilize the experiences of the participants to stimulate debate and encourage active participation by the members. Members typically meet weekly in community centers and local clinics, or in the homes of participants. The participants select study materials relevant to poverty alleviation, wealth creation, community development, and civic education. Civic education materials receive a positive reaction as the participants are thereby enabled to debate such topics as democracy, governance, and human rights – all significant issues in Zimbabwe.

On the other hand, the workshops in Gokwe North focused on agriculture since those communities were more interested in learning about cattle marketing, grazing, dip tanks, and farming. In meeting the needs of the communities, the ABDT provided relevant study materials to all workshop participants. The participants particularly appreciated the language and content of the materials concerned with cattle rearing since cattle have special significance not only in Zimbabwe but also in many African societies, both materially and culturally. Through this study circle workshop, the participants in Gokwe North were able to resolve cattle-related problems encompassed within their study materials. This prompted them also to occasionally contact their local veterinary office for support.

In addition, the study circles workshop brought about improvements in community relationships and welfare. For example, another study circle in Gokwe North focused its discussions on the problem of unsafe drinking water and the participants were able to propose measures to address the problem. Prior to the workshops, these communities lacked the knowledge and confidence to freely express their concerns surrounding community-related problems. Their participation in study circles acted to increase their knowledge and confidence to discuss important issues and to formulate strategies through which to overcome their problems. The study circle program also potentially helps the participants to develop and set up income-generating activities in their villages, as they learn such specific skills as poultry farming and carpentry (Naido, 2001).

Summing up the views of the ABDT on the study circle pedagogical approach provides an innovative channel through which to distribute civic education resources to marginalized communities (Naido, 2001). This is, Naido (2001) concludes, needed more especially in Global South countries, such as Zimbabwe, where civic education has received little attention and has only been provided through nationwide civic education workshops. The workshops provide an effective mechanism through which to share information widely and the shared learning approach, or study circle, enables participants to study at their own pace and provides them with sufficient opportunities to thoroughly discuss civic issues. Case study 2 includes a discussion of how civic issues have also been discussed in study circles in Sweden.

CASE STUDY 2: SWEDEN

Study Circles in Sweden

The current population of Sweden is a little over 10 million (UN World Population Prospects, 2019a). The country has for quite some time had an international reputation for having developed a welfare regime based on the principles of social equality, solidarity, and democracy. It also has an international reputation for its generous immigration policies as well as for its social inclusion of migrants. This will be discussed later in the chapter after an explanation of how the study circle concept developed in Sweden.

The study circle concept is widely linked to civic movements in Sweden in the 1890s (Christie, 1998). The movement for the study circle in Sweden started as a result of the failure of the government to alleviate the suffering of its population from rural poverty, overpopulation in cities, illiteracy, inequality, a rise in alcohol consumption, and threats of civil disturbances (Torstensson, 1994).

These social problems stem from rapid industrial changes witnessed by Sweden during the 1890s (Torstensson, 1994). These changes forced many Swedes to move from rural areas to cities, and even to other countries, seeking employment (Torstensson, 1994). The changes also led to the formation of many trade unions and the Social Democratic Party in 1889 (Torstensson, 1994). Equally, some of the trade unions established libraries financed by endowments, union fees, and other related fees (Torstensson, 1994). What is interesting is that the libraries were considered as an alternative way of supporting the working classes to attain education upon leaving the "folkskola," or elementary school (Torstensson, 1994). Initially, the government tried to encourage its citizens, especially the working class, to meet and study together so as to reduce the spread of alcohol consumption (Christie, 1998).

This idea of meeting and studying together – later known as a study circle – was spread and promoted throughout Sweden by Oscar Olsson from 1902 onward within the workers' libraries (Torstensson, 1994). The meeting and study rooms, as discussed previously, differed from those seen with traditional forms of schooling (Torstensson, 1994). The acceptance of the study circle by the working classes led to the creation of 254 study circle libraries operating in Sweden in 1917 (Torstensson, 1994). The Swedish Parliament had approved formal funding for these libraries in 1912 (Oliver, 1987).

The popularity and spread of study circles in Sweden were credited to the Swedish concept of "folkbildning." The term "folkbildning," as coined by the Swedish citizens themselves, and as interpreted in much literature, denotes the unequivocal importance of education and knowledge for all and their link to the development of society as a whole. The word is an amalgam of two smaller words, "folk" and "bildning." "Bildning" is translated in English as "learning" while "folk" typically refers to "people." Upon combining these two words, "folkbildning" can be literally translated as the Swedish form of "non-formal adult education." Folkbildning is a loose label often used in the Swedish language to describe lifelong learning as an "integrating alternative" to class conflict and confrontation between the upper and lower classes; Torstensson (1994) reports on how this happened by analyzing three different views of class in Sweden in the 1890s.

The first is the socialist emancipatory view of "folkbildning," which suggests that workers should enlighten themselves and increase their knowledge base in order to become moderate in their judgment of matters affecting their lives and their country (Torstensson, 1994, p. 2). Second is the liberal view of "folkbildning," which recognized that Swedish society in the 1890s was divided between the educated upper class (bildade) and the undereducated lower class (obildade); coupled with swift cultural changes at the time, this division could have led to social problems. Thus, the "bildade" took their social responsibility to the "obildade" by supporting voluntary forms of education for the working class, who would regularly agitate for revolution, in order for the "obildade" to become responsible and do that which was objectively judged to be in the best interests of society as a whole rather than engage in social unrest. Implicitly, "Folkbildning" in this sense is correlated with establishing a reciprocal relationship between the "bildade" and "obildade" through education.

In addition to this, factory owners copied the trade unions by establishing their own libraries aimed at circumventing possible conflict and confrontation with workers who might be provoked by the swift changes occurring at the time (Torstensson, 1994). This is the third and conservative view of "folkbildning," which attempts to include the working class in building on the progress made in preserving social order and which in turn sustains the rule and privileges of the upper class.

It follows from the above that Swedish folkbildning is the collective name for the activities organized by the country's Study Associations and FHS. FHS, as shown in the preceding paragraphs, have long existed in Sweden; indeed dating back to the 1880s. FHS deviate from the espoused ideals of conventional schools. Presently, in Sweden there are approximately 155 FHS offering both short and long courses accessible to 30,000 or more students each year (Fejes, Dahlstedt, Olson, & Sandberg, 2018). The program of studies and activities conducted by FHS are neither initiated by the Swedish government nor organized from the top (Oliver, 1987). The sessions and studies (teaching as referred to in conventional schools) in FHS are delivered in the form of study circles. This pedagogical approach, as discussed earlier, is experience based, collaborative in nature, and promotes a democratic relationship between members of the group. Although FHS are very concerned about competition and demands for academic achievement, fewer FHS offer courses that lead to qualifications (Christie, 1998). This type of reward is more apparent in the other major adult education institution in Sweden, Municipal Adult Education (MAE).

The MAE initiative was set up in 1968 and has developed over time (Dahlstedt & Fejes, 2019). MAE follows traditional forms of schooling and consists of three different forms of education: compulsory and upper secondary school levels, special education for adults and Swedish education for immigrants. These forms of education are mostly managed by the municipal authorities but are also partly run by non-governmental organizations receiving financial support from the government (Christie, 1998). The education largely focuses on skills development for the labor market and the teaching and learning processes are similar to those observed in formal schooling. It is estimated that more than 10,000 students are enrolled in these types of schooling every year (Fejes et al., 2018). The school programs also offer some form of certification as part of the formal education system (Fejes et al., 2018). The aim of this formal education system is to increase the adult education students' chances of success when applying for higher education and employment and to prepare them for life as citizens more generally (Dahlstedt & Fejes, 2019).

A research project focusing on this citizenship education provision in FHS and MAE in Sweden was presented by Fejes et al. (2018). This study examined a particular FHS maintained by a county council situated in a mid-sized Swedish urban area. A range of courses was offered including basic courses, vocational courses, cultural courses, and commissioned courses. A number of prospective students applied for these programs and they were routinely offered study places. The MAE institution, on the other hand, was located in a large Swedish town and managed by a municipality. The students at the FHS and MAE were both male and female and derived from different ethnic and social backgrounds. They were mostly young adults that were either unemployed or employed on zero-hour contracts. Fejes et al. examined these students' lives as citizens and their experiences in the FHS and MAE institutions. The study also examined teachers' perceptions of their teaching practices and motivations in the institutions. The key findings reached include, normalization, role modeling, non-belonging, and will-formation. Some of these findings are briefly discussed in the next section.

DISCUSSION OF ALE AND THE SDG 4 TARGETS

This section examines how ALE brings about social change by comparing the use of the study circles, or community learning (henceforth these terminologies will be used interchangeably), implemented in Sweden and Zimbabwe.

Zimbabwe is a country where previously (and even presently) there have been serious reports on welfare inequality, lack of access to formal learning and education, and extreme mismanagement, corruption and poverty. These problems are resulting in increasing apathy and loss of confidence among the majority of Zimbabweans to participate in development processes, especially in the Matabeleland South and Midlands Provinces which benefit least from society (Naido, 2001). Transforming this society into an equal society requires, as Lather (1991) suggests, heightened consciousness and collective action. The aim of community learning was to increase the awareness of the marginalized and disadvantaged citizens in the provinces of democracy, governance, and human rights (Naido, 2001). On the other hand, Sweden is a diverse country with (as stated earlier) comparatively better social welfare, fewer cases of discrimination toward ethnic minorities and fewer social problems surrounding race, class, and immigration. The country continues to support its principles of democracy, social equality, and solidarity by providing equal opportunities to everyone in the country to engage in education. Such education, especially in FHS, is provided in the form of study circles supported by the Swedish government as part of its drive to promote social democracy (Brevskolan, 1980).

It follows from the above that community learning in Zimbabwe and study circles in Sweden were inspired by Oscar Olsson's notion of FHS. Both forms of learning have promoted education for social transformation and education linked to community problems. Learning in both contexts has underscored the importance of learners' experiences and learning in a democratic manner. These points are elaborated upon briefly below.

As discussed in the preceding sections, study circles in Sweden have emerged entirely out of "folkbildning" (Christie, 1998; Torstensson, 1994). Community learning in Zimbabwe meanwhile cannot be linked to social movements originating in the country. Again, while study circles in both Zimbabwe and Sweden were or are run by NGOs (ABDT and Study Associations), community learning in Zimbabwe is comparatively independent of government support, in contrast to the Swedish study circles which are partly financed by the government. Another noticeable difference is that community learning in Zimbabwe has been more concerned with securing social and economic justice through social liberation in the Matabeleland South and Midlands Provinces – the most deprived and isolated communities in the country. Community learning, in this sense, follows a radical approach to adult education, which is interpreted in much literature as a process aimed at correcting injustices, freeing people from oppression, and educating them to take part in decision-making that affects their lives. This means adult education, in the form of community learning, can help local communities in Zimbabwe to transform the social structures of their provinces.

Conversely, the notion of education in the Swedish study circles and the country's approach to social change is strongly linked to humanistic adult education. This is, as conceived in this chapter, more concerned with voluntary forms of education aimed at responding to the needs and concerns of individuals. Individuals can be empowered through social interactions, in non-formal settings, facilitated through shared learning about the root causes of their problems and possible solutions (Oliver, 1987). This also underlines democratic principles and suggests that democracy is likely to be sustained by providing individuals with the skills and opportunities necessary to participate in transforming their social conditions. Unequivocally, this reflects the philosophy of folkbildning which has supported many workers and farmers in the continuation of their education through study circles, and which in turn has enabled the people to bring about some changes in their lives and society (Torstensson, 1994).

It is important to note here the subtle difference between community learning in Zimbabwe and study circles in Sweden. The latter emphasizes "individual empowerment" by providing everyone, irrespective of his/her educational background or social circumstances, with the opportunity to continue with his/her education, such to enable him/her to make a difference to his/her life and society. The former, on the other hand, has focused on "social empowerment" by targeting marginalized, less powerful local communities in Zimbabwe in the Matabeleland South and Midlands provinces. These communities, with their lower social positions, meet and discuss such local issues as poverty alleviation, wealth creation, civic education, unsafe drinking water, and cattle-related problems in an attempt to identify ways in which to overcome the problems. It is clear that "individual" and "social empowerment" are, as shown above, inseparable because they both represent a process that involves social interaction, shared learning, enriching individual life, and social justice (Wallerstein & Bernstein, 1988).

This reaffirms the importance of ALE, as discussed previously, both as a value in itself and as a valuable medium in addressing current global challenges. This suggests that education has enabled both individuals and societies in developed and developing countries to achieve their (SDGs) goals. The challenges ahead are, however, enormous because there are in excess of 700 million adults who can neither read nor write, and an even greater number who have never completed basic education or have no upper secondary education certificate (Croso, 2018).

Considering these huge challenges, this chapter is restricted to an analysis of ALE within the 2030 Sustainable Development plan and the Education 2030 Framework for Action. These plans, described earlier in the chapter, were adopted by Member States in 2015 and include ambitious ALE-related targets that are intended to be achieved between 2015 and 2030. These ALE-related targets are examined in this section. This section also shows how adult community learning and study circles in Zimbabwe and Sweden contribute to SDG 4 targets.

The 2030 Sustainable Development plan and the Education 2030 Framework for Action give ALE a unique global potential as a catalyst for moving development forward. At the 2015 WEF in Incheon, Republic of Korea, Member States committed to ensuring that

> all youth and adults, especially girls and women, achieve relevant and recognized functional literacy and numeracy proficiency levels and acquire life skills, and that they are provided with adult learning, education and training opportunities. (UN, 2016)

The Education 2030 Framework for Action identifies "children, youth and adults" as its major beneficiaries (UNESCO, 2016).

Among the 17 SDGs, SDG 4 is the most strongly linked to ALE. It requests that Member States "ensure inclusive and equitable quality education and promote lifelong learning opportunities for all" (UN, 2016). SDG 4 also has 10 targets, as detailed in the Education 2030 Framework for Action. Five of the targets under SDG 4 that relate directly to ALE are analyzed below.

Target 4.3 urges Member States to ensure that all women and men have equal access to affordable and quality technical, vocational, and tertiary education. The Education 2030 Framework for Action follows through, advising Member States to make available "lifelong learning opportunities for youth and adults" and emphasizing that lifelong learning covers "a variety of modalities: formal, non-formal and informal learning" (UIL, 2015, p. 2). The participation of adults in community learning and study circles in both Zimbabwe and Sweden can be considered an indicator to this SDG 4: target 4.3. Although community learning in Zimbabwe covers only non-formal learning, study circles in FHS and MAE institutions in Sweden encompasses both formal and non-formal education.

Target 4.4 calls on Member States to train youth, women and men with skills for decent jobs. The Education 2030 Framework for Action reminds Member States to provide learners not only with work-specific skills but also with entrepreneurship skills such as problem-solving, creativity, and networking. The Education Framework also cautions the government on the need to provide adult learners with opportunities to upgrade their skills through lifelong learning. Although the related indicator is limited to the information and communications technology skills acquired by many adult learners, the range of subjects, including drama, arts, and music, studied at study circles in both Sweden and Zimbabwe are likely to equip learners with transferable skills too.

Target 4.5 aims to eliminate gender disparities in education and provide equal access to ALE for women and men. The Education 2030 Framework for Action states that parity in education and equal access to ALE should be extended to other vulnerable groups, such as persons with disabilities, indigenous people, and children in vulnerable situations. The participation of marginalized and oppressed people from the Matabeleland and Midlands Provinces in community learning and the provision of free adult education to farmers, the working class, the upper class, and migrants in Sweden are indications of the promotion of equality in education and the extension of access to ALE to everyone, irrespective of educational background or social circumstances. This, however, necessitates the daunting task of establishing parity indices on the basis of disaggregated data for all the indicators related to Goal 4.

Target 4.6 reminds governments to ensure that "all youth and a substantial proportion of adults achieve literacy and numeracy." The Education 2030 Framework for Action draws the attention of Member States to the fact that literacy and numeracy exist on a continuum, suggesting that individuals are literate at different levels. Consequently, the Education 2030 Framework encourages governments to ensure that all individuals achieve literacy and numeracy proficiency equivalent to the successful completion of primary education and lower secondary education. Many local people in Gokwe North (which has an adult illiteracy rate as high as 85 percent) in Zimbabwe, as well as migrants and other undereducated lower class in Sweden, have been or are participating in adult literacy and numeracy programs. Of course, in ABDT '...literacy classes – people who can read, teaching those who can't...' (Lessing, 1999 cited in Naido, 2001, p. 728).

Target 4.7 is focused on education for sustainable development, human rights, gender equality, peace, and global citizenship. As discussed in the two case studies and in this section, ALE has a major effect on these domains. The Education 2030 Framework for Action calls on governments to develop effective guidelines directed narrowly toward curricula and student assessment in schools. This, however, indicates valuing the role played by "all learners" in creating peaceful, healthy, and sustainable societies. The teaching of civic education in study circles, as exemplified in the case studies, may "create spaces for participants to learn across cultures" (Fejes, 2019, p. 244). This in turn may also (re) establish a relationship and understanding between different social classes (Kurawa, 2019). Other scholars have critically problematized the role of ALE in relation to the fostering and shaping of citizens (see Fejes et al., 2018).

To sum up, the 2030 Education Framework and SDG 4 provides a strong political imperative for investment in ALE to improve labor-market outcomes and develop individuals as full citizens, as recapped in the conclusion section.

CONCLUSION

This chapter has shown that study circles and community learning were inspired by the notion of folkbildning, with both being delivered in a democratic manner. The needs and interests, in addition to the existing knowledge, of all individuals are accorded equal respect and are equally considered during study sessions. This form of democratic learning can be, as this chapter has argued, linked to humanistic education and radical education. Education, in the form of study circles, commenced within the context of local communities and considered local issues, conditions, implications, and other locally generated information.

The study circles in the two case studies are also linked to social movements through which the participants can bring about social change. The social change theories followed in the study circles and community learning have however differed as a result of their dissimilar sociocultural contexts and social issues to address, which are visible in the group membership and management of the learning program.

The social context of the Metabeleland South and Midlands Provinces is as the most deprived and isolated regions in the country. During the learning sessions, the participants would have learnt about community development theories and would have taken up a radical approach to education to support their marginalized communities in changing social structure. The learning programs were organized by an NGO, ABDT, and this minimizes government interference in the collective learning and action taken by the participants. On the other hand, the Swedish study circles were founded within a social environment that adopted democratic principles and provided equal opportunities to everyone in the society. The aim of their study circles is the formation of an ideal citizen (Fejes, 2019). This is apparent in the way the program focuses on changing participants' traditional beliefs of who they are and who they should become through education, and on the capacities and skills they must develop in order to become "full" citizens in society (Fejes, 2019). The humanistic approach of the program is reflected in its pedagogy which is experience based, collaborative in nature, and aims to promote an egalitarian relationship between participants. The program is part-financed by the government.

This provides an improved understanding of the two contexts and uncovers the collective actions taken by individuals and communities in their attempts to bring about sustainable social development.

It is important to note that the 2030 SDGs are a major improvement on the MDGs; indeed, while inadequate attention was previously given to ALE, much focus is now given in the 2030 Agenda for Sustainable Development. In particular, the agenda identifies the needs of adults and perhaps other learners, describes different ALE pathways (i.e., formal, non-formal, and informal) and provides an improved understanding of literacy within the framework of lifelong learning. There remains much to be done on the progress of ALE however and the Recommendation on ALE (UNESCO, 2016a) serves as an opening in this regard. The three areas of learning mentioned in the Recommendation – literacy, continuing training and professional development, and active citizenship – reflect SDG targets.

In sum, the Recommendation on ALE, the Education 2030 Framework for Action and the 2030 Sustainable Development agenda are powerful, integrated tools that will drive progress in ALE between 2015 and 2030.

REFERENCES

Brevskolan. (1980). *The study circle: A brief introduction*. Stockholm: Brevskolan.

Christie, M. (1998). Sweden's Folk University. *Australian Journal of Adult and Community Education*, *38*(2), 81–88.

Cooley, M. (1993). Skills and competence. Paper presented to the ILTD 24th national conference, Galway.

Croso, C. (2018). After Dakar, where to from here? The Global Campaign for Education's (GCE) reflections from the GPE Financing Conference and thoughts on the future of education financing. Global Partnership for Education [blogpost 15 February]. Retrieved from https://www.globalpartnership.org/blog/after-dakar-where-here. Accessed on June 18, 2019.

Dahlstedt, M., & Fejes, A. (2019). Futures in line? Occupational choice among migrant adult students in Sweden. *International Journal of Lifelong Education, 38*(1), 76–87

Daniele, V. N., & Raul, V. C. (2018). *Promoting lifelong learning for all: The experiences of Ethiopia, Kenya, Namibia, Rwanda and the United Republic of Tanzania*. Hamburg: UNESCO Institute for Lifelong Learning (UIL).

Delors, J., Mutfi, I. A., Amagi, I., Carneiro, R., Chung, F., Geremek, B., …, Nanzhao, Z. (1996). *Learning: The treasure within*. Paris: UNESCO.

Faure, E., Herrera, F., Kaddoura, A. R., Lopes, H., Petrovsky, A. V., Rahnema, M., & Ward, F. C. (1972). *Learning to be: The world of education today and tomorrow*. Paris: UNESCO.

Fejes, A. (2019). Adult education and the fostering of asylum seekers as "full" citizens. *International Review of Education, 65*, 233–250.

Fejes, A., Dahlstedt, M., Olson, M., & Sandberg, F. (2018). *Adult education and the formation of citizens*. London: Routledge.

Kurawa, G. (2019). Examining teachers' professional development needs for promoting inclusive education in northeast Nigeria. In B. Rice (Ed.), *Global perspectives on inclusive teacher education* (p. 263). Pennsylvania, PA: IGI Global.

Lather, P. (1991). *Getting smart: Feminist research and pedagogy with/in the postmodern*. New York, NY: Routledge.

Leighninger, M. (1996). Measuring the outcomes of community-wide study circle programs. *Public Management, 78*, 39–41.

Lessing, D. (1999). Books for the hungry. *Index on Censorship, 2*, 158.

Naido, S. (2001). Community empowerment through lifelong community learning in developing countries. In D. N. Aspin, J. D. Chapman, M. Hatton, & Y. Sawano (Eds.), *International handbook of lifelong learning* (pp. 713–732). Dordecht: Kluwer Academic Publishers.

Oliver, L. P. (1987). *Study circles*. Newport Beach, CA: Seven Locks Press.

Ranson, S. (1994). *Towards the learning society*. London: Cassell Education.

Ranson, S., Rikowski, G., Nixon, J. Mckeown, P., & Butterfield, S. (1995). *Institutional systems, capacity for agency and wealth creation in a learning society*. Research proposal for the learning society programme. The ESRC learning society programme. Birmingham: University of Birmingham, School of Education.

Rikowski, G., Ainley, P., & Ranson, S. (1996). The learning society for the learning city. A paper presented at the annual conference of the Royal Geographical Society and the Institute of British Geographers at University of Strathclyde, January 3–6.

Ruber, I. E., Rees, S., & Schmidt-Hertha, B. (2018). Lifelong learning: Lifelong returns? A new theoretical framework for the analysis of civic returns on adult learning. *International Review of Education, 64*,543–562.

The Zimbabwe Vulnerability Assessment Committee (ZIMVAC). (2019, January). *Lean Season monitoring report*. Zimbabwe: ZIMVAC.

Torstensson, M. (1994). Expectation and a worthy, respectable position in society. Means and aims of library work within the early Labour Movement in Sweden. Paper presented at the 60th IFLA General Conference, August 21–27.

UNESCO Institute for Lifelong Learning (UIL). (2010). *Belém framework for action: Harnessing the power and potential of adult learning and education for a viable future*. Hamburg: UIL.

UNESCO Institute for Lifelong Learning (UIL). (2015). *Lifelong learning. UNESCO Institute for lifelong learning technical note*. Hamburg: UIL.

United Nations (UN). (2015a). *Transforming our world: The 2030 Agenda for sustainable development*. New York, NY: United Nations.

United Nations (UN). (2015b). *The millennium development goals report 2015*. New York, NY: United Nations.

United Nations (UN). (2016). *Sustainable development goal 4: Targets and indicators*. New York, NY: United Nations.

United Nations Educational, Scientific and Cultural Organization (UNESCO). (2016a). *Incheon declaration and Framework for action for the implementation of Sustainable Development Goal 4. Towards inclusive and equitable quality education and lifelong learning opportunities for all. Education 2030*. Paris: UNESCO.

United Nations Educational, Scientific and Cultural Organization (UNESCO). (2016b). *Education for people and planet: Creating sustainable futures for all. Global Education Monitoring Report 2016*. Paris: UNESCO.

United Nations Educational, Scientific and Cultural Organization (UNESCO). (2017). *Education for sustainable development goals: Learning objectives*. Paris: UNESCO.

Wallerstein, N., & Bernstein, E. (1988). Empowerment education: Freire's ideas adapted to health education. *Health Education Quarterly*, *15*(4), 379–394.

World Education Forum (WEF). (2000). *The Dakar framework for action. Education for all: Meeting our collective commitments*. Paris: UNESCO.

World Education Forum (WEF). (2016). *Incheon declaration and Framework for action for the implementation of sustainable development goal 4. Towards inclusive and equitable quality education and lifelong learning opportunities for all. Education 2030*. Paris: UNESCO.

World Education Forum (WEF). (2019a). *Sweden population 2019*. New York, NY: World Population Division, United Nations.

World Population Prospect. (2019b). *Zimbabwe population 2019*. New York, NY: World Population Division, United Nations.

Yang, J., & Yorozu, R. (2015). *Building a learning society in Japan, the Republic of Korea and Singapore*. Hamburg: UIL.

Yorozu, R. (2017). *Lifelong learning in transformation: Promising practices in Southeast Asia*. Hamburg: UNESCO Institute for Lifelong Learning.

CHAPTER 12

STUDENT PERCEPTIONS OF ENGINEERS' VERSUS TEACHERS' ROLES AND RESPONSIBILITIES IN CONTRIBUTING TO SUSTAINABLE DEVELOPMENT

Karin Edvardsson Björnberg, Inga-Britt Skogh and Lena Gumaelius

ABSTRACT

In this study, we critically examine how students enrolled in a combined engineering and teacher education program given at the KTH Royal Institute of Technology, Sweden, understand the concept of sustainable development (SD) and the professional responsibilities of engineers versus teachers in contributing to this goal. A questionnaire was used to collect and analyze data based on five research questions: (1) How do students conceptualize the notion of SD? (2) What aspects of SD are students interested in? (3) Are there any gender differences in what aspects of SD students are interested in? (4) How do students perceive the roles and responsibilities of engineers versus teachers in contributing to SD? and (5) How confident are students in their abilities to address SD issues vocationally? The data indicated a conventional view of SD among the students; a clear interest in sustainability issues, especially for ecologically linked questions; a tendency to ascribe significant but

Teaching and Learning Strategies for Sustainable Development:
Innovations in Higher Education Teaching and Learning, Volume 19, 177–195

ISSN: 2055-3641/doi:10.1108/S2055-364120200000019015

differentiated responsibilities to engineers/teachers; and a low degree of confidence in their own ability to adequately address SD issues vocationally. The data also indicated differences between male and female students when looking at interest in different aspects of SD. Overall, female students were found to be slightly more interested in SD than the male students. This gender difference is larger in relation to social aspects than ecological or economic aspects. It is suggested that future sustainable development education needs a shift of focus from what separates female and male students to what unites them. The observed "confidence gap" that exists between stated degree of interest in, and perceived importance of, sustainability issues, suggests the potential for significant improvement of the design of the Master of Science in Engineering and in Education program (CL-program).

Keywords: Engineering education; teacher training; sustainable development; student perceptions; confidence gap; gender

1. INTRODUCTION

Engineers and teachers are key players in the work toward creating sustainable living conditions for present and future generations – through technical innovation, design, and educational efforts directed at those who will be responsible for developing and managing society's future institutions. That engineers are expected to shoulder these responsibilities is clear from the educational requirements of various accreditation boards as well the codes of conduct of many engineering associations. For example, the U.S. National Society of Professional Engineers' (NSPE) Code of Ethics encourages engineers "to adhere to the principles of sustainable development in order to protect the environment for future generations" (NSPE, 2019, para III. 2d). The Swedish Association of Graduate Engineers annually awards scholarships to its members in support of sustainable development (SD) projects.[1] Furthermore, the United Nations Sustainable Development Goals, in particular Goal 4 on education, have important implications for how engineering education should be structured and implemented (ASCE, 2015; Zelinka & Amadei, 2017). Expectations are obviously also put on graduate teachers. Important international policy documents like UNESCO's *Roadmap for Implementing the Global Action Programme on Education for Sustainable Development* (2014) have been developed to foster and support the transition toward sustainability thinking in all forms of education (see also UNESCO, 2017). In Sweden, the national diploma objectives for engineering and teaching degrees are well aligned with the intentions of the international community. The qualifications for bachelor's and master's degrees of science in engineering contain clear statements regarding knowledge about SD.[2] The corresponding objectives for a teacher degree are not as clearly formulated;

however, since the curricula for most school subjects include a sustainability perspective, teachers' competence in the SD area is implied.[3]

Although research on SD in engineering (Enelund, Knutson Wedel, Lundqvist, & Malmqvist, 2013; Glassey & Haile, 2012; Mulder, 2017; Mulder, Segalàs, & Ferrer-Balas, 2012; Segalàs, Ferrer-Balas, Svanström, Lundqvist, & Mulder, 2009; Segalàs, Mulder, & Ferrer-Balas, 2012) and teacher training education (Andersson, Jagers, Lindskog, & Martinsson, 2013; Bertschy, Künzli, & Lehmann, 2013; Cebrián & Junyent, 2015; Firth & Winter, 2007; Summers, Childs, & Corney, 2005) abound, few studies address how the students themselves conceptualize the notion of SD and how they perceive their future professional roles and responsibilities in contributing to it.[4] In this chapter, we aim to address this lack of attention by critically examining how SD educational efforts within a combined engineering and teacher education master program (henceforth "CL-program"), run by the KTH Royal Institute of Technology and Stockholm University (SU) in cooperation, are assimilated by the students: How do students conceptualize SD and the professional roles and responsibilities of engineers and teachers in contributing to this goal?

Against the background of the debate in Sweden, and in other countries, about possible differences between how women and men relate to SD issues, we decided to include this aspect in our study. Here, available research findings are somewhat inconclusive. A number of studies reported minor (Mohai, 1992) or no gender differences (Al-Naqbi & Alshannag, 2018; Miller & Brumbelow, 2016; Watson, Noyes, & Rodgers, 2013). Some studies reported male students showing stronger concern for environmental problems (Shields & Zeng, 2012; Tang, 2018), while other studies reported female students expressing pronounced environmental concern (Awan & Abbasi, 2013) and greater risk perception than male students (Johnson, 2002). In relation to the latter findings, researchers have even suggested that "[b]eing female means more for sustainability activity than being a male" (Sammalisto, Sundström, von Haartman, Holm, & Yao, 2016, p. 12).

Based on these observations, we identified five research questions that formed the backbone of our investigation:

1. How do CL students conceptualize the notion of SD? (RQ1)
2. What sustainability aspects are students interested in? (RQ2)
3. Are there any gender differences in what SD aspects students are interested in? (RQ3)
4. How do the students perceive the roles and responsibilities of engineers versus teachers in contributing to SD? (RQ4)
5. How confident are the students in their abilities to contribute to SD in their future professions as engineers versus teachers given the education that they have received at KTH? (RQ5)

With these research questions in mind a questionnaire was designed and distributed to students enrolled in the CL-program, a program that leads to a double diploma in engineering and teaching.[5] It should be noted that the local degree objectives for this combined program are based on the national objectives for the engineering degree/diploma. The above-mentioned difference in national degree requirements regarding SD competences of engineers and teachers is, consequently, in practice non-existent for this educational program. At the end of their studies, all CL students should be able to "show the ability to develop and design products, processes and systems with regard to people's conditions and needs and society's goals for economic, social and ecologically sustainable development" (see footnote 2). Since the CL-program includes optional subject courses, some of which contain SD-related contents, the SD education that they have received may vary. This variation of SD experience among the students gave us the opportunity to present an overall picture of the state of SD knowledge, which, in turn, provides a basis for future development of both courses and the program as a whole. However, the aim of the present study was not to evaluate the SD education at the CL-program. Instead, our focus was on capturing the knowledge and experience that these students, based on their respective experiences of SD teaching, expressed at the time of the study.

In Section 2, our methodological approach is described in further detail, including sample, data collection, and analysis. In Sections 3–4, findings from the survey research are presented and analyzed. In Section 5, the implications the study has on future research and curriculum design are elaborated on.

2. RESEARCH METHODS

2.1 Sample

The subjects in this study were fourth- and final-year students enrolled in a combined engineering and teacher educational program offered collaboratively by KTH and SU during one specific academic year (autumn and spring term). In the academic year under consideration, there were 40 fourth-year and 20 fifth-year students enrolled in the CL-program. All students had been taught SD within the framework of their various subject courses and via a mandatory 6.0 European Credit Transfer System (ECTS) credit SD course offered during their third year of studies. As noted above, depending on which subject courses the CL students choose to take, their SD education may vary. However, through the mandatory 6 credit SD course all students are introduced to the concept of SD and how theories about SD can be translated into practice.

2.2 Data Collection

A modified version of Watson et al.'s (2013) questionnaire was used with the addition of questions explicitly dealing with the concept of SD and the engineer's versus teacher's responsibilities in contributing to SD within the scope of each profession. A preliminary version of the questionnaire was circulated among three persons involved in SD education at KTH to establish content validity. The questionnaire was distributed to the CL students during two mandatory lectures.

The questionnaire consisted of 10 questions divided into three categories:

1. Items designed to collect information about the students' gender, year of study, and specialization within the program (Question 1).
2. Open-ended questions where the students were asked to write down words and draw a picture that they associated with SD and comment on the sustainable development education (SDE) they had received while studying at the KTH (Questions 2–3, 10).
3. Seven-point scale self-rating items where the students were asked to rate how great responsibility they believed engineers versus teachers versus private citizens have in contributing to SD (Questions 4–6), how interested they were in 21 different SD aspects (Question 7), how important they believed it is for engineers versus teachers to contribute to the same 21 SD aspects (Question 8), and how confident they were in their abilities to make a contribution to SD in their future roles as engineers versus teachers regarding the SD aspects (Question 9). The SD aspects are listed in Table 1. Low rating by the informant equals low degree of responsibility/interest/importance/confidence.

When ticking the boxes, the students were given the opportunity to tick an "I don't know" box. Some students chose to use a more fine-grained scale than the 1–7 grades provided in the questionnaire and put a cross between the pre-defined

Table 1. Sustainability Aspects Covered in Questions 7–9.

No.	Sustainability Aspect	Sustainability Dimension
A1	Poverty reduction and international aid	Social
A2	Corporate social responsibility (CSR)	Economy
A3	Globalization and international trade	Economy
A4	Green building/buildings	Environment
A5	Green biotechnology (agriculture, forestry, aquaculture, GMO)	Environment
A6	Sustainable infrastructure (VA-systems, waste, roads)	Environment
A7	Sustainable communications (IT, mobile communications)	Environment
A8	Sustainable cities/town planning	Environment
A9	Sustainable transportation	Environment
A10	Sustainable agriculture, forestry, fishery, and reindeer husbandry	Environment
A11	Health and well-being	Social
A12	Climate change	Environment
A13	Life-cycle assessment (LCA) and environmental impact assessment	Environment
A14	Food security	Social
A15	Environmental/ecological economics, including circular economy	Economy
A16	Ethics and justice, including responsibility for future generations and gender aspects	Social
A17	Environmental pollution (environmental toxins, acidification, eutrophication, etc.)	Environment
A18	Environmental law	Economy
A19	Environmental conservation, biodiversity, and ecosystem services	Environment
A20	Clean/renewable energy and energy efficiency	Environment
A21	Religious/existential aspects	Social

steps in the scale. In those cases, the grade immediately above the grade used by the students was used in the analysis.

Since the questionnaire was distributed during mandatory lecture time, the response rate was fairly high. The 24 fourth-year and 19 final-year students who completed the questionnaire corresponded to a response rate of 60% of all fourth-year and 95% of all final-year students. The distribution of male and female students was 24–16. Three students did not wish to indicate their gender.

2.3 Data Analysis

The questionnaire data were first systemized in search for common patterns. The data were then analyzed statistically using Statistical Package for the Social Sciences,[6] both to see if the patterns found were of significant nature and if other undefined patterns could be detected. This was done by looking at the descriptive statistics for all data and by conducting independent sample *t*-tests for comparing the mean values for our groups of interest, that is, female/male students, and by conducting paired sample *t*-tests for comparison between the environmental, economic, and social aspects for questions 7–9 (Table 2).

3. RESULTS

3.1 The Concept of Sustainable Development (RQ1)

Two questions were asked in order to identify how the students conceptualize the notion of SD. In Question 2, the students were asked to write down up to four words that they associated with SD. In Question 3, the students were asked to draw a picture that they associated with SD.

3.1.1 Words

A total of 41 students answered Question 2. The words that were written down were compiled, sorted alphabetically, and translated into English using a free online Swedish–English dictionary.[7] The six most frequently listed words among the students were:

1. Environment/ecology/ecological (23 hits).
2. Economy/economic (15).
3. Society/social (13).
4. Future (13).
5. Ethics/justice/fairness/equality (6).
6. Interaction/cooperation (5).

3.1.2 Pictures

A total of 38 students answered Question 3. The most commonly drawn picture was that of three overlapping circles representing the three sustainability dimensions of ecology, economy, and society (nine pictures).[8] In most cases, the drawn circles were supplemented with words like "economy," "ecology," "society," or

Table 2. Descriptive Statistics for Question 7 (Q7), Q8a, Q9a, Q8b, and Q9b.

Interest for Sustainability				Precieved Importance - Engineer				Degree of Confidence - Engineer				Precieved Importance - Teacher				Degree of Confidence - Teacher			
Descending order. highest interest in top	Number of students answered	Mean	Conf. Inerv. (±)	Descending order. highest importance in top	Number of students answered	Mean	Conf. Inerv. (±)	Descending order. highest confidence in top	Number of students answered	Mean	Conf. Inerv. (±)	Descending order. highest importance in top	Number of students answered	Mean	Conf. Inerv. (±)	Descending order. highest confidence in top	Number of students answered	Mean	Conf. Inerv. (±)
A20	40	5.85	0.42	**A20**	40	5.68	0.48	**A20**	37	5.16	0.47	**A16**	39	5.72	0.58	**A16**	36	5.44	0.62
A12	40	5.65	0.50	**A7**	39	5.49	0.52	**A12**	38	4.66	0.51	**A11**	38	5.53	0.51	**A12**	36	5.22	0.49
A11	40	5.55	0.39	**A9**	39	5.46	0.43	**A16**	37	4.65	0.58	**A12**	38	5.50	0.52	**A17**	35	5.06	0.51
A9	41	5.41	0.46	A12	39	5.36	0.50	A17	37	4.62	0.52	A20	38	5.45	0.47	A20	35	5.00	0.56
A8	40	5.38	0.49	A13	39	5.23	0.46	A7	38	4.39	0.59	A17	38	5.05	0.51	A13	34	4.56	0.56
A17	41	5.29	0.39	A17	40	5.23	0.54	A13	36	4.36	0.59	A7	39	5.00	0.47	A11	36	4.53	0.60
A4	39	5.21	0.53	A8	39	5.13	0.49	A4	37	4.27	0.58	A9	39	4.90	0.48	A9	35	4.17	0.66
A7	40	5.18	0.50	A6	40	5.13	0.47	A9	38	4.11	0.66	A5	38	4.84	0.49	A4	35	4.09	0.55
A5	37	5.08	0.53	A2	37	5.08	0.58	A3	37	3.97	0.52	A1	39	4.79	0.56	A7	36	4.03	0.57
A16	41	5.05	0.64	A16	40	5.03	0.58	A2	34	3.97	0.53	A10	39	4.72	0.55	A8	36	3.86	0.55
A6	40	4.93	0.55	A3	40	4.93	0.47	A6	38	3.95	0.62	A13	37	4.62	0.45	A19	34	3.82	0.64
A10	40	4.83	0.56	A11	38	4.89	0.45	A8	38	3.76	0.61	A8	39	4.62	0.52	A5	35	3.80	0.61
A3	39	4.72	0.53	A4	40	4.88	0.48	A11	36	3.67	0.56	A19	37	4.59	0.51	A21	32	3.78	0.69
A13	39	4.72	0.53	A5	40	4.88	0.52	A5	36	3.50	0.67	A3	39	4.59	0.57	A6	35	3.77	0.59
A2	38	4.71	0.53	A10	39	4.41	0.59	A19	36	3.47	0.55	A14	36	4.47	0.55	A2	31	3.58	0.55
A14	38	4.71	0.56	A19	39	4.36	0.52	A10	36	3.19	0.60	A4	39	4.46	0.48	A10	35	3.57	0.61
A15	31	4.68	0.66	A15	34	4.35	0.53	A1	36	3.03	0.47	A18	37	4.41	0.55	A3	36	3.47	0.55
A1	41	4.51	0.59	A18	37	4.27	0.52	A18	36	2.97	0.50	A6	39	4.38	0.56	A1	35	3.46	0.54
A19	38	4.47	0.54	**A1**	40	4.13	0.53	**A14**	35	2.94	0.62	**A15**	34	4.29	0.53	**A18**	34	3.26	0.62
A18	39	3.85	0.62	**A14**	39	4.08	0.57	**A15**	35	2.74	0.55	**A21**	33	4.27	0.76	**A15**	33	3.12	0.58
A21	39	3.31	0.70	**A21**	36	2.56	0.58	**A21**	32	2.69	0.64	**A2**	36	4.03	0.54	**A14**	33	3.06	0.66

The confidence interval has been calculated as 1.96* standard error.

"ecological," "economic," and "social." The second most commonly drawn picture was that of a closed loop of arrows pointing toward each other (six pictures). The third most commonly drawn picture was that of a landscape scenery/tree/animal (five pictures).

3.2 Degree of Interest in Sustainability Issues (RQ2)

In Question 7, the students were asked to rate their interest in the 21 different SD aspects. When calculating the mean value for each of the aspects all question marks or empty boxes were not included in the calculation. The sum was divided by the number of students ticking a box for that particular aspect.

The descriptive statistics for Question 7 is compiled in the first column in Table 2. All mean values were ranked depending on interest level. The aspect (henceforth, A=aspect) highest up in the list corresponds to the aspect that students ranked as the most interesting one. A 95% confidence interval is shown to give an estimation of how dispersed the values are for each aspect. Cronbach's alpha was calculated to be 0.948, indicating a high level of internal consistency. It can be noted that A20 "Clean/renewable energy and energy efficiency," was found to be in top being graded to a mean of 5.85 ± 0.42.

All aspects, except two, were ranked above the border of being neutral, which means that the students felt a positive interest for the majority of the SD aspects. At the bottom, we found A21 "Religious/existential aspects."

Most students answered the majority of the questions. However, for some of the bottom-ranked aspects, fewer answers were obtained. For example, for A15 "Environmental/ecological economics" only 31 out of 41 students responded, and for the bottom-ranked aspect, A21 "Religious/existential aspects," 15 students marked the lowest number, 1 (4 students did not mark this aspect).

To get a more general picture of students' interest in SD issues, the results for the three different sustainability areas (environmental, social, and economic) were compared. The presented means are calculated as the average of the mean values for all aspects that belonged to the respective area according to Table 1. Table 4 shows these mean values for questions 7–9. Confidence intervals are presented in the Table 1 to give an estimate of the significance of the different means. Paired sample *t*-test was also conducted to prove the significance of the comparative differences (see Table 4).

Tables 3 and 4 show clearly that the students have a significantly higher interest in the environmental aspects than in the economic and social aspects.

Table 3. Mean Value of Q7, Q8a, Q9a, Q8b, and Q9b for Environmental, Economic and Social Sustainability Aspects.

Sustainability Aspect	Degree of Interest	Perceived Importance – Engineer	Degree of Confidence – Engineer	Perceived Importance – Teacher	Degree of Confidence – Teacher
Environmental	5.19 ± 0.31	5.29 ± 0.41	4.15 ± 0.41	4.81 ± 0.39	4.23 ± 0.45
Economic	4.37 ± 0.49	4.64 ± 0.37	3.36 ± 0.41	4.26 ± 0.41	3.26 ± 0.49
Social	4.40 ± 0.45	4.18 ± 0.37	3.44 ± 0.41	4.95 ± 0.43	4.07 ± 0.43

Confidence intervals are calculated as 1.96* standard error of the means.

Table 4. Paired Samples *t*-Test Analyzing the Significance of Differences Regarding the Three Sustainability Areas for Questions 7, 8a, 9a, 8b, and 9b.

	Pair	Mean	SD	*t*-value	df	*p*-value
Degree of interest	**env-eco**	**0.77**	**1.01**	**4.93**	**40**	**0.00**
	env-soc	**0.54**	**1.27**	**2.73**	**40**	**0.01**
	eco-soc	−0.23	1.43	−1.05	40	0.30
Perceived importance engineer	**env-eco**	**0.65**	**1.06**	**3.89**	**39**	**0.00**
	env-soc	**1.11**	**1.32**	**5.32**	**39**	**0.00**
	eco-soc	**0.46**	**1.08**	**2.70**	**39**	**0.01**
Degree of confidence - engineer	**env-eco**	**0.79**	**1.33**	**3.64**	**37**	**0.00**
	env-social	**0.71**	**1.31**	**3.33**	**37**	**0.00**
	eco-social	−0.08	1.24	−0.38	37	0.71
Perceived importance - teacher	**env-eco**	**0.56**	**0.73**	**4.77**	**38**	**0.00**
	env-social	−0.14	0.97	−0.91	38	0.37
	eco-social	**−0.70**	**0.88**	**−4.97**	**38**	**0.00**
Degree of confidence - teacher	**env-eco**	**0.97**	**1.32**	**4.42**	**35**	**0.00**
	env-social	0.16	1.26	0.76	35	0.45
	eco-social	**−0.82**	**1.35**	**−3.61**	**35**	**0.00**

Significant differences are given in bold values.

3.3 Differences in Interest Between Male and Female Students (RQ3)

In line with Awan and Abbasi (2013) and Johnson (2002), we expected no differences regarding the interest among females and males. However, our data suggested that this was not the case.

Fig. 1 presents a graph of the results for female and male respondents indicating that female students at the CL-program are slightly more interested in the sustainability aspects than the male students. The female respondents gave a higher mark for 19 of the 21 aspects. Significant differences were found for five aspects (Table 5): **A1, A9, A14, A15** and **A16**. No correction has been done to prevent a type 1 error,

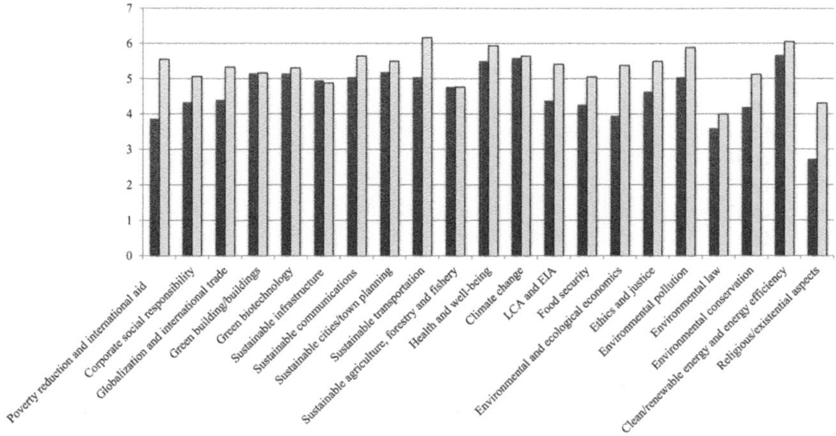

Fig. 1. Degree of Interest (Mean Value) in Sustainability Aspects for Male Students (Dark Grey) and Female Students (Light Grey).

Table 5. Independent Samples *t*-Test for Female and Male Students.

	Gender	N	Mean	Standard Deviation	*t*-value	*p*-value
A1	**Male**	**22**	**4**	**2.0**		
	Female	**16**	**6**	**1.3**	**−3.08**	**0.00**
A2	Male	21	4	1.8		
	Female	14	5	0.8	−1.83	0.08
A3	Male	20	4	1.9		
	Female	16	5	1.1	−1.71	0.10
A4	Male	20	5	1.6		
	Female	16	5	1.6	−0.43	0.67
A5	Male	20	5	1.5		
	Female	16	5	1.6	−0.19	0.85
A6	Male	22	5	1.9		
	Female	15	5	1.0	−0.51	0.62
A7	Male	22	5	1.5		
	Female	16	6	1.4	−0.96	0.34
A8	Male	21	5	1.7		
	Female	16	6	1.0	−1.45	0.13
A9	**Male**	**22**	**5**	**1.6**		
	Female	**16**	**6**	**0.7**	**−2.27**	**0.03**
A10	Male	22	5	1.8		
	Female	16	5	1.5	−0.41	0.68
A11	Male	22	6	1.3		
	Female	15	6	1.0	−0.43	0.67
A12	Male	22	6	1.7		
	Female	15	6	1.5	−0.39	0.70
A13	Male	21	4	1.8		
	Female	15	5	1.2	−1.77	0.09
A14	**Male**	**19**	**4**	**1.7**		
	Female	**16**	**6**	**1.0**	**−2.79**	**0.01**
A15	**Male**	**18**	**4**	**2.0**		
	Female	**11**	**6**	**0.9**	**−2.60**	**0.01**
A16	**Male**	**22**	**5**	**2.2**		
	Female	**16**	**6**	**0.9**	**−2.78**	**0.01**
A17	Male	22	5	1.3		
	Female	16	6	1.4	−1.47	0.15
A18	Male	22	4	2.0		
	Female	15	4	1.8	−1.26	0.22
A19	Male	21	4	1.7		
	Female	15	5	1.4	−1.43	0.16
A20	Male	21	6	1.6		
	Female	16	6	1.0	−0.78	0.44
A21	Male	22	3	2.3		
	Female	14	4	1.9	−1.99	0.06

and therefore there is a chance that the number of significant aspects are higher than they should be. Three of the aspects where significant differences were found belonged to the social area, one to the economic area and one to the environmental area. This suggests that the gender difference is larger in relation to social aspects than ecological or economic aspects.

Five students showed an overall mean below 4, meaning that the overall interest in SD was generally lower than being neutral. Four of these respondents were male students and the fifth student did not include any gender information. This raises the question of different perceptions of SD among female and male students.

3.4 The Role/responsibilities of the Engineer versus Teacher (RQ4)

In questions 4–6, the students were asked to indicate how large a responsibility they believe engineers versus teachers have to contribute to SD in their professional lives. The students were also asked to indicate how large a responsibility they believe that private citizens have to contribute to SD. A total of 43 students answered one or several questions (4–6). The data showed that the overall mean value for the three categories (engineer, teacher, and private citizen) is almost the same: 5.44 for engineer compared to 5.57 for teacher and 5.29 for private citizen. No significant differences were observed in the independent sample *t*-test.

In question 8, the students were asked to indicate how important they think it is for engineers versus teachers within their area of specialization to contribute to the 21 SD aspects. The column 2 of Table 2 shows the descriptive statistics of perceived importance for the role of being an engineer. The analysis showed that the students found the SD aspects very important in this role. Highest ranked was A20 "Clean/renewable energy and energy efficiency," which is in line with the results for what aspects were considered most interesting. Only one aspect was ranked to be of minor importance, that is, the mean was below 4, namely A21 "Religious/existential aspects." Table 3 shows that the environmental aspects received the highest mean when asked about the importance of the engineer.

The analysis of the importance for a teacher showed a list of top three and bottom three aspects that looked a bit different from the ones reflecting the role of an engineer. For a teacher, A16 "Ethics and justice," was top-ranked. A21 "Religious/existential aspects," was still among the bottom three aspects. All aspects showed an average higher than 4, that is, were considered important to the respondents.

Analysis of the three sustainability areas (environmental, economic, and social) in relation to the perceived roles/responsibilities of engineers versus teachers showed that the environmental aspects were the highest ranked. For the role of the engineer, the economic aspects were ranked as second, and for the teacher role the social aspects were ranked almost as high as the environmental aspects. In the latter case, no significant difference was seen between the environmental and the social area.

3.5 Degree of Confidence in Sustainable Development Issues (RQ5)

In question 9, the students were asked how confident they feel, given the education that they have received at KTH, that they will be able to contribute to the 21 SD aspects in their professional roles as engineers and teachers (within their respective fields of specialization).

In the engineering role, students expressed insecurity rather than security in 13 of the 21 aspects (13 aspects had a mean below 4), even though they considered most aspects to be very important for an engineer. Again, A20 "Clean/renewable energy and energy efficiency" was top-ranked. Four aspects were ranked very low, below 3, namely A21 "Religious/existential aspects," A15 "Environmental/ecological economics," A14 "Food security," and A18 "Environmental law."

For their teacher role, the students also expressed insecurity, as the mean ranking was below 4 in 12 of the 21 aspects. They felt most comfortable in relation to A16 "Ethics and justice." They felt least comfortable in relation to A14 "Food security," A15 "Environmental/ecological economics," and A18 "Environmental law." Similarities were seen for the confidence in being an engineer and being a teacher, with the exception that A21 "Religious/existential aspects" was ranked fairly high for confidence in being a teacher.

The students expressed confidence that they could make a significant contribution to environmental sustainability, both in their role as engineer and teacher. However, in their role as engineer, both the economic and the social aspects were ranked significantly lower than the environmental aspects, and both areas were also ranked below 4, indicating that the students were generally less confident in those areas. In their teacher role, the students felt confident in the environmental and social areas.

The overall trend was that students' self-confidence in contributing to SD was low compared to how important they considered their professional role to be.

4. DISCUSSION

4.1 The Concept of Sustainable Development

In this chapter, the students' perceptions of the concept of SD were surveyed by asking them to list words and draw pictures that they associated with the concept. Based on the data we received some points are worth stating.

A great variety of interpretations of the concept of SD exist in the literature. This has led some authors to argue that SD is an "essentially contested concept" (Connelly, 2007). The most widespread definition of SD is the Brundtland definition: "meeting the needs of the present generation without compromising the ability of future generations to satisfy their needs" (World Commission on Environment and Development, 1987, p. 43). The concept is generally understood as consisting of three dimensions – ecological, social, and economic sustainability – although there are different views on how the dimensions are related. An attempt to operationalize the ecological dimension of SD was made through the concept of "planetary boundaries," that is, ecological limits that should not be exceeded if we want to avoid irreversible and potentially catastrophic ecological changes (Rockström et al., 2009). The social dimension of SD has been operationalized analogously through the concept of "social boundaries," below which no human being should be allowed to fall (Raworth, 2012). Baker (2016) identified a set of normative principles that underlie the concept of SD, namely the principles of need, inter- and intragenerational equity, common but differentiated responsibilities, justice, participation, and gender equality. Jacobs (1999) similarly identified six constituents that he believed make up the core of SD: environment–economy integration, a futurity focus, a commitment to environmental protection, in particular reducing pollution, and making room for more efficient use of resources, equity, a recognition that human welfare cannot be reduced to income growth, and a recognition that SD requires the political involvement of all stakeholders in society.

Our data can be said to reflect the prevailing views on the concept of SD. The words most frequently recorded through our questionnaire correspond well with the core ideas outlined in the above-mentioned literature. Among the most frequently recorded words were those that related to the three aspects of SD ("environment/ecology/ecological," "economy/economic," and "society/social") and words denoting a futurity-focus ("future"). Also the equity aspect of SD was captured through the students' choices of words such as "ethics/justice/fairness/equality." The aspect of stakeholder involvement was captured through the words "interaction/cooperation."

Moreover, the three dimensions of the sustainability concept were also captured by the drawings made by the students. Nine students chose to illustrate their understanding of SD though the classic Venn diagram, with three overlapping circles representing ecological, economic, and social sustainability. It is interesting to note that none of the students drew the "nested circles" model (Carter & Moir, 2012). In the sustainability literature there is a discussion of the merits and downfalls of different sustainability models/symbols. Several writers have criticized the Venn diagram, believing that it does not adequately capture the relations that exist between the dimensions (Giddings, Hopwood, & O'Brien, 2002). For instance, Mebratu argued that the Venn diagram is an "epistemological trap" that fails to account for "[t]he 'parts,' the 'whole,' and, most importantly, the interaction between the parts and the whole" (Mebratu, 1998, p. 513). The nested circles model gives a more adequate account, it is argued, since it better captures the fact that economy is a subset of society and that both the economic and social dimensions are ultimately bounded by and depend on the natural environment (Carter & Moir, 2012).

4.2 Degree of Interest in Sustainability Issues

According to the survey data the students were most interested (calculated as mean value) in aspects that in our study were classified as environmental, followed by social and economic aspects. The interests for the last two areas are fairly similar. When comparing which aspects received the highest/lowest grades in our survey to the ranking reported in other studies both similarities and differences emerged.

In Watson et al. (2013), the students (civil and environmental engineering) were asked to indicate their level of interest in 24 sustainability aspects (a similar list to the one used in our study). In general, most of the aspects that were top/bottom ranked in our study also received top/bottom scores in their study, including clean/renewable energy and energy efficiency, pollution, environmental health, and sustainable transportation (top scores) and religious/existential aspects and environmental law (bottom scores). However, the students in Watson et al.'s (2013) study generally took a greater relative interest in sustainability aspects that related to infrastructure, transportation, city planning, and community development, which could be explained by the fact that they were enrolled in a civil and environmental engineering program. In our study, aspects such as climate change, ethics, and justice were ranked relatively high in comparison to how they were ranked in Watson et al. (2013).

In a study conducted by Cebrián and Junyent (2015), student teachers were asked to design curriculum for SD. It was found that the students prioritized activities for aquisition of knowledge related to nature and natural sciences, rather than activities strengthening ethical values or positive attitudes. Our findings align with this study as our students also showed higher interest for environmental aspects.

The data indicated that female students are slightly more interested in sustainability issues. This result deviates from, for example, Watson et al.'s (2013) study in which no such gender differences were reported, however, is consistent with a large body of literature from outside the educational field reporting greater risk perception and concern regarding the environment among women than among men (Finucane, Slovic, Mertz, Flynn, & Satterfield, 2000; Flynn, Slovic, & Mertz, 1994; Mohai, 1992). Reported findings are ambiguous. It may well be more constructive to ask whether gender matters in SDE. According to Meinzen-Dick, Kovarik, and Quisumbing (2014) the answer is yes. Not that women and men differ in terms of environmental awareness but to point out the importance of taking into account both women's and men's "intellectual and inherent motivations and their material conditions and means" (Meinzen-Dick et al., 2014, p. 47).

4.3 The Role of the Engineer versus Teacher

When asked to indicate how large responsibility students believe that engineers versus teachers have to contribute to SD in their professional lives compared to that of private citizens, no significant differences could be discerned. On the other hand, a significant difference could be seen as they expressed that social sustainability was as important as ecological sustainability in their role as teachers, but not as engineers. This shows that our informants had reflected on their professional role and believes that teachers have a slightly different role to play in relation to SD.

4.4 Degree of Confidence in Sustainable Development Issues

The survey data showed that the mean value of confidence is surprisingly low among the students, both in terms of their role as engineers and teachers. A comparison of the self-reported degree of confidence with the stated degree of interest and the perceived importance of SD issues revealed a significant confidence gap (Table 2). Table 2 also shows that the degree of interest is correlated to the degree of confidence. This could imply that students are interested in SD issues and believe that both engineers and teachers have an important role to play in furthering SD, however, feel somewhat unequipped to address those issues in their imagined roles as engineers/teachers. A similar confidence gap was reported in Watson et al. (2013).

The somewhat contradictory image of self-confidence in SD issues expressed by the students is interesting. The importance of tying the acquisition of knowledge to personal experience cannot be underestimated. In educational research there is a seldom questioned consensus that "skills and activities must be the basis of learning" (Dewey, 1999, p. 231) and the individuals' attitudes (self-confidence) are "based on both cognitive standpoints and emotional experience" (Ahlgren, 1991, p. 31). Cech (2014) showed that engineering education as such may have a negative effect on students' attitudes toward SD, as the engineering culture, developed throughout the engineering program in general, may cause disengagement for SD-related educational issues. Jointly, these two studies show that it is very important not only to implement education for SD but to follow how students' attitudes and self-confidence develop during engineering and/or teacher education.

5. CONCLUSION

In the present study, we investigated how students enrolled at the CL-program during one specific academic year understood the concept of SD and the roles and responsibilities of engineers versus teachers as contributors to SD. A limitation of this study is that only two cohorts of students at a specific engineering-teacher program at KTH were studied, and they were not studied or compared longitudinally. Moreover, the fact that the students' experience of SD teaching varied, depending on chosen subject courses, could be seen as a methodological weakness. Thus, the results of the study need to be treated with some caution. Further empirical data would have to be gathered, for example, through interviews, in order to be able to draw more robust conclusions. However, bearing this in mind, we believe that the following tentative conclusions could be drawn based on the presented data.

First, the CL students embraced the prevailing three-partite view of SD, which includes environmental as well as economic and social aspects. The tendency to identify SD with environmental and/or technical issues, which has been reported in other studies of engineering students' perceptions of SD, was less pronounced in our study. It remains to be investigated what factors have contributed to this relatively "balanced view" of SD detected among the CL students. Such knowledge may be useful in informing engineering curriculum toward including more social and economic sustainability aspects.

Second, the most well-known graphical model of the sustainability concept among the CL students was the Venn diagram. Although the Venn diagram has endured some criticism in the sustainability literature, we believe that in the context of engineering education it could serve as a heuristic tool for anchoring sustainability to what is already familiar to the students, namely mathematical and logical thinking. However, further research into the relative advantages and disadvantages of the different sustainability models in engineering education is needed.

Third, the CL students showed interest in sustainability issues, and female students took a greater interest in such issues than their male peers did. Although the students were most interested in aspects that were classified as environmental in our study, social aspects such as ethics and justice were ranked relatively high in comparison to other studies. Investigating in further detail what factors contribute to students taking an interest in sustainability issues will be useful in designing courses and attracting students to the CL-program and other engineering programs. Emphasizing the role of sustainability in the engineering curriculum might be a way of attracting more women to engineering, as suggested by our data.

Fourth, the data showed that CL students believed engineers and teachers have a somewhat different responsibility in contributing to SD, in particular for the social aspects of SD. For teachers, "Ethics and justice" was ranked the most important sustainability aspect among the final year students.

Fifth, the data indicated a surprisingly low degree of confidence in SD issues in both student groups. A comparison of the self-reported degree of confidence with the stated degree of interest in and perceived importance of sustainability issues revealed a significant "confidence gap." Perhaps this contradiction between interest and confidence can be understood in the light of a perceived uncertainty about what may be required of them as members of each profession.

Finally, our findings suggest a statistically significant difference between female and male students' attitudes to SD. The question of how to deal with this knowledge is important. Maybe a shift of focus from what separates individuals to what unites them is a viable route. In line with Meinzen-Dick et al. (2014), future SDE needs to be built on an awareness of both women's and men's interests, experiences, and conditions. This suggests the potential for significant improvement of the design of the CL-program.

ACKNOWLEDGMENTS

The authors would like to thank the student informants for their participation in our study.

NOTES

1. https://www.sverigesingenjorer.se/om-forbundet/vara-fragor/miljo/#5817 (in Swedish, accessed on August 8, 2019).
2. Swedish Council for Higher Education, Higher Education Ordinance, 1993, p. 100, Annex 2, Degree of Bachelor/Master of Science in Engineering, https://www.uhr.se/en/start/laws-and-regulations/Laws-and-regulations/The-Higher-Education-Ordinance/Annex-2/ (accessed on August 8, 2019).
3. See footnote 2, Degree of Master of Arts/Science in Secondary/Upper Secondary Education.
4. For exceptions, see Carew and Mitchell (2002), Azapagic, Perdan, and Shallcross (2005), Summers and Childs (2007), Kilinc and Aydin (2013), and Watson, Noyes, and Rodgers (2013). See also Kagawa (2007), Barth and Timm (2011), Yuan and Zuo (2013), and Zeegers and Clark (2014) on student perceptions of sustainable development outside the engineering/teacher training field.
5. https://www.kth.se/student/kurser/program/CLGYM/20172/mal?l=en (accessed on August 8, 2019).
6. http://www.ibm.com/analytics/us/en/technology/spss/ (accessed on August 8, 2019).
7. http://sv.bab.la (accessed on August 8, 2019).
8. The raw data, including the drawn pictures, are archived in the Division of Philosophy, KTH, and are available upon request.

REFERENCES

Ahlgren, R.-M. (1991). Jag – en social varelse. In P. Björklid & S. Fischbein (Eds.), *Individens samspel med miljön* (pp. 29–42). Stockholm: HLS.

Al-Naqbi, A. K., & Alshannag, Q. (2018). The status of education for sustainable development and sustainability knowledge, attitudes, and behaviors of UAE University students. *International Journal of Sustainability in Higher Education, 19*(3), 566–588. https://doi.org/10.1108/IJSHE-06-2017-0091

Andersson, K., Jagers, S. C., Lindskog, A., & Martinsson, J. (2013). Learning for the future? Effects of education for sustainable development (ESD) on teacher education students. *Sustainability, 5*(12), 5135–5152. https://doi.org/10.3390/su5125135

ASCE. (2015). Civil engineering education and the United Nations sustainable development goals. Retrieved from https://collaborate.asce.org/blogs/william-kelly/2015/12/15/civil-engineering-education-and-the-united-nations-sustainable-development-goals

Awan, U., & Abbasi, A. S. (2013). Environmental sustainability through determinism: The level of environmental awareness, knowledge and behavior among business graduates. *Research Journal of Environmental and Earth Sciences, 5*(9), 505–515.

Azapagic, A., Perdan, S., & Shallcross, D. (2005). How much do engineering students know about sustainable development? The findings of an international survey and possible implications for the engineering curriculum. *European Journal of Engineering Education, 30*(1), 1–19. https://doi.org/10.1080/03043790512331313804

Baker, S. (2016). *Sustainable development* (2nd ed.). Abingdon: Routledge.

Barth, M., & Timm, J. M. (2011). Higher education for sustainable development: Students' perspectives on an innovative approach to educational change. *Journal of Social Science, 7*(1), 13–23. https://doi.org/10.3844/jssp.2011.16.26

Bertschy, F., Künzli, C., & Lehmann, M. (2013). Teachers' competencies for the implementation of educational offers in the field of education for sustainable development. *Sustainability, 5*(12), 5067–5080. https://doi.org/10.3390/su5125067

Carew, A. L., & Mitchell, C. A. (2002). Characterizing undergraduate engineering students' understanding of sustainability. *European Journal of Engineering Education, 27*(4), 349–361. https://doi.org/10.1080/03043790210166657

Carter, K., & Moir, S. (2012). Diagrammatic representations of sustainability: A review and synthesis. In S. D. Smith (Ed.), *Proceedings 28th annual ARCOM conference*, September 3–5, Association of Researchers in Construction Management, Edinburgh (pp. 1479–1489).

Cebrián, G., & Junyent, M. (2015). Competencies in education for sustainable development: Exploring the student teachers' views. *Sustainability, 7*, 2768–2786. https://doi.org/10.3390/su7032768

Cech, E. A. (2014). Culture of disengagement in engineering education? *Science, Technology, and Human Values, 39*(1), 42–72. https://doi.org/10.1177/0162243913504305

Connelly, S. (2007). Mapping sustainable development as a contested concept. *Local Environment, 12*(3), 259–278, https://doi.org/10.1080/13549830601183289

Dewey, J. (1999). *Demokrati och utbildning*. Göteborg: Daidalos.

Enelund, M., Knutson Wedel, M., Lundqvist, U., & Malmqvist, J. (2013). Integration of education for sustainable development in the mechanical engineering curriculum. *Australasian Journal of Engineering Education, 19*(1), 51–62.

Finucane, M. L., Slovic, P., Mertz, C. K., Flynn, J., & Satterfield, T. A. (2000). Gender, race, and perceived risk: The 'white male' effect. *Health, Risk and Society, 2*(2), 159–172. https://doi.org/10.1080/713670162

Firth, R., & Winter, C. (2007). Constructing education for sustainable development: The secondary school geography curriculum and initial teacher training. *Environmental Education Research, 13*(5), 599–619. https://doi.org/10.1080/13504620701659079

Flynn, J., Slovic, P., & Mertz, C. K. (1994). Gender, race, and perception of environmental health risks. *Risk Analysis, 14*(6), 1101–1108. https://doi.org/10.1111/j.1539-6924.1994.tb00082.x

Giddings, B., Hopwood, B., & O'Brien, G. (2002). Environment, economy and society: Fitting them together into sustainable development. *Sustainable Development, 10*(4), 187–196. https://doi.org/10.1002/sd.199

Glassey, J., & Haile, S. (2012). Sustainability in chemical engineering curriculum. *International Journal of Sustainability in Higher Education, 13*(4), 354–364. https://doi.org/10.1108/14676371211262308

Jacobs, M. (1999). Sustainable development as a contested concept. In A. Dobson (Ed.), *Fairness and futurity: Essays on environmental sustainability and social justice* (pp. 21–45). Oxford: Oxford University Press.

Johnson, B. B. (2002). Gender and race in beliefs about outdoor air pollution. *Risk Analysis*, *22*(4), 725–738. https://doi.org/10.1111/0272-4332.00064

Kagawa, F. (2007). Dissonance in students' perceptions of sustainable development and sustainability: Implications for curriculum change. *International Journal of Sustainability in Higher Education*, *8*(3), 317–338. https://doi.org/10.1108/14676370710817174

Kilinc, A., & Aydin, A. (2013). Turkish student science teachers' conceptions of sustainable development: A phenomenography. *International Journal of Science Education*, *35*(5), 731–752. https://doi.org/10.1080/09500693.2011.574822

Mebratu, D. (1998). Sustainability and sustainable development: Historical and conceptual review. *Environmental Impact Assessment Review*, *18*(6), 493–520. https://doi.org/10.1016/S0195-9255(98)00019-5

Meinzen-Dick, R., Kovarik, C., & Quisumbing, A. R. (2014). Gender and sustainability. *Annual Review of Environment and Resources*, *39*(1), 29–55. https://doi.org/10.1146/annurev-environ-101813-013240

Miller, G. R., & Brumbelow, K. (2016). Attitudes of incoming civil engineering students toward sustainability as an engineering ethic. *American Society of Civil Engineers*. https://doi.org/10.1061/(ASCE)EI.1943-5541.0000306

Mohai, P. (1992). Men, women, and the environment: An examination of the gender gap in environmental concern and activism. *Society and Natural Resources*, *5*(1), 1–19. https://doi.org/10.1080/08941929209380772

Mulder, K., Segalàs, J., & Ferrer-Balas, D. (2012). How to educate engineers for/in sustainable development: Ten years of discussion, remaining challenges. *International Journal of Sustainability in Higher Education*, *13*(3), 211–218. https://doi.org/10.1108/14676371211242535

Mulder, K. F. (2017). Strategic competences for concrete action towards sustainability: An oxymoron? Engineering education for a sustainable future. *Renewable and Sustainable Energy Reviews*, *68*, 1106–1111. https://doi.org/10.1016/j.rser.2016.03.038

National Society of Professional Engineers (NSPE). (2019). Code of ethics for engineers. Retrieved from https://www.nspe.org/sites/default/files/resources/pdfs/Ethics/CodeofEthics/NSPECodeofEthicsforEngineers.pdf

Raworth, K. (2012). *A safe and just space for humanity*. Oxfam Discussion Papers. Oxfam. Retrieved from https://www-cdn.oxfam.org/s3fs-public/file_attachments/dp-a-safe-and-just-space-for-humanity-130212-en_5.pdf

Rockström, J., Steffen, W., Noone, K., Persson, Å., Stuart Chapin, F., Lambin, E. F.,..., Foley, J. A. (2009). A safe operating space for humanity. *Nature*, *461*, 472–475. https://doi.org/10.1038/461472a

Sammalisto, K., Sundström, A., von Haartman, R., Holm, T., & Z. Yao. (2016). Learning about sustainability: What influences students' self-perceived sustainability actions after undergraduate education. *Sustainability*, *8*(6), 510. https://doi.org/10.3390/su8060510

Segalàs, J., Ferrer-Balas, D., Svanström, M., Lundqvist, U., & Mulder, K. F. (2009). What has to be learnt for sustainability? A comparison of bachelor engineering education competences at three European universities. *Sustainability Science*, *4*(1), 17–27. https://doi.org/10.1007/s11625-009-0068-2

Segalàs, J., Mulder, K. F., & Ferrer-Balas, D. (2012). What do EESD "experts" think sustainability is? Which pedagogy is suitable to learn it? Results from interviews and Cmaps analysis gathered at EESD 2008. *International Journal of Sustainability in Higher Education*, *13*(3), 293–304. https://doi.org/10.1108/14676371211242599

Shields, T., & Zeng, K. (2012). The reverse environmental gender gap in China: Evidence from "The China Survey". *Social Science Quarterly*, *93*(1), 1–20, https://doi.org/10.1111/j.1540-6237.2011.00802.x

Summers, M., & Childs, A. (2007). Student science teachers' conceptions of sustainable development: An empirical study of three postgraduate training cohorts. *Research in Science and Technological Education*, *25*(3), 307–327. https://doi.org/10.1080/02635140701535067

Summers, M., Childs, A., & Corney, G. (2005). Education for sustainable development in initial teacher training: Issues for interdisciplinary collaboration. *Environmental Education Research*, *11*(5), 623–647. https://doi.org/10.1080/13504620500169841

Tang, K. H. D. (2018). Correlation between sustainability education and engineering students' attitudes towards sustainability. *International Journal of Sustainability in Higher Education, 19*(3), 459–472. https://doi.org/10.1108/IJSHE-08-2017-0139

UNESCO. (2014). *Roadmap for implementing the global action programme on education for sustainable development*. Paris: United Nations Educational, Scientific and Cultural Organization. Retrieved from https://www.voced.edu.au/content/ngv:70467

UNESCO. (2017). *Education for sustainable development goals. Learning objectives*. Paris: United Nations Educational, Scientific and Cultural Organization, ISBN 978-92-3-100209-0.

Watson, M. K., Noyes, C., & Rodgers, M. O. (2013). Student perceptions of sustainability education in civil and environmental engineering at the Georgia Institute of Technology. *Journal of Professional Issues in Engineering Education and Practice, 139*(3), 235–243. https://doi.org/10.1061/(ASCE)EI.1943-5541.0000156

World Commission on Environment and Development. (1987). *Our common future*. Oxford: Oxford University Press.

Yuan, X., & Zuo, J. (2013). A critical assessment of the higher education for sustainable development from students' perspectives: A Chinese study. *Journal of Cleaner Production, 48*, 108–115. https://doi.org/10.1016/j.jclepro.2012.10.041.

Zeegers, Y., & Clark, I. F. (2014). Students' perceptions of education for sustainable development. *International Journal of Sustainability in Higher Education, 15*(2), 242–253. https://doi.org/10.1108/IJSHE-09-2012-0079

Zelinka, D., & Amadei, B. (2017). A methodology to model the integrated nature of the sustainable development goals: Importance for engineering education. Paper presented at 2017 ASEE annual conference & exposition. Retrieved from https://www.asee.org/public/conferences/78/papers/18668/view

CHAPTER 13

WHAKAWHITINGA KŌRERO: DIALOGUES ON SUSTAINABILITY

Tonya Sweet, Andrea Milligan and Meegan Hall

ABSTRACT

Interdisciplinary approaches to sustainability curriculum and pedagogy remain a particular challenge internationally. This chapter shares insights from a 2016 attempt to establish a first-year undergraduate Design course with an interdisciplinary approach to sustainability education. A series of video dialogues between university and community-based sustainability experts was created to enable students to access understandings and research evidence about sustainability issues and the United Nations Sustainable Development Goals, through different disciplinary lenses. The video dialogues provided students with opportunities to learn reflexively through exposure to differing visions for sustainable development, including Indigenous perspectives. In doing so, the video dialogues provide material for critical, creative, and iterative design thinking. Drawing on feedback from students enrolled in the course, this chapter offers reflections about enhancing course design through using video dialogues to support students' critical openness to addressing sustainability concerns.

Keywords: Design thinking; interdisciplinarity; pedagogy; sustainability; sustainable development goals; video dialogues

Like many universities around the world, Victoria University of Wellington (VUW) in New Zealand is engaging with its responses and responsibilities to

Teaching and Learning Strategies for Sustainable Development:
Innovations in Higher Education Teaching and Learning, Volume 19, 197–211

ISSN: 2055-3641/doi:10.1108/S2055-364120200000019016

complex sustainability issues. In recent years, for example, it established a Sustainability Office with a broadly mandated focus on campus operations, student engagement, and teaching and learning. It also identified a distinctive, interdisciplinary research strength for the university called *Te Auroa: Enhancing Resilience and Sustainability*. Te Auroa refers to a water current that continues to flow without end, indicating both resilience and sustainability. In 2017, it became the first New Zealand University to sign an international *University Commitment to the Sustainable Development Goals* agreement, an Australasian/Pacific initiative to show that universities can be leaders in sustainability. Accordingly, every academic unit now offers courses with sustainability content and many degrees are shaped with a strong sustainability focus.

However, the experience of academics championing sustainability indicates that interdisciplinary approaches to curriculum and pedagogy remain a particular challenge (Wood, Cornforth, Beals, Taylor, & Tallon, 2016). VUW is, of course, not alone in this. As Howlett, Ferreira, and Blomfield (2016) explained, "higher education institutions remain notoriously stubborn in changing their unidirectional, hierarchical and disciplinary approach to teaching" (p. 310). In many ways, affirming this challenge this chapter shares insights from 2016 attempt to establish a first-year undergraduate course with a focus on sustainable development. Emerging from an impasse in the course development process, the course's eventual reincarnation in 2018 within the School of Design as *Design Thinking for Sustainability* (DSDN183) offered unexpected opportunities to engage in an interdisciplinary approach to sustainability education.

In our chapter, we consider how interdisciplinary approaches to sustainable development education can be enhanced through course design. We focus particularly on a key pedagogical element developed for DSDN183 – a series of video dialogues between university and community-based sustainability experts. The videos were created to enable students to access understandings and research evidence about sustainability issues and each of the United Nations Sustainable Development Goals (SDGs), through different disciplinary lenses. The development of the video dialogues was supported by a *VicTeach* grant that assisted the development of creative and interdisciplinary, community-building, learning, and teaching initiatives. In contrast to strongly content-driven and normative approaches, the video dialogues were intended to provide opportunities to learn reflexively through exposure to differing visions for sustainable development, including perspectives from the Indigenous Māori people of New Zealand. Used in this way, the video dialogues provided material for critical, creative, and iterative design thinking as a process-based approach to problem-solving. Drawing on student focus groups and written reflections, our chapter examines the impact of the video dialogues on the students' responses to a wide range of complex sustainability issues related to the SDGs. Our chapter concludes with thoughts and reflections on enhancing the course design through the use of pedagogical tools and transformative approaches that support students' critical openness to addressing sustainability concerns.

INTERDISCIPLINARY LEARNING FOR SUSTAINABILITY

Many courses are capable of effectively addressing sustainability concerns through specified disciplinary perspectives. However, sustainability as a collective aspiration is, by nature, interdisciplinary. While there is limited research that compares the outcomes of disciplinary and interdisciplinary approaches to sustainability education in higher education contexts (Remington-Doucette, Hiller Connell, Armstrong, & Musgrove, 2013), advocates of interdisciplinary sustainability curricula emphasize that responding to the interpenetrated nature of sustainability issues requires opportunities to bring together multiple ways of knowing. Universities can be challenging places for such work. The complexities of organizational change, power relationships, traditional institutional structures, and economic pressures (Filho et al., 2019; Hoover & Harder, 2014; Krizek, Newport, White, & Townsend, 2012) present substantial obstacles to interdisciplinarity. Even for committed higher education institutions and individuals, bringing together academic and disciplinary insight across a university is replete with theoretical and practical challenge, particularly in terms of maintaining learning cohesiveness, continuity, and depth (Caviglia-Harris & Hatley, 2004).

VUW's experience highlights enablers and constraints of "top down" (senior management led) and "bottom-up" (teacher driven) interdisciplinary sustainability curriculum development. In 2016, a newly appointed Assistant Vice-Chancellor (Sustainability) (AVCS) was charged with leading a small but capable Sustainability Office and transforming the University's sustainability practices and outcomes. Among the AVCS' priorities was establishing a new sustainability course that was accessible to all university students and collaborative in nature. The project quickly gathered momentum and a large potential teaching team was assembled and embarked on a complex course design process. The United Nations' SDGs were to provide the architecture for a multifaceted approach to introducing sustainability and a vision for transformation "for people, planet and prosperity" (Sustainable Development Solutions Network, 2015, p. 6). It was felt that the SDGs provided a holistic context that reinforced the interconnectivity between sustainability challenges, including synergies and potential conflicts and trade-offs, and the need for awareness of their collective demands. The SDGs are understood as inherently interdisciplinary in scope and applicability, in that they are informed by, and call for further research across, multiple disciplines.

Despite being strategically important, the proposal that went forward for approval was rejected by a central university committee because the course had not secured an administrative "home" within the institutional structure. That could have been the end of the story. However, this time in a bottom-up approach, a small subset of the initial course developers saw the potential to recast the original course within a more conventional structure, while still allowing for interdisciplinarity. Out of the ashes arose *Design Thinking for Sustainability, DSDN183*, a first-year undergraduate Faculty of Architecture and Design course that used design thinking and its application to complex sustainability challenges. The five-week, blended course considered sustainability through different perspectives, disciplines, spatial, and temporal scales, and employed a student-led, project-based, and reflexive pedagogical orientation. DSDN183 retained the original vision for an interdisciplinary framework scaffolded by the SDGs, but with Design as the anchor, as the learning outcomes indicate:

- Describe relationships between the SDGs according to local, national, and global sustainability contexts.
- Explain existing and future sustainability challenges from disciplinary, Māori, and Treaty perspectives.[1]
- Explain the principles of design thinking.
- Apply design thinking in a collaborative process (https://www.victoria.ac.nz/courses/dsdn/183).

Crucially, DSDN183 accommodated students from across the university, irrespective of their skill level or major field of study, and was offered in the Summer trimester when student schedules availed greater flexibility. Entry was not restricted by co- or pre-requisites that may otherwise hinder interdisciplinary enrollment. As an introductory-level course, DSDN183 presented a comprehensive overview of the SDGs. This overview addressed local, national, and global contexts inclusive of examples of synthesis/reciprocity and of conflict. Examples of external actors/forces that have the potential to impede sustainable development were examined in course materials, in-class discussions and assessments.

CRITICAL OPENNESS: DESIGN THINKING AS A SIGNATURE PEDAGOGY

Later in this chapter we consider a resource developed for DSDN183, a series of video dialogues between university and community-based sustainability experts. Before that, this section looks more widely to the design thinking approach used in DSDN183, within which the video resource was nested. Borrowing from Shulman's (2005) work in the area of professional practice, we characterize design thinking as a "signature" course pedagogy with potential to support students' *critical openness* as they respond to complex sustainability challenges.

A key objective in DSDN183 was to introduce students to the principles of design thinking as a practical skill-set for addressing sustainability issues. Equally applicable to designers and non-designers, design thinking has gained traction as a process that can be applied systematically across disciplines (Seidel & Fixson, 2013) and to the navigation of sustainability challenges (Garcia & Dacko, 2016). Design thinking can be understood as a human-centered and process-based approach to problem-solving. Its deep structure that is "assumptions about how best to impart a certain body of knowledge and know-how" (Shulman, 2005, p. 55) involve building empathy with a person's problem, applying non-linear divergent/convergent thinking to produce multiple potential solutions, and using abductive reasoning to review, test, and apply the best option (Brown, 2009; Kelley & Kelley, 2013; Martin, 2007). In the context of sustainability education, design thinking acknowledges the "long now" (Brand, 1999), that is, the shortsightedness that has given rise to our current sustainability challenges and the need for long-term responsibility that considers potential effects over long horizons of time (Irwin, 2015).

Shulman (2005) emphasized that signature pedagogies are not values-neutral acts. Arguably, design thinking offers one approach to a central ethical dilemma in sustainability education: how to balance the need for urgent, collective responses to sustainability challenges with the recognition of uncertainty and plural societies embody multiple perspectives and diversity (e.g., Öhman, 2016; Sund & Öhman, 2014; Van Poeck, Goeminne, & Vandenabeele, 2016). Design thinking navigates this balancing act by developing cognitive, affective, and volitional and motivational competencies to empower students to make positive contributions to sustainable development (UNESCO, 2015; Weinert, 2001). At the same time, it responds to the highly complex and evolving nature of sustainability challenges by nurturing collaborative, critical, and creative thinking to strike a clear deviation from traditional tactics that created our sustainability challenges in the first place. The latter is particularly notable, given the observation by Wood et al. (2016) that one barrier to interdisciplinary curriculum design lies in "embracing" the kinds of pedagogies that can support students to navigate the perspectival and contested dimensions of sustainability issues.

We contend that the "deep structures" (Shulman, 2005) of design thinking hold considerable potential to support students' critical openness to addressing complex sustainability issues. This is because the iterative nature of design thinking is useful in generating alternative and ongoing responses to complex and wicked problems (Buchanan, 1992), where root causes are uncertain or entangled, and where there is unlikely to be a simple blueprint for change. Design thinking also develops a disposition toward abductive and integrative thinking, that is, to "hold two conflicting ideas in constructive tension" (Martin, 2007, p. 7) and to create an outcome that is potentially more effective than the sum of its parts. The process therefore entails the expansive generation of ideas through spontaneous, wide brushstrokes as well as through the analysis of patterns and organized constraints. Importantly, and a discussion that is returned to later in this chapter, the collaboration of diverse disciplines and perspectives play a vital role in this process; as Tim Brown (2009), CEO of IDEO proclaims, "all of us are smarter than any of us" (p. 26). Collective contribution and engagement across disciplines is a decisive requirement of sustainability education where partnership is seen as central to achieving shared goals and is, in fact, reflected in SDG 17: Partnership for the goals (UN General Assembly, 2015).

Indigenous knowledge and its relevance and contribution to sustainability education also provide an important underpinning of the design thinking process in DSDN183. Students examined the principles of sustainability and the consequences of non-sustainable development on global, national, and individual scales. Through guest lectures and integration within the video resource, students were introduced to local contexts, inclusive of cultural concepts and Indigenous values, including: mātauranga Māori (the Indigenous Māori knowledge, comprehension and understanding of everything visible and invisible existing in the universe), kaitiakitanga (the Māori concept of guardianship, care, and conservation of nature, people, and ideas) and whanaungatanga (the Māori concept of close relationships and bonds that are formed through collective experiences, as evidenced through the interdisciplinary and collaborative learning and teaching environment).

WHAKAWHITINGA KŌRERO: DIALOGUES ON SUSTAINABILITY

A bespoke resource was produced for DSDN183 to support the learning objectives and to facilitate blended learning through synthesizing in-class and online educational activities. The resource, *Whakawhitinga Kōrero: Dialogues on Sustainability* (2019),[2] entailed a series of 14 videos that introduced the SDGs as they relate to (a) regional, national, and global sustainability and (b) interconnections between economic, social, cultural, and environmental dimensions of sustainability. The Māori term "whakawhitinga kōrero" means dialogue and discussion. It stems from the Māori word "whiti" which translates to cross over, swap, or exchange but, in another sense, "whiti" can also mean "to shine." With both interpretations in mind, the videos shine a light on the importance of dialogue, both in person and on screen, as a key pedagogical approach to teaching sustainability. The series served as the dominant source of online content, functioned to complement project-based learning, and supported internationally recognized dimensions of global competence, including: "the capacity to examine issues and situations of local, global, and cultural significance," "the capacity to understand and appreciate different perspectives and worldviews," and "the capacity and disposition to take constructive action toward sustainable development and collective well-being" (OECD, 2018, pp. 7–8).

The videos supported the student's engagement in design thinking in two key respects. They firstly embedded an interdisciplinary approach to introducing principles of sustainability, by presenting diverse perspectives through dialogues between pairs of academics, local representatives from business and government sectors, and university alumni. This afforded a democratic frame of reference in understanding the SDGs and mirrored the complexity and universality inherent in the SDG framework. Importantly, through the dialogues, students were exposed to conflicting attitudes and viewpoints on topics of sustainability and invited to consider and develop personal positions. A layer of animated content supported the students understanding of the connectivity and interdependence between the goals, and clarified complex concepts as they were raised. For example, in the first video, an icon (visual symbol) associated to SDG 1 appeared as the two participants initiated their conversation about poverty as a sustainability challenge. As the conversation evolved additional icons (in this case, for SDG 2: Zero Hunger; SDG 3: Good Health and Well-being; and SDG 6: Clean Water and Sanitation) appeared, linked to the icon representing SDG 1 by branching dashed lines. Additionally, as more complex concepts on the topic of poverty were raised, simple hand-drawn images appeared that depicted the concepts narrated.

A second support for the students' design thinking was the priority given to local context and personal actions in discussing sustainability challenges as they related to the SDGs. Although the dialogues did not follow a prescriptive direction, the participants were asked in advance of recording to (i) reflect on the relevance of their assigned SDG in the context of Wellington and New Zealand; (ii) share examples of their everyday sustainable actions; and (iii) suggest strategies for the adaptation of sustainable behaviors. Through this place-based, contextualized lens, students were afforded with avenues of identification in understanding how sustainability and the SDGs related to them personally. Many of the dialogues drew connections between sustainability, Indigenous knowledge, and cultural values, including addressing specific considerations as they apply to New Zealand's Māori population and constitutional context.

The videos were explicitly linked to the course learning objectives through an online assessment task. Weekly reflective journals required the students to write a summary of150–500 words in length, and responding to two or three of the following questions:

- Why is this SDG is important – in your life, locally, nationally, and/or globally?
- How does this SDG connect with, or present challenges for, other SDGs?
- How do Māori and Treaty of Waitangi perspectives relate to or challenge this SDG?
- What could you do – individually, with others and/or politically – to take action toward achieving this SDG?

Another assignment project specifically required students to work in interdisciplinary groups to identify points of synthesis between three SDGs and, through the application of a design thinking process, to devise an awareness campaign for the university that highlighted the interconnections.

EDUCATIONAL OUTCOMES

All 18 students enrolled in DSDN183 in Trimester 3, 2018 participated in a small-scale study about the educational outcomes of the use of the videos within the course. The study was approved by the VUW Human Ethics Committee (Approval number 26995). The students were invited to submit their reflective journals after the course was completed and/or take part in a focus group interview about how they used the video dialogues to learn, the strengths and weaknesses of this teaching tool, and how the videos could be used in future courses (see Appendix for questions). The Course Coordinator (one of the co-authors of this chapter) did not participate in the focus group discussion and did not have access to the data until after the final grades were released. Five students agreed to participate in the focus group interview and provide their assignments, and another student agreed to provide their assignment only. All students involved in the study have been given a pseudonym. Across both data sources, a directed content analysis (Hseih & Shannon, 2005) was employed, using the analytic constructs of interconnectedness and interdisciplinarity, critical thinking and polyvocality. Through Westheimer and Kahne's (2004) typology, we were also interested in how the videos may have inspired *personally responsible, participatory* (collective), and/or *social-justice oriented* (focused on a deep understanding of the structural underpinnings of issues) actions for change.

An initial question in the focus group interview revealed a range of motivations that led the students to enroll in DSDN183, including "needing the points" ($n = 3$), the course's connection to workplace learning ($n = 2$), and having enjoyed a previous course with the lecturer ($n = 2$). While one student stated that they felt familiar with the SDGs, three out of the five participants were interested in the course because they were less familiar with this framework. One student reflected that:

> I felt quite bad as before coming into this course I really didn't have any interest or knowledge towards sustainability in general and had no idea what the SDGs were or that they existed. As an architecture student I knew that we do need to become better sustainable architects which pushed me to take this course. I was instantly dreading it because I felt almost ashamed of my lack of knowledge towards the topic. (Aheli)

Regardless of their starting point, it was striking that the students' perception was that the course had significantly amplified their understanding of the SDGs and sustainability issues. While it is difficult to assess the role that the video dialogues alone played in this, all the students commented positively on this pedagogical tool. The students felt that the video dialogues were supportive of their assignment work, found them to be more engaging than print media, and especially liked the way they could be used flexibly within their independent learning time. The local contextualization of the dialogues and their conversational style significantly supported the students to access the concepts and debates by making global issues seem less overwhelming, presenting the issues as possible for the students to address, and inviting their own responses. Tying the videos to an assessment task provided the students with a strong purpose for viewing. One student, Aheli, commented that the written reflections particularly enabled her to "create a personal connection to them [the SDGs] while also thinking about the larger scale." Another student, Richard, said that his favorite part of the journaling was "seeing the different chemistries between different people, and how this affected the shape of the conversations they had."

All the students clearly understood the interconnected nature of SDGs and were able to provide multiple examples of this, drawn from the videos. They found the animations within the videos that highlighted connections between the SDGs very helpful. However, the students much more strongly emphasized seeing the interconnections between the SDGs in the videos than the role of interdisciplinary thinking. A somewhat latent and ambivalent understanding of interdisciplinarity was evident in two suggestions: (a) that other faculties could take up responsibility for particular SDGs and (b) that a series of issues centric rather than SDG-led videos should be created. While these are not necessarily mutually exclusive suggestions, it was notable that the students perceived the videos as being relevant to their own and other disciplines rather than as supportive of interdisciplinary approaches. The students did not articulate why the role of interdisciplinarity did not resonate as well, but it is possible that this was because the connections between disciplines received less visual emphasis that those between the SDGs.

When asked about the extent to which the videos supported their critical thinking, the students strongly emphasized the polyvocal nature of the series of dialogues. The convivial, open-minded conversations were particularly appreciated because they felt less threatening – to the extent that the students called for more debates of this nature within the videos. To them, perspectival differences are a fact of sustainability issues but need to be debated with intellectual humility and empathy. They felt that the videos had opened up conversations about important topics that were sometimes contentious within the class. The videos reinforced the idea that, because there are no simple solutions, appreciating new and/or different perspectives was important. The students felt that the non-directive nature of the videos provided a valued opportunity to reflexively engage with the ideas and arguments presented in the videos, that is, to use them as a counterpoint to their own perspectives. Milos expressed it this way:

> The fact that the videos were showing two people having a discussion allowed me to form my own views and reflections on the SDGs. As we know that there isn't a straightforward answer to these wicked problems, having a discussion rather than a video that 'teaches' made it more engaging as well as providing me with the necessary space to think.

The students strongly equated this feature with the credibility of the videos. Emlin expressed this as:

> Their opinions, that are not necessarily being presented as right or wrong, helped you engage and made it credible as well because they're not telling you that this is how you should be thinking for sustainability, they're just voicing their opinions and making it open that you can voice your opinion too.

In sum, the focus group participants strongly connected the videos to critical thinking dispositions or traits (Foundation for Critical Thinking, n.d.) especially intellectual autonomy and fairmindedness. However, the students were less likely to question what was presented in the videos, such as the assumptions, implications, or points of view. The students struggled to identify perspectives that were missing from the videos, one suggestion being that a male perspective could have enhanced the discussion about Gender Equality (SDG5). Their other observation was that Māori perspectives were more evident in relation to some SDGs. They commented favorably on the organic inclusion of Māori perspectives and were interested in learning more but not if such perspectives were "forced" into each video. One student, Aheli, recognized that there may be different perspectives in relation to sustainability but did not explore these deeply in her reflective journal. Another, Milos, questioned the efficiency of volunteering and then provided a counter-argument in relation to enhancing good health and well-being (SDG3) and creating sustainable cities and communities (SDG11). A third student, Bess, demonstrated the strongest levels of criticality in her writing, particularly through questioning Western assumptions about what constitutes a "good" quality of life and the cultural relevance of the SDGs for Indigenous communities. This student also most strongly engaged with Māori perspectives, across multiple journal entries.

The students reflections on the links between the video dialogues and sustainability actions indicated that the wider course had opened up a level of personal awareness and that the use of the SDG framework had drawn attention to the urgency for change. It was particularly encouraging that the videos had supported everyday conversations with family and friends and offered encouragement for small personal changes. Overwhelmingly, the students emphasized the importance of personal responsibility for change (citing actions such as re-evaluating their own transport options and patterns of consumption) and the need for participatory, collective change. Richard, for instance, noted that:

> Half way through the video, SDG 17 is brought into focus – Partnership For The Goals – relating to collective action, that climate change for instance is not going to be solved by one person, it is something that needs to be worked on together.

The students emphasized social-justice oriented action to a much lesser extent. In one instance, this form of participation was regarded with concern: "this leads to a strong-willed but perhaps narrow-minded 'sustainability activists' that may cause conflicts with other 'activists' with varying priorities" (Milos). One student, however, emphasized an imperative for democratic political engagement to bring about change:

> Change is currently happening too slowly and individually and as the public, we need to put pressure on governments. Governments respond to what people are demanding to keep their own party in power so if local communities across the nation demand better public transport systems, bicycle/scooter/skateboard spaces, more windmills and solar panels to make electricity cheaper then the change will come. (Bess)

VIDEO DIALOGUES AS A MECHANISM FOR CRITICAL OPENNESS?

Although the students' feedback suggests that the video resource played a positive role in their understanding of the SDGs and sustainability issues, their comments also highlight potential avenues for improvement. A first avenue is that the resource may have benefited from a more diverse representation of genders and socio-cultural perspectives in supporting the course learning objectives. In particular, the inclusion of additional Māori perspectives could have better connected to the emerging literature on the contribution of Indigenous knowledge to sustainability and the SDGs. This would assist in conveying local sustainability contexts and the reinforcement of the importance of Indigenous voices in the sustainability discourse for the enhancements they provide (Folke, 2004; Hill et al., 2012; Magni, 2017; Yap & Watene, 2019). This would more effectively support the objectives assigned to the resource, and facilitate a connection to three aspects of the SDG framework: the inclusion of Indigenous peoples as one of their nine major groups, their human rights basis, and their focus on "achieving balance between people and the environment" (Yap & Watene, 2019, p. 5).

In reflecting on the production of the videos, the thread of each dialogue was – to a certain extent – shaped by the post-production editing process whereby the director/editor of the videos determined which material to keep or cull. Although the editing process was driven by the parameters and objectives assigned to the learning and teaching resource, subjective influence is unavoidable. This recognition illuminates the need for collaborative oversight in the creation of resources such as *Whakawhitinga Kōrero: Dialogues on Sustainability* in which polyvocality is a central theme.

A second potential avenue for enhancement relates to the videos support for students' critical thinking. As they indicated, the conversational style of the dialogues – whereby participants engaged in an organic exchange of ideas and opinions – enabled them "space to think" about their individual perspectives and, from this, to construct personalized viewpoints around sustainability issues. This dimension of learning underpins a key aspect of global competence whereby globally competent people effectively combine knowledge about the world with critical reasoning in forming their own opinion about a global issue (OECD, 2018). The recognition that perspectives and behaviors are shaped by multiple influences is an important aspect of this competency. However, the structure attributed to the discourse may have benefited from showcasing participants engaged in additional divergence, expressed as an opportunity to facilitate greater critical thinking. In retrospect, the discussions may have erred on the side of convivial and the animations possibly inadvertently reinforced notions of connectedness between ideas, rather than productive disjunctions. That the students placed less emphasis on interdisciplinarity suggests that, in particular, further consideration could be given to the different epistemic perspectives that each participant was bringing to the discussion. While each participant title (noted on the screen at the beginning of each video) included their discipline or organization, it was interesting that the students did not directly pick up on this. A specific discussion prompt, such as "what perspectives seemed to be shaping the discussants' viewpoints?" may have encouraged the students to consider the relationship between individual positions and the disciplines/organizations represented.

A further support for students' criticality relates to the debate in the literature that has centered around the differences between Western and Indigenous ways of knowing related to sustainability (Berkes, 1999; Johnson et al., 2016; Kealiikanakaoleohaililani & Giardina, 2016). It has been noted, for example, that the "persistent and intimate relationships" that Indigenous people have with their surroundings contrast with "Western sustainability's anonymous and ephemeral market-based consumer relationships" (Kealiikanakaoleohaililani & Giardina, 2016, p. 59) that take a short-term view of sustainability issues. Interestingly, the students that engaged with Māori perspectives tended to do so in a positive and unquestioning manner.

A third consideration with regard to improving the videos relates to the ways in which change was envisaged. It is perhaps unsurprising, given the prevalence of neoliberal discourses, that students emphasized the individual (and, to a lesser extent, collective) sustainability actions that they and others could engage in. Again, we suggest that a specific discussion prompt could have highlighted the political dimensions of sustainability action, particularly in relation to the mandate that New Zealand universities are given to act as critic and conscience of society.

It could have been valuable for students to learn, for example, how each of the participants conceived their research or organizational contribution to a national and global debate on sustainability issues.

A fourth consideration relates to strengthening the relationship between the video dialogues and their application to design thinking. The introduction to sustainability and the SDG framework according to varying contexts, including local, national, and global scales, reflects the pattern of convergence and divergence that is at the heart of the design thinking process (Brown, 2009). Design thinking is particularly useful as a collaborative problem-solving process where multiple perspectives and (interdisciplinary) points of expertise are warranted. However, design thinking may be employed by individuals as a means to work divergently and convergently in the investigation of potential solutions. While the structure of the videos inherently supports these modes of cognitive thinking, this attribute was not explicitly illuminated in the video resource or to the students enrolled in DSDN183. Likewise, just as design thinking is pursued as an iterative and non-linear process (Brown, 2009), this process is mirrored in the SDGs whereby the means of implementation does not follow a prescriptive path (UN General Assembly, 2015). It was salutary to note that, within the focus group discussions and reflective journals, none of the students articulated how the videos contributed to their design thinking. This may have been an artifact of the interview questions and journal prompts, however, it was notable that the students tended to position the video dialogues as information, albeit encompassing differing perspectives, rather than as material to think with, *within* the design process.

CONCLUSION

This chapter explored the role that the video resource *Whakawhitinga Kōrero: Dialogues on Sustainability* played within a course that aimed to harness interdisciplinary, polyvocality, and design thinking to address sustainability challenges and the SDGs. We have contended that the critical, creative, and collaborative nature of design thinking holds considerable potential to address the uncertain and perspectival nature of sustainability issues. Located within this conceptual and pedagogical framing, the video dialogues fulfilled a function that is arguably less typical of content-driven sustainability learning resources. That is, they offered a mechanism for students to engage with a holistic and synoptic view of sustainability concerns, and at the same time opened a window to the plural and contested nature of this landscape. Perhaps most vitally, the open-ended, respectful, and quietly challenging nature of the videos achieved this in an invitational manner. The videos invited students to consider their own perspectives and experiences, engage in dialogue with peers and family, and consider how they could take action for change. There is, no doubt, further scope for enhancing this pedagogical resource and, of course, the views expressed are a window in time. However, we suggest that the use of iteratively developed video dialogues within a design course offers fertile transformative potential in relation to encouraging students' critical openness to sustainability concerns.

NOTES

1. Signed in 1840, the Treaty of Waitangi is the agreement between Māori and the British Crown that established the nation now known as New Zealand. "Treaty perspectives" refers to views informed by the bicultural relationship established by the signing of the Treaty of Waitangi.
2. https://www.youtube.com/playlist?list=PLV_dlHiN2dYDhSCYMkaotRT9LKJu7jBPC

REFERENCES

Berkes, F. (1999). *Sacred ecology: traditional ecological knowledge and management systems.* Philadelphia, PA: Taylor & Francis.

Brand, S. (1999). *The clock of the long now: Time and responsibility.* New York, NY: Basic.

Brown, T. (2009). *Change by design: How design thinking transforms organizations and inspires innovation.* New York, NY: Harper Business.

Buchanan, R. (1992). Wicked problems in design thinking. *Design Issues*, *8*(2), 5–21. http://www.jstor.org/stable/1511637

Caviglia-Harris, J. L., & Hatley, J. (2004). Interdisciplinary teaching: Analyzing consensus and conflict in environmental studies. *International Journal of Sustainability in Higher Education, 5*(4), 395–403. https://doi.org/10.1108/14676370410561090

Filho, W. L., Raath, S., Lazzarini, B., Vargas, V. R., de Souza, L., Anholon, R., …, Orlovic, V. L. (2018). The role of transformation in learning and education for sustainability. *Journal of Cleaner Production, 199*, 286–295. https://doi.org/10.1016/j.jclepro.2018.07.017

Folke, C. (2004). Traditional knowledge in social–ecological systems. *Ecology and Society*, *9*(3), 7. http://www.ecologyandsociety.org/vol9/iss3/art7/

Foundation for Critical Thinking. (n.d.). The essential dimensions of critical thinking. Retrieved from http://www.criticalthinking.org/pages/critical-thinking-where-to-begin/796

Garcia, R., & Dacko, S. (2016). Design thinking for sustainability. In M. Luchs, S. Swan, & A. Griffin (Eds.), *Design thinking: New product development essentials from the PDMA* (pp. 381–400). Hoboken, NJ: Wiley.

Hill, R., Grant, C., George, M., Robinson, C., Jackson, S., & Abel, N. (2012). A typology of Indigenous engagement in Australian environmental management: Implications for knowledge integration and social-ecological system sustainability. *Ecology and Society*, *17*(1), 23. http://dx.doi.org/10.5751/ES-04587-170123

Hoover, E., & Harder, M. K. (2015). What lies beneath the surface? The hidden complexities of organizational change for sustainability in higher education. *Journal of Cleaner Production*, *106*, 175–188. https://doi.org/10.1016/j.jclepro.2014.01.081

Howlett, C., Ferreira, J.-A., & Blomfield, J. (2016). Teaching sustainable development in higher education: Building critical, reflective thinkers through an interdisciplinary approach. *International Journal of Sustainability in Higher Education, 17*(3), 305–321. https://doi.org/10.1108/IJSHE-07-2014-0102

Hseih, H.-F., & Shannon, S. E. (2005). Three approaches to qualitative content analysis. *Qualitative Health Research*, *15*(9), 1277–1288. https://doi.org/10.1177/1049732305276687

Irwin, T. (2015). Transition design: A proposal for a new area of design practice, study, and research. *Design and Culture*, *7*(2), 229–246. doi:10.1080/17547075.2015.1051829

Johnson, J. T., Howitt, R., Cajete, G., Berkes, F., Louis, R. P., & Kliskey, A. (2016). Weaving Indigenous and sustainability sciences to diversify our methods. *Sustainability Science*, *11*(1), 1–11. https://doi.org/10.1007/s11625-015-0349-x

Kealiikanakaoleohaililani, K., & Giardina, C. P. (2016). Embracing the sacred: An Indigenous framework for tomorrow's sustainability science. *Sustainability Science*, *11*(1), 57–67. https://doi.org/10.1007/s11625-015-0343-3

Kelley, T., & Kelley, D. (2013). *Creative confidence: Unleashing the creative potential within us all.* New York, NY: Crown Business.

Krizek, K. J., Newport, D., White, J., & Townsend, A. R. (2012). Higher education's sustainability imperative: How to practically respond? *International Journal of Sustainability in Higher Education*, *13*(1), 19–33. https://doi.org/10.1108/14676371211190281

Magni, G. (2017). Indigenous knowledge and implications for the sustainable development agenda. *European Journal of Education*, *52*(4), 437–447. https://doi.org/10.1111/ejed.12238

Martin, R. (2007). *The opposable mind: How successful leaders win through integrative thinking*. Boston, MA: Harvard Business School Press.

OECD. (2018). Preparing our youth for an inclusive and sustainable world: The OECD PISA global competence framework. Retrieved from www.oecd.org/pisa/Handbook-PISA-2018-Global-Competence.pdf

Öhman, J. (2016). New ethical challenges within environmental and sustainability education. *Environmental Education Research*, *22*(6), 765–770. https://doi.org/10.1080/13504622.2016.1165800

Remington-Doucette, S. M., Hiller Connell, K. Y., Armstrong, C. M., & Musgrove, S. L. (2013). Assessing sustainability education in a transdisciplinary undergraduate course focused on real-world problem solving: A case for disciplinary grounding. *International Journal of Sustainability in Higher Education*, *14*(4), 404–433. https://doi.org/10.1108/IJSHE-01-2012-0001

Seidel, V. P., & Fixson, S. K. (2013). Adopting design thinking in novice multidisciplinary teams: The application and limits of design methods and reflexive practices. *Journal of Product Innovation Management*, *30*(1), 19–33. https://doi.org/10.1111/jpim.12061

Shulman, L. S. (2005). Signature pedagogies in the professions. *Daedalus*, *134*(3), 52–59. https://doi.org/10.1162/0011526054622015

Sund, L., & Öhman, J. (2014). On the need to repoliticise environmental and sustainability education: Rethinking the postpolitical consensus. *Environmental Education Research*, *20*(5), 639–659. doi:10.1080/13504622.2013.833585

Sustainable Development Solutions Network. (2015). Getting started with the sustainable development goals. Retrieved from http://unsdsn.org/wp-content/uploads/2015/12/151211-getting-started-guide-FINAL-PDF-.pdf

Sweet, T. (2019). Whakawhitinga kōrero: Dialogues on sustainability. Retrieved from https://www.youtube.com/playlist?list=PLV_dlHiN2dYDhSCYMkaotRT9LKJu7jBPC

UN General Assembly. (2015). Transforming our world: The 2030 Agenda for sustainable development. Retrieved from https://sustainabledevelopment.un.org/post2015/transformingourworld

UNESCO. (2015). *Global Action Programme on Education for Sustainable Development*. Paris: UNESCO.

Van Poeck, K., Goeminne, G., & Vandenabeele, J. (2016). Revisiting the democratic paradox of environmental and sustainability education: Sustainability issues as matters of concern. *Environmental Education Research*, *22*(6), 806–826. doi:10.1080/13504622.2014.966659

Weinert, F. E. (2001). Concept of competence: A conceptual clarification. In D. S. Rychen & L. H. Salganik (Eds.), *Defining and selecting key competencies* (pp. 45–65). Ashland, OH: Hogrefe & Huber Publishers.

Westheimer, J., & Kahne, J. (2004). What kind of citizen? The politics of educating for democracy. *American Research Journal*, *41*(2), 237–269. https://doi.org/10.3102/00028312041002237

Wood, B. E., Cornforth, S., Beals, F., Taylor, M., & Tallon, R. (2016). Sustainability champions? Academic identities and sustainability curricula in higher education. *International Journal of Sustainability in Higher Education*, *17*(3), 342–360. https://doi.org/10.1108/IJSHE-12-2014-0171

Yap, M. L.-M. & Watene, K. (2019). The sustainable development goals (SDGs) and Indigenous peoples: Another missed opportunity? *Journal of Human Development and Capabilities*, *2019*, 1–17. doi:10.1080/19452829.2019.1574725

APPENDIX: SEMI-STRUCTURED FOCUS GROUP INTERVIEW QUESTIONS FOR DSDN183 STUDENTS

1. Why did you enroll in this course and what did you hope to gain from it? Thinking about the video dialogues that you have used in this course:
2. In what ways have the video dialogues supported your learning?
3. In what ways have the video dialogues helped you to think critically about sustainability issues and the SDGs?
4. How did they help you to think about the interconnected and interdisciplinary facets of sustainability?
5. In what ways have the video dialogues helped you to think about different perspectives related to sustainability issues, including Māori worldviews?
6. Were any perspectives missing from the videos?
7. What suggestions do you have for how the videos could be used in future courses?
8. In what ways have the video dialogues inspired change in your everyday lives?

CHAPTER 14

CAMPUS AS A LIVING LAB: CREATING A CULTURE OF RESEARCH AND LEARNING IN SUSTAINABLE DEVELOPMENT

Angelique Pilon, John Madden, James Tansey and John Metras

ABSTRACT

Over the last 30 years, the University of British Columbia (UBC) in Vancouver, Canada has advanced sustainable development on campus and created a culture of sustainability, with ambitious goals, and strong collaborative relationships. Launched in 2010, the Campus as a Living Laboratory (CLL) initiative utilizes the campus buildings and infrastructure as opportunities for research, teaching, and learning. Projects under the CLL bring together academic researchers, students, staff, and partners to demonstrate, test, research, and learn from new ideas for sustainable development. These projects range in scale from small and discrete educational or research projects, often led by students, to the design and construction of innovative buildings, with multiyear interdisciplinary research programs. CLL projects are opportunities for UBC students to engaged in applied research and learning that enhances their educational experience at the university, and may serve as models for other universities interested in expanding sustainable development on their campuses.

Keywords: Sustainable development; green buildings; institutional enablers; living lab; institutional culture; applied learning

Teaching and Learning Strategies for Sustainable Development:
Innovations in Higher Education Teaching and Learning, Volume 19, 213–227

ISSN: 2055-3641/doi:10.1108/S2055-364120200000019017

INTRODUCTION

Located in the west coast province of British Columbia, Metro Vancouver is one of the fastest growing urban areas in Canada and has been recognized as one of the most sustainable regions in the world (Arcadis, 2018). Within the region, the University of British Columbia (UBC) has been operating at the frontier of sustainability for the last 30 years, advancing the design of sustainable buildings, low-carbon energy systems, and human health and well-being initiatives. Over 220 UBC faculty across 50 programs engage in research generating more than $80m in funding, and teach over 650 sustainability courses (UBC, 2018). UBC is also unique among leading research universities because its Vancouver campus effectively operates like a small city. The University independently manages 16.5 million square feet of buildings on the 400 hectare campus, along with landscape, roads, utilities, and other infrastructure.

The concept of the Campus as a Living Laboratory (CLL) was developed at UBC to demonstrate leadership in sustainable development, through the integration of research and learning with the planning, design, construction, and operation of buildings, landscape, and infrastructure. It uses the campus as a giant sandbox in which there is freedom to creatively and collaboratively explore and solve big problems. CLL embodies the belief that universities have an important role in responding to the complex challenges we are facing in the twenty-first century, not only as drivers of innovation through the generation of new knowledge, but also as the educators of the next generation of policy-makers, practitioners, and citizens. It is an approach to knowledge generation and dissemination that can be replicated in universities and cities to enhance both sustainable development practices and academic learning experiences.

This chapter describes the context at UBC that has led to the establishment of CLL, an overview of the initiative, and case studies that illustrate a selection of CLL projects. It discusses some of the enablers and challenges of the initiative as an opportunity for research and learning. UBC's experience with the CLL initiative may provide a useful approach for other universities seeking to engaging students in sustainable development on their campuses.

SUSTAINABILITY AT THE UBC

Institutional actions in the early 1990s laid the foundation for UBC's sustainability journey over the subsequent 30 years. In 1990, UBC signed the Talloires Declaration which committed signatories to a 10-point action plan to incorporate sustainability into institutional decision-making and led UBC to become Canada's first university to formulate a sustainable development policy "to ensure integration of ecological, economic, and social consideration at all levels of strategic planning and operations within the University" (Sustainable Development, 1997, p. 1). A year later, UBC signed the Halifax Declaration, an on-going commitment to the principles and practices of sustainable development within the university, as well as at the local, national, and global levels.

During this time, a number of UBC faculty were laying the groundwork to establish sustainability as a key aspect of the academy. These included research on the Ecological Footprint analysis for urban planning (Wackernagel & Rees, 1996) and high-performance buildings in architecture (Cooper, 2017), as well as the establishment of the Sustainable Development Research Institute (now part of the Institute for Resources, Environment and Sustainability) to study the long-term economic, social, and environmental impacts of urban policies. While these ideas were gaining a foothold, there was a shift in the strategic approach to physical development on the campus. UBC launched the *World of Opportunities* campaign which resulted in the largest infusion of University funds targeted at building state-of-the-art research facilities in support of the academic mission, and started a 30-year building boom. These new development projects increasingly incorporated the emerging sustainable design approaches and strategies.

In 1997, UBC's Board of Governors adopted a policy that formally positioned sustainability as a core pillar of UBC's strategic plans: *Sustainable Development Policy #5*. This policy provides a high-level mandate for the institution to foster collaboration between the academy and operational units. It encourages the engagement of academic thought leaders, students, and staff in innovative approaches to campus operational issues and to use these as a basis for research, learning, and advancing sustainability beyond the campus boundaries. Following the adoption of this policy, UBC opened a Campus Sustainability Office (CSO) in 1998. The CSO worked to systematically institutionalize sustainability in every aspect of campus life, operating under a model where money saved through energy and water conservation was reinvested into campus sustainability programs.

In 2007, UBC participated in the United Nations Colloquium of University Presidents on the role of universities in climate change policy. During the conference former US President Bill Clinton, a guest speaker, highlighted UBC as one of three universities that he described as sustainability leaders (Toope, 2008). This pronouncement sparked enthusiasm and helped to motivate the executive leadership to raise the bar on UBC's sustainability commitments.

With recognition and visibility came the opportunity to expand the CSO to include the creation of the UBC Sustainability Initiative in 2010, with a greater focus on advancing sustainability in academic curriculum, teaching, and research. The CSO's operational functions were integrated into the Sustainability and Engineering unit within UBC's Campus and Community Planning Department and would eventually expand into other operational units, such as a dedicated Energy and Water Services unit. The establishment of these departments provided a direct link between the executive level of the university, operational department heads, and academic faculty.

In parallel, a number of additional policies were created to advance the sustainability mandate. The *UBC Sustainability Academic Strategy* (2009) and the *UBC 20-year Sustainability Strategy* (2014) were developed by faculty, students, and staff working groups and serve as mechanisms for translating high-level policy into department level activities. They outline the primary principles in UBC's approach to sustainability: that "the university should explore the various dimensions of sustainability through research, teaching and learning" and "should exemplify sustainability in its operations and related activities both on and off campus" (Exploring and Exemplifying Sustainability, 2009, p. 1). In addition, these strategic documents provide recommendations and guidelines for the integration of academic and operational dimensions of the campus as a means toward achieving sustainability goals.

These strategies articulate two key themes that would become the bases of UBC's current approach to sustainability. The first is the concept of the university as an agent of change. As a public academic institution, UBC has an obligation "to foster active engagement with local, national and global communities … [in order] to become a catalyst for change in society" (Exploring and Exemplifying Sustainability, 2009, p. 2). The second concept is that of the university CLL. As a research university, UBC can "combine campus operations and administration … with the education, research and outreach mandates of the university" to create an environment where new ideas are tested and examined to optimize learning and improvements (Exploring and Exemplifying Sustainability, 2009, p. 2). In short, UBC positioned itself as an institution that can pilot and demonstrate new ideas, study the outcomes, and then share that knowledge and experience beyond the campus.

UBC CAMPUS AS A LIVING LABORATORY

The strategy behind UBC's CLL initiative is to utilize the physical infrastructure of the campus for the purpose of demonstrating, testing, researching, and learning about sustainable development. Projects on campus have leeway to experiment, in a venue where innovative designs and technologies can be deployed and studied in real-world conditions. The applied research opportunities created by these projects serve as pathways to engage students on challenging sustainability issues and to enhance their education.

The original priority of the CLL initiative was to identify and implement projects that would help UBC achieve its greenhouse gas (GHG) reduction targets, open up interesting avenues for research, and demonstrate cutting-edge technologies. In 2010, UBC committed to reducing GHG emissions below 2007 levels by 33% by 2015, and 67% by 2020, and to eliminate 100% of GHG emissions by 2050 (Climate Action Plan 2020, 2010). UBC leadership recognized that in order to successfully achieve these ambitious goals, a collaborative and learning-based approach was necessary to leverage new ideas and technological innovation (UBC News, 2010).

The UBC Campus as a Living Lab Steering Committee was first convened in May 2010 and included representatives from the Vice-President of Research's Office, Faculty of Applied Science, UBC Sustainability Initiative, Infrastructure Development, Building Operations, and Campus & Community Planning. However, the concept of using the campus as a living lab was compelling and attracted interest from UBC faculty and staff, who saw it as an opportunity to connect their own research interests and operational needs. Additional stakeholders joined the committee, and the focus quickly expanded beyond GHG reduction targets to sustainable development more broadly.

In order to achieve the CLL initiative's mandate of strategically advancing operational goals while providing a platform for research and applied learning, the following principles were established to govern decisions and selection of projects (UBC Campus as a Living Lab, 2017):

- *Create sustainable solutions*: projects must be ecologically, socially, and economically sustainable.
- *Deploy innovative technology*: implement new technologies that are operable but may not yet be fully or widely commercialized, with plans to test and improve them.
- *Build with a long-term vision*: select creative, innovative solutions that will create value for the campus community over decades.
- *Be inclusive*: engage a broad and interdisciplinary range of UBC faculty, students and staff, as well as community members and external partners.

Case Study: Centre for Interactive Research on Sustainability

The flagship CLL project was the Centre for Interactive Research on Sustainability (CIRS). The concept for CIRS – a high-performance sustainable building and research facility – built on UBC's sustainability efforts since the 1990s and imagined a building that demonstrated the best practices in sustainable design and technologies, while also serving as a long-term research subject to study its performance and inhabitants behavior.

CIRS was designed to be the most sustainable building of its time, and to show that a building can influence "the active restoration and regeneration of the environment; and the active pursuit of improvements in the well-being of the community" (UBC Sustainability, 2019c, para. 2). CIRS was the first building project at UBC to document the design development and decision-making around its sustainable features and systems, and to make project information accessible for use by others, whether those were students studying the building or design and construction professionals (Perkins+Will Architects, 2012).

As part of the CIRS project, a new interdisciplinary graduate program was created in the Institute for Resources, Environment and Sustainability. Funded through a federal government grant, the Sustainable Building Science Program (SBSP) was open to graduate research students from any discipline. Student attended seminars and project-based courses together, in addition to the curriculum in their degree program, and undertook research focused on sustainable building technologies, and their interaction with people. The objective of SBSP was to create a program where

> graduate students will learn to actively integrate science and engineering concepts with knowledge from the other key disciplines in order to creatively and interactively develop, for and with the relevant stakeholders, buildings that are more sustainable from social, environmental and economic perspectives. (UBC, 2010, p. 2)

SBSP was housed within the CIRS building and numerous students utilized it as the basis of their research. Many graduate theses focused on engineering topics, such as indoor environmental quality (Lei, 2014), building systems controls and operations (Fedoruk, 2013), energy performance gaps between predictions and actual data (Chu, 2016), and life cycle assessments (LCA) (Storey, 2014). However, a notable subset studied social and behavioral issues, including strategies to better engage people with their buildings (Reckermann, 2014) and how buildings can enhance inhabitant well-being and sense of community (Coleman, 2016). Because of the plethora of project design materials available, as well as real-time performance data, another common area of study was the difference between design intentions and actual performance of the building, and why it had fallen short (Fedoruk, Cole, Robinson, & Cayuela, 2015; Salahi, Terim Cavka, Frisque, Whitehead, & Bushe, 2015). The research was used by UBC to help improve the operation and performance of CIRS, and has informed other building and CLL projects.

Although the SBSP program closed after six years (when the grant was not renewed), CIRS remains a subject of research. It is the most visited, documented, and studied building on UBC's campus, and has continued to be a source of learning for students, researchers, designers, and others. CIRS is a hub for sustainability on campus and home to academic groups and operational departments focused on sustainability-related research, applied learning, planning and operations, and community engagement.

The CLL initiative has continued to evolve and expand since its creation at UBC. It includes university-initiated capital projects, like the CIRS building, that incorporate new and emerging technologies and approaches to sustainable design and development. The Steering Committee awards annual seed funding for CLL projects proposed by both faculty and staff. The funding typically is part of a larger grant application or supports the first step in a larger endeavor, frequently to facilitate data collection by faculty and students for research and teaching. A recent example is the installation of a smart and integrated water monitoring system at UBC Farm to enable the creation of a water innovation lab to study and test strategies for reducing the water footprint of agriculture practices (Johnson, 2018). Beyond these formal projects, CLL has become a widely used framework for any academic research or student learning that uses the campus as the subject of study or as a demonstration site.

CLL PROJECTS: CASE STUDIES OF RESEARCH AND LEARNING

In 2017, during the development of UBC's new Green Building Action Plan, an effort was made to categorize the different types of CLL projects occurring on the Vancouver campus, recognizing that they required different levels of resources, expertise, and management, while providing different types of opportunities for student learning (Green Building Action Plan, 2018). The three levels are: (1) educational and engagement activities; (2) small scope research studies; and

(3) large-scale research projects. The Plan explicitly incorporated these projects into a cycle of research, benchmarking, and piloting sustainable developments, in order to continuously improve green buildings on campus (see Fig. 1).

Level 1: Education and Engagement

The first level is comprised of education activities that communicate about CLL projects, their purpose, and results. The focus is on engaging the campus community, and raising awareness of sustainability issues through interesting displays of information.

Case Study: Bird Friendly Glass Competition and Design Guidelines
Positioned on a prominent peninsula and surrounded by forests, UBC is home to many birds and is on the flyway for coastal migrations. Collisions with window glass on campus buildings are common, caused when birds become confused by reflections of sky or greenery in the glass. Preliminary estimates indicate that up to 10,000 birds could be dying on campus each year from collisions. In response, UBC has developed *Bird Friendly Building Design Guidelines for Buildings* which includes strategies such as avoiding large panes of clear and reflective glass, creating patterns on the glass that break up the reflections, and reducing light pollution that increase reflections at night.

In 2018, UBC's Campus and Community Planning Department held a student design competition to create a bird-friendly window application that would demonstrate a creative solution to integrating the design guidelines into building windows.

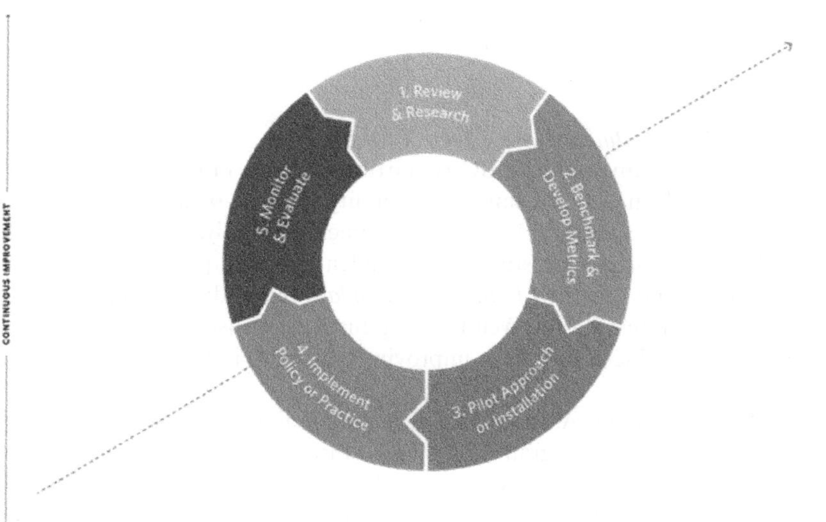

Fig. 1. The Green Building Action Plan's Structured Cycle of Research, Benchmarking, Piloting, and Implementation and Monitoring (Credit: UBC Campus and Community Planning Department).

The competition was open to students in any UBC program, and was judged based on the successful application of the design guidelines and the education potential of the proposal. Fifteen students submitted nine designs. The winning design, by a UBC PhD student in the English department, showed stylized images of the local birds and plants commonly found on campus in a pattern that disrupted reflections. It was installed as a pilot on the windows of the CIRS building (UBC Campus Planning, 2018), as a means to educate the campus community about bird biodiversity on campus and the importance of reducing bird collisions with buildings in urban areas.

The competition and pilot were developed and managed as projects under the Sustainable Environmental Economic Development Studies (SEEDS) Program. Situated within UBC's Campus and Community Planning Department, the SEEDS Program creates applied research projects between students, faculty, and staff. The aim is to advance sustainability ideas, policies, and practices that create societal impacts by engaging students in the development and operation of their campus, and in the achievement of sustainability goals (UBC Sustainability, 2019d). The SEEDS program has been operating since 2001, and has developed a model that consists of four project typologies to engage students: curricular, volunteer (as in the case of this competition), paid, and a mixed approach.

Level 2: Small Scope Research Studies

The second level is comprised of small-scale, discrete research projects that respond to specific questions or address gaps in knowledge that can inform sustainable development at UBC. These projects are often the first step in a series of actions to develop policies or campus regulations, or to secure grants and other resources for larger research projects.

Case Study: WELL Building Assessment Project

Like many other universities, UBC is starting to focus more attention on the health and well-being of its campus community. As part of a sustainable campus, UBC buildings should be healthy environments to study, work, and live. The WELL Building Assessment study was a student research project conducted in 2018 to understand the *WELL Building Standard* (a building certification program run by the International Well Building Institute focused on human health), and to assess its value as a tool for improving the health impacts of institutional buildings on campus.

The WELL Building Assessment Study was undertaken by a student in the Master of Architecture program who studied three academic buildings on campus, with different functions and features. The student researched campus policies, building designs, and operational documentation, and conducted interviews with facilities managers and other operational staff to gain their first hand understanding of the buildings.

The findings were used to assess how the buildings performed against the *WELL Building Standard*, and indicated that UBC has opportunities to do more to design and deliver a healthier campus. The study also identified gaps of information that can become topics for future research, such as the impacts of certain interior materials on human health and air quality (Parsian, 2018). The results of the WELL Building Assessment study are helping to inform the development of design guidelines and policies for healthier campus buildings.

The WELL Building Assessment study was conducted through the Sustainability Scholars program, a funded summer internship for graduate students that matches them with partners to work on applied research projects that improve sustainability in the region. Research questions are developed by staff at the partner organizations and students apply for them through a competitive hiring process. In the internship, the students develop a research project plan, lead the work, and produce a report or other final deliverable for the partner's use (UBC Sustainability, 2019e). The Well Building Assessment project was the first Sustainability Scholars project on-campus and has proven to be an effective model. The work was funded and supported by staff in UBC's Wellbeing Initiative, Sustainability Initiative, and Campus and Community Planning Department. Internships, like the Sustainability Scholars program, are increasingly becoming part of graduate degree requirements at UBC, and provide an opportunity for students to explore career options and gain experience in research beyond their core academic program.

Level 3: Large-Scale Research Projects

The third level of CLL projects encompasses major projects that pilot innovative ideas, support sustained academic research over multiple years, and address core campus operational needs. These projects have often included significant capital investments and grant funding, and involve both external partners and interdisciplinary teams of academic faculty and students.

Case Study: Bioenergy Research and Demonstration Facility

The Bioenergy Research and Demonstration Facility (BRDF) is an innovative utility plant that converts renewable biomass (wood waste) into a synthetic gas (syngas) to generate thermal energy powering the academic campus district energy system. Completed in 2012, the system included an experimental cogeneration engine that used the syngas to produce electricity, in addition to thermal energy. This experiment, however, was unsuccessful, resulting in the conversion of the cogeneration engine to use renewable natural gas. Since the deployment of experimental technologies is one of the principles of CLL, the failure was viewed as an opportunity for academic research that could improve the functionality of this technology in future applications. The BRDF currently produces 8.4 MW of thermal energy, which accounts for 25–32% of the total campus heating and hot water needs each year, and 2 MW of electrical energy, which accounts for 5% of the total campus electricity requirements each year. The facility displaces around 8,500 tons of emitted fossil fuel-based CO_2 annually (UBC Sustainability, 2019a).

In addition to piloting new technology, BRDF supports research in bioenergy, biomass, chemical engineering, and environmental engineering. The building contains an onsite research lab that provides access to the biomass supply, syngas, and system by-products. Four graduate students have done or are currently finalizing their research on BRDF. One of the key objectives of this research has been to improve the system operations using the syngas, by developing better processes for addressing the buildup of tar, a by-product of the wood gasification, and the cause of the cogeneration engine's failure (Madadkhani, 2016; Oveisi et al., 2018). Other research topics include issues in quality and logistics of fuel supply (Oveisi et al., 2018; Quirion-Blais, Taje Malladi, Sowlati, Gao, & Mui, 2019) and the health impacts of emissions from the plant (Petrov, 2018).

The BRDF has an operational mandate, which means its primary function is meeting campus operational needs. This puts constraints on the type of research that can be conducted there. The facility does not support controlled experiments, since changes to the system could negatively impact operations, but does allow for observational research or for the system by-products to be used in lab experiments. Additionally, the operation of the facility and its role in the reduction of campus energy and emissions are studied by students in sustainability and engineering courses, through projects and tours of the facility. Lastly, the facility, and the research associated with it, contributes to a working demonstration of the feasibility, benefits, and challenges of operating a biomass energy utility at a scale that could be applicable for other communities outside the university.

Case Study: Brock Commons Tallwood House

Brock Commons Tallwood House is an 18-story (54m) student residence, with an innovative mass timber hybrid structure. While the foundation, ground floor, and stair cores are concrete, the majority of the structure is composed of mass timber: the floors are made of cross-laminated timber panels supported on glue-laminated timber or parallel strand lumber columns. The tallest contemporary wood building in the world when it was completed in 2017, Brock Commons is a demonstration of innovation in terms of building design and construction processes, advancing building codes, and use of building information modeling and prefabrication techniques.

As a CLL project, Brock Commons was the subject of a multiyear research study led by the UBC Sustainability Initiative in collaboration with research faculty in Wood Science and Civil Engineering (UBC Sustainability, 2019b). Four graduate students from these departments were embedded with the project team and studied the design, construction, and commissioning process for the building, collecting documentation, and interviewing key project stakeholders. This research and the data collected from the project formed the basis for their graduate theses (Calderon, 2018; Fallahi, 2017; Kasbar, 2017; Moudgil, 2017). Because it was their graduate research, the students were able to spend significant time with the project teams and build relationships while collecting detailed information. In fact, upon graduation, three of the four students secured jobs with members of the project team.

In addition to this core research program, detailed studies were also conducted on the LCA of environmental impacts, and life cycle costing (LCC) of Brock

Commons and a second UBC student residence (Teshnizi, Pilon, Storey, Lopez, & Froese, 2018). These studies were undertaken by an interdisciplinary team of students working as paid interns with the UBC Sustainability Initiative, and collaborating with professional LCA and LCC consultants. The internship structure enabled students in professional, course-based Masters programs and upper level undergraduate courses to participate in the research. The team included students from construction management, architecture, wood science, and engineering leadership programs.

Equally important to the research of Brock Commons was knowledge dissemination. Brock Commons has received significant interest from design and building industry professionals, policy-makers, and building owners, as well as researchers, educators, and students from all over the world. UBC Sustainability Initiative brought on students, again in internship positions, from disciplines such as architecture, landscape architecture, civil engineering, planning, and environmental science to work with staff on the development of a variety of educational materials. The students synthesized and summarized information from the research projects described above, and created materials to describe different aspects of the building, strategies for design and construction, and lessons learned from the project. The resulting case studies have been used at professional and industry conferences, for lectures in UBC courses, for campus green building tours, and are made public online as a resource for other students, researchers, or professionals interested in mass timber buildings (UBC Sustainability, 2019).

ENABLERS AND IMPACT OF CLL ON CAMPUS

A strong culture of sustainability, campus physical attributes and infrastructure, and favorable governance context have created an "ecosystem" at UBC that enables the CLL initiative. The CLL projects support collaborations between academic researchers, students, staff, and partners, leading to new sustainable development policies and practices.

Leadership and support from the executive level have been instrumental in creating a culture of sustainability which in turn creates capacity for pursuing CLL projects. Part of this institutional culture has been the establishment of clear policy objectives and campus-wide goals, such as the GHG emission reduction targets. The ambitious nature of these goals has required innovative approaches in order to meet them. In addition, these goals are supported by a road map of action plans, strategies, and operational priorities that create opportunities for new CLL projects. This leadership provides an important signal of UBC's values and commitments to sustainability across the entire institution.

The history of sustainability at UBC has been marked by initiatives arising from both academic researchers and operational staff, and which have required participation from multiple stakeholders in order to be successful. Sustainability is no longer seen as a specialized discipline or the responsibility of a single department, but rather an approach to academic learning and operational decisions that should be incorporated across multiple disciplines. This has created an environment of positive collaborative relationships, including a willingness to learn and experiment together, as well as actively involving students in policy development and operational activities.

Students are central to the CLL initiative. They conduct the research, under the direction of faculty and with staff support, which illuminates the lessons learned from the CLL projects. Projects can be operated within academic curriculum or as extracurricular activities, and create a range of different types of educational experiences for students in different programs and at different points in their academic tenure. Short-term projects, like those illustrated in Levels 1 and 2, are often more accessible to undergraduate students or to students in professional, course-based Master programs. The larger and longer-term research on capital projects, illustrated in Level 3, are more aligned with the multiyear work of research-oriented graduate students and postdoctoral fellows. Involvement with CLL projects can enhance the educational experience for UBC students.

The CLL initiative is a balance between operational needs and research opportunities. Incorporating research is paramount, however, the need to maintain operational functionality places some constraints on the types of research that can be conducted. Operationally focused CLL projects lend themselves to research that is more observational than controlled experimentation. Conversely, this opens up opportunities for a broader range of research topics and collaborations between different disciplines on a specific project. The BRDF supports technical research on an equipment failure, as well as research on the air quality around the plant. Brock Commons supports research on new design and construction techniques, not just the characteristics of the mass timber structure.

CONCLUSION

As one of Canada's largest and leading post-secondary research institutions, UBC plays a strategic role as a positive change agent. To fulfill its sustainability aspirations, the university is committed to fostering a culture that internalizes considerations of social, economic, and environmental impacts in long-term strategic planning, operational decision-making, and through teaching and research. The culture of sustainability, ambitious goals, and strong relationships combine to create an institutional environment where calculated risk, through experimental and demonstrative projects, is permissible to achieve long-term goals and support the academic mandate.

The CLL initiative is the embodiment of this sustainability culture of UBC. CLL provides a structured approach to sustainable development through academic research, while providing unique learning opportunities for all students. Projects under CLL initiative may be small-scale research or educational projects, undertaken by students as part of a course, internship, or extracurricular activity. They may also be large-scale capital projects, funded by the University, that serve as the subject of long-term research projects, contributing to a student's Master thesis or PhD dissertation. In all cases, the results from the research are used to inform future policy or projects on campus, and are shared beyond UBC.

UBC recognizes that the university campus provides a unique testbed for student learning through engagement in the CLL initiative. Students are exposed to real sustainable development and operational challenges, often working in collaboration with professionals, and the results of their work are used to inform and advance policy and decisions for future developments. Through CLL, UBC is working to realize the 2035 Vision outlined in the *20-year Sustainability Strategy*: "sustainability embedded across the University through teaching, learning, research, partnerships, operations and infrastructure, and the UBC community" (UBC 20-year Sustainability Strategy, 2014, p. 1).

REFERENCES

Arcadis. (2018). Sustainable Cities Index. Retrieved from https://www.arcadis.com/en/global/our-perspectives/sustainable-cities-index-2018/citizen-centric-cities/

Calderon, F. (2018). *Quality control and quality assurance in hybrid mass timber high-rise construction: A case study of the Brock Commons*. Master's thesis. Retrieved from https://open.library.ubc.ca/collections/ubctheses/24/items/1.03

Chu, A.-M. (2016). *Understanding the performance gap: an evaluation of the energy efficiency of three high-performance buildings in British Columbia*. Master's thesis. Retrieved from https://open.library.ubc.ca/cIRcle/collections/ubctheses/24/items/1.0300046

Climate Action Plan 2020, University of British Columbia Vancouver Campus. (2010). Retrieved from https://sustain.ubc.ca/about/plans-policies-and-reports

Coleman, S. (2016). *Normalizing sustainability in a regenerative building: The social practice of being at CIRS*. Ph.D. thesis. Retrieved from https://open.library.ubc.ca/cIRcle/collections/ubctheses/24/items/1.0319909

Cooper, I. (2017). The socialization of building science: The emblematic journey of R. J. Cole. *Building Research and Information, 46*,(5), 463–468. doi:10.1080/09613218.2018.1400328

Exploring and Exemplifying Sustainability: UBC Sustainable Academic Strategy. (2009). Retrieved from https://sustain.ubc.ca/about/plans-policies-and-reports

Fallahi, A. (2017). *Innovation in hybrid mass timber high-rise construction: A case study of UBC's Brock Commons project*. Master's thesis. Retrieved from https://open.library.ubc.ca/collections/ubctheses/24/items/1.0345634

Fedoruk, L. (2013). *'Smart' energy systems and networked buildings: Examining the integrations, controls, and experience of design through operation*. Master's thesis. Retrieved from https://open.library.ubc.ca/cIRcle/collections/ubctheses/24/items/1.0165715

Fedoruk, L., Cole, R., Robinson, J., & Cayuela, A. (2015). Learning from failure: Understanding the anticipated-achieved building energy performance gap. *Building Research and Information, 43*,750–763. doi:10.1080/09613218.2015.1036227

Green Building Action Plan, University of British Columbia. (2018). Retrieved from https://sustain.ubc.ca/about/plans-policies-and-reports

Johnson, M. (2018). *A living laboratory for water sustainability at UBC farm* (Project proposal). UBC Faculty of Land and Food Systems (internal document).

Kasbar, M. (2017). *Investigating the performance of the construction process of an 18-storey mass timber hybrid building*. Master's thesis. Retrieved from https://open.library.ubc.ca/collections/ubctheses/24/items/1.0347252

Lei, Y. (2014). *An investigation of the indoor environmental quality of a sustainable building at UBC*. Master's thesis. Retrieved from https://open.library.ubc.ca/cIRcle/collections/ubctheses/24/items/1.0167414

Madadkhani, S. (2016). *Red mud as an iron-based catalyst for catalytic cracking of naphthalene*. Master's thesis. Retrieved from https://open.library.ubc.ca/collections/ubctheses/24/items/1.0340503

Moudgil, M. (2017). *Feasibility study of using cross-laminated timber core for the UBC Tall Wood building*. Master's thesis. Retrieved from https://open.library.ubc.ca/collections/ubctheses/24/items/1.0355221

Oveisi, E., Sokhansanj, S., Lau, A., Lim, C., Bi, X., Ebadian, M.,..., Gill, R. (2018). In-depot upgrading the quality of fuel chips for a commercial gasification plant. *Biomass and Bioenergy*, *108*, 138–145. https://doi.org/10.1016/j.biombioe.2017.10.036

Oveisi, E., Sokhansanj, S., Lau, A., Lim, J., Bi, X., Preto, F., & Mui, C. (2018). Characterization of recycled wood chips, syngas yield, and tar formation in an industrial updraft gasifier. *Environments*, *5*(7), 84. https://doi.org/10.3390/environments5070084

Parsian, M. (2018). *Understanding the applicability of the WELL Building standard to UBC's academic context*. Vancouver: UBC Sustainability Scholars.

Perkins+Will Architects. (2012). *CIRS building manual*. Vancouver: University of British Columbia. Retrieved from Building Manual: http://cirs.ubc.ca/building/building-manual/

Petrov, O. (2018). *Forest residues to energy: Local air quality, health risks and greenhouse gas emissions*. Ph.D. thesis. Retrieved from https://open.library.ubc.ca/collections/ubctheses/24/items/1.0365819

Quirion-Blais, O., Taje Malladi, K., Sowlati, T., Gao, E., & Mui, C. (2019). Analysis of feedstock requirement for the expansion of a biomass-fed district heating system considering daily variations in heat demand and biomass quality. *Energy Conversion and Management*, *187*, 554–564. https://doi.org/10.1016/j.enconman.2019.03.036

Reckermann, J. (2014). *CIRS pre-occupancy evaluation: Inhabitant feedback processes and possibilities for a regenerative place*. Master's thesis. Retrieved from https://open.library.ubc.ca/cIRcle/collections/ubctheses/24/items/1.0167655

Salahi, M., Terim Cavka, B., Frisque, A., Whitehead, D., & Bushe, K. (2015). A case study: The energy performance gap of the Center for Interactive Research on Sustainability at the University of British Columbia. *Building Engineering*, *4*, 127–139. https://doi.org/10.1016/j.jobe.2015.09.002

Storey, S. (2014). *Application of life-cycle approaches for the evaluation of high performance buildings*. Ph.D. thesis. Retrieved from https://open.library.ubc.ca/cIRcle/collections/ubctheses/24/items/1.0167331

Sustainability Development, University of British Columbia Policy #5. (1997). Retrieved from https://universitycounsel.ubc.ca/files/2018/09/policy5.pdf

Teshnizi, Z., Pilon, A., Storey, S., Lopez, D., & Froese, T. M. (2018). Lessons learned from life cycle assessment and life cycle costing of two residential towers at the University of British Columbia. *Procedia CIRP*, *69*, 172–177. https://doi.org/10.1016/j.procir.2017.11.121

Toope, S. (2008, September 29). *Speech to Vancouver Board of Trade*. Vancouver: Records of the Office of the President.

UBC Campus as a Living Lab, Terms of Reference. (2017). University of British Columbia (internal document).

UBC Campus Planning. (2018, May 1). Bird friendly art saves feathered lives. Retrieved from https://sustain.ubc.ca/news/bird-friendly-art-saves-feathered-lives

UBC News. (2010, March 4). UBC sets aggressive new targets to reduce greenhouse gas emissions. Retrieved from https://news.ubc.ca/2010/03/24/ubc-sets-aggressive-new-targets-to-reduce-greenhouse-gas-emissions/

UBC Sustainability. (2019a). Bioenergy research and demonstration facility. Retrieved from https://sustain.ubc.ca/research/research-collections/bioenergy-research-demonstration-facility

UBC Sustainability. (2019b). Brock Commons Tallwood House. Retrieved from https://sustain.ubc.ca/research/research-collections/brock-commons-tallwood-house

UBC Sustainability. (2019c). Centre for Interactive Research on Sustainability. Retrieved from https://sustain.ubc.ca/research/research-collections/centre-interactive-research-sustainability

UBC Sustainability. (2019d). SEEDS Sustainability Program. Retrieved from https://www.sustain.ubc.ca/teaching-applied-learning/seeds-sustainability-program

UBC Sustainability. (2019e). Sustainability Scholars Program. Retrieved from https://sustain.ubc.ca/teaching-applied-learning/ubc-sustainability-scholars-program

UBC 20-Year Sustainability Strategy. (2014). Retrieved from https://sustain.ubc.ca/about/plans-policies-and-reports

University of British Columbia (UBC). (2010). *Sustainable Building Science Program (CREATE Training Program Proposal)*. Vancouver, BC: University of British Columbia.

University of British Columbia (UBC). (2018). *UBC Annual Sustainability Report 2016–17*. Vancouver, BC: University of British Columbia.

Wackernagel, M., & Rees, W. (1996). *Our ecological footprint: reducing human impact on the earth*. Gabriola Island, BC: New Society Publishers.

ABOUT THE CONTRIBUTORS

Patrick Baughan, PhD is a Senior Adviser at Advance HE, having joined the organization in April 2019. His role involves supporting universities in the UK and internationally with all aspects of pedagogy. In addition, he has affiliated roles at the Society for Research in Higher Education and the European Educational Research Association. His research interests lie in the study of higher education as well as areas of educational development, and encapsulate issues including: sustainability in higher education, higher education curricula, assessment and feedback, and academic integrity. He has been involved in a range of sustainability initiatives and policies, and has written and presented on many aspects of sustainability in higher education/education for sustainable development (ESD). Prior to his current position, he worked as a Programme Director and a Principal Teaching Fellow at the UCL Arena Centre for Research-based Education, University College London, following earlier roles at City, University of London, and the University of Leicester. He has taught at several overseas institutions, particularly in Hong Kong, Singapore and Malaysia, accumulating many years of experience in the management and teaching of postgraduate distance learning programs. In all, he has more than 20 years of teaching experience, based in several subject areas, including academic practice, and training and human resource management. He is a Senior Fellow of the Higher Education Academy.

Karin Edvardsson Björnberg is an Associate Professor of environmental philosophy with the Division of Philosophy, KTH Royal Institute of Technology. Her main research interests are in environmental philosophy, public policy analysis, and law. She has taught courses on sustainable development in computer science and engineering and is particularly interested in the normative foundations of the concept of sustainable development.

Patrick Blessinger, Ed.D., is an Adjunct Associate Professor of education at St John's University, a Math and Science Teacher with the New York State Education Department, and a Chief Research Scientist of the International Higher Education Teaching and Learning Association (in consultative status with the United Nations). He has edited and authored many books and articles, and he is an Educational Policy Analyst and a Contributing Writer with UNESCO's Inclusive Policy Lab, University World News, The Hechinger Report, *The Guardian*, and Higher Education Tomorrow, among others. He teaches courses in education, leadership, and research methods, and he serves on doctoral dissertation committees. He founded and leads a global network of educators focused on teaching and learning, and he is an Expert in inclusion, equity, leadership, policy, democracy, human rights, and sustainable development. He provides professional development workshops to teachers and professors and regularly gives presentations and keynote addresses at academic conferences around the world. He was a recipient of several educational awards, including: Fulbright Senior Scholar to Denmark (Department of State, USA), Governor's Teaching Fellow (Institute of Higher Education, University of Georgia, USA), and Certified Educator (National Geographic Society, USA).

Audrey M. Dentith, PhD, is a Professor and the Director of the Center for Teaching Excellence (CTE) at North Carolina A&T State University in Greensboro, North Carolina, USA. The CTE is the hub of all activities directed at the enhancement of faculty teaching in the university. She holds a PhD in Curriculum & Instruction from the Pennsylvania State University, an M.Ed. in Psychological Educational Processes from Temple University in Philadelphia. She also holds a BS and an MS in Education from Bloomsburg State University in Pennsylvania. Her dissertation work and subsequent research is on women's issues in leadership, feminisms, curriculum theory, and adult learning. She has written about ecological issues and the implementation of ecological perspectives and knowledge into the all levels of education from elementary through graduate school. Recently, she has edited a volume entitled, *Ecojustice Adult Education: Theory and Practice in the Cultivation of the Cultural Commons* which was published in the series, New Directions for Adult and Continuing Education at Jossey-Bass publishers. Her essays on environmental education have appeared most recently in *Theory and Practice* published by EcoJustice Press in Eugene, OR, and *The Routledge Encyclopedia of Education*. A mentee of the late prominent environmental education scholar, Chet Bowers, she recently chaired two panels one at American Educational Research Association (AERA) in New York City (NYC) and the other at the Bergamo Conference in Ohio that reflect on his work and legacy. She is currently working on an edited book with David Flinders, John Lupinacci, and Jennifer Thom that considers the direction of Bowers' work for the next generation of teachers in the US and around the world. In addition to her scholarship, she also conducts week-long seminars and institutes that focus on the cultivation of educational efforts that encourage teachers and faculty to integrate ecological content in their curriculum.

Christopher E. Grice is a Professor at Brookhaven College, one of seven independently accredited colleges of the Dallas County Community College District, the largest community college district in Texas. As a teaching sociologist, he focuses on community and youth program development, racialized educational disparities and media representations of race and difference. He currently serves as the Chair of the Departments of Sociology and Human Development. He has previously worked as a Consultant for the Harris County Department of Education, Lipkins Group, LLC, and as an Education Pioneers Fellow. He earned his Doctorate in Sociology from Texas Woman's University in 2015. He additionally has graduate degrees in Community Counseling and Urban-Applied Sociology from Texas Southern University. He has taught an array of undergraduate college courses in Racial and Ethnic Groups in the United States, Minority Studies,

Social Inequality, Urban Sociology, and Social Psychology. His current research interest focuses on constructing sustainable programs for cultural diversity, social equity, and institutional inclusion.

Lena Gumaelius is an Associate Professor, leading a research group named "Engineering education in Society" at KTH. This group consists of around 10 persons and focus on research projects related to learning in technology and engineering. Lena has a background in biotechnology, but has worked in the field of education for the last 15 years, building up research in Learning and establishing teacher education at KTH.

Meegan Hall is the Assistant Vice-Chancellor (Mātauranga Māori) at Victoria University of Wellington and provides strategic academic leadership to increase the awareness of and grow engagement with Māori (the Indigenous people of New Zealand) knowledge and people in learning, teaching, and research contexts. This complements her academic development role with Victoria's Centre for Academic Development, where she works with academic staff and teaches about Māori culturally responsive teaching and learning practices. Her research interest focuses on the achievement of Māori people in higher education, which combines her interest in higher education learning and teaching with her disciplinary background in Māori studies and her development work with Māori academic staff and students. She is interested in the way that Māori values such as kaitiakitanga (guardianship) and whanaungatanga (kinship connections) interact with the Sustainable Development Goals (SDGs) and how Indigenous perspectives can be incorporated into sustainability-related goals and actions.

Margaret Jollands is the Director of the Science Health and Engineering Education Research Centre in the College of Science Engineering and Health and an Associate Dean Student Experience in the School of Engineering, at RMIT University. She introduced sustainability criteria for design in a spine of project based learning courses in chemical engineering at RMIT, which were then evaluated and published in several papers. Students developed their own criteria to choose the optimum design for new technology, using FIDIC Project Sustainability Management core project indicators and the GEMI Navigator methodology. Her research interests include the work readiness of graduates and project-based learning, as well as how students learn about sustainability.

Gwadabe Kurawa is a Member of Inclusive Education Task Team: Inter-Agency Network for Education in Emergencies. He has extensive experience working in mainstream and challenging schools, colleges and universities in the UK and Nigeria. His teaching experience includes undergraduate and postgraduate supervision levels. His research interests are in the areas of school improvement and leadership, teacher professional development, inclusive education and education in fragile, and conflict-affected contexts. His current focus is on Education and Development in the Global South. His experience extends across all levels of the system from policy development, through curriculum development to service delivery.

Hilligje van't Land, PhD, is the Secretary General of the International Association of Universities (IAU) and the Executive Director of the International Universities Bureau. For the past two decades, she has worked at IAU committing to make higher education a key driver of societal change. Over the past years, she co-supervised the overall programmatic activities of the IAU and the everyday work of the secretariat, she engaged in developing the IAU Membership base and strengthening the IAU membership development strategy. She positioned the IAU as partner in the UNESCO Global Action Programme on ESD by promoting the role of higher education and research in addressing the goals set in the context of Agenda 2030. She engaged the Association in strategic partnerships to advance HESD and represents IAU at external events to foster leadership engagement and advance action at all institutional levels. She strongly believes in the importance of intercultural understanding and developed projects and other initiatives to promote higher education's actions in this field. She represents IAU in various working groups and expert committees including at the Council of Europe where she contributed to intercultural understanding initiatives and related publications, and more recently the development of a European Framework for Competences for Democratic Citizenship. Prior to joining the IAU, she taught comparative francophone literature at the Universities of Groningen, Laval and Avignon et des Pays du Vaucluse. For five years, she also headed the Institute for American Universities in Avignon. Since 1987, she has been very active in the field of Canadian Studies. She holds a PhD in comparative contemporary francophone literatures from Groningen University, and completed the postdoctoral research at Laval University. She has authored a number of publications related to higher education and speaks six languages.

Sharyn Lowenstein is Associate Professor of Humanities at Lasell College in Newton, MA. From 2001 through 2019, she was the founding Director of the Center for Community-Based Learning. Sharyn initiated the 4th credit option (Linked-Credit) for Service-Learning and the Service-Learning minor. She led the team that successfully applied for the Carnegie Community Engagement classification. She has applied for and supervised community-based VISTA volunteers for more than a dozen years and consults with faculty regarding service-learning projects. Annually, the Center offers two Alternative Breaks, applying the Break Away model that incorporates student leaders who assume responsibility for identifying geographic location, partnership outreach, team development, student accommodations, and logistics. She teaches in the First Year Seminar, Honors, and Core programs. In 2017, she used her Sabbatical to explore democratic practice in the higher education classroom, focusing on Deliberative Dialogs, Peacemaking/learning Circles, and Restorative Justice practices. She wrote the guide Doing Democracy: Urgency and Hope that explores democratic practice in higher education with a focus on Lasell College (available electronically, by request) and completed the study Assessing Student Outcomes through a Qualitative Approach: The ASB as a Meaning-making and Change-making Experience (posted on Break Away website (alternativebreaks.org). She is co-facilitating Lasell's civic engagement learning outcomes task force, and, with faculty across several disciplines, is integrating deliberative dialogs on pressing social topics. Most recently, she presented at the National Coalition for Dialogue and Deliberation, Frontiers of Democracy, and the Civic Learning and Democratic Engagement Meeting of NASPA. She is a Member of Communities for Restorative Justice (c4rj.org), a 23 town/city coalition in Massachusetts, promoting restorative justice for youth and young adults.

John Madden is the Director of the Sustainability and Engineering unit within Campus and Community Planning at the University of British Columbia. The unit is responsible for setting policies and resource and infrastructure management plans for both the Vancouver and Okanagan campuses. He oversees operational sustainability planning and reporting, creating incentives for sustainable behaviors among staff, faculty and students, green building programs and engineering services for land use planning and permitting processes. He brings over 18 years of experience working for local municipal government, international agencies and nonprofit consulting to advance sustainability policies and implementation strategies. While working in the Middle East, he led efforts in the design and implementation of an innovative green building and sustainability program which was awarded the "Best Regional Sustainability Initiative" by the World Green Building Council. He is also a Sessional Instructor at the Harvard's Graduate School of Design teaching on the subject of Sustainable Master Planning. He holds a BA from the University of British Columbia as well as graduate studies at the UBC's School of Community and Regional Planning.

Jackie Malcolm is the Associate Dean for Learning and Teaching at the Duncan of Jordanstone College of Art & Design (DJCAD), University of Dundee, Scotland. She worked as a professional graphic designer before setting up her own business, Arc Visual Communications Ltd in 1999, joining DJCAD part time at the same time. She moved into full time academia in 2015 and has diverse teaching skills across most design disciplines. She was an Associate Director of the Centre for Environmental Change and Human Resilience, until it closed in July 2018, where she contributed to the management of the Centre. She contributes to the MSc Sustainability at the University of Dundee and has been newly appointed as External Examiner for the MSc Ecological Design Thinking at Schumacher College, Devon. Her research interests span Food as a Trigger for Memory, Biomimicry, Biophilia, Sustainable Design, Transdisciplinary Design, and Design for Healthcare.

Stefanie Mallow is a Programme Officer at the International Association of Universities (IAU), in charge of the Association's strategic priority Higher Education and Research for Sustainable Development (HESD). In her position, she maps and analyses developments in sustainable development through the IAU Global Portal on HESD and coordinates the newly established IAU Global HESD Cluster. She is also part of the IAU team taking part in the UNESCO Global Action Programme on ESD (GAP ESD). In 2016, she developed together with Dr Hilligje van't Land the first IAU Global Survey on HESD to identify global and regional trends and map what universities worldwide are doing for sustainable development. She also coordinated the work on its second iteration. Together with the steering committee of the Global Action Programme's Partner Network 2, she was involved in conducting and analyzing a survey on the Whole Institution Approach at educational institutions, including universities, worldwide. She holds a Master's degree in cultural anthropology from Uppsala University and a Bachelor's degree in international social work from Germany. She has worked and studied in multiple countries, including New Zealand, Indonesia, and Costa Rica. Her research interests include power relations and inequality in knowledge production, cultural diversity in sustainable development, and transformations of higher education.

Gavin Melles is an Associate Professor in the Faculty of Health, Arts and Design, Swinburne University. He is affiliated with the Centre for Urban Transitions, the Centre for Design Innovation, and the Collaborative Research Centre for Low Carbon Living. He holds a PhD (Education), MSc (Sustainable Development), MSc Linguistics, B Arts and Postgraduate Diploma of Teaching. He has taught at Melbourne University and Swinburne University and has been recipient of seven international fellowships in Germany, Sweden, Switzerland, India, and the UK. His current research and teaching interests are in the areas of Education for Sustainable Development, Design for Social Innovation, Human-centered Design, and Sustainability. He is an Associate Member of IEMA and active in several other areas including Gender & Equity in STEMM, and social impact assessment for SAN (India). He is an Assessor for the Australian Research Council, Leverhulme Trust, FNS Switzerland, the Singapore Ministry of Education, and the EURIAS Program. He has also been particularly active in DFAT (Australia) funded study tours to India and was also a project leader in the 2009–2012 EU ICP Project focused on Design innovation in seven Australian and European Universities.

John Metras is an Associate Vice-President, Facilities at the University of British Columbia (UBC). He and his team are responsible for the planning, development, and operation of institutional facilities and utilities infrastructure at UBC, collaborating with campus stakeholders to provide great spaces for learning, research, and campus life. He has over 20 years of experience in facilities development and operations including his previous positions as the Managing Director, Infrastructure Development and Director, Plant Operations at UBC. He has played an integral role in helping UBC evolve into a global leader in sustainability, working on a wide range of initiatives including the Campus as a Living Lab program, the 20-Year Sustainability Strategy, LEED Platinum and Gold certified building projects and the development of the Brock Commons Tall Wood student residence. He has a Bachelor of Engineering Science from the University of Western Ontario and an MBA from UBC.

Andrea Milligan is an Associate Dean (Teacher Education) in the School of Education at Victoria University of Wellington. She was also a Steering Group Member of Victoria's Te Auroa: Enhancing Resilience and Sustainability theme, which has been named as a distinctive, interdisciplinary research strength for the university. She researches in a range of areas related to citizenship education, social and environmental justice, sustainability, and the role of philosophy in education. Her research draws on critical perspectives to explore how education can support people to address complex social and environmental issues. Her recent research explores how local environments and cities can be sites of informal and nonformal learning. She is particularly interested in the intersections between critical thinking, the relational and embodied dimensions of people's lives, and societal transformation.

Angelique Pilon is the Director of Urban Innovation Research within the University of British Columbia's (UBC's) Sustainability Initiative. This is an interdisciplinary collaborative with a portfolio of research and educational programs focused on sustainable buildings, community and urban development, climate change, and the future of cites. Working under the Campus as Living Lab initiative, her team develops partnerships and projects that take advantage of UBC's growing role as a model for urban sustainability and utilize campus plans, buildings, and infrastructure as sources of innovation and learning. She has 15 years' experience in research and practice relating to the built environment, with previous professional positions at architectural firms in the United States and Canada. She has a Bachelor of Science in Architecture from the University of Michigan and a Master of Architecture from UBC. She is a certified Project Management Professional and a LEED Accredited Professional with a specialization in Building Design and Construction.

Enakshi Sengupta, PhD, serves as an Associate Director of HETL and is responsible for the advancement of HETL in Asia, Middle East, and Africa. She works closely with the executive director to fulfill the mission of HETL. She is also the Director of the Center for Advanced Research in Education (CARE), an Associate Series Editor of the book series, *Innovations in Higher Education Teaching and Learning*, Emerald Group Publishing. She is the Managing Editor of the *Journal of Applied Research in Higher Education*, Emerald Publishing, and serves as the Vice Chair for the Editorial Advisory Board of the Innovations in Higher Education Teaching and Learning book series, Emerald Publishing. She is the Senior Manager of the Research, Methodology, and Statistics in the Social Sciences forums on LinkedIn and Facebook responsible for managing all aspects of those forums. She is a PhD holder from the University of Nottingham in research in higher education, prior to which she completed her MBA with merit from the University of Nottingham and Master's degree in English Literature from the Calcutta University, India. She has previously held leadership positions in higher education institutions.

Keith R. Skene was born in the beautiful cathedral city of Armagh in Northern Ireland, in 1965. Having gained a First Class Honours degree in Botany and a PhD in Ecology (during which time he was awarded the Australian Association of Rhodes Scholars Scholarship), he was appointed as a Principle Investigator in the world-renowned College of Life Sciences at the University of Dundee. He has carried out research across the planet, from Kenya to Vietnam and from Australia to the West Indies. Currently, he is the Director of the Biosphere Research Institute, where he is responsible for vision enhancement, facilitation, and development. He has authored four books and 30 papers in international peer-reviewed journals, applying ecology to global issues such as economics, sustainability, and social progress. He regularly reviews papers for many of the leading international academic journals. He has been a Visiting Research Fellow at both the University of Winchester Business School and the University of Leeds Business School and has been a Consultant at the Centre for Low Carbon Futures, University of York. He has been a Keynote Speaker at conferences globally, while also regularly contributing to popular science events such as the Edinburgh Science Festival and Greenbelt Festival. He has made numerous appearances on radio and television documentaries and news programs in the UK and the USA, including Countryfile, BBC World Service, British Television, and GTV. He has served as a Co-ordinator of the European Plant Ecophysiology Consortium, a consortium of eight European universities focusing on teaching and research and as National Consultant for Ecology in the Life Sciences Teaching Network Discipline for Ecology in the UK. He has represented Summer School Access Courses in Higher Education at the 15th Commonwealth Meeting of Leaders. In 2018, he was invited to join the Taylor and Francis Advisory Board to the United Nations Education Programme on Sustainable Development Goals and was further invited to join the Register of Scientific Experts for the Ministero dell' Istruxione, dell' Universita e della Ricerca, advising the Italian Government on fundamental research. He has worked as an Assessor for scientific funding councils in the UK and Switzerland. Married with a young son, he currently lives in rural Angus in Scotland. He enjoys playing blues guitar and studying philosophy, which, he claims, are inextricably linked!

Inga-Britt Skogh is a Professor at the Department of Learning, School of Industrial Technology and Management, KTH Royal Institute of Technology. Inga-Britt is primarily working with pedagogical–philosophical research with a particular focus on children's and young people's attitudes toward technology/engineering and related areas.

Tonya Sweet is a Senior Lecturer in the School of Design at the Victoria University of Wellington. She is also a Coordinator of the *Critical Resilience through Innovative Solutions in Sustainability* (C.R.I.S.I.S.) Design Research Innovation Lab that supports design-led responses to sustainability challenges impacting Aotearoa New Zealand and beyond. Her research interests include sustainable design, resilient design, speculative design, social design, creative practice, and design pedagogy. She has developed pedagogy and taught courses across the disciplines of design, including design thinking. She is an advocate of facilitating heuristic and empirical learning opportunities that synthesize critical thinking, theory, and practice, and that foster an innovative, conscientious, and inclusive approach to design development.

James Tansey is an Associate Professor at the University of British Columbia's (UBC's) Sauder School of Business, and a former Executive Director of UBC's Sustainability Initiative. His academic research includes the social impacts and acceptability of new technologies, industrial ecology, social innovation and impact investing, clean technology policy, and ecosystem services. He is the Executive Director of the Centre for Social Impacting Investing, and has led the creation of the UBC Impact Accelerator and the UBC Impact Fund. He has over 20 years' experience in innovation, environmental consulting, and climate change. He founded NatureBank Asset Management and has worked as an Advisor and Contributor to a wide range of organizations including the World Economic Forum, the UK National Audit Office, Oxford Analytica, Environment Canada, the Federal and Provincial Governments, and the Canadian Environmental Assessment Agency. He received his PhD in Environmental Sciences from the University of East Anglia and has taught in MBA, EMBA, Executive Education, MSc, and Undergraduate programs in the UK and Canada.

Bland Tomkinson is a Visiting Lecturer in the School of Mechanical, Aerospace and Civil Engineering at the University of Manchester, having spent 45 years in the public service – civil service, local government, university and a spell with the Royal Institute of Public Administration. His most recent full-time role as a University Adviser on Pedagogic Development had two principal aspects. First, the development of academic staff and others who teach and, second, the undertaking and encouragement of research and development into teaching and learning. In the former role, he has been engaged on studies looking at the embedding in the curriculum of education for sustainable development and also smaller studies on the use of portfolios for academic and personnel decision-making. He has authored or edited a number of books in the field of human resource and educational development and contributed chapters to others. He has contributed a number of articles to professional journals and a substantial number of papers to international conferences. His particular areas of interest are the management of change, sustainable development, approaches to learning, and the use of portfolios.

Rosemary Tomkinson recently retired from the position of Academic Support, Teaching Innovation and Development Adviser in the Faculty of Science and Engineering in the University of Manchester. She had previously undertaken the role of Programme Director to the UMIST PG Certificate in Academic Practice and PG Certificate in Teaching Science and Engineering in English. She was much involved in the introduction of course units in Sustainable Development, which led to a Green Gown Award. In her later role, she gave presentations on Portfolio Development, Reflective Practice, Presentation Skills, Aspects of Sustainable Development, Student Support and Mentoring and provided individual and group mentoring/counselling to staff on request. She has taught in China and on the International Teachers Programme in Milan and has contributed to a number of academic papers and conference sessions.

Jenny S. Wakefield is an Instructional Designer/Learning Designer at Dallas County Community College District supporting faculty with online course design and technology implementations toward student success. She has previously held similar positions at the University of Texas at Dallas and the University of North Texas (UNT). She earned her Doctorate in Learning Technologies/ Instructional Design from UNT in 2016 where she is also currently an Adjunct Professor. She additionally has a graduate minor in Philosophy and 18 graduate hours in Education. She has taught online undergraduate, graduate, and PhD-level courses at UNT in Computer Applications, Instructional Design, and Proposal Writing and Grant Administration. Additionally, she has taught continuing education, face-to-face courses at Collin. She has presented at many prominent conferences (AERA, AECT, AACE, CELDA, ISTE) and published research and theory journal articles and book chapters on instructional design, the use of social media, games for learning, simulations, virtual worlds, and the use of transmedia in education. Her current research interest focuses on how we may include sustainability-infused curriculum in all types of courses bringing out awareness to students about our fragile, changing world and how we can all work toward a sustainable future.

Nancy V. Winfrey, PhD, is an Adjunct Faculty for the Center for Creative Leadership, a Consultant for the NCA&T Center for Teaching Excellence, and a Team Member of Insprius Consulting. Her teaching and training experience span 20 years of work with adults in Nonprofit Management, Leadership Development, Corporate Training, and Higher Education. She is also an Experienced Instructional Designer. For 14 years, she directed a nonprofit organization supporting education in Central America and is experienced with the principles and practices of sustainable engagement in cross-cultural partnerships, and the process of educating for global citizenship. She holds certification from Global Learning Partners in Dialogue Education. Her current research interests are the critical theory underpinning learning from experience, action research, and group processes in nonformal learning environments, and the scholarship of teaching and learning in higher education.

Taisir Subhi Yamin is a Professor of gifted education. He has a B.Sc. in Physics, an M.A. in Special Education, and a Ph.D. in Gifted Education and Computer Assisted Learning from Lancaster University in England. He was a recipient of academic prizes and fellowships from Jordan, England, and the USA including the Fulbright Award (1996), the Leadership in Gifted Education from the WCGTC (2013), and the British Council Scholarship. He is active in the field of science popularization, and has written 20 books, a large number of articles, chapters in edited books, and research papers. In addition, he has developed a number of training packages to develop productive thinking skills (creative thinking, critical thinking, creative problem solving, and future problem solving). He is an active member of an impressive list of academic institutions including: the British Educational Research Association, the European Council for High Ability, Bahrain Association for the Gifted and Talented; Former President, Jordanian

Association of Physicists, the National Committee for Gifted Education; Founder, the Qatari Centre for the Gifted and Talented. He is also the National Chancellor and the Vice President of the International Association of Educators for World Peace. He was a Delegate of the World Council for Gifted and Talented Children (WCGTC) for about 10 years. In 2002, he was elected as a Member of the executive committee of the WCGTC. He was involved in developing UAE project for the gifted and talented in Ulm University. In addition, he has established, in cooperation with Todd Lubart and Sandra Linke, the International Centre for Innovation in Education (ICIE). The ICIE has seven branches in: France, Germany, Sweden, Turkey, Canada, Kenya, and Jordan. In 2005, he was named the Editor-in-Chief of Gifted and Talented International. In March 2009, he was elected as the President of the WCGTC for four years. More recently, he is the General Director of ICIE in Germany, and a Research Fellow at Université Paris Descartes. In 2013, he founded, in cooperation with Ken McCluskey, the *International Journal for Creativity and Talent Development* (IJTDC). This ICIE publishes the IJTDC in partnership with a number of American and European universities. In 2018, he joined the Faculty of Education-University of Winnipeg, Canada, as a Visiting Professor.

NAME INDEX

Abbasi, A. S., 179
Abbott, J., 85
Abu-Ghaida, D., 43
Achankeng, I, F., 85
Adams, C. A., 144
Adams, W. M., 124
Agnelli, S., 58
Agombar, J., 11, 77
Ahlgren, R. -M., 191
Ainger, C. M., 124
Ainley, P., 162, 163
Airasian, P. W., 60, 61, 67
Al-Naqbi, A. K., 179
Albertini, C., 16
Alonso-Almeida, M., 126
Alshannag, Q., 179
Alsobrook, M., 151
Álvarez, J. B., 118–119
Alvesson, M., 127
Amadei, B., 178
Amador, F., 124
Amin, S., 42
Anderson, L. W., 60, 61, 67
Andersson, K., 179
Angulo, Y., 118–119
Anholon, R., 199
Arias-Maldonado, M., 75, 79
Armstrong, C. M., 199
Ashford, 124
Attaran, A., 43
Audrey M., 7
Avitabile, C., 118–119
Awan, U., 179
Azapagic, A., 126
Azarnoosh, M., 91

Bacelar-Nicolau, P., 124
Bailey, I., 126, 133
Bailey, P., 34, 35, 37, 38
Baillie, C., 61, 64, 68
Baker, S., 126, 188
Banerji, R., 42
Banister, D., 77
Banta, T. W., 61, 63, 64
Barker, D., 86
Barlett, P., 75
Barnett, J., 76
Barrie, S. C., 61
Barron, B., 62
Barrows, H. S., 30
Barth, M., 126
Battisti, B., 124
Baughan, P., 11, 75, 78
Beals, F., 77, 198
Beliavsky, N., 24
Berger, D., 85, 93
Berkes, F., 207
Bernstein, E., 163, 170
Bernstein, W., 44
Bertschy, F., 179
Bessant, S., 34, 35, 37, 38
Bi, X., 222
Bierema, L., 24
Biggs, J. B., 61
Biggs, J., 59, 60, 61, 63, 67
Björnberg, Karin Edvardsson, 9, 177
Blessinger, P., 37
Blincoe, K., 44
Blomfield, J., 198
Bloom, A., 144
Boast, R., 34, 35, 37, 38
Bone, E., 11, 77
Bonneuil, C., 11, 74, 76, 78
Bonoli, A., 113
Boud, D., 59, 63
Bowers, C. A., 19, 20, 21, 22, 25
Braithwaite, C., 124
Branch, R. M., 60

Brand, S., 200
Brannen, J., 127
Breidlid, A., 42
Brent, R., 60, 67
Brew, A., 76
Brinkworth, R., 127
Brody, S. D., 126
Brown, N. J., 68
Brown, T., 200, 201, 208
Brumbelow, K., 179
Brundtland, G. H., 30, 58
Buba, I. A., 52
Buchanan, C., 85
Buchanan, R., 201
Buckler, C., 110
Bushe, K., 218
Butler, C. D., 42
Butterfield, S., 162, 163
Byrne, E. P., 59, 62, 66, 67

Caeiro, S., 124
Cahir, J., 76
Cajete, G., 207
Calderon, F., 222
Campbell, J., 76
Campbell, O., 42
Caradonna, J., 76, 77, 81
Carew, A. L., 58, 61, 63, 67
Carter, K., 189
Castree, N., 76, 81
Caviglia-Harris, J. L., 199
Cayuela, A., 218
Cebrián, G., 133, 179, 190
Cech, E. A., 191
Ceulemans, K., 126
Chase, G., 75
Childs, A., 179
Chirwa, E., 42
Christie, B. A., 124, 126
Christie, M., 164, 166–168, 169
Chu, A. -M., 218
Church, M., 155
Clark, I. F., 126
Clark, S., 74, 77
Clarke, D. F., 91
Clarke, R. M., 31
Claudio, F., 42
Cleaver, E., 126, 130
Clemens, M. A., 42
Cocis, A., 126, 129
Cocklin, C., 124
Coffey, 124
Cole, R., 218
Coleman, S., 218
Collender, G., 42
Colley, A., 68
Collis, K. F., 61
Connelly, S., 188
Conombo, G., 42
Cooke, R., 126
Cooley, M., 163
Cooper, A., 59
Cooper, I., 215
Corney, G., 126, 179
Cornforth, S., 77, 198
Cotton, D. R. E., 144
Cotton, D., 126, 133
Cox, M. D., 145
Creech, H., 110
Creswell, J. W., 150
Croso, C., 170
Cruickshank, H. J., 124
Cruikshank, K. A., 60, 61, 67
Crutzen, P., 74, 75, 76
Cruz, Y., 59
Curry, A., 46

Dackman, C., 59
Dacko, S., 200
Dahlstedt, M., 168, 172
Daniele, V. N., 161
de Souza, L., 199
Dedrick, J., 86
Dei, G. J. S., 47
Delbecq, A. L., 37
Delgado, M., 65
Delvaux, T., 42
Dentith, A., 24, 25
Derek, A., 86
DesJardins, J. R., 144
Devanathan, S., 44
Dewey, J., 190
Dieltiens, V., 42
Dienstfrey, H., 86

Dillard, J., 85
Dillard, K., 85
DiPaolo, Terry, 7
Djordjevic, A., 144
Dmochowski, J. E., 147
Dobson, H., 37
Doherty, J., 85, 95
Drayson, 11
Drayson, R., 77
Dripps, W., 126
Drury, S., 85
Durand-Delacre, D., 43

Earl, A., 84
Ebadian, M., 222
Edmundson, J., 19, 22, 25
Egron-Polak, E., 111
Enelund, M., 179
Engel, C. E., 30, 31, 38
Engel, C., 37
Engel, Charles, 8, 30
Ereira, A., 47
Eyben, R., 43
Eyler, J., 62

Fallahi, A., 222
Farland, M., 85
Faud-Luke, A., 44
Featherstone, L. 16
Fedoruk, L., 218
Fehr, R., 64
Feilzer, M. Y., 127
Fejes, A., 168, 172, 173
Felder, R. M., 60, 62, 64, 67
Feletti, G. I., 38
Fenner, R. A., 124
Ferreira, J. -A., 198
Ferrer-Balas, D., 59, 62, 65, 179
Ferreyra, M. M., 118–119
Filho, W. L., 199
Finucane, M. L., 190
Firth, R., 179
Fisher, P. B., 144
Fisher, S., 147
Fisk, S., 85, 93
Fixson, S. K., 200
Flateby, T. L., 61, 63, 64
Flynn, J., 190
Foley, J. A., 188
Folke, C., 206
Follett, M. P., 26
Foss, S., 78
Fressoz, J., 11, 74, 76, 78
Frisque, A., 218
Froese, T. M., 223
Fukuda-Parr, S., 42, 43
Fullan, M., 59

Gaffney, O., 54
Gambogi, D., 147
Gao, E., 222
Garcia, R., 200
Garofalo, D., 147
Gastil, J., 85
Giardina, C. P., 207
Gibbard, P., 11, 74, 76
Gibbs, D. C., 124
Giddings, B., 189
Gill, R., 222
Glassey, J., 179
Goddard, S., 85
Goeminne, G., 201
Goleman, D., 22, 26
Gore, A., 16
Grace, M., 133
Graham, A., 75
Graham, R. H., 62
Grattan, L., 86
Green, T. L., 133
Greene, A., 147
Grice, C. E., 7, 143
Grierson, D., 124
Griffin, M., 61, 63, 64
Griggs, D., 54
Grimm, K., 124
Gubrium, J., 127
Gumaelius, L., 9, 177
Gustafson, D. H., 37
Gustafson, K. L., 60
Gustler, S., 85
Guthrie, P. M., 124

Hadgraft, R. G., 60, 62, 67
Haile, S., 179

Hall, B. L., 108, 112
Hall, J. W., 43
Hall, M., 10, 197
Hammer, D., 4
Harder, M. K., 199
Harell, K., 91
Hargreaves, L. G., 110
Harriger, K., 85
Hatley, J., 199
Hattie, J., 63, 65, 67
Held, H., 43
Hercot, D., 42
Hernandez, M., 75
Hickel, J., 43
Higgins, B., 126
Hiley, A., 37
Hill, F., 37
Hill, P. S., 42
Hiller Connell, K. Y., 199
Hmelo-Silver, C., 152
Holden, E., 77
Holm, T., 179
Holmberg, J., 58–59, 63, 65, 67–68, 127
Hoover, E., 199
Hopkinson, P., 11, 76
Hopwood, B., 189
Horst, N., 127
Howitt, R., 207
Howlett, C., 198
Hseih, H. -F., 203
Hugé, J., 126
Hughes, P., 11, 76
Huisingh, D., 65, 108, 126
Hulme, D., 43
Humphris, D., 133
Hutt, I., 35
Hyland, C., 124

Irwin, T., 201
Isaacs, D., 26

Jacobs, M., 188
Jagers, S. C., 179
Jensen, H., 118–119
Jickling, B., 74
Johnson, B. B., 179
Johnson, J. T., 207
Johnson, M., 44
Johnston, L., 75
Jollands, M., 9, 59, 61, 62, 66
Jolly, L, 62
Jonassen, D. H., 32
Jones, J., 132
Junyent, M., 179, 190

Kagawa, F., 126
Kahn, S., 61, 63, 64
Kaner, S., 85, 93
Kanie, N., 54
Kaplan, D. M., 91
Kargazari, H. R., 91
Karreman, D., 127
Kasbar, M., 222
Kealiikanakaoleohaililani, K., 207
Keith R., 8
Kelley, D., 200
Kelley, T., 200
Kemp, S., 11, 77
Kenny, C. J., 42
Khalid, M., 58
Klasen, S., 43
Klein, N., 16, 43
Kliskey, A., 207
Knobloch, K., 85
Knutson Wedel, M., 179
Kolbe, T., 145
Kopnina, H., 6, 52, 126, 129
Kovarik, C., 190
Krathwohl, D. R., 60, 61, 67
Kriegler, E., 43
Krizek, K. J., 199
Kroll, C., 43
Kumar, N., 42
Kumar, S., 42
Künzli, C., 179
Kurawa, G., 8, 159, 172

Lakoff, G., 44
Lam, S., 91
Lamberton, J., 85
Lambin, E. F., 188
Lambrechts, W., 108
Land, Hilligje van't, 12
Langford, M., 42

Lather, P., 163, 169
Lattuca, L. R., 60, 62, 67
Lau, A., 222
Lawrence, W., 85
Lawson, A., 37
Layer, G., 11, 76
Lazzarini, B., 199
Leal Filho, W., 126
Leary, H., 62, 64, 67
Leeder, S. R., 38
Lehmann, M., 179
Lei, Y., 218
Leighninger, M., 164
Lenton, T. M., 43
Lessing, D., 172
Leung, C. F., 61
Lewis, S., 75, 76
Lidstone, L., 77
Liedtke, C., 45
Lim, C., 222
Lind, J., 85, 93
Lindskog, A., 179
Linnerud, K., 77
Litzinger, T. A., 60, 62, 67
London, S., 85, 89
Longhurst, J., 124
Looker, J. T., 45
Lopez, D., 223
Louis, R. P., 207
Lovren, V. O., 126
Lowenstein, S., 12, 83
Lozano, F. J., 65, 108, 126
Lozano, R., 108, 126
Lucht, W., 43
Lucio-Villegas, E., 23, 24
Lukman, R., 108
Lundqvist, U., 59, 179
Lupinacci, J., 19, 22, 25
Lutz, W., 4

Madadkhani, S., 222
Madden, J., 11, 213
Magni, G., 206
Maher, M., 44
Maher, R., 44
Maiboroda, O., 126, 133
Malcolm, J., 8
Mallow, S., 12, 107
Mallow, S., 107
Malmqvist, J., 179
Mann, S., 44
Mansoor, G. F., 42
Marston, 124
Martin, R., 200, 201
Martinho, A. P., 124
Martinsson, J., 179
Martusewicz, R. A., 19, 22, 25
Martusewicz, R., 25
Marzano, R. J., 67
Maslin, M. A., 75, 76
Mathews, D., 85
Matthews, C., 127
Maurice, J., 43
Mayer, R. E., 60, 61, 67
McAdams, E., 144
McAlpine, C. A., 44
McCann, B., 127
McDonough, W., 53
McDorman, T. D., 85
McKenzie, M., 77
Mckeown, P., 162, 163
McKeown, R., 84
McMichael, A. J., 42
McMillan, J., 85
McNeill, J., 74
Mebratu, D., 189
Meinzen-Dick, R., 190
Melles, Gavin, 12, 123
Mendes, P., 126, 130
Merriam, S., 24
Mertz, C. K., 190
Metras, J., 11, 213
Mezirow, J., 36
Miller, G. R., 179
Miller, K. K., 126
Miller, W. R., 43
Milligan, A., 10, 197
Mitchell, C. A., 58, 61, 63, 67
Mohai, P., 179, 190
Moir, S., 189
Molyneaux, T., 62
Mora, O. -G., 118
Morrison, K., 155
Moss, T. J., 42

Moudgil, M., 222
Mui, C., 222
Mulder, K. F., 59, 62, 65, 124, 179
Mullally, G., 59, 62, 66, 67
Murray, A., 43
Musgrove, S. L., 199
Muttarak, R., 4

Naeem, M. A., 124
Nagel, R., 58, 61, 62, 63, 66
Naido, S., 165, 166, 169, 172
Natkin, L. W., 145
Nejati, M., 126
Neufeld, V. R., 30
Newport, D., 199
Newstetter, W. C., 60, 62, 67
Nicholas, K. A., 126
Nixon, J., 162, 163
Njeru, S. N., 45
Noone, K., 188
Nordström, K., 127
Novak, J. D., 65
Noyes, C., 179, 180, 189, 190

O'Brien, G., 189
O'Byrne, D., 126
O'Connell, D., 54
Öhman, J., 6, 201
Oliveira, C. P., 124
Oliver, L. P., 163, 164, 167–168, 170
Olson, M., 168, 172
Orlovic, V. L., 199
Ormerod, R. M., 34, 35, 37, 38
Orr, D., 44, 53
Ouedraogo, C., 42
Oveisi, E., 222

Pace, P., 126
Paletta, A., 113
Papanek, V., 44
Pappas, E., 58, 61, 62, 63, 66
Parsian, M., 221
Parthasarathy, R., 62, 66
Paz, F. H., 118–119
Peach, N. W., 124
Perdan, S., 126
Perkins, D., 154
Perrault, E., 74, 77
Persson, Å., 188
Petocz, P., 74, 126, 144
Pierrakos, O., 58, 61, 62, 63, 66
Pilon, A., 11, 213, 223
Pintrich, P. R., 60, 61, 67
Price, J., 68
Prince, M. J., 60, 62, 64, 67

Quirion-Blais, O., 222
Quisumbing, A. R., 190

Raath, S., 199
Rahmstorf, S., 43
Ramani, K., 44
Ramanujan, D., 44
Ranson, S., 162, 163
Raul, V. C., 161
Raworth, K., 188
Reckermann, J., 218
Redman, C. L., 59, 60
Rees, S., 163
Rees, W., 215
Reid, A., 74, 126, 144
Remington-Doucette, S. M., 199
Renard, M. K., 91
Reyers, B., 54
Richard, F., 42
Rikowski, G., 162, 163
Ritchhart, R., 154, 155
Rittel, H. W., 32
Robinson, J., 218
Robinson, Z., 34, 35, 37, 38
Rockström, J., 188
Rodgers, M. O., 179, 180, 189, 190
Roman, M., 75
Ruber, I. E., 163
Ryan, A., 126
Rydhagen, B., 59
Ryu, H., 126

Sachs, J. D., 43
Sachs, J., 109
Saith, A., 43
Salahi, M., 218

Salleh, A., 52
Samake, S., 42
Sammalisto, K., 179
Samuelsson, B. E., 58, 59, 63, 65, 67, 68
Sandberg, F., 168, 172
Satterfield, T. A., 190
Schapper, J., 11, 76, 147
Schellnhuber, H. J., 43
Schmidt-Hertha, B., 163
Schmidt-Traub, G., 43
Scholz, R., 75
Schultz, W., 46
Schwarz, N. U., 130
Segalàs, J., 59, 62, 65, 66, 67, 179
Seidel, V. P., 200
Serra, M. A., 118
Shallcross, D., 126
Shannon, S. E., 203
Shen, J. -P., 110
Sherman, Z., 22
Sherren, K., 124, 126
Shields, T., 179
Shing, C. K., 59
Shiva, V., 16
Shulman, L. S., 200, 201
Sipos, Y., 124
Skene, K. R., 43
Skenea, 8
Skogh, I, 9, 177
Slovic, P., 190
Small, M. L., 127
Sokhansanj, S., 222
Sowlati, T., 222
Spangenberg, J. H., 44
Spirn, A. W., 44
Stafford-Smith, M., 54
Steffen, W., 74, 188
Steigelbauer, S., 59
Stephens, J., 75
Sterling, S., 84
Stern, N., 4
Stigson, B., 54
Storey, S., 218, 223
Straka, T., 84
Stuart Chapin, F., 188
Stubbs, 11
Stubbs, W., 76, 124, 147
Summers, M., 179
Sund, L., 201
Sundström, A., 179
Sutherland, J. W., 44
Svanström, M., 59, 179
Sweet, T., 10, 197
Sylvestre, P., 124, 126

Taje Malladi, K., 222
Tallon, R., 77, 198
Tang, K. H. D., 179
Tansey, J., 11, 213
Taylor, M., 77, 198
Taylor, P., 74
Tejedor, G, 62, 65, 66
Teksoz, K., 43
Terim Cavka, B., 218
Teshnizi, Z., 223
Theis, J., 85
Thomas, C., 126, 130
Thomas, I., 126
Thompson, O., 24, 25
Tilbury, D., 126
Timm, J., 126
Timmerman, L., 85
Toldi, C., 85, 95
Tomkinson, B., 8, 30–31, 33, 35, 37
Tomkinson, C. B., 34, 35, 37, 38
Tomkinson, R., 8, 34, 35, 37, 38
Toohey, S., 61, 65, 68
Toope, S., 215
Torstensson, M., 166–167, 169, 170
Townsend, A. R., 199
Trowler, P., 59
Tuncer, G., 126
Turner, J. P., 68
Turunen, H., 132

Ullah, F., 54
Unterhalter, E., 42
Urzúa, A. S., 118–119

Vaismoradi, M., 132
Valsiner, J., 24, 25, 26
van Dam-Mieras, R., 32

Van de Ven, A. H., 37
Van der Veer, R., 24, 25, 26
Van Norren, D. E., 43
van Olmen, J., 42
Van Poeck, K., 201
Van Wynsberghe, R., 84
van't Land, H., 107
Vandemoortele, J., 42
Vandenabeele, J., 201
Vargas, V. R., 199
Vaughter, P., 77
Vieira, M. -J., 118
Vivekadhish, S., 42
von Haartman, R., 179

Waage, J., 42
Waas, T., 126
Wackernagel, M., 215
Wakefield, J. S., 7, 143, 151
Walker, A., 11, 62, 64, 67
Walker, M., 74, 76
Wallerstein, N., 163, 170
Wals, A., 36, 74
Walter, P., 84
Warburton, K., 84
Warner, R., 30
Warren, M. F., 126, 133
Warren, S. J., 151
Watene, K., 206
Waters, W., 78
Watson, M. K., 179–180, 189–190
Watts, J., 75, 78
Webber, M. M., 32
Wentzel, J., 85
Wheeler, D., 4
White, J. G., 126
White, J., 199
Whitehead, D., 218
Wiek, A., 59, 60
Wilson, E., 48
Winter, C., 179
Witham, H., 79
Withycombe, L., 59, 60
Wood, B. E., 198
Wood, B., 77
Wright, T., 77, 124, 126–127
Wu, Y. -C. J., 110

Yang, J., 161
Yao, Z., 179
Yap, M. L. -M., 206
Yorozu, R., 161

Zeegers, Y., 126
Zelinka, D., 178
Zeng, K., 179
Zhao, F., 44
Ziai, A., 52

SUBJECT INDEX

Academic culture, 26
Academies, 16–19
  learning in, 23–25
Acceptability, 33
Active citizenship, 23
Adult education, 23–24
Adult Learning and Education (ALE), 160, 169–172
Adult learning theories, 16
Africa Book Development Trust (ABDT), 165–166
Agenda 2030, 108–110
AIGA's Living Principles, 53
Anthropocene, 74–76
  outcomes, 78–80
  research approach, 77–78
  sustainability in higher education, 76–77
"Anthropocene-friendly" understanding of sustainability, 79
Anthropocenic Turn, 79
Applied learning, 217–218
Assessment, 10, 59, 67
  current practice assessments, 68
  design on student approaches to learning, 63
  research in, 63–64
Assistant Vice-Chancellor (Sustainability) (AVCS), 199
Association for Advancement of Sustainability in Higher Education (AASHE), 147–148

Big Tent Consortium, 108
Biggs' 3P model, 60
Bioenergy Research and Demonstration Facility (BRDF), 221–222
Biomimicry, 45–46
Biophilia, 45–46
Bloom's revised taxonomy, 60
Brain function, 22
Brock Commons Tallwood House case study, 222
Brookhaven College (BHC), 144
"Buy and throw" mentality, 144

Campus as a Living Laboratory (CLL), 11, 214
  case studies of research and learning, 218
  CIRS, 217–218
  education and engagement, 219–220
  enablers and impact of CLL on campus, 223–224
  large-scale research projects, 221–223
  small scope research studies, 220–221
  sustainability at UBC, 214–216
  types of opportunities, 218–219
  UBC CLL, 216–217
Campus Sustainability Office (CSO), 215
Capacity building programs, 5
Centre for Interactive Research on Sustainability (CIRS), 217–218
Chief executive officer (CEO), 163
CL-program, 179–180
CLAQWA rubrics, 63–64
"Closed-loop" PjBL, 67–68
Coalition, 24
Code of Ethics, 178
Cognitive functioning, 24
Coherent framework, 61
Collective awareness and attention, 22–23

Community
college, 145–148, 151
community-oriented approaches, 61–62, 68
engagement, 118
learning, 170
Concept map (Cmap), 64–65, 68
Confidence gap, 9, 190, 192
Consensus, 129–130
Contextualization for sustainability, 69
Corporate social responsibility (CSR), 147
Corporate sustainability (CS), 147
Covert method, 151
Critical openness, 200–202
video dialogues as mechanism for, 206–208
Critical thinking, 152
Cultural commons, 17, 20
embracing, 20–21
revitalization of, 21
Cultural ecologies, 21
Curriculum, 59, 75, 78
strategies, 4, 6
structure, focus, and history, 132–133
sustainability in, 79

Dallas County Community College District (DCCCD), 147–148
Deep learning principles, 84
Deliberation, 84–85, 95
Deliberative democracy principles and practices, 85–86
Deliberative Dialogue (DD), 12, 84–86
author's context, 86–87
general flow of activity, 87
issue guide, 87–88
questions and ponderings, 93–95
rationale, 88
reflections and findings, 88–91
scaffolded activities, 87
session implementation, 88
at work, 87–91
Democracy, 170
Democratic classroom practices, 86
Descriptive research design, 150
Design thinking, 208
as signature pedagogy, 200–202
Design Thinking for Sustainability (DSDN183), 10, 198–201, 208
semi-structured focus group interview questions for DSDN183 students, 211
Diagnosis-solution problems, 32–33
Digital Interaction, 45
Disagreement, 129–130
Discipline considerations and views, 133

Early College High School (ECHS), 149
Earth system science, 75
Eco-centric and Anthropocentric Attitudes toward Environment scale (EAAT SD), 126
Eco-intelligence, 21, 23
Eco-Schools, 110
Ecojustice curriculum framework, 19
embracing cultural commons, 20–21
redressing conceptions of intelligence, 21–23
Ecojustice Leadership Academy, 17–18
Ecological/ecology, 21, 44
of democracy, 86
dimension of SD, 188
Footprint analysis, 215
intelligence, 22
Economic
inclusion, 163
market system, 144
sustainability, 188
Education, 5, 16, 154, 160–161, 163, 172
adult, 170
civic, 165–166, 172
in FHS, 169
forms of, 167–168
free adult provision, 172
gender disparities in, 171
rural residents in accessing, 165
Education 2030 Framework for Action, 160, 171

Education for Sustainable Development (ESD), 5, 84, 109, 124
transformative nature of, 36–37
Educational outcomes, 203–206
Educational reforms in ecojustice education, 19
Effectiveness, 33
Employability, 23
Empowerment, 163
Engineers, 178
role/responsibilities in SD, 187, 190
English for speakers of other languages (ESOL), 149
Environment, economy and social equality (Three "Es"), 77
Environmental protection, 42
Environment–economy integration, 188
ePortfolios, 63–64
Ethics, 153
Examinations, 59, 64, 67
Exercises, 59

Facilitators, 35, 92
Faculty awareness, 146
Faculty interviews, 132
curriculum structure, focus, and history, 132–133
discipline considerations and views, 133
lecturer experiences and transformation, 134–135
organizational contrasts and tensions, 135
strong and weak sustainability, 133–134
students characteristics and consequences, 136
sustainability principles, definitions, and practices, 135–136
Faculty Learning Communities (FLC), 145–146
Folk High Schools (FHS), 164, 168–169
"Folkbildning", 167–168
Formal education system, 168
Forward Thinking Conference in Oslo, 45
Frameworks for sustainability teaching, 61
Future scenarios, 46
building, 46–48
ethical journey, 47–48

Gender Equality, 205
Geology, 74–75
Global Action Programme (GAP), 12
Global Action Programme on Education for Sustainable Development (GAP ESD), 108
Global Goals (*see* Sustainable development goals (SDGs))
Graphic Design, 45
Green Building Action Plan, 218–219
Green-washing, 81
Greenhouse gas (GHG), 216

Halifax Declaration, 214
Hannover Principles, 53
Higher education (HE), 86, 108, 144–145
sustainability in, 76–77
Higher education institution (HEI), 6, 109
Holism, 6
Human Capital theory, 162

Incheon Declaration, 161
Indigenous knowledge, 47
Indigenous wisdom, 47
Informal feedback from students, 38
Institutional culture, 223
Institutions, 127–128
Instructional design on student achievement, 60
Intelligence, redressing conceptions of, 21–23
Interdisciplinarity, 198–199, 204, 207
Interdisciplinary approach, 146–147
Interdisciplinary learning for sustainability, 199–200
Interdisciplinary problem-based approach, 30

beginnings, 30–31
development of approach, 33–36
pilot, 31–33
preparing ground, 31
transformative nature of education for SD, 36–37
Interdisciplinary thinking, 204
Interior and Environmental Design, 45
International Association of Universities (IAU), 108
Involve (European-based organization), 85

Jewellery & Silversmithing, 45

Kaitiakitanga, 201–202
Knowledge of engaged curriculum, 16

Leadership, 223
in sustainable development, 214
Learning (*see also* Sustainability learning)
in academies, 23–25
activities, 59
lifelong, 160–162
models, 60–61
objectives, 61
service, 62
shared, 164
society, 160, 162–163
strategies, 5
Learning and Teaching as Communicative Action theory (LTCA), 151
Lecturer experiences and transformation, 134–135
Life cycle assessments (LCA), 218
Life cycle costing (LCC), 222–223
Life's Principles, 53
Lifelong learning, 160–162
Linkage density, 52
Local democracies, 21

Manoa scenario building method, 46
Market-led growth, 131
Master program, 179, 224
Mātauranga Māori, 201
Mediation, 26
Meta-analyses of student achievement, 63
Meta-cognitive awareness of assessment practices, 63
Metro Vancouver, 214
Millennium Development Goals (MDGs), 42–43, 160–161
Modified essay questions, 32, 38
Montréal Design Declaration, 45
Moral imperatives, 77
Municipal Adult Education (MAE), 168–169

Narrative assignment, 152
National funding, 35
National Issues Forum/Kettering Institute (NIFI), 86–88
Natural commons, 20
Nature-based intelligences, 45
Negotiated syllabus (*see* Syllabus Deliberation method)
"Nested circles" model, 189

Online assessment communities, 63–64
Online working, 35
Open-book "power" exams, 68
Organizational contrasts and tensions, 135
Oslo Manifesto, 45
Overt method, 151

Paired sample *t*-test, 184–185
Paradigm shifts in higher education, 37
Participants, 149
Personal stakes, 93
Phenomenology, 7, 150
Philosophy course, 153
Pluralism, 6
Polling techniques, 93
Postgraduate curriculum in UK, 124
ladder framework, 126–127
material and methods, 127–136
postgraduate taught courses, 124–126
Potential learning, 24

"Power" examinations, 64
Presentations, 64
PricewaterhouseCoopers (PwC), 44
Problem-based learning, 30, 37, 152
Process syllabus (*see* Syllabus Deliberation method)
Product Design, 45
Professor as mediator, 25–26
Programs, 127–128
Project-based learning (PjBL), 61–62
Proposals, 93
Public investment, 4

Qualitative method, 127
Quantitative method, 127

"Radical" positions, qualitative comments on, 130–132
Real-world learning, 146, 149
Reason Design Process, 53
Recruitment, 149
Recycle Mania events, 148
Reductionist approach, 59
Reliability, 150
Research
 in assessment, 63–64
 reporting, 146–147
Resilience, 45–46
"Returning to subjects" process, 150
Revitalization of cultural commons, 21

Scaffolding, 38
Scepticism, 132
Self-confidence in SD, 190–191
Self-realisation, 47–48, 52, 54
Semi-structured focus group interview questions for DSDN183 students, 211
Semi-structured interview, 126
Service learning, 62
Shared learning, 164
Shared pool of attention, 22
Siam University, 116–118
Signature pedagogy, design thinking as, 200–202
Skills revolution, 162
Social
 awareness, 22
 boundaries, 188
 brain, 22, 26
 dimension of SD, 188
 empowerment, 170
 exclusion, 163
 facility, 22
 intelligence, 22, 26
 issue, 88
 science, 74, 76, 78
 social-justice oriented actions, 204, 206
 sustainability, 190
SOLO taxonomy, 61
Statistical analysis, 182
Statistical Package for Social Sciences, 182
Students, Staff, and Surrounding Communities (3S), 117
Students
 characteristics and consequences, 136
 student-based studies, 76–77
Study circles, 160, 163–164
 in Sweden, 166–169
 in Zimbabwe, 164–166
"Summer School" approach, 35
Summit on Climate Change and Indigenous People, 17
Sustainability, 4–5, 11, 33, 74, 144, 149, 151, 208
 curriculum, 79, 145–150, 152, 155
 education, 5
 in higher education, 76–77
 interdisciplinary learning for, 199–200
 principles, definitions, and practices, 135–136
 strong and weak, 133–134
 teaching, 60–61
 at UBC, 214–216
Sustainability development (SD), 144
Sustainability learning (*see also* Learning), 58, 60
 assessment design on student approaches to learning, 63

current practice in assessment for sustainability, 64–65
frameworks for sustainability teaching, 61
instructional design on student achievement, 60
learning models, 60–61
publications on sustainability instructional design, assessment, and research outcomes, 66
through reflective paper submissions toward changed mindset, 155
research in assessment, 63–66
teaching approaches in engineering sustainability classes, 61–62
visible by starting with text, 155
visible through story and participatory action, 155
Sustainability Scholars program, 221
Sustainability Summit Conference, 148
Sustainable Building Science Program (SBSP), 217
Sustainable development (SD), 4, 9, 35, 37, 58, 108, 178, 182, 188–189
CLL to, 224
data analysis, 182
data collection, 180–181
degree of confidence in SD issues, 187–188, 190–191
degree of interest in sustainability issues, 184–185, 189–190
descriptive statistics for question, 183
differences in interest between male and female students, 185–187
in engineering, 179
leadership in, 214
literature review, 5–6
pictures, 182, 184
policy, 214–215
research methods, 180
role/responsibilities of engineer *vs.* teacher, 187, 190
sample, 180
teachers responsibilities in, 180
whole institution approach for, 109–112
words, 182
Sustainable development education (SDE), 181
Sustainable Development Goals (SDGs), 42–43, 50, 52, 108, 160–169, 198
ALE and SDG 4 targets, 169–172
awareness, 48
and design, 43–45
design, 43–45, 48–50
example, 51–52
framework, 208
framing research, 45–46
future scenario building, 46–48
insights, 53–54
learning society, 162–163
lifelong learning, 161–162
methods, 48
results, 48–52
SDG Fund, 111
SDG Wheel, 118
SDG3, 205
SDG4, 8, 161–162, 169–172, 178
SDG5, 205
SDG11, 205
study circles, 163–164
study circles in Sweden, 166–169
study circles in Zimbabwe, 164–166
UN 2030 plan, 160–161
values, 49–50
Sustainable Development Policy #5, 215
Sustainable Development Solutions Network (SDSN), 110
Sustainable Education, 84
Sustainable engineering practice, 58, 69
Sustainable Environmental Economic Development Studies Program (SEEDS Program), 220
Sweden
study circles in, 166–169
sustainable development in, 178
Syllabus Deliberation method, 12

Syllabus deliberations (SD), 86, 91
questions and ponderings, 93–95
reflections and findings related to, 91–93
Symbiosis, 45–46
Syngas, 222
Systems theory, 43, 50
Systems-level thinking, 84

Talloires Declaration, 146
Taxonomic frameworks, 60
Teachers, 178
role/responsibilities in SD, 187, 190
Teaching
approaches in engineering sustainability classes, 61–62
strategies, 5
sustainability, 6
of sustainability, 74, 76
Teaching Research and Development Network (TRDN), 30–31
Teaching sustainability mini-pilot model (TSMP model), 144, 146
conceptual framework, 147–148
data collection, 149–150
educating sustainability, 146–147
essence of experience, 154
FLC, 145–146
higher education, 144–145
limitations, implications, and outcomes, 155–156
methodology, 148–150
objective, 149
participants, recruitment, and subjects taught, 149
presentation of data, 150–154
Texas Core Curriculum, 145
Texas Education Code, 145
Textile Design, 45
Thailand, 116–117
Three-pillar model, 11, 75, 77
Time-tested indigenous methods, 53
Traditional engineering assessment methods, 58
Transferable skills, 37
Transformative learning, 36
Transformative nature of education for sustainable development, 36–37
"Transforming our World" (*see* UN 2030 Agenda for Sustainable Development)

U.S. National Society of Professional Engineers (NSPE), 178
UN 2030 Agenda for Sustainable Development, 160–161, 171
UNESCO Institute for Lifelong Learning (UIL), 160
United Nations Educational, Scientific, and Cultural Organization (UNESCO), 84, 160
University faculty, 26
University Leaders for Sustainable Future (ULSF), 146
University of Bologna, 113–114
University of British Columbia (UBC), 11, 214
CLL, 216–217
Sustainability Academic Strategy, 215
sustainability at, 214–216
20-year Sustainability Strategy, 215
University of Costa Rica (UCR), 118–119
University of Ghana, 114–115
University of Manchester Institute of Science and Technology (UMIST), 30
University of Regina (UofR), 115–116
Unsustainable lifestyle, 144

Value-based design, 46, 54
Venn diagram, 189
VicTeach, 198
Victoria University of Wellington (VUW), 10, 197–198
Video dialogues, 198
as mechanism for critical openness, 206–208
Video resource, 206
Vygotsky's theory, 24

WELL Building Assessment Project, 220
Whakawhitinga kōrero: Dialogues on Sustainability, 202–203, 207
Whanaungatanga, 202
Whole Institution Approach (WIA), 12, 108
  case studies, 112–119
  for sustainable development, 109–112
Whole School Approach, 110
Wicked problems, 32
World Education Forum (WEF), 160

Zimbabwe, study circles in, 164–166
Zone of Proximal Development, 24

Printed and bound by CPI Group (UK) Ltd, Croydon, CR0 4YY

13/09/2026

14961064-0004